Y0-BOB-693

Historical Gems of the San Francisco Bay Area

© 2015 Magnifico Publications
ISBN-13: 978-0-9853006-6-1

Credits:

I would like to thank the docents, curators, and volunteers at the historical sites and museums for their assistance with this book. They dedicate countless hours to educate the community about the wonderful historical gems entrusted to their care. Without their tireless efforts, many of these sites and the artifacts contained within them would not be available to the public for viewing. Their passion for local and state history is inspirational. Their outreach efforts contribute greatly to the state's educational and cultural advancement. They make visitors from around the world feel welcome to their sites and leave them with a better understanding of California's rich heritage and contributions to the history of the world.

I would also like to thank geologists Kent Fogelman and Phil Stoffer for their generous assistance with the section on California's geological history.

Cover photos from top left to bottom right: Wings of History-San Martin; San Jose Fire Museum; Ravenswood Historical Site-Livermore; Rengstorff House-Mountain View; The South Bay Historical Railroad Society-Santa Clara; Ravenswood Historical Site-Livermore

"Bay Area county map" by Kryston - based upon image: California Bay Area county map.svg. Licensed under Public domain via Wikimedia Commons - http://commons.wikimedia.org/wiki/File:Bay_Area_county_map.png#mediaviewer/File:Bay_Area_county_map.png.

Back cover photo: Olompali State Historic Park

Table of Contents

Introduction

Whether you are a visitor to the San Francisco Bay Area or a long-term resident of the area, it's not uncommon to focus on the major, well-known attractions and overlook lesser-known sites that offer more local flavor and background. Many people think that it is necessary to travel to places that are far from the San Francisco Bay Area in order to see important historical sites. When one thinks about famous historical sites, places like Gettysburg, Boston, Philadelphia, or Washington, D.C., come to mind. The truth is, however, that the San Francisco Bay Area is loaded with fascinating and unique historical sites that represent a broad range of historical events and eras. A resident of the Bay Area or a tourist in town for a few days can see a wide range of historical sites all within a day's drive of San Francisco.

This book may also be useful for a teacher or parent who is looking for an educational field trip which ties in with the child's curriculum in a history, literature, or science class. Others may find it interesting to learn more about the Native Americans or pioneer settlers in a local community. So, whether you are just curious about what is inside that old historical house in your neighborhood, want to know how a specific historical event played out in your area, or are just looking for an interesting day trip, this book has something for you.

Many people are familiar with the more famous sites in California. It is not uncommon to see tourists make a trip to see all of the California missions or Gold Rush towns, but there are also scores of lesser-known sites within the Bay Area that highlight a particular historical event or offer a comprehensive overview of the history of that town or region.

Still other sites preserve the homes of local literary figures and contain many interesting artifacts from their lives and legacies. Some sites commemorate the spot where a famous historical event took place. Military sites abound for every major conflict in which America has fought. Most people do not realize what an important role California played in many of these wars. There are even a handful of battle sites in the Bay Area that are largely unknown to the general public.

California has also been the home of many important technological and scientific advancements. There are sites that demonstrate and preserve that legacy as well. Many museums highlight the role that transportation has played in the region. The Bay Area has its share of train, trolley, automobile, aircraft, fire-fighting, and nautical museums with a wide variety of historical vehicles that are in well-preserved condition.

There are also museums related to industry and commerce. Mining, in particular, has had a huge impact on the region and there are sites where you can learn about gold, silver, coal, sand, and quicksilver mines. In addition, there are many places that commemorate the area's agricultural heritage. Visitors can see antique farm equipment, historical farm products, and historic structures. In some cases, there are working farms in which farming is still done using traditional methods.

Furthermore, there are many fine museums that are dedicated to particular ethnic groups and the roles that they have played in the area. The region has some serious academic museums, such as those dedicated to art history, anthropology, or archeology, but there are also quirky pop culture museums that preserve the history of such items as blue jeans, cartoons, silent movies, and popular toys. There is even a museum dedicated to Agnews Mental Hospital.

In short, there is something for everyone. Whether you want to see a large, state-of-the-art comprehensive museum or a small, eclectic collection of "old junk", there is a museum to suit your tastes in the Bay Area. Many are free or low-cost and make a great family outing, an affordable vacation destination, or are just an interesting way to fill a free afternoon.

Unfortunately, finding information about this wide variety of museums and historical sites can be difficult. Some of the sites are open at inconvenient or infrequent times. Many of the smaller museums are staffed by volunteers, and if the volunteers are unavailable, the museum may not be open at the advertised times. A few do not even have webpages. Reaching the staff by phone can be difficult in some locations. Popular tour books often only mention the major attractions and leave some of the minor sites out. Some of the few books that have previously been written on this subject are already out of date or have a different scope.

That is why I wrote this book. As a history buff and a history teacher who loves to travel, I found it difficult to find information about local museums. I have visited almost every place in this book personally. When I began to visit various historical sites, I heard some common complaints from the staff members. Many mentioned being under-funded, dependent on volunteers with limited availability, and being short on display space. They all felt like they had many interesting items and stories to share with the public, but many people in their own community did not know their museums even existed. This book meets this need. It is designed to bring together the friendly and knowledgeable staff members from these museums and historical sites, who are passionate about the importance of their facilities, with the general public that needs to know more about local history.

In order to qualify for this book, a site must be an actual museum, historical home, or park that is open to the public with at least some items of a historical nature. There are numerous historical societies, archives, California Historical Landmarks plaques, and privately owned historical homes or businesses that have nothing on display for the public to see. These are not included in this book. For more information about these places see the National Register of Historic Places or the California State Parks Office of Historic Preservation websites: http://www.nps.gov/nr/ and http://ohp.parks.ca.gov/?page_id=21387 respectively.

Some states, like Texas and Virginia, require their students to take a course on their state's history. Inexplicably, California has no such requirement. California students study the Native Americans in third grade and the Mission Period and Gold Rush in the 4th grade. After that, in the grades that follow, things are much more hit and miss. Even though California played a huge role in the development of the agricultural and industrial revolutions and was a major staging area and weapons supplier for the wars of the 20th Century, it is totally up to the discretion of the history teacher as to whether or not to make a local connection to these national events. A similar problem exists for political movements such as the Progressive Era, or the Civil Rights, Anti-war, Environmental, Labor, and Women's Movements. Nor is anything specifically tied to California in the realm of entertainment, aerospace, computers, or other scientific advances in most high school U.S. History courses.

This is unfortunate and should be changed. Students would be much more motivated to learn about history if they knew there was a local connection to these events. Even though early California history is taught in primary grades, it is done at an age where the students do not really have the maturity to understand the complexities of the events. The end result is that many Californians do not know much about their state's history. Even though there are local history resources available, many people do not know about them.

No matter how long a person has lived in the San Francisco Bay Area, there are bound to be some new places that are unfamiliar to them. New museums open all the time and some established ones have shortened their hours or closed due to tough economic times. There is no point in driving out to an old familiar site, only to find that it is closed. This book will give you the latest information available on local museums.

Even less is known about local history by the millions who moved to California from other states or countries or by most visitors to the region. They may have studied a little about California in school, but are often surprised about how influential it was in historical events. Transplanted residents may know about their birthplace, but most would like to get to know their adopted home better. Often they are surprised at how many connections there are in California to their homeland or region of America. The events that took place in California have truly shaped the entire world, and any visitor to its museums and historical sites can learn from them, whether he or she is a California native or not. Only by visiting these sites can one get a true appreciation for how important California and its people are to the rest of the world.

Finally, I'd like to offer a brief description of the structure or organization of the book. Each chapter in this book will have a brief historical overview of a time period, followed by a listing of the sites that best relate to that era. A fun activity for your family or students is to make a quest to see all of the sites for a particular era. Checklists have been provided for each chapter with a place for a museum staff member to sign off when you have completed the quest. This would be an ideal activity to conduct when a young person is studying the era in a particular grade in school. This would help them immensely if they have a project or paper due on a particular historical subject. However, these quests are primarily designed to be fun and educational. If you don't make it to every last site on the list, not to worry, you will still learn a lot from visiting several sites.

The main section of the book will have detailed individual listings on each museum or historical site. Each listing in this book contains the following helpful information:

1. Name of the museum or historical site
2. Location

3. Website
4. Phone number(s)
5. E-mail address
6. Hours of operation
7. Cost
8. Permanent exhibits
9. Special exhibits
10. Historical era that is best featured
11. Targeted age groups
12. Special activities for children
13. Guided tour information
14. Hands-on activities
15. The best-kept secrets about the museum or site
16. Hidden treasures
17. Unique features of the museum or site that can't be found anywhere else
18. The most important things about local, state, or American history that can be learned at the museum or site
19. Annual events held at the site or elsewhere in the community
20. Research facilities or archives at the site
21. The kind of a gift shop and what is for sale
22. Additional information (if any)

Finally, there are listings of museums and sites by county, type of site, and major theme of the collections. You may also want to make a quest to see all of the museums in a particular county or all of those of a particular theme. The possibilities are endless. The main thing is to have fun with it and learn from your visits.

Fireplace carving detail at Ravenswood Historical Site-Livermore   **The Dunsmuir House-Oakland**

The San Francisco Bay Area Before Spanish Contact

In the remote past, the Bay Area looked quite different than it does today. At various times, the coastline has changed with the rise and fall of sea level during the ice ages. The oceans shrunk during periods of glaciation and expanded during times of melting. As continental glaciers formed during ice ages, the shoreline moved westward and the exposed continental shelf became a coastal plain, extending as far as a small series of hills that are today the Farallon Islands. During warm periods between ice ages, sea level rose flooding inland valleys. For instance, the San Francisco Bay is the flooded lower valley of the prehistoric Sacramento River.

Tectonic forces cause mountains to rise, whereas erosion wears down the landscape. The region's famous earthquake faults exist along the boundaries of great blocks in the crust that are slipping past each other. These faults are generally oriented in a northwest-southeast direction. Erosion along these fracture zones formed canyons. The larger valleys of the San Francisco Bay region are locations where large blocks in the crust sank relative to the rising mountains. These valleys flooded, forming the arms of the San Francisco Bay. Many of the area's mountains have sedimentary rocks that contain fossils. These fossils provide evidence that proves that they were once under the sea. As new mountains arose, old hills eroded. Rivers and streams slowly eroded the land away, exaggerating the contrasts between highlands and low lands. Nutrient-rich sediments derived from the ancient rocks exposed in the upland regions helps to account for the unusually rich soil in the region.

While the Bay Area never had glaciers, it was nonetheless affected by glaciation. After the glaciers melted, a large inland lake in the Central Valley of California formed and began to seek outlets to the sea. At first it flowed out through the Salinas River Valley. Later, when land shifted due to the movement of the San Andreas Fault, it began to drain into a lake in the present San Francisco Bay region. The bay itself started out as merely a canyon of the Sacramento River as it flowed to the sea. It gradually widened and deepened as time went by. When sea levels rose, the Golden Gate widened and seawater flowed in and mixed with the fresh water to form an estuary.

In general, the climate during the ice ages was much wetter than today. During wetter periods there were far more marshes, ponds, lakes, and active streams than at present. During drier periods, many of the streams and rivers only occasionally reached the bay, creating much more wetlands and a higher water table. As a result, the area had much different kinds of vegetation and wildlife than during the current dry period. When humans reached the area, they began to change the lands to suit their needs. Each successive wave of settlement altered the landscape, flora, and fauna more dramatically, unto the point that today's bay would be scarcely recognizable to its first inhabitants.

To the surprise of many, the Bay Area has had its share of volcanic activity as well. One need look no further than the obsidian, geysers, and petrified forests of the Napa Valley and Sonoma County for evidence of this, but there are tiny volcanoes, hot springs, and volcanic rocks scattered throughout the Bay Area. All of this geological activity explains why the one thing not found in the Bay Area is the type of land dinosaur fossils with which most people are familiar. Most of Coastal California was under the ocean during most of those eras in which dinosaurs lived. However, some less familiar prehistoric mammal and sea life fossils have been found. Large swimming reptiles called Mosasaurs have been found in the Panoche Hills, and Mesozoic-age marine fossils are abundant in some locations where these rocks are exposed.

Some Bay Area museums, such as The Oakland Museum of California, the Fremont Area Museum, the Antioch Historical Museum, and the California Academy of Sciences have small collections of local fossils. Other samples of local fossils are scattered here and there in small museums throughout the Bay Area. The best collection of fossils in the Bay Area is at a research collection at the UC Berkeley Museum of Paleontology, but alas, the displays are only open to the public once a year on Open House day. The rest of the year, they may be viewed on their website. Displays about the geologic history of the Bay Area can be found at The Lawrence Hall of Science, The Oakland Museum of California, the California Academy of Sciences, and the US Geological Survey. Other small science, natural history, and historical museums, as well as park visitor centers throughout the Bay Area, also have geologic history displays and exhibits.

Native American settlement in the region has left far more traces than is commonly realized. The Indians of the Bay Area left large deposits of oyster shells in coastal regions of the bay, such as in Vallejo, Napa, the Presidio in San Francisco, San Bruno Mountain, Emeryville, Alameda, and Fremont. One turn-of-the-century survey listed hundreds of such places around the bay. The Native Americans also conducted burns to clear away unfavorable plants and to help round up insects and small animals for food. They made bedrock mortars for grinding acorns and other seeds. They decorated rocks with fascinating petroglyphs that have still not been fully deciphered. Traces of these Native American alterations of the land can be seen throughout the Bay Area.

Due to the fact that there are no large Indian reservations in the Bay Area, many people are not aware that they lived here at all. Sadly, many local Native American settlements, burial grounds, and remains were never studied or documented before they were unceremoniously covered over by highways, roads, and housing developments. Miraculously, some sites and artifacts survived and are preserved in local museums all across the region. In a few extremely rare cases, the actual sites of Native American settlements are still preserved, such as Olompali State Historic Park, Chitactac-Adams Heritage County Park, and the Sanchez Adobe. Many Bay Area residents go about their daily lives with little thought as to who owned the land before them. Still more have a vague notion that Indians once lived here, but mistakenly assume that nothing remains of their material culture. Meanwhile, interesting artifacts sit in a nearby museum awaiting their discovery.

Because of the shortcomings of social studies instruction before the 1980s, some adults were incorrectly informed that all of the California Indians are gone and are astonished to learn that that their descendants still live among us. One Native American acquaintance of mine recalls being quite surprised to hear this in school and had to respectfully inform her teacher that she and her people were still here!

Very few people know that the Bay Area has settlements going back as far as 12, 000 years ago or that the Bay Area was settled in several waves of Native Americans who originally came from all over North America.

The most widespread group in the Bay Area was the Ohlone Indians (sometimes known as Costanoans), but there were also portions of the Bay Area that were settled by Coastal and Bay Miwoks, Esselen, Pomo, Wintun, and Wappo Indians as well. The various tribes shared a similar material culture of hunting and gathering acorns, seeds, and many other plants. While their cultures were similar across the region, the languages from each local settlement were so diverse that even members of the same tribe from different parts of the Bay Area could not understand one another. The Native Americans of the Bay Area did not build permanent structures. Most used tule or other grasses to build their dwellings, although those who lived in mountainous areas used tree bark.

Native Americans migrated from area to area to follow seasonal changes in the availability of plants and animals for food. They did not conduct farming, but instead relied on an extremely wide variety of gathered plants and animals for food. They were masters of their own environment. They also had very detailed knowledge of useful medicinal plants. They developed many ingenious tools for trapping, hunting, or fishing. Most impressive was the fact that they managed to prepare and cook a wide variety of plants without the use of pottery or metals. California Indian basketry and arrow making are among some of the finest in North America. Because of this, they seldom went hungry. Consequently, California was one of the most densely populated areas of North America, even in pre-Hispanic times.

Trade was widespread throughout the region. Coastal tribes would trade abalone, olivella, and other prized shells for the much-prized obsidian (used for arrow and spear heads) from the volcanic regions of the Bay Area or the Sierra Nevada Mountains. Other trade items included furs, medicines, dyes, and other useful minerals and plants.

Warfare among the tribes was very rare and none tried to subjugate the others. When intertribal conflicts did arise, they were usually mediated or settled through small ritualistic conflicts involving a few chosen champions. These staged skirmishes were quickly resolved after someone was injured and therefore resulted in very little bloodshed. Tribal government was informal, consisting of tribal councils, elders, and village leaders with no strong central authority.

Women spent most of their time gathering and preparing food, child-rearing, and making clothing, baskets, and other household items. The men did most of the hunting. The religion of the local Indians generally consisted of reverence for ancestors, sponsorship from spirit guides from nature, vision quests, sweat lodges, and shamanistic healing. Favorite leisure activities included story telling, singing, dancing, and wagering on games.

The world of the Bay Area's Native Americans changed dramatically with the arrival of the Spanish. The initial contact between the cultures was friendly. The Spanish accounts state that both cultures were impressed with the other's music and dance. Foods and trade goods were exchanged. The Indians were intensely curious about the inventions and clothing and appearance of the Spanish. Droves of curious onlookers went to the Spanish to learn their ways, especially the young people. Later, the Spanish went on expeditions throughout the hills to find isolated groups of Indians as far away as the Central Valley. They eventually emptied villages from hundreds of miles around to settle the Indians in the Spanish missions. Their goals were to convert the Indians to Christianity and to teach them agriculture, building, and other technologies of Spanish civilization.

The unforeseen result of this crowding together of thousands of Indians from many different tribes from all over the Bay Area was a loss of cultural identity and a massive die-off due to the rapid spread of diseases inadvertently introduced by the Spanish. Within 100 years of Spanish contact, most of the Indians were gone. Those who remained intermarried with European settlers, and, for the most part, assumed their cultures. Native American lands were taken from them and their villages destroyed. This is why there are no Indian Reservations in the Bay Area. Countless numbers of cultural relics, burial sites, and dwelling places were wiped out without a thought to preservation. It is a miracle that any survived at all. The natives' village-based hunter-gatherer culture was gone forever. Instead, they adopted occupations such as farmers, ranchers, and other jobs from European culture.

Beginning with the pioneering work of Alfred Kroeber and other ethnologists and anthropologists in the early 1900s, an effort was begun to preserve the material culture, music, language, and oral traditions of the Native Americans of the Bay Area before they disappeared completely. Many descendants of the Bay Area Indian tribes have taken up the torch themselves, and are laboring extensively to resurrect the languages, stories, music, dance, basket making, and other crafts of their ancestors.

A cultural renaissance has taken place in the last few years, with tribal gatherings being held at Coyote Hills Park, Henry Cowell Park, Rancho San Antonio, Indian Canyon, Monterey, Olompali State Historic Park, the Museum of the American Indian in Novato, and other locations. These pow-wows, festivals, and other events have provided a fantastic opportunity to see story telling, dances, cooking, arrow-making, basket making, and many other demonstrations. Hands-on activities allow participants to try out many Native American crafts and skills for themselves. A wide variety of guest speakers, cultural activists, and craftspeople are also in attendance. Food sales and nature hikes focusing on plants used by Native Americans are also usually a part of the events. These can be a great opportunity to meet tribal members and other cultural experts and learn from them. This is a particularly valuable activity for California students from the third grade who are currently studying their local Indian tribes. Most of these events are held in the fall. Check the websites for each individual site for details.

The following sites are great places to learn more about local Native Americans. They have been arranged by tribal group:
(The numbers after the description of the historical site refer to the individual listings later in this book).

A. Ohlone sites:

✓	Museum or historical site	Date Visited
	1. The Alameda Museum: large collection of stone mortars, beads, necklaces, arrowheads, and other stone and bone tools. #5	
	2. New Almaden Quicksilver Mining Museum (San Jose): a display explaining the ways in which the Ohlone used cinnabar for pigmentation; an acorn pounding bowl, mortar and pestle, and replicas of baskets and other tule items. #142	
	3. Alviso Adobe (Pleasanton): a few Ohlone Indian artifacts and a large collection of replicas used for hands-on demonstrations. There are also bedrock mortars near the creek. #8	
	4. Aptos History Museum: original Ohlone mortars, spear tips, and arrowheads; replicas of Ohlone foods and cooking utensils, baskets, furs, playing pieces, beads, tule mats, hunting decoys, bows, fish traps, other tools and implements. #11	
	5. The Botanical Gardens at UC Berkeley: The California Natives: Plants and People tour. Learn about the plants used by California Indians for food, shelter, clothing, tools, medicine, games, and music. Become familiar with the varied customs and skills of California's earliest human inhabitants. No listing.	
	6. The California Academy of Science (San Francisco): occasional cultural and educational events related to Native Americans. No listing.	
	7. Chitactac-Adams Heritage County Park (Gilroy): a beautiful site with acorn pounding holes and rare petroglyphs. #43	
	8. Contra Costa County History Center (Martinez): a few Ohlone and other Indian artifacts. #49	
	9. Coyote Hills Park (Fremont): a replica of an Ohlone village, shell mounds, interpretive programs, and good display in the Visitor's Center, including a full-scale canoe replica. The annual Ohlone cultural festival in October is the largest in the Bay Area. #51	
	10. Deer Hollow Farm in Rancho San Antonio County Park (Cupertino): learn about the local Native Americans through hands-on activities in a replica Ohlone village. #56	
	11. The deSaisset Museum at Santa Clara University: Native American baskets, jewelry, ornaments, and hand tools; a replica of an Ohlone house and a good Missions Period collection. #58	
	12. Evergreen Valley College Library's Heritage Room (San Jose): a few Ohlone artifacts. #66	
	13. The Filoli Education Center (Woodside): The Native Plants/Native Ways program explains the traditional use of plants and animals by California Indians and provides hands-on activities, such as making cordage or beads and playing traditional California Indian games. #68	

	14. The Phoebe A. Hearst Museum of Anthropology (Berkeley): Native Californian artifacts are supplemented by large and well-documented collections of photographs, films, and sound recordings. #160	
	15. History San Jose: Ohlone objects and related historical records are available for viewing by appointment with the museum's collections staff. One rare historical Ohlone basket is currently on display at the Diridon Train Station. #88	
	16. Indian Canyon (near Hollister): Indian Canyon has been opened up to all indigenous peoples who are in need of traditional lands for ceremonies. This remote and beautiful canyon has a fire circle, sweat lodges, a dance center, and a cultural resource room. No listing.	
	17. Lafayette Historical Society: a small collection of arrowheads. #98	
	18. The Lindsay Wildlife Museum (Walnut Creek): an Ohlone display, including animals that were important to them. No listing.	
	19. Los Altos History Museum: a display on the manufacture of Ohlone baskets and arrowheads. Some Ohlone artifacts and replicas are also displayed. #104	
	20. Mission Dolores (San Francisco): an Ohlone burial site and a scale model replica of an Ohlone house; Ohlone objects on display. #117	
	21. Mission Santa Clara: the mission church and the nearby deSaisset Museum (see listing above). #120	
	22. Mission Santa Cruz: an exhibit featuring the Mission Period. Nearby is the Santa Cruz Mission State Historic Park, featuring the only remaining example of neophyte (new convert) housing in the California missions. #121	
	23. Mission San José: several Ohlone objects prominently displayed. An Ohlone burial site is nearby. #118	
	24. Mission Carmel: an Ohlone burial site. Exhibits featuring the Mission Period. #116	
	25. Museum of the San Ramon Valley (Danville): a few artifacts from the Ohlone and other Indians. #135	
	26. The Oakland Museum of California: California Indian and Spanish Missions exhibits; educational programs. #147	
	27. Pacific Grove Museum of Natural History: Ohlone baskets sometimes on display. No listing.	
	28. Point Lobos Whaling Station (near Carmel): a few Ohlone items. #165	
	29. Sanborn County Park (Saratoga): bedrock mortars along the creek and near the youth hostel. No listing.	
	30. The Sanchez Adobe (Pacifica): an Ohlone Indian village once located at the site that is the only known Indian village in the region directly associated with the remains of a mission outpost. The museum also offers activities for school groups, such as cattle roping,	

	corn grinding, adobe brick, and candle making. #182	
	31. Santa Cruz Natural History Museum: artifacts, baskets, images, and a giant mural of life on the Central Coast 200 years ago. #187	
	32. San Mateo County History Museum (Redwood City): an interactive exhibit explaining how the natural resources of the Peninsula were used by the Ohlone. #185	
	33. Wildlife Education and Rehabilitation Center (Morgan Hill): a guided walk introduces students to local wildlife and their habitats and to California Early Native American plant use. No listing.	
	34. The Pacific House in Monterey: an Early California adobe building. The Monterey Museum of the American Indian, located upstairs, presents beautiful baskets, pottery, and other Native American artifacts. #128	
	35. The Peralta House Museum of History (Oakland): a display on Ohlone foods, a few Ohlone artifacts, signage about Ohlone life and artwork, classes on Ohlone life. #156	
	36. Salinas Valley Memorial Hospital Museum of Medical History: murals depicting Native American and Spanish colonial medical practices in the area. #179	
	37. Saratoga Historical Foundation Museum: mortars and a few other objects; a small display about the Ohlone. #189	
	38. Shellmound Memorial (Emeryville): a park preserving a small portion of the once vast oyster shellmound in the area. No listing.	
	39. Sunnyvale Heritage Park Museum: a mural that includes a bayside Ohlone village; items from an archaeological dig at The Moffett Towers in Sunnyvale including shell beads, stone mortars, and tools made from animal bones and obsidian. Another display showcases a dig at Santa Clara University, which includes impressive facial masks that are based upon skeletal remains that show what the Ohlone looked like in real life. #202	
	40. Ulistac Natural Area (Santa Clara): a garden planted with native plants, including signs explaining how the Ohlone used them. #209	
	41. Youth Science Institute: visitor centers at the Alum Rock, Sanborn, and Vasona County Parks in Santa Clara County offer educational programs. No listing.	
	42. San Leandro History Museum & Art Gallery: a basket, mural, and shellmounds. #183	
	43. Millbrae Historical Museum: a small Ohlone display containing arrowheads and a mortar. #113	
	44. Morgan Hill Historical Society: The Amah Mutsun Exhibit includes models of homes in transition from native to Spanish, language, tools, and culture of the local Ohlone. #227	

B. Miwok sites:

✓	Museum or historical site	Date Visited
	1. The Museum of the American Indian (Novato): a wide variety of Native American items from the Bay Area and other parts of the country; rotating special exhibits. The museum is part of a park that was built on the site of an Indian village that has a guided nature trail. #137	
	2. Olompali State Historic Park (near Novato): a Miwok village including mortars and shelters. Also includes a native plant garden and a timeline in the visitor's center. #148	
	3. Summit Visitor Center -Mt. Diablo (Walnut Creek): a cultural history display that includes the local Indians. #130	
	4. Mission Solano (Sonoma): Miwok mortars and displays about the Miwoks. #197	
	5. Angel Island: Miwok artifacts are located in the visitor center. #9	
	6. Kule Loklo: a reconstructed Coast Miwok Village with signs explaining the uses of native plants. There is also a display in the Bear Valley visitor's center that includes a mortar and a ceremonial headdress. #17	
	7. Tomales Regional History Center: Miwok Indian artifacts including rare trade beads thought to be given to the Miwok Indians by Russian traders, mortars, arrow and spear heads. #206	
	8. Mission San Rafael Arcangel: the Miwok lived and worked at this mission. #119	
	9. Petaluma Adobe State Historic Park: a display on Miwok Indians and a few artifacts. #158	
	10. Petaluma Historical Library and Museum: The collection of Miwok artifacts is quite extensive. It includes beads, basketry, tools, mortars, arrowheads, etc. #159	
	11. Novato History Museum: a mortar and pestle. #145	
	12. Bolinas Museum: baskets, beads, spear and arrowheads, fishing weights; displays explaining how tools were made. #26	
	13. Antioch Historical Museum: a replica of a native shelter, mortars and other tools. #10	
	14. Western Sonoma County Historical Society West County Museum (Sebastopol): mortars and other tools. #221	
	15. Marin Headlands Visitor Center: interactive Miwok display. #71	
	16. Marin History Museum: a display on Miwok Indians and a few artifacts. #109	
	17. The Phoebe A. Hearst Museum of Anthropology (Berkeley): Miwok artifacts. #160	

C. Wappo sites:

✓	Museum or historical site	Date Visited
	1. Napa Valley Museum (Yountville): Displays on basket and tool making; beads, charm stones, spear points etc. #139	
	2. Sharpsteen Museum (Calistoga): Large display with a map and many artifacts including beads, baskets, arrowheads, scrapers, etc. #194	
	3. Healdsburg Museum: Wappo Indian artifacts. #85	

D. Pomo Sites:

✓	Museum or historical site	Date Visited
	1. Healdsburg Museum: Pomo Indian artifacts. #85	
	2. Cloverdale Historical Society Museum: basket making, grinding stones, and flake tools. #45	
	3. Depot Park Museum (Sonoma): arrowheads, baskets, etc. #57	
	4. Jesse Peter Native American Art Museum (Santa Rosa): many types of Native American basketry. #95	
	5. Western Sonoma County Historical Society West County Museum (Sebastopol): Pomo Indian artifacts. #221	
	6. The Phoebe A. Hearst Museum of Anthropology (Berkeley): Pomo artifacts. #160	
	7. Fort Ross:(Jenner): very important site for the Kashaya Pomo #227	

I certify that _____ has visited the majority of the sites for the _____ people and has been declared an honorary tribal member.

X _____ (museum staff member).

Bolinas Museum

The Spanish and Mexican Periods

California was the furthest outpost of the Spanish Empire. There were many other more desirable places to go in the colonies. California was considered a wild frontier. If someone were to be sent there, they might conceivably ask the king, "Why? What did I do to deserve such a punishment?" Northern California was the extreme fringe of the Spanish domain in North America, so Bay Area settlement was very light and sporadic. Even though the Spanish first explored the coast of California in the 1500s, they did not begin serious settlement until the 1700s. California had no immediate magnet to draw settlers like the established colonies in Mexico or South America with their large treasures of gold and silver. Even though California had a large amount of gold, the Spanish were unaware of it, because they had only made preliminary surveys of the Sierra Nevada region. One has to wonder if they would have taken the settlement of California more seriously if they had known about the vast deposits of gold lying in those mountains.

By the time the Spanish determined to make permanent settlements in California, they had a tried and true method of developing a colony that had been refined over and over again since the days of Columbus. First they would build missions to Christianize the Indians, then they would try to turn them into Spanish citizens by forcibly changing their culture from hunting and gathering to agriculture. Instead of traveling over a wide area to search for food, the Indians would be taught to live in permanent dwellings and do European style jobs such as farming, ranching, and crafts. The Indians' cultural identity was further diluted by forcing them to marry members of other tribes or the Spanish themselves. They were forbidden to perform their traditional rituals, speak their language, hunt, or return to their ancestral villages once they joined the mission. Punishments for breaking the rules could be quite harsh. Most of the early converts and their children died of European diseases within a few years of moving to the missions and many of them are buried there.

The Bay Area missions were also set up as a first wave of settlement to stop the Russian advance into Northern California. The Russians were trapping furs in Alaska, but when the large Alaskan otters were nearly hunted to extinction, they began to hunt the smaller ones in Northern California. They established Fort Ross as a base to trade with the Indians and grow food for their starving colonies in Alaska. Some of our best accounts of how the Indians lived or what life was like in the Spanish missions are from Russian explorers. Once the bulwark against Russian advancement was established, however, further development was delayed due to the declining fortunes of the Spanish Empire in general. Centuries of expansion, colonization, and endless European wars were draining Spanish resources to the breaking point. Plans were made to start a new string of missions in the Central Valley, but these never were completed. Unlike in New Mexico and Southern California, no large towns were established in the Bay Area. The pueblos of Monterey, San Jose, and San Francisco were tiny in comparison to those that were further south.

Consequently, most of the permanent buildings that remain from Spanish times are the missions themselves and a few scattered adobe houses belonging to prominent families. These dons were given vast tracks of land that were more land than anyone could ever possibly farm by themselves. These land grants covered so much area that when overlaid upon a modern map of the region, they often include several cities or sometimes whole counties. They were typically operated as cattle ranches with thousands of head of cattle in their herds. Since they were not fenced in, the cattle tended to roam over a large area freely and were only culled once a year for their hides and tallow. The Spanish cattle industry attracted the attention of Yankee merchants from New England and they sent ships out to buy these products from the missions. They used the leather for their burgeoning textile factories and the tallow for soap, candles, and lamps. The meat could not be safely transported over such a long distance, so it was consumed on the spot. This is why visitors to the missions often mention how well fed they were with steak dinners! One of these Yankee sailors, named Richard Henry Dana, was sent to California by his doctor to improve his health. It must have worked because Dana wrote of hauling hides onto boats for weeks on end in the dead of winter in the chilly surf off of Big Sur and Mendocino! While working in California, he could not help but notice how nice the weather was and how fertile the soil seemed to be. Acting as an unofficial recruiter for American expansion, he was also keen to point out how few Spanish there were here and how easily a determined nation might snatch this paradise from them. Dana's writings and similar accounts from other visitors were best sellers in the United States. Soon, settlers began coming to California from the East Coast.

Things changed even more dramatically when Mexico gained its independence from Spain in 1821. The Mexican government actually encouraged foreign settlers as a way to populate their tenuously held lands in Alta California. A generation of Americans and Europeans began to settle in places like Monterey, San Francisco, and other places around the Bay Area. They soon intermarried with Spanish landowners and became wealthy merchants and landowners themselves. As their numbers increased, they began to clamor for America's annexation of California. They achieved this goal after the Mexican American War of 1848.

The Mexican Revolution had been inspired by the American War for Independence, so it had similar goals of liberty, freedom, and independence. However, it was also a social revolution. The revolutionaries felt that the landowners and the Catholic Church had had too much wealth and influence in the Spanish colonies. Therefore, they believed in redistributing land to the poor and severely restricting the land ownership and political influence of the Roman Catholic Church over the government. This meant that the missions were taken away from the monastic orders that had founded and administered them and their lands were to be distributed to the Indians that lived in them. In theory this sounds fair, but in practice, the Indians did not have the experience to run farms on their own because they had become dependent upon the missions since they had left their ancestral homes and lost their hunter-gatherer cultures. They knew little of how to administrate a land grant and how to take care of taxes, land titles, and other legal obligations. As a result, within a few short years, most of them had been swindled out of their land and forced to work on their own land under new owners.

The mission buildings themselves did not fare much better. They were purchased by secular owners and fell into disrepair. Some were even put to such shameful uses as barns or saloons. Over the years, earthquakes and fires damaged their fragile adobe bricks and since very little maintenance was done, many were destroyed or fell into ruin. As a result, most of what you see today of Spanish buildings are actually artful reconstructions (not without controversy as to their authenticity, I might add). Very few original buildings have survived unchanged. Most have been reconstructed in whole or in part based on original records or photographs. Many of the surrounding buildings have disappeared and only the church or a few other buildings have survived. Sometimes even the church itself is a modern reconstruction. Therefore, it is worth asking when you visit a Spanish or Mexican site how much of it was original and how much was restored and how the restoration choices were made. To the credit of the modern day caretakers of the missions and adobes, a great deal of effort has gone into acquiring the property, preserving these sites, and stocking them with the appropriate artifacts. Considering what they went through, it is a miracle that any of them survived.

The Mexicans were just as unlucky in their quest for gold as the Spanish had been. It is one of the great ironies of history that gold was discovered in Sutter's Mill just one year after Mexico lost control of Alta California. Again, one has to think Mexico would have fought a lot harder to keep California had they known how much gold was there. There were only a few battles in California during the Mexican American War and most of the large ones were in Southern California. There were small battles in Monterey, San Francisco, Olompali, and Santa Clara. These are well documented in the Presidio museums and in the Headen-Inman House in Santa Clara. Incidentally, there has never been a major battle in the entire history of the world in the Bay Area, thus making it one of the most peaceful places on earth. In Sonoma, a group of self-styled patriots proclaimed the Bear Flag Republic, so for a few months California was an independent country until it was annexed by the United States in 1850. These events are commemorated in the town square near where they happened.

Under the Treaty of Guadalupe-Hidalgo, Mexican citizens residing in California were allowed to remain and become American citizens. Therefore, Spanish influence in the region still pervades. Ironically, the Mexicans themselves (including many who had supported the revolt against the government of Mexico due to its ineffectual management and corruption) were often moved off of their own land as ever-increasing waves of settlers challenged their land claims. Crude, hand-drawn maps and the lack of easily identifiable landmarks or boundary markers made the Mexican land claims easy to contest in American courts. Their once vast land grants were whittled away piece by piece until little or nothing remained.

Nonetheless, Spanish place names abound in the Bay Area and Spanish and Mexican-inspired foods remain popular. The most lasting legacy, however, is in architecture. The "mission style" architecture has been replicated in many homes and public buildings throughout the region. Elements such as ranch style houses, patios, verandas, fountains, and interior gardens have become standard features of many Bay Area buildings.

Juan Jesus Vallejo Adobe-Fremont

(The numbers after the description of the historical site refer to the individual listings later in this book).

Sites for the Spanish and Mexican periods:

✓	Museum or historical site	Date Visited
	1. The Peralta House Museum of History-Oakland: An historic saddle, sword, historic photos, home furnishings, and items excavated from the site. #156	
	2. Drake's Bay: site of English exploration, the Kenneth C. Patrick Visitor Center in Point Reyes National Seashore contains exhibits that focus on 16th century exploration. #17	
	3. Fort Ross-Jenner: a Russian fort with trade items and an historic chapel. #73	
	4.History San Jose: rotating exhibits at the Arbuckle Gallery often contain items from this time period. #88	
	5. Oakland Museum of California: exhibits on Spanish and Mexican settlement, maps, historical documents, and artifacts. #147	
	6. Mission San Jose-Fremont: numerous items belonging to the priests and the church, priceless art objects from Mexico and Spain, an historic cemetery with many famous Californio names on the tombstones. #118	

	7. Mission Santa Clara: historic statues, paintings, and other items of interest; mission gardens and ruins of earlier mission buildings. #120	
	8. deSaisset Museum- Santa Clara : many items from the Santa Clara Mission, Spanish and Mexican settlers. #58	
	9. Peralta Adobe- San Jose: a horno (an outside working oven), inside the home are two rooms furnished as they might have been when they were occupied by the Gonzales and Peralta families. #157	
	10. Sanchez Adobe-Pacifica: original household furnishings from the Mexican era, ranch tools and equipment. #182	
	11. Juan Jesus Vallejo Adobe-Fremont: no displays, only a rental hall. #215	
	12. Mission San Rafael Arcangel: the mission museum contains artifacts, paintings, and other objects for public viewing, including three of the original bells from Mission San Rafael Arcangel. #119	
	13. Mission Dolores-San Francisco: the basilica and mission grounds, which include a historic cemetery and garden. There are a few rooms dedicated to displaying mission artifacts. #117	
	14. Mission Santa Cruz: original mission housing, a fine collection of Mission era vestments from the original mission. There are also sacred vessels used in the Catholic Mass and silver candlesticks on display. #121	
	15. Mission Carmel: the mission church, gardens, priests' vestments, relics, artwork, Munrás family items, and Junipero Serra's memorial. #116	
	16. Mission Soledad: mission art, relics, and furnishings, and items found in the archaeological digs. #122	
	17. Sonoma State Historic Park: includes General Vallejo's Home, Mission San Francisco Solano, The Sonoma Barracks, and the Servants Quarters (the remains of La Casa Grande). Many mission, ranch, personal, and military items are on display. In the plaza is a marker commemorating the Bear Flag Revolt. #197	
	18. Depot Park Museum-Sonoma: items belonging to the Vallejo family, a display about the raising of the Bear Flag. #57	
	19. Boronda Adobe History Center-Salinas: clothing, household items, saddles, and other ranch equipment. #127	
	20. Petaluma Adobe State Historic Park: the large two-story ranch house contains a loom and weaving room, bread ovens, leather processing and storage areas, a gristmill, dining room, parlor, and living quarters where fandangos were held. #158	
	21. The Higuera Adobe-Fremont: the adobe has been restored and furnished with handcrafted redwood furniture. It is available for visits to view the exterior only. There are some signs explaining the historical significance of the property. #86	
	22. Museum of Monterey: information on Spanish explorers. #136	

	23. Monterey State Historic Park: numerous public and private buildings spanning the Spanish, Mexican, and Early American periods; some have original artifacts and furnishings. #128	
	24. Los Altos History Museum: a few items from the rancho era. #104	
	25. San Mateo County History Museum-Redwood City: a few items from the rancho era. #185	
	26. Presidio Visitor's Center and The Officers' Club - San Francisco: Spanish cannons on the grounds, and historic maps, uniforms, etc., can be seen in the visitor's center. #169	
	27. Martinez Adobe-Martinez on the grounds of the John Muir National Historic Site: de Anza Expedition display, Mexican era artifacts, historic documents, maps, pictures, artifacts, etc. #96	
	28. The Headen-Inman House-Santa Clara: an original drawing of the little known Battle of Santa Clara, a bayonet from the battle and early Californio objects; family trees and genealogical information on early California families. #84	
	29. Berryessa Adobe-Santa Clara: clothing and other items belonging to the Berryessa family, and an exhibit about the de Anza Expedition; historic home and gardens. #23	
	30. Contra Costa County History Center-Martinez: a few items from the rancho era, historic documents and maps. #49	
	31. Angel Island: information about Spanish explorer Juan Manuel de Ayala. #9	
	32. Napa Valley Museum-Yountville: a few items from the rancho era. #139	
	33. Ulistac Natural Area-Santa Clara: plants used by Hispanic settlers. #209	
	34. Evergreen Valley College Library's Heritage Room: a few items from the rancho era, historic documents and maps. #66	
	35. Novato History Museum: a few items from the rancho era, historic documents and maps. #145	
	36. Petaluma Historical Library and Museum: exhibits on the Vallejo and other Californio families. #159	
	37. Museum of the San Ramon Valley-Danville: a few items from the rancho era, historic documents and maps. #135	
	38. Alviso Adobe- Pleasanton: replicas of ranch items, hands-on activities like adobe brick making for kids. One of the buildings is an original adobe. #8	
	39. Agricultural History Project Center and Museum- Watsonville: a few items from the rancho era, historic documents, and maps; the history of the rodeo. #3	
	40. The Pena Adobe-Vacaville: historic home furnishings and farm equipment. #155	

	41. Jose Maria Alviso Adobe-Milpitas (currently closed but the exterior may be viewed). No listing.	
	42. Alvarado Adobe-San Pablo: bricks from the original adobe, an antique piano, period furniture that belonged to the family. #7	
	43. Royal Presidio Chapel-Monterey: only structure remaining from the Spanish Presidio of Monterey, founded in 1770, #128	

I certify that _____ has visited all of the
above sites. He or she is an honorary Californio.
X _____ (museum staff member).

The Gold Rush Era

Gold is typically formed in volcanic areas, and while the Bay Area has had a few small gold mines that played out after only a few years, the largest deposits were found in the Sierra Nevada Mountains to the east. The discovery of gold at Sutter's Mill in 1848 changed California dramatically. The news spread quickly and people came from all over the world to search for more. The sleepy little village of Yerba Buena suddenly transformed into San Francisco, an all-important staging ground for gold seekers.

Most people are familiar with the emigrants coming to California by covered wagon over the Oregon, California, and Santa Fe Trails and their various offshoots. Some are unaware that the majority of gold seekers came by ship around the horn of South America and from other points around the Pacific. Just as Sutter's Fort and then Sacramento became a point for rest and re-provisioning for the lucky survivors of the overland routes, San Francisco provided the same benefits to those who came by sea. Hundreds of buildings sprang up overnight to meet the needs of those heading off to the gold fields after disembarking in San Francisco. They purchased mining equipment, clothing, food, and other supplies. They stayed in its hotels and ate in its restaurants, and then headed off up the rivers by steamboat to the gold fields of the Sierras. They traveled through the bay and up to the Sacramento Delta, disembarking at points such as Stockton or Sacramento. Then they traveled the rest of the way to the mining camps by stagecoach. If they found gold, they returned to San Francisco to have it assayed and banked, spending some of it on saloons, entertainment, or luxury goods as well.

Cities do not grow up in a certain spot by accident. In his famous book, *The Geography Behind History*, William Gordon East explains the theory of cities being magnets that attract people to them. He also states that cities are often founded in areas of transition from one region to the other, near water, and along transportation crossroads. San Francisco was chosen because it met several of these criteria. It has little arable land and is very hilly, so it was difficult to build upon. Nevertheless, its central location and access to waterways made it Northern

California's largest city, which it remained until it was finally surpassed by San Jose in the 1980's. The smaller cities and towns around the Bay Area initially grew up in order to provide food and goods to the rapidly growing San Francisco because it had so few resources and very poor soil. Most of the local museums in this book have excellent displays on the particular industries and farm products that their area produced in order to support San Francisco.

The San Francisco Bay and the Pacific Ocean provided shrimp, fish, clams, oysters, and whale oil for lamps. Fishing communities are found along the coasts of the bay and the ocean. From the north came redwood trees for lumber, farm produce, poultry, and wild game for San Francisco's hotels and restaurants. From Sonoma and Napa came dairy products, wine, and other foods. The northeast provided grains, dairy, and other foods. The East Bay provided farm goods, livestock, oaks and redwoods, and one of the few sources of coal in California. The peninsula provided lime and sand for building, farm products, and some of the largest redwood trees.

Vast forests around the bay were felled to feed San Francisco's greed for lumber. In fact, most of the historic mansions described in this book were built of redwood. The wood's special resistance to insects helps explain the longevity of these homes. Astonishingly, there are redwood pipes that are more than a century old that are still working in the sewers of San Francisco.

Finally, the South Bay provided grains, fruit, and most importantly, quicksilver, the mineral that produces mercury. Mercury is an essential ingredient for removing gold from hard rock gold ores such as quartz. If you examine the mercury bottles from any gold mill, you will see that they came from the New Alamaden mine in San Jose. It is safe to say that the Gold Rush as we know it could not have happened without San Jose. The down side of this is that there are still high levels of toxic mercury in the bay to this day because of runoff from the mines. This had a disastrous effect on Bay Area fisheries.

Once the placer gold ran out, mining switched from panning to hard rock, which involved tunneling, blasting rock, and then crushing it in a stamp mill. Some of these mines are still open today. Many of the lone miners who had scoured the hills of California looking for new gold claims were forced to work for large mining companies when the smaller claims didn't pay out well enough. In the final stage of the Gold Rush, large companies created massive hydraulic mining to wash away entire hillsides in search of gold. Beautiful pristine pine forests were left as barren as the Grand Canyon as millions of tons of topsoil were hosed away for a few ounces of gold. This had a devastating effect on the Central Valley and Delta communities downstream as they were inundated with water and mud. This led to some of the nation's first environmental laws, created to stop hydraulic mining. Other areas had huge dredges that moved tons of riverbed silt to sift for gold. The bay itself was choked with sediment and so much dirt was washed into it that it actually became one-fourth smaller. This had a devastating effect on its wildlife.

The human impact of the Gold Rush on the region was profound as well. The Gold Rush brought an ethnic mixture to the Bay Area that had never been seen before. The flood of immigrants drowned out the earlier inhabitants and they lost their land very quickly. In addition to Americans, immigrants included hopeful gold seekers from Australia, China, Hawaii, Latin America, and Europe. These various cultures clashed and the rivalries over gold claims were seldom settled amicably. Americans felt that the land was theirs through Manifest Destiny and they resented anyone else searching for gold.

Mexicans were important in the early stages of the Gold Rush because experienced miners from the Sonora region of Mexico introduced much of the technology for mining gold to other miners. Although the Treaty of Guadalupe Hidalgo allowed Mexicans to remain in California after the Mexican-American War, the American miners treated them like foreigners and tried to drive them from the camps. A disproportionate number of men convicted of jumping claims, stealing horses, or robbing people of their gold were Hispanic. Often, "kangaroo courts" were held on the spot and the accused did not even speak enough English to defend themselves. Trials were short and hangings were swift.

The Chinese fared even worse. Stereotyped as being heathen and called "yellow devils", they were driven from the camps completely. The only solution for these oppressed groups was to make a camp of their own, away from the Americans, if possible. These new camps were often only allowed in areas with inferior gold deposits. Many chose to leave the gold fields entirely and seek work in farms, ranches, or urban restaurants, laundries, and other businesses. Hence, Chinatowns began to spring up in the Bay Area and Sacramento Valley cities. Consequently, Chinese workers were hired to work on major construction projects, such as building the transcontinental railroad or paving roads in the Bay Area. They were also employed to harvest ice and timber in the Tahoe region. The Chinese also formed fishing communities, such as China Camp in Napa, and other fishing camps on the San Francisco Peninsula. Discrimination remained rampant for many years, leading to a series of laws restricting Chinese immigration. Finally, in 1882, the Chinese Exclusion Act banned any further immigration from China. This is the only ethnic group that was expressly banned by law in its entirety from entering the US. The history of the Chinese in California is very well documented at the Chinese Historical Society Museum in San Francisco.

Worst of all was the fate of the Indians of California. Their culture was obliterated and their lands were taken from them. Miners literally hunted them as if they were vermin, posting bounties upon their heads. Many of them died of disease, and the ones who survived only did so by intermarrying with other cultures. That is why most Native Americans in California today have Western last names. Also, by marrying non-Indians, they could gain citizenship. After the secularization of the missions, most Indians found work as ranch or farm hands. Some became unemployed. An indigent law was passed by the new state of California in 1850 that effectively allowed whites to force an Indian into indentured servitude for several months if it could not be proved that he had gainful employment. Another portion of the law allowed for minor Indian children to be "apprenticed" for a period of several years. As the Native Americans had no standing in court, it was pretty easy to have this claim approved, regardless of the evidence. Many Indians were forced to work under these conditions with little or no pay until the law was finally repealed during the Civil War due to the Emancipation Proclamation.

By contrast, the American settlers during the Gold Rush often prospered greatly, though not always through gold. Few miners actually struck it rich. Some died on the way to California or due to illnesses, accidents, fights, or crimes in the gold fields. Some found nothing at all or merely enough gold to cover their expenses and then either returned home or gave up and became farmers, merchants, etc. Some would continue to scour every hillside and valley stream in California looking for new gold deposits, usually with little success. Some miners went on to other gold and silver rushes in the northern part of the state, or in Nevada, Colorado, Arizona, New Mexico, and Alaska. Most ordinary folks simply homesteaded farmland or set up shop in the new towns and achieved modest prosperity. Several survivors of the infamous Donner-Reed expedition went on to settle in the Bay Area. Their stories and artifacts can be found in such diverse places as the museums in Calistoga, Saratoga, and San Jose.

A few, though, had the good fortune of being in the right place at the right time and became millionaires. They made their fortunes by catering to the needs of the miners and other settlers. One such example was Levi Strauss. He noticed that many of the sailing ships that came to San Francisco were abandoned at anchor because the sailors aboard had gone off to the gold fields along with the passengers. He had heard from a miner that they had difficult getting pants strong enough to withstand the harsh conditions of the gold field. So it dawned on him to use the sailcloth to make pants, adding rivets for added strength. The result was the Levi Strauss Company, which continues to make clothing to this day. At their museum and store in San Francisco, you can see historic jeans from the miners and even buy a replica pair!

Philip Armour started his company Armour Meat, in response to the miners' need for fresh meat. Henry Wells and William Fargo met the need of safely transporting and storing gold. You can visit the Wells Fargo History Museum in San Francisco to see a stagecoach and items from the Gold Rush. Many other businesses that still have a huge economic impact in the region today got their start in the Gold Rush, with familiar names like Stanford, Crocker, Hopkins, etc. San Francisco has grown into the financial capital of the West as a direct result of the Gold Rush. One of the oldest federal deposit banks is still open to display in the city. Also, one of the owners of the fabulously productive Empire Gold Mine built a mansion near Woodside and called it Filoli.

The Gold Rush also had an influence on American literature. Many famous writers, such as Bret Harte, Mark Twain, Jack London, and Robert Louis Stevenson wrote about the Gold Rush. Many of them had homes built in the Bay Area. Easterners were thrilled to read of these adventures and the western literary genre was born. Similarly, artists helped to capture the beauty and the grandeur of the West for skeptical but curious eyes from the East. Landscape paintings became very popular, many of which can be found in museums such as the Legion of Honor, de Young, or California Historical Society in San Francisco. The Cantor Arts Center, Oakland Museum of California, and Napa Valley museums also have fine pieces of landscape art. These fine paintings also adorn the homes of many historic mansions around the Bay Area, such as the homes of John Muir, the Pardee family, and many others.

(The numbers after the description of the historical site refer to the individual listings later in this book).

Gold Rush sites:

✓	Museum or historical site	Date Visited
	1. The San Francisco History Museum: Gold Rush artifacts, historical photos. #192	
	2. New Almaden Quicksilver Mining Museum -San Jose: quicksilver mining artifacts. #142	
	3. Filoli-Woodside: a home owned by the wealthy owner of the Empire Mine. #68	
	4. Chinatown- San Francisco: some buildings date back to the Gold Rush era, pictures and artifacts from Chinese miners are in the Chinese Historical Society of America Museum. #42	
	5. Agricultural History Project Center and Museum- Watsonville historic farm equipment. #3	
	6. Oakland Museum of California: Gold Rush artifacts, photos and interactive displays. #147	
	7. Sunnyvale Heritage Park Museum: The Murphy Party predated the Donner Party. A comprehensive display about this important pioneer tells his story. #202	
	8. Los Altos History Museum: Gold Rush artifacts. #104	
	9. San Mateo County History Museum: Gold Rush artifacts and local food that supplied the miners. #185	
	10. Presidio Visitor's Center and The Officers' Club -San Francisco: early San Francisco fortifications and historic photos. #169	
	11. San Francisco Fire Dept. Fire Museum: early fire fighting equipment. #191	
	12. San Francisco Maritime National Historic Park: historic sailing ships and models. #190	
	13. Wells Fargo History Museum- San Francisco: an original Wells Fargo wagon, bank items, gold, etc. #219	
	14. Levi's Plaza Store and Historical Archives-San Francisco: historic blue jeans. #102	
	15. Museum of Monterey: historic photos, artwork, and nautical items. #136	
	16. Point Pinos Lighthouse-Pacific Grove: an historic lighthouse still in operation. #166	
	17. Bale Grist Mill-St. Helena: an historic mill. #15	
	18. Fischer-Hanlon House-Benicia: a house built from the era when Benicia was the state's capital. #19	

	19. Benicia Historical Museum: Gold Rush tools, river dredging, and pictures of Gold Rush era buildings; display about the first announcement of the discovery of gold from Sutter's Mill which took place in Benicia. #21	
	20. Contra Costa County History Center-Martinez: Gold Rush artifacts and documents. #49	
	21. The Robert Louis Stevenson Museum: personal items of Stevenson's, original manuscripts, first printings, etc. #177	
	22. Napa Valley Museum-Yountville: Gold Rush artifacts. #139	
	23. Ulistac Natural Area-Santa Clara: plants used by early settlers to the region. #209	
	24. Murrietta's Well-Livermore: a well used by the notorious Gold Rush bandito. #132	
	25. Antioch Historical Museum: a giant wheel from a Gold Rush era steamboat. #10	
	26. Colton Hall and several buildings in the Monterey State Historic Park: site of the first state constitution and many other events of the era. #128	

I certify that _____ has visited all of the above sites. He or she has "seen the elephant" and is an honorary forty-niner.
X _____ (museum staff member).

Sharpsteen Museum-Calistoga

The Civil War

Many people would probably assume that the majority of activity in the Civil War took place on the East Coast and that California had nothing to do with it at all. They would be surprised to learn how many links California had to the conflict. In some ways, it can be said that the admission of California to the union in 1851 started the Civil War. For decades before that time, the North and the South had made a series of compromises over which states would enter the union as free and slave states. The most important of these, the Missouri Compromise of 1820, stated that new states above the 36° 30' parallel would be free and those below it would be slave holding, with the exception of Missouri itself, which would be free. This held true through the following decades until California applied for admission to the Union shortly after the Gold Rush began. The Missouri Compromise line would have cut California in half, something that nobody wanted. Pro-slavery forces lobbied hard for California to be a slave state at the Constitutional Convention. They got a surprisingly high number of votes because many Southerners had come to California. Some even tried bringing slaves to dig their gold for them, but in the end, the anti-slavery forces narrowly prevailed.

This issue forced Congress to make a new deal called the Compromise of 1850. Under it, California would be admitted as one free state, the rest of the West would vote one by one whether to be free or slave upon admission, and slavery would be banned in Washington, D.C. The South would get a tougher Fugitive Slave Law that would force Northerners to cooperate with slave hunters to return runaway slaves hiding in the North. When Northerners effectively ignored or defied this law, the compromise broke down. Congress tried one last compromise called the Kansas-Nebraska Act, which called upon territories to decide for themselves their slavery status when applying for admission to the Union. This merely led to a rush of settlers from both sides to the disputed territories. Rioting and then armed conflict broke out, which continued until the outbreak of the Civil War. California's narrow brush with secession and its journey to statehood are well documented at the Benicia Capitol State Historic Park. Another site related to this dispute is the Daly City History Museum. The town was the site of the famous Broderick-Terry duel, which was an important showdown over whether California would enter the Union as a free or slave-owning state.

By the time the war broke out, most Californians had settled firmly upon the side of the Union. California volunteers formed armies that traveled to the East to fight for the Union. About 17,000 volunteers for the Union came from California, the highest per capita of any state. Large portions of the West were defended and occupied by California troops. The uniforms and arms of these units can be seen at the California State Military Museum in Sacramento. These troops fought faithfully for the Union and participated in many key battles, including Gettysburg and the campaign to free New Mexico from Confederate control. They were even present when Robert E. Lee surrendered to U.S. Grant at Appomattox Court House, Virginia in 1865. The most famous Civil War volunteer was General Joseph Hooker. At first Lincoln liked him because he was called "Fighting Joe", but when Lee defeated him, he was demoted. Later, he was given a lesser command by General Grant. Details of Hooker's life and the ups and downs of his career can be seen at his home in Sonoma. Californians contributed more to the United States Sanitary Commission than any other state. This was the most important organization responsible for the medical treatment of the numerous military casualties suffered on the Union side.

Abraham Lincoln realized the importance of California's gold to bankroll the war, so he took measures to protect the new state from Confederate attack. Forts were built on Alcatraz Island and Fort Point (which is now under the Golden Gate Bridge). Troops were stationed at the Presidio in San Francisco and at Angel Island. At Fort Point, visitors can see impressive fortifications and practice firing a Civil War era cannon. During the annual Civil War Days, re-enactors march and drill, play music, etc. Angel Island has some of the oldest and best-preserved Civil War Era barracks in the nation. Students may even stay in the barracks overnight and re-enact the lives of the soldiers, including baking bread in the original ovens. The park visitor's center has Civil War uniforms and flags. The American Civil War Association has a Northern California chapter and they often stage battle reenactments in Bay Area parks. See their website at http://www.acwa.org/ for details. The Civil War fortifications on Alcatraz Island were covered by later forts and then the infamous Penitentiary, but if you ask the Park Rangers, they can point out which portions of the buildings are from the Civil War Era.

Troops were also stationed in the Benicia Barracks. The U.S. Navy's first base located on the Pacific coast was Mare Island. The founding commander was future Union Admiral David Farragut (the first to hold that title). His famous quote, "Damn the torpedoes! Full speed ahead!" demonstrated his courage. He is also famous for his exploits in attacking the defenses at Mobile Bay. Visit the Benicia Historical Museum and Mare Island Historic Park to learn more about many little known contributions the Bay Area made to the Civil War.

Despite Northern California's pro-Union sentiments, there were still many Confederate sympathizers. In March of 1863, a plot to capture the San Francisco Bay was foiled. The plan was to arm the schooner, J.M. Chapman, and use it to capture a steamship, which would then be used to raid commerce in the Pacific. Everyone was arrested, however, and the arms were confiscated. In October 1863, a suspected Confederate vessel was spotted in the bay headed towards U.S. military installations. It was fired upon by Alcatraz Island batteries. No casualties resulted from the engagement and the ship turned out to be British! Confederate privateers had sunk several ships in the Pacific, so they did try to raid the bay, but did not get there before the end of the war.

In the Santa Clara Valley, conspirators tried to arrange to hijack two Wells Fargo wagons near Placerville, which were filled with silver from Nevada. They hoped to use the treasure to fund recruiting of troops for the Confederate Army. Local law enforcement killed some of the robbers and arrested others and the silver was recovered. Also, Confederate sympathizers in Los Angeles organized a company of mounted rifles that marched through the desert all the way to Texas, where they joined Confederate units. Their leader, Albert Sidney Johnston, went on to be one of the highest-ranking officers in the Southern army.

28

(The numbers after the description of the historical site refer to the individual listings later in this book).

Civil War sites:

✓	Museum or historical site	Date Visited
	1. Fort Point: cannons and coastal defenses. #72	
	2. Alcatraz Island: cannons and coastal defenses. #6:	
	3. Presidio Visitor's Center and The Officers' Club -San Francisco: parade grounds, cannons, and coastal defenses. #169	
	4. The South Bay Historical Railroad Society-Santa Clara: Civil War era train station. #199	
	5. Angel Island: Civil War uniforms and flags, parade grounds, barracks, bakery, and coastal defenses. #9	
	6. Salinas Valley Memorial Hospital Museum of Medical History: a surgery kit from the Civil War. #179	
	7. The General Joseph Hooker House-Sonoma: historic pictures, documents and some personal items belonging to the general. #74	
	8. Mare Island Historic Park: the U.S. Navy's first base located on the Pacific coast, historic pictures and model ships. #216	
	9. Daly City History Museum: photos and documents about the Broderick-Terry duel over secession for California. #54	
	10. Lathrop house-Redwood City: a Civil War era house with pictures of Lincoln and his cabinet. #99	
	11. Benicia Capitol State Historic Park: exhibits on the battle over secession during the drafting of California's constitution. #19	
	12. The Benicia Historical Museum: pictures of the Civil War generals who served at Benicia, a few Civil War era artifacts, and a copy of a book that Lincoln read about Benicia shortly before he died. #21	
	13. Vallejo Naval and Historical Museum: models and pictures of Civil War era ships. #216	
	14. Antioch Museum: a Civil War drum. #10	
	15. Crockett History Museum: Civil War bullets and currency. #52	
	16. Presidio Museum of Monterey: Civil War Encampments with musket, cannon, and cavalry demonstrations during Monterey's History Fest in October. #168	
	17. Museum of the African Diaspora-San Francisco: compelling slave narratives #124	
	Note: Some Civil War items are to be found in museums scattered throughout the Bay Area, such as the occasional Civil War medal, gun, bullets, currency, or photo. If you find one, mark it here.	

I certify that _____ has visited all of the
above sites and has preserved California for the Union.
X _____ (museum staff member).

Camron-Stanford House-Oakland

Settlers From Around the World

In the years following the Gold Rush, people came to California from all around the world. They were drawn here by the mild climate, inexpensive land, fertile soil, and varied job opportunities. The older populations in California were overwhelmed by the tide of immigrants. California Indians declined in numbers, but Indians from other parts of the country began to move to the state and eventually outnumbered the local Indians. The rich diversity of California's Indians can be seen at the Museum of the American Indian in Novato. Mexicans have been a part of the Bay Area for centuries, but the newer Mexican immigrants far outnumbered the old Californios, and they continue to come to this day. The newer immigrants brought a slightly different culture and did not always relate well with the older settlers. Russia gave up its claims to California when it sold Alaska to the U.S. in 1867, but Russian immigrants have come to California, the Bay Area in particular, in ever increasing numbers to this day.

Chinese immigrants held to their neighborhoods with determination despite rampant discrimination and hostility from other groups. The Chinese Exclusion Act of 1882 banned further immigration by the Chinese, but relatives could be admitted to the U.S. with the proper paperwork. An unexpected boon to Chinese immigrants was created by the 1906 Earthquake. Many buildings were burned and records were lost. If a Chinese immigrant could prove to immigration officials that his or her parents lived in Chinatown before the earthquake, admission would be granted due to the lost records. These so-called "paper sons" were detained on Angel Island for up to two years while investigations were conducted to verify their relations to U.S. citizens. An entire industry grew up to provide hopeful Chinese immigrants with the necessary paperwork and to coach them with minute details about their fathers' homes in China that they would need to know to pass the Immigration Department's questioning. Most were eventually cleared, but some got sent back to China due to failing the interviews or due to medical quarantines. The fascinating story of these and many other immigrants can be seen at The Angel Island Immigration Station.

Their heartbreaking poetry about loneliness and hopelessness can still be seen on its walls. The immigrants could not understand why they were being detained if they had committed no crime. They missed the old country and were tantalized by the hope of San Francisco's Chinatown being so near, but just out of reach.

Other Asians came to California as well. Japanese came in large numbers and found work in the fisheries, orchards, and greenhouses around the bay, particularly in the Santa Clara Valley. Their story is told at the Japanese American Museum of San Jose and other places. Filipinos came to work in the farms of the Bay Area and Santa Cruz and Monterey Counties. They eventually became the largest Asian group in the state. Other settlers included people from Latin America and the Caribbean, the Pacific Islands, and smaller East Asian countries. The Oakland Museum of California and The San Mateo County History Museum in Redwood City have especially good displays on immigration. Many agricultural museums in the area highlight these Asian and Hispanic migrant workers. Some examples are the Boronda Adobe History Center and National Steinbeck Center in Salinas and The Agricultural History Project Center and Museum in Watsonville.

Ever since Hawaii's discovery by Captain Cook in 1778, the fate of Hawaiians has been inextricably intertwined with California. Young Hawaiian men were highly sought after for the whaling industry because of their skills at sea. Many whaling ships also operated in California's waters or stopped there for supplies. Some Hawaiians subsequently decided to settle in California. They were even among those to build the Petaluma Adobe. Sandalwood from Hawaii was highly prized in America as well. Hawaiians worked to harvest it in such large quantities that the trees became nearly extinct. In the following years, large sugar plantations were planted in Hawaii and a brisk business was conducted to satisfy America's ever-growing sweet tooth. C&H sugar became one of the most powerful companies in the Pacific by producing the majority of cane sugar from Hawaii and beet sugar from California, hence the name C&H. The Crockett Historical Museum sits in the shadow of the largest sugar refinery in the West, and has interesting displays on the history and influence of sugar in California. The sugar plantation owners, such as the Spreckels and Dole families, became very influential in the movement that led to the annexation of Hawaii by America.

This annexation was bitterly opposed by Hawaii's monarchs. They traveled to California several times to protect their interests. One of them, Joseph Kalakaua, died in San Francisco during one such trip. The Spreckels and Dole families had homes and farms scattered throughout the Bay Area. The Doles are best known for their pineapples, but they established many farms and built canneries in the agricultural communities of the Bay Area. They still own many farms and food processing plants in Santa Cruz and Monterey Counties. In several Victorian homes in the Bay Area, it is common to see pineapples as an ornamentation carved into staircase banisters or doorposts. This ornamentation is said to represent hospitality because visiting sea captains from Hawaii often brought fresh pineapples with them.

European immigrants came in large numbers to California as well. English, Dutch, French, Germans, Scandinavians, and Swiss settlers came to the Bay Area to become farmers and merchants. They were attracted by California's wide-open spaces and peaceful landscape, which were very much welcomed after the overcrowding and incessant wars of Europe. These groups tended to blend in with the rest of the white population rather quickly and therefore faced little discrimination. The Irish faced more difficulty, particularly if they were Roman Catholic. Southern and Eastern Europeans had a tougher time due to their different appearance, languages, and customs as compared to those of the Northwestern European immigrants. Large numbers of Italians, Portuguese, Greeks, and Slavic people settled in the Bay Area because the climate reminded them of the Mediterranean. Initially, they tended to do the jobs that nobody else wanted, such as garbage collectors, fishermen, or farm and factory laborers. Even some Middle Easterners and Africans came to California in these years. African Americans came to California in large numbers after emancipation from slavery in 1865 because the Golden State represented a fresh start away from the discrimination and lack of opportunity in the South. Many of these groups faced initial hardships, but eventually prospered. Their jobs and social status improved over time. While there was still some racism and discrimination in California, immigrants and migrants achieved wealth and influence that would not have been possible in their homelands or home regions. Each of these groups brought with them their traditions, customs, and foods, making the Bay Area one of the most ethnically diverse regions in the world. In fact, it has the greatest variety of restaurants, ethnic schools, and places of worship on the planet.

Due to their large numbers, the group of settlers that had the biggest impact on the development of the Bay Area was the Americans who flooded in from the East Coast. They had the advantages of possessing the dominant language, customs, and laws. They brought with them the social institutions with which they were familiar, such as churches, schools, and courts. Frontier justice soon gave way to established courts, government, and the rule of law. Unfortunately, this meant that it was very easy for American settlers to defraud Indian and Hispanic landowners of their land claims. The requirements for proving ownership of land were much more stringent under American law and the complete domination of the legal system by whites meant that previous landowners almost always lost their lawsuits. Many Americans were also able to buy up land very cheaply from destitute Indians and Hispanics. They were then able to reap immense profits after developing and improving the land. Many of the Bay Area's fortunes were begun during this era. Even if the white settlers came from humble origins, they could strike it rich in California, not by mining gold, but by farming or conducting commerce.

The architecture of the period reflects this American influence. So much so, that when Hollywood location scouts are looking for a historic locale to represent New England, they often come to Northern California to shoot. Some of the early American settlers in California purchased and modified old adobes. Sometimes the transition from adobe brick, dirt floors, and tiled roofs to brick or linoleum floors and wood paneling or plastered walls can be seen in the same house. Examples of this are to be seen in adobes in Monterey, San Jose, Pleasanton, and other places. Some were torn down and rebuilt in a grander Mission style. Eventually, when these houses were all taken, Americans began to build in the styles that were familiar to them in the East, particularly that of New England. At first, modest cottage style homes were built, followed by ever larger Neoclassical, Italianate, and

Victorian style homes and mansions, which began to crop up in the cities as fortunes increased. Often, homes were an odd mixture of several of these architectural influences, mixed in with Mission elements and some original materials and experimental building techniques. Perhaps the biggest experimental builder of them all was Sarah Winchester. It is said that she never stopped building during her lifetime. Her vast mansion in San Jose (the Winchester Mystery House) is still visited by thousands of people each year, making it the one of the most popular historical sites in the state.

There is enough variety in the Bay Area to keep an architectural historian happy for a lifetime. Many of the homes that survived from this era became the historical house museums listed in this book. The details of each site are too many to be described here, so please refer to the listings for each museum later in this book. Soon, every town had streets laid out in a grid pattern with American street names. Public squares, parks, gardens, concert halls, and Carnegie libraries sprouted up in every locale. The wealthy built private retreats to escape from the press of the big city. These elaborate mansions had many rooms and the grounds had large formal gardens, fountains, grottos, and nature paths. These became common in the scenic rural areas of the mountains and foothills of the region. Fortunately, most of these were opened up for the masses to enjoy in the twentieth century and have become popular destinations for cultural and social events in the Bay Area today.

On April 18, 1906, a terrible earthquake shook the region. The horrific damage and dislocation caused by this disaster can be seen at the San Francisco Fire Dept. Fire Museum, The San Francisco History Museum, The South San Francisco Historical Museum, and The Daly City History Museum. The earthquake was such a catastrophe that popular accounts of the event at the time were bundled and sold with accounts of the destruction of ancient Pompeii by the volcano Mount Vesuvius. Most people have heard of the devastation caused by this quake and subsequent fires in San Francisco, but not as many know that it caused damage at many locations outside of San Francisco. On The Earthquake Trail, near the Bear Valley Visitor's Center in Point Reyes National Seashore, you can see posters explaining how the quake happened and how much damage there was. One section of a ranch fence along the trail shifted twenty feet apart from the original line of the fence! In fact, the highest casualties from the earthquake were at Agnews Mental Hospital in Santa Clara due to the collapse of its brick buildings. They even have a skull from one of its victims on display! Many buildings were leveled in downtown San Jose and other places. Many fine buildings were destroyed and extensive remodeling subsequently occurred in many Bay Area towns and cities. Most of the historic buildings in this book sustained some damage from the 1906 Earthquake, but miraculously survived it, sometimes when all the buildings around it were destroyed. Ask your docent for the details of how the quake affected the building you are visiting during your tour. You will be certain to hear some amazing stories.

(The numbers after the description of the historical site refer to the individual listings later in this book).

Sites for Settlers from Around the World:

✓	Museum or historical site	Date Visited
	1. Rio Vista Museum: artifacts from early settlers such as an antique buggy, mail carriage, and organ. #176	
	2. Salinas Valley Memorial Hospital Museum of Medical History: historic medical instruments and books. #179	
	3. Agricultural History Project Center and Museum- Watsonville: fruit jar, milk bottle, and dairy artifact displays; restored horse drawn equipment including plows, binders, reapers and planters, tractors and many other forms of farm equipment. #3	
	4. Petaluma Historical Library and Museum: shipping and transportation items, poultry farming, a schoolroom, kitchen, an antique carriage, and firearms. #159	
	5. The San Lorenzo Valley Museum: schoolroom, farming and logging items. #184	
	6. Evergreen Valley College Library's Heritage Room: pictures and documents related to local schools, mining, agriculture, and historic buildings. #66	
	7. Jack Mason Museum of West Marin History-Inverness: pictures related to local schools, fishing, agriculture, and historic buildings. #93	
	8. Tomales Regional History Center: pictures related to fishing, agriculture, railroad items, historic buildings, and extensive school records. #206	
	9. Ravenswood Historical Site-Livermore: historical home with Victorian era clothing and furnishings. #172	
	10. Ulistac Natural Area-Santa Clara: garden with historic plants used by settlers from various times. #209	
	11. Agnews Historic Cemetery and Museum: historic mental hospital equipment. #2	
	12. Sharpsteen Museum-Calistoga: stagecoaches, local resorts, farms, blacksmith shops, Robert Louis Stevenson, Sam Brannon, and the Donner party. #194	
	13. Robert Louis Stevenson State Park-Calistoga: site of Stevenson's cabin. #177	
	14. Point Pinos Lighthouse-Pacific Grove: light-keeping equipment, buoys, maps, photos, etc. #166	
	15. Point Lobos Whaling Station: whaling and fishing equipment. #165	
	16. Museum of Monterey: maritime items, and local artwork. #136	
	17. The Daly City History Museum: newspapers and photos of the San Francisco Earthquake and the resettlement that followed it. #54	

	18. Aptos History Museum: pioneer families, Spreckels, the "sugar king", the coming of the railroad, Asian immigration, the lumber industry, apples and other farming, flight pioneer John Montgomery, and resort building in the 1920's and 30's. #11	
	19. The Museum of Art & History at the McPherson Center-Santa Cruz: farming and ranching items, household items, and logging tools. #203	
	20. Ygnacio Peralta Home-San Leandro: historical home. Open by appointment only. No listing	
	21. Union City Historical Museum: household items of every kind and objects and photos from local businesses. #210	
	22. History San Jose: mini-museums dedicated to many different ethnic groups that moved to the area with a large variety of historic artifacts; reconstructed historical buildings from the turn of the century and beyond. #88	
	23. Museum of the San Ramon Valley-Danville: railroad, farming, and cowboy items. #135	
	24. Oakland Museum of California: many historical artifacts from the late 1800s and early 1900s. #147	
	25. Camron-Stanford House-Oakland: historical home with Victorian era clothing and furnishings. #33	
	26. Winchester Mystery House-San Jose: historical home with Victorian era clothing and furnishings, outstanding historical gun collection. #223	
	27. Sunnyvale Heritage Park Museum: Murphy family, early pioneers, orchards and farm equipment, historic businesses, etc. #202	
	28. Rengstorff House-Mountain View: historical home with Victorian era clothing and furnishings. #174	
	29. Montalvo Arts Center-Saratoga: the historic villa and gardens of James Duval Phelan. #216	
	30. Hakone Gardens- Saratoga: historic Japanese gardens. #79	
	31. Chinese Historical Society of America Museum-San Francisco: many interesting artifacts from the different occupations held by Chinese immigrants, anti-Chinese propaganda, etc. #42	
	32. Pacific Heritage Museum-San Francisco: photographic exhibits that often include immigrant themes. #151	
	33. Los Altos History Museum: orchards, farming, diorama of the town including model railroads. #104	
	34. San Mateo County History Museum-Redwood City: exhibits on the agriculture and industry of the region, immigrant profiles in their own voices, and model ships. #185	

	35. African American Museum & Library-Oakland: unique focus on the Black experience in the East Bay, historic photos and documents, a reconstructed store. #1	
	36. Shinn Historic Park & Arboretum-Fremont: historic gardens and an historical home with Victorian era clothing and furnishings. #195	
	37. Alameda Museum: antique home furnishings, farms, and nautical items; Neptune Park amusement park. #5	
	38. Ardenwood Historic Farm- Fremont: agricultural tools, buildings, farm animals, and living history. #12	
	39. Prusch Farm-San Jose: agricultural tools, buildings, farm animals, and living history; an historic home. #170	
	40. Museum on Main-Pleasanton: farm items, early pioneer families, household objects, business and entertainment items. #163	
	41. Niles Essanay Silent Film Museum-Fremont: items from the silent film era including famous actors such as Charlie Chaplin. #144	
	42. Black Diamond Mines -Antioch: historic coal and salt mines, mining equipment, and an historic graveyard. #24	
	43. Clayton Historical Society Museum: farming, mining, and antique household items. #44	
	44. East Contra Costa Historical Society Museum-Brentwood: antique farm equipment, household items, river and delta transport. #63	
	45. John Muir National Historic Site-Martinez: historic furnishings, paintings and books of Muir's, and an historic orchard and farm buildings. #96	
	46. Martinez Museum: shipping, an antique barbershop, other local businesses, kitchen, toys, and clothing. #111	
	47. Pittsburg Historical Society: a vintage saloon, movie theater, military items, bridal gowns; items from the ranching, mining, fishing, canning, and river transport industries. #162	
	48. Richmond Museum of History: early settlers, a general store, farm tools, antique automobiles, and shipping items. #175	
	49. Shadelands Ranch Historical Museum-Walnut Creek: historical home with Victorian era clothing and furnishings. #193	
	50. Western Railway Museum- Suisun City: electric trolleys and streetcars. #220	
	51. Alcatraz Island: an historic prison. #6	
	52. Cable Car Museum San Francisco: close up view of the cables, and displays on how the cable cars work. #28	
	53. Presidio Visitor's Center and The Officers' Club -San Francisco: military housing, historic cannons, Buffalo Soldiers, uniforms, military items and a film of Teddy Roosevelt's visit. #169	
	54. San Francisco Fire Dept. Fire Museum: antique fire fighting	

	equipment and fascinating items from the 1906 earthquake. #191	
	55. San Francisco Maritime National Historic Park: sailing and steam ships from the era. #190	
	56. Ainsley House-Campbell: historical home with Victorian era clothing and furnishings. #4	
	57. Cupertino Historical Museum: farming, pioneers, photos of historic buildings, and a general store. #53	
	58. The Gilroy Museum: American pioneers, local businesses, local resources, ranching, hot springs resorts, schools, and items belonging to women and children. #75	
	59. Harris-Lass House Museum-Santa Clara: historical home with early 20th century era clothing and furnishings. #81	
	60. New Museum Los Gatos: farming, mill items, local pioneers, clothing and household items. #105	
	61. The Headen-Inman House-Santa Clara: historical home with early 20th century era clothing and furnishings. #84	
	62. Saratoga Historical Park & Museum: American pioneers, local businesses, wineries, logging, hot springs resorts, schools, household items, etc. #189	
	63. Dunsmuir House & Gardens-Oakland: historical home with Victorian era clothing and furnishings. #62	
	64. Hayward Area Historical Museum-Hayward: objects showing the agricultural and industrial roles of the area. #83	
	65. McConaghy House- Hayward: historical home with turn-of-the -century clothing and furnishings; an antique buggy, gas pump, clothing, and sports items. #112	
	66. Pardee Home Museum-Oakland: historical home with Victorian era clothing and furnishings. #154	
	67. Antioch Historical Museum: bridal room, toys and other children's items, the military, local businesses, movies and theaters, a lady's bedroom, cameras, saloon, government offices, a parlor, and musical instruments. #10	
	68. Point Reyes Light Station District: historic lighthouse equipment. #167	
	69. Falkirk Cultural Center-San Rafael (open for special events only): historic home. No listing.	
	70. Marin History Museum-San Rafael: maps, paintings, furniture, tools, household objects and clothing, objects from the 1906 earthquake and two World Fairs, Northwest Pacific Railroad & Ferry Company, San Quentin Prison, and personal effects of arctic explorer Louise Boyd. #109	
	71. China Camp Historic District-San Rafael: historic Chinese fishing area; boats, nets, shrimp dryers, etc. #41	
	72. Point Bonita Light House: historic lighthouse equipment. #164	
	73. Forts Baker, Barry, and Cronkhite Marin County Headlands:	

	remains of historic gun emplacements that you can explore. #71	
	74. Haas-Lilienthal House-San Francisco: historical home with Victorian era clothing and furnishings. #78	
	75. Kohl Mansion-Burlingame (open for special events only): historical home with Victorian era clothing and furnishings. No listing.	
	76. Lathrop House-Redwood City: historical home with Victorian era clothing and furnishings. #99	
	77. Octagon House-San Francisco: colonial furnishings and items related to the Founding Fathers and signers of the Declaration of Independence. #149	
	78. Fallon House-San Jose: Victorian era clothing and furnishings. #157	
	79. Casa Peralta-San Leandro: displays on settlers from around the world. #37	
	80. Cohen-Bray House-Oakland: historical home with Victorian era clothing and furnishings. #46	
	81. Wilder Ranch State Park-Santa Cruz: turn-of-the-century ranch with antique autos and farm equipment. #222	
	82. Pajaro Valley Historical Association-Watsonville: historical home with Victorian era clothing and furnishings, and an archive with photos and documents. #152	
	83. California Historical Society-San Francisco: an archive of historical documents about California. #29	
	84. Bancroft Library-Berkeley: an archive of historical documents about California. #16	
	85. Hayes Mansion-San Jose: historical home that has a few items that belonged to the Hayes family. #82	
	86. Gilroy Hot Springs: ruins of the historic hot springs resort. #76	
	87. Novato History Museum: American pioneers, Victorian household items, and farm and ranch items. #145	
	88. The Berkeley Historical Society: historical photos and documents, farming tools, and historic buildings. #22	
	89. Judah L. Magnes Museum-University of California, Berkeley: items pertaining to Jewish immigrants. #108	
	90. Crockett Historical Museum: household items, antiques and general store items, vintage toys, etc. #52	
	91. South San Francisco Historical Museum: vintage wedding gowns and other clothing, a teacup collection, photos and artifacts, an historic kitchen, local industries and businesses. #200	
	92. The Woodside Store: general store items, logging, blacksmithing, etc. #225	
	93. Pine Ridge Museum-Henry Coe State Park: an historic ranch house. #161	
	94. The Museum of Local History-Fremont: farming, The Early	

	Mission Mercantile, livery stable, film-making in Niles, early post offices, horse carriages, farm and ranch equipment, school exhibits, and a home kitchen exhibit. #134	
	95. The South Bay Historical Railroad Society-Santa Clara: historic railroad equipment, a railcar, and model train layouts. #199	
	96. San Jose Fire Museum: antique fire-fighting equipment. #181	
	97. Contra Costa County History Center-Martinez: farmers, ranchers, the oil industry, shipping, historical maps and documents. #49	
	98. Lafayette Historical Society: historical photos, historical clothing, tools, a blacksmith's anvil and other artifacts. #98	
	99. The David and Eliza Glass House Museum-San Ramon: historical home with early 20th Century era clothing and furnishings. #70	
	100. Angel Island: military camps and other buildings and the immigration station. #9	
	101. Alviso Adobe- Pleasanton: dairy and farming equipment. #8	
	102. Centennial Light Bulb-Livermore: a light bulb that has burned for more than 100 years. #38	
	103. The Livermore Heritage Guild: models of historic buildings, local wineries and farms, clothing and household items. #103	
	104. Cowell Lime Works Historic District- Santa Cruz: lime production facilities. #50	
	105. Soquel Pioneer and Historical Association: pictures and artifacts of farming, fishing, logging, and other industries. #198	
	106. Santa Cruz Boardwalk Historium- Santa Cruz: pictures of the historic amusement park and ballroom. #186	
	107. Vacaville Museum: varies by display, but often features local historical clothing and pioneer items. #214	
	108. Blume House and Bunk House- San Pablo: an historical home with early 20th Century era clothing and furnishings. #7	
	109. Jack London State Historic Park-Glen Ellen: many personal items belonging to London, original manuscripts, first printings, etc. #92	
	110. Monterey County Agricultural & Rural Life Museum: The Spreckels House, Schoolhouse, Train Depot and Olson Blacksmith Shop; farm equipment. #123	
	111. Lick Observatory: historic telescopes #131	
	112. The Woodside Store: general store, dentist office, hardware shed, and blacksmith shop. #225	
	113. Burlingame Hillsborough History Museum: founding fathers, railroads, and historic trees #27	
	114. Millbrae Historical Museum: many interesting household items and other artifacts. #113	
	115. The San Francisco History Museum: exhibit on vanished landmarks such as the Sutro Baths and the Cliff House. #192	
	116. Bear Valley Visitor's Center in Point Reyes National Seashore: earthquake trail and Morgan Horse Corral. #17	

I certify that _____ has visited the at least 5 historic homes and 5 local community museums, a transportation, industrial, and an agricultural museum. He or she is now an honorary California settler.

X _____ (museum staff member).

World War One and the Early Twentieth Century

As we have reached the centennial of the outbreak of World War I, some historians are now calling it the Forgotten War because it is mentioned so seldom these days. All one has to do is compare the number of films made about WWI and WWII to get a sense of the popular interest in this event. There are literally hundreds of WWII movies that have been made and perhaps a dozen that have been made about WWI. The last known veteran of the war, Florence Green, died on February 8, 2012, and with her, living human memory of the event vanished forever. From now on, we only have written accounts and a small amount of historical footage to go on for direct memory of these events. I am fortunate that an oral history of WWI has been passed down in my family, but for many others, the events of WWI are known only in history books. My Italian grandfather was a machine gunner in the Battle of Caporetto. He faced relentless enemy gas attacks and was captured (along with thousands of others) and subsequently tortured by the Germans. After the war, he was sent home without even the clothes on his back.

Even though it was far from the action, California sent many soldiers to the war. Memorials to the fallen of the war exist at The University of California Memorial Stadium in Berkeley, The Palace of the Legion of Honor in San Francisco, and in many Bay Area parks and cemeteries. Home guards were also organized in California after the famous Zimmerman Telegram was intercepted and decoded. It was discovered that Germany had been conspiring with Japan and Mexico to invade the United States and return to Mexico some of its lost territory. Fortunately, nothing ever came of this plot. Mexico and Japan denied any involvement and Germany never had the means to carry it out. This discovery, along with the sinking of ships with Americans aboard, led to the U.S. declaring war on Germany.

Bay Area military bases expanded, with troops being trained at the Presidio, Angel Island, and other facilities. Huge gun emplacements were built at various locations around the Golden Gate to protect the Bay Area. The region's naval bases, such as Mare Island, Vallejo, and Alameda played an especially important role. Their museums contain many interesting artifacts from the war.

America's involvement in WWI was much shorter than most nations, but it was nonetheless decisive regarding its outcome. America was only in the war from 1917 to 1918, but it supplied much needed reinforcements, materiel, and air support for the Allies. Faced with a two front war and the strains of a long stalemate on the Western Front, Germany asked for an armistice. If America had not intervened, Germany might still have had a chance to win due to Russia dropping out of the war because of the Russian Revolution. In fact, the harshness of the peace terms that Germany demanded from Russia in exchange for withdrawing from the war probably led to Germany being given even more harsh terms by the Allies after the ceasefire. Instead of it merely being an armistice, Germany's acquiescence was treated like a surrender. Under the Treaty of Versailles, they lost many lands and colonies, were demilitarized, and were forced to pay huge reparations. The treaty established most of the modern borders of Europe and forced the relocations of millions of people.

The economic collapse that followed the war led to a new wave of immigration to the U.S. (which included my grandfather). It also led to the rise of totalitarian governments in Europe, and subsequently, the Second World War. One lesser-known result of the war was the worldwide influenza epidemic of 1919, aided by those mass migrations. Sadly, this epidemic claimed my grandfather's brother shortly after he arrived in America, as well as millions of others around the globe. Even a far away place like California was affected by this event. Thousands died here as well. Contemporary accounts in the Bay Area recall seeing people walking the streets of its cities with scarves covering their faces and quarantines being enforced everywhere.

The biggest contribution that California made to WWI was in the area of aviation. California was attractive to aviation pioneers because of its fair weather and coastal location. The best places for us to learn about the role that aviation played in WWI are the Moffett Field Historical Museum, Travis Air Force Base Heritage Center in Fairfield, The Hiller Air Museum in San Carlos, The Oakland Aviation Museum, and The Wings of History Museum in San Martin. The last two museums mentioned even have full-scale replicas of the Wright Brothers' first airplane. About the same time as the Wright brothers, John Joseph Montgomery conducted a series of manned glider flights in San Jose. Unfortunately, Montgomery perished on one of these flights in 1911 or he might have been even more famous than the Wright Brothers. Details of this flight can be seen at Evergreen Valley College's library in San Jose.

WWI was the beginning of the age of dirigibles in the U.S. Moffett Field in Mountain View was the home of fleets of blimps, which would patrol the coast for enemies until after WWII. Hangar Number One was built in 1933 to hold the Navy dirigible *USS Macon*. The hangar is so large that it visible from most of the South San Francisco Bay Area. The *USS Macon* was based at Moffett from October 1933 until it crashed in a storm at sea in February 1935. Hangar Number One also sheltered several smaller non-rigid lighter-than-air ships at the same time as the Macon. The hangar is an incredible 1,133 feet long and 308 feet wide. Its floor covers eight acres, big enough to accommodate 10 football fields! The massive hangar doors weigh 500 tons apiece.

After WWI, aviators continued to experiment with new aircraft and tried to set records for speed and distance traveled. One of the most famous, Amelia Earhart, departed from Oakland on her ill-fated attempt to circumnavigate the globe. Some of her personal items are on display at The Oakland Aviation Museum. Many interesting experimental aircraft were developed in the area. Some of them can be seen at The Hiller Air Museum in San Carlos. The famed China Clippers, the first transoceanic passenger airplanes, began to fly out of Oakland in the 1930's.

One that was used in the filming of an Indiana Jones movie can be seen at the Oakland Aviation Museum.

There was a certain amount of anti-foreigner hysteria during WWI. Enemy aliens were forced to register with the government. German language schools were closed and German books were banned. Some people changed their names to appear more American. Many items of German origin were renamed to avoid sympathy with the enemy. Frankfurters became "liberty pups" and sauerkraut was dubbed "liberty cabbage" for example. Even the color of bottles changed, as the minerals used to color the glass blue were no longer available from Germany due to the Allied blockade. This is demonstrated very nicely in the impressive canning display at the Agricultural History Project Center and Museum in Watsonville. Another remarkable exhibit, found at the Hoover Institute at Stanford University, includes propaganda posters from many nations during the war and subsequent revolutions. Sadly, many people only remember President Herbert Hoover because he was unfairly blamed for the Great Depression. They do not realize that he was also a great humanitarian. Herbert Hoover made his name by organizing famine relief for Europe's refugees after the war. He also contributed greatly to education. This is why the Hoover Tower at Stanford bears his name. From the top of this tower, great panoramic views of the entire South Bay Area can be seen. Displays inside Hoover Tower chronicle his many important accomplishments.

As a result of the war, many refugees came to California. The Armenian Genocide committed by the Ottoman Turks resulted in many Armenian survivors moving to California. Russian refugees from the Revolution also immigrated to the Bay Area, especially San Francisco. However, suspicions of radical activities by immigrants in the U.S. led to restrictions on immigration. Quotas for each country were set up for the first time. For example, my grandfather had to state on his application for citizenship that he was not an anarchist. Suspected radicals were rounded up during the war, union activities were curtailed, and the railroads were nationalized to prevent disruption to the economy.

The war also helped boost California's economy. Farm goods helped feed the troops and America's blockaded Allies. Foods from the Bay Area's canneries were particularly prized in Europe. Kelp was made into potash following Germany's embargo. Potash is an important fertilizer for soil. Bay Area farmers also unwittingly helped Germany's development of poison gas weapons before the war by selling them their apricot pits, which were used to make the poison gas.

Transportation networks expanded to handle this new volume of goods. Many of the region's railroads and streetcars were built in the years after WWI. Their story can be learned at the Western Railway Museum near Suisun City, The Niles Depot Model Railroads and Museum near Fremont, The South Bay Historical Railroad Society in Santa Clara, Railroad & Ferry Museum in Tiburon, Depot Park Museum in Sonoma, the Museum of the San Ramon Valley in Danville, The Cable Car Museum in San Francisco, and other museums. Many of the area's best-known roads, such as the Alameda, the El Camino Real, the famous streets of San Francisco and Oakland, and many others were paved in the postwar era. Some of these roads would later become highways. In the 1920s and 1930s, bridges began to be built to cross the San Francisco Bay. One of these, The Golden Gate Bridge, became a world famous landmark. The Visitor's Center at the southern entrance of the bridge explains how it was built.

When peace resumed, California continued to grow and prosper through the 1920s. For a time, the Niles area was even a rival to Hollywood for silent filmmaking. Charlie Chaplin and others filmed at the Essanay Studios. His famous tramp sequence was filmed in the nearby Niles Canyon. A museum is housed in the Edison Theater in Niles that hosts silent film nights. These make a fun family outing. The museum has many interesting cameras, films, and even Charlie Chaplin's cane! Several of the historical homes listed in this book were built in this era. Literary and cultural figures such as John Steinbeck, Jack London, and many others chose to build homes in the area.

After the Great Depression began in 1929, many refugees from the Dust Bowl, the East, and the South sought California as a place to try to rebuild their lives and seek a new fortune. They found employment in the orchards and farms of the region. Steinbeck chronicles the hardships and discrimination suffered by the Okie and Mexican migrant farm workers in several of his famous novels, such as *The Grapes of Wrath, Tortilla Flats*, and *Cannery Row*. These novels and others are beautifully displayed at The National Steinbeck Center in Salinas. The cannery industry was particularly hard hit when they were forced to close due to over-fishing in the 1930s and 40s. Cannery Row went from the sardine capital of the world to a virtual no man's land by the 1950's. Over time, the circumstances of farm and cannery workers improved, however, and some of them eventually bought land and later made great fortunes selling to postwar developers. Overall, the economy of California suffered in the 1930s, but was not as hard hit as other regions in the Great Depression. The build up for World War Two pulled the economy out of the doldrums in a dramatic fashion.

(The numbers after the description of the historical site refer to the individual listings later in this book).

WWI and Early 20th Century sites:

✓	Museum or historical site	Date Visited
	1. Hoover Tower-Stanford: Herbert Hoover's life and accomplishments. #89	
	2. The Hoover Institute-Stanford: posters, historic documents, etc. related to twentieth century conflicts. #89	
	3. Oakland Museum of California: domestic items from the era. #147	
	4. Blackhawk Museum-Danville: historic automobiles. #25	
	5. WWI memorials at: The Palace of the Legion of Honor in San Francisco, The University of California Memorial Stadium in Berkeley, The Saratoga WWI Memorial, The Piedmont WWI Memorial, and Oak Hill Cemetery in San Jose. No listings.	
	6. Vallejo Naval and Historical Museum: photos and artifacts from	

	WWI-era vessels. #216	
	7. Hiller Air Museum-San Carlos: WWI and other early aircraft. #87	
	8. Oakland Aviation Museum: WWI and other early aircraft. #146	
	9. Richmond Museum of History: historic photos and models of WWI vessels. #175	
	10. Alcatraz Island: remnants of WWI era defenses and the historic prison. #6	
	11. The Presidio Visitor's Center and The Officers' Club -San Francisco: WWI troop housing, training eras, and WWI artillery. #169	
	12. San Francisco Fire Dept. Fire Museum: WWI-era fire fighting equipment. #191	
	13. San Francisco Maritime National Historic Park: historic tugboats and fishing vessels. #190	
	14. Museum of American Heritage-Palo Alto: domestic appliances and other early 20th century items. #125	
	15. Forts Baker, Barry, and Cronkhite-Marin County Headlands: remnants of historic gun emplacements. #71	
	16. Eugene O'Neill National Historic Site-Danville: the famous playwright's home containing many of his personal belongings. #65	
	17. Capitola Historical Museum: historic beach resort items. #35	
	18. Musee Mecanique-San Francisco: vintage coin-operated arcade games. #133	
	19. Alameda Museum: many items from the Neptune Beach amusement park. #5	
	20. Golden Gate Railroad Museum-Sunol: historic trains. No listing.	
	21. The Niles Depot: model railroads and museum, historic trains. #143	
	22. Millbrae Train Museum: model railroads, train station furnishings, historic photos, and an historic train car. #114	
	23. Davenport Jail Museum: historic items from the jail, historic cement plant, and other items of local interest. #55	
	24. The National Steinbeck Center-Salinas: many of Steinbeck's personal items, original manuscripts, and clips from movies based upon his books. #141	
	25. The South Bay Historical Railroad Society-Santa Clara: a huge model railroad display, a historic railcar, and train equipment. #199	
	26. Angel Island: WWI-era military facilities. #9	
	27. Agnews Historic Cemetery and Museum–Santa Clara: items from the famous mental health hospital. #2	

	28. Salinas Valley Memorial Hospital Museum of Medical History: the office of John Steinbeck's doctor and WWI-era medical tools. #179	
	29. Wings of History Museum-San Martin: WWI aircraft, weapons, equipment, and other artifacts. #224	
	30. Oakland Aviation Museum: WWI aircraft, weapons, equipment, and other artifacts; personal items of Amelia Earhart. #146	
	31. Travis Air Force Base Heritage Center-Fairfield: WWI aircraft, weapons, equipment, and other artifacts. #208	
	32. Moffett Field Historical Museum–Mountain View: historic photos and artifacts related to blimps, observation planes and other early aircraft. #126	
	33. Luther Burbank Home & Gardens-Santa Rosa: historic experimental orchards that Burbank used. #107	
	34. Colma Historical Society: WWI display. #47	
	35. Tor House-Carmel: historic home of poet Robinson Jeffers. #206	
	36. Campbell Historical Museum: schoolhouse, historic orchards. #32	
	37. The San Francisco History Museum: San Francisco Earthquake and Golden Gate Bridge photos and artifacts. #192	
	38. Duarte Garage-Livermore: historic garage. #60	

I certify that _____ has visited the majority of the above sites and has come through the trenches.

X _____ (museum staff member).

Cohen-Bray House-Oakland

World War Two

When the Japanese attacked Pearl Harbor on December 7th, 1941, the nation was reluctantly drawn into war. Public opinion polls changed overnight from heavily isolationist to wanting immediate revenge on Japan. California became an immediate part of the conflict. Many of the ships sent to Hawaii had been part of the fleets in San Diego and the Bay Area. Numbers of tourists and other civilians from California were trapped in Hawaii and were unable to come home. The San Jose State College football team was in Honolulu the day before the attack. Unable to get home and wanting to do their part, many members of the team enlisted in the Armed Forces and they never finished their season. Several of them never came home, having died while fighting in the war. In Hawaii, most people assumed that the naval assault would be soon followed by an amphibious landing in the islands. They prepared for the worst, but thankfully, the land invasion never came.

Since Alaska had already been invaded, Californians naturally assumed that they were in line for an attack because they were the next nearest territory to Japan. This had been the pattern of Japanese expansion to date. Californians hastily constructed coastal defenses and marshaled their forces. They organized civil defense efforts, such as blacking out windows, conducting air raid drills, and patrolling coastlines for enemy submarines. A submarine net was dragged across the Golden Gate. Barrage balloons and sea mines were put into place. Commercial radio stations were silenced and people patrolled the coastline looking for enemy vessels. Beaches were strewn with barbed wire and merchant ships were held in the harbor.

Little did Californians know that the taking of the two Alaskan islands, Attu and Kiska, had been just a diversion to draw attention away from the attack on Pearl Harbor and that the much dreaded invasion of California would never materialize. They mobilized for war and prepared for invasion just the same. Civilians supported the war effort with rationing, scrap drives, and by conducting civil defense preparations. California's gold mines were shut down during the war so that miners could be diverted to mining minerals that were more critical to the war effort. As a result, unfortunately, many historic mining structures were dismantled and sent to scrap yards in the Bay Area to provide raw materials for building weapons.

The Bay Area would soon become the major staging ground for the war in the Pacific. Its vast calm harbors and the availability of inexpensive undeveloped land made it the best place on the West Coast for preparing for war. Airfields, harbors, shipyards, and war industries sprung up around the bay overnight. Attracted by high wages, people flooded into the Bay Area from all over the country to find jobs. Many women and minorities found work in places like the Kaiser Shipyards, Bethlehem Alameda Shipyard, and many other wartime industries. The Kaiser shipyards produced an astounding number of ships. About 13% of the nation's wartime ships were built there. They also hold the record for the fastest victory ship construction. The Liberty Ship *Robert E. Perry* was built in just 5 days!

Henry Kaiser also pioneered the development of daycare centers and hospitals to maintain the health and productivity of his workers. This is the genesis of the vast Kaiser Permanente healthcare network of today. Ford Automobiles, The Farm Machine Corporation, and many other local industries converted from making cars and farm vehicles to tanks and other military vehicles. Lockheed, Hiller, and other aircraft manufacturers provided many important advancements in aeronautics during the war. The frequent clear skies of the Bay Area provided ideal testing grounds for new models and technologies. These can be seen at the Hiller Air Museum and the air museums at San Martin, Oakland, Moffett, Hamilton, and Travis.

Farming boomed as well, as California exported huge amounts of food for the war effort. A severe housing shortage caused multiple workers to rent the same room and take turns sleeping in it while others were away at their work shifts around the clock. Federally subsidized housing was built to help ease the housing shortage. This story is demonstrated very well at the Rosie the Riveter-WWII Home Front National Historical Park-Richmond, Richmond Museum, and other local military and air museums.

Things did not go so well for Japanese, German, and Italian immigrants during the war, however. The Japanese were rounded up and put into internment camps far from the Bay Area. Most had to sell their homes and possessions in a very short period of time at far less than market value. The Italians and Germans were excluded from living in coastal areas, but only a few were sent to internment camps. Resident aliens were held suspect and many were brought in for questioning to determine their loyalty to the U.S. Many Italian fishermen (including Joe DiMaggio's father) had their boats confiscated by the Navy with no compensation. Their means of making a living was taken from them and they were forced to relocate far from the sea. Many of them fell onto hard times due to their lost incomes.

The Japanese flower industry was particularly hard hit. It took them many years to rebuild and recover from their wartime losses. The Japanese American Museum of San Jose and the San Mateo County History Museum in Redwood City tell this story well. Oddly, some Japanese were employed as translators and code crackers at the Presidio in San Francisco during the war because it was so hard to find other Americans with fluency in Japanese. Their story is told at the Military Intelligence Service Historic Learning Center in San Francisco.

One group that was particularly well motivated to fight the Japanese was California's Filipinos. The Philippines was still an America possession in 1941, and they were invaded at the same time as the attack on Pearl Harbor. Filipinos in California formed the all-volunteer 1st Filipino Infantry Regiment in the Army. This unit fought very bravely to help liberate their homeland. After the war, the U.S. granted independence to the Philippines. Filipinos who fought with America were granted U.S. citizenship, if they so chose, so many of them immigrated with their families to the U.S. The U.S. maintained large military bases in the Philippines throughout the Cold War. Many Filipinos gained medical training at these bases and then came to California to become an important part of its medical industry.

Many key facilities around the Bay Area played an important role in the Pacific campaign. Yerba Buena Island and Treasure Island became major naval facilities during the war. The Navy used Treasure Island as a location for transporting people and equipment to the Pacific Theater. The Treasure Island Naval Station, which also included a portion of Yerba Buena Island, was established on April 1, 1941. The islands would host a Coast Guard post, Marine district headquarters, and the West Coast office of Pan American Airways. The civilian passenger clippers provided regular air travel between the U.S. and Asia, but were pressed into military service after the Battle of Pearl Harbor. They ferried military personnel and medical supplies between San Francisco and Pearl Harbor every day. Treasure Island also served as a forward base and docking station for the blimps flying out of Moffett Field in search of submarines near the Golden Gate.

During World War II, the Mare Island shipyard turned out large numbers of ships and submarines. They assembled new destroyer escorts with prefabricated sections that were transported from locations as far away as Colorado. Repairs were also made on warships that were damaged in battle. By the end of the war, Mare Island had produced 17 submarines, four submarine tenders, 31 destroyer escorts, 33 small craft, and more than 300 landing craft. Moffett Field became the West Coast headquarters for coastal patrol blimps. Throughout the war, Navy blimps could be seen hovering over the Golden Gate patrolling for submarines and mines. In 1943, Hangar Number Two and Hangar Number Three were constructed to keep pace with the Navy's increasing demand for space. Many different forms of naval aviation were conducted at the facility over the years, including carrier support and surveillance. The Moffett Field Historical Museum has many fascinating artifacts from WWII, including captured Japanese weapons, flags, and uniforms. There are also U.S. uniforms, ordinance, and navigational equipment.

The Benicia arsenal supplied ports with weapons, artillery, parts, supplies, and tools during the entire war. The arsenal is most famous for supplying munitions to Lieutenant Colonel Jimmy Doolittle for the first bombing raid on Tokyo on April 18, 1942, launched from the *U.S.S. Hornet*. Fort Mason and the piers of San Francisco also served as important embarkation points for troops headed out to the Pacific. There were also important army bases in Oakland, Fort Ord, and the numerous forts surrounding San Francisco. The Letterman General Hospital was an important recovery destination for thousands of returning wounded servicemen. Camps Hydle, Stoneman, Clayton, Ashby, and Fremont became World War II training centers. You might even say that during WWII, the Bay Area went to the dogs. A training facility in San Carlos trained about 4,500 dogs for use as sentries, scouts, messengers, mine detectors, and attack animals.

Another key munitions facility, Port Chicago, was the home of one of the greatest wartime tragedies on domestic soil. The Navy was in such a rush to load munitions that the pier could support the loading of two ships simultaneously. Loading went on around the clock. Due to the racial segregation of the times, African-American sailors were assigned to the dangerous work at Port Chicago. Only the officers of these units were white. The dockworkers had not been properly trained to handle munitions and the Navy's safety standards were not upheld. Competitions were held to see how quickly the ships could be loaded instead of how safely.

On the evening of July 17, 1944, a shell was dropped to the deck of The *SS E.A. Bryan*, which set off the explosives and fuel oil on the ship. Soon after, it and the nearby *Quinault Victory*, carrying 4,606 tons of ammunition exploded. The seismic shock wave was felt as far away as Boulder City, Nevada. The *E.A. Bryan* and the surrounding pier were completely disintegrated. The pillar of fire and smoke stretched over two miles into the sky. 320 men were killed instantly. The blast smashed buildings and rail cars near the pier and damaged every building in Port Chicago. Military and civilian buildings were damaged for miles. Even San Francisco sustained damage 48 miles away!

The Navy improved its safety procedures after this tragedy, but it also had far-reaching social consequences. The surviving men who had experienced the horror were ordered to resume loading munitions at Mare Island. Of the 328 men of the ordnance battalion, 258 African-American sailors refused to load ammunition. They were put on trial for mutiny and severely punished. After much protest and court proceedings, they were eventually given clemency. Some people trace these protests as the beginnings of the modern Civil Rights Movement.

Port Chicago Naval Magazine National Memorial is administered by the National Park Service and the United States Navy. It honors the memory of those who gave their lives and were injured in the explosion on July 17, 1944. It recognizes those who served at the magazine and commemorates the role of the facility during World War II. The memorial is on an active military base, so advance permission must be granted in order to visit. You must contact the Park Service for information.

Several important naval vessels from WWII have been refurbished and turned into historical museums. These include the Liberty ship, the *O'Brien* , which is fully operational and even goes on cruises, and the *U.S.S. Pampanito*, which is a small submarine that can be toured at the San Francisco Maritime National Park . In Alameda, the *Red Oak* Victory Ship and the *U.S.S.*, an aircraft carrier that sunk many enemy vessels during the war, are also on display. Perhaps the most interesting is President Franklin Roosevelt's private yacht, the *USS Potomac*, moored in Oakland, which is also available for tours and charter trips. There are even a few unrestored WWII vessels remaining in the famous "Mothball Fleet" of Benicia. This fleet once held hundreds of ships, but now only a few remain. Soon, they will all be gone. Cruises from Martinez allow you to see the vessels up close, but they may not be boarded.

As the war progressed, the Bay Area's military facilities expanded to overflowing. After the war, many of them were converted to civilian uses and are actively in service in their new roles today as public or commercial buildings.

The Bay Area also played an important role in the end of the war. The atomic bomb was originally developed to defeat Hitler, but when Germany surrendered in 1945, the bomb was instead used to induce Japan to surrender and speed up the end of the war. The plutonium that was developed at The Lawrence Berkeley Lab was instrumental in developing the physics needed to make the atomic bomb. A tour of the sites where history was made at the lab is available with reservations. The Lawrence Livermore Lab also played an important role in the weapon's development. The visitor's center at Lawrence Livermore tells of this remarkable project and the pioneering scientists and technicians who made it possible. It was undoubtedly the biggest secret weapon of all time.

The first atomic bomb used against Japan secretly departed from Mare Island aboard the *USS Indianapolis* on its way to Tinian Island to be placed on the bomber, the *Enola Gay*. One has to wonder how different history might have been if Japan had sunk that ship during it's crossing of the Pacific, since only one other bomb was ready for use. Would Japan still have surrendered after only one atomic bomb was dropped on them?

As the war drew to a close, the United Nations Charter was signed in San Francisco. Many of the early proceedings of the U.N. were conducted in San Francisco until the new permanent site was ready in New York. During WWII, the Allies had pledged to one another not to make separate peace treaties, but in the aftermath of the war, when tensions broke out between the U.S. and the U.S.S.R., the negotiations for a comprehensive peace treaty broke down. The U.S. had no choice but to sign a separate peace treaty between Japan and many of the nations it had fought. The peace treaty was finally signed in San Francisco in 1951, based upon the principals of the U.N. charter. Japan lost its conquered territories and pledged non-aggression in the future, collective security would be used to maintain the peace, and Japan would be allowed to regain self-rule and peaceably return to the family of nations.

(The numbers after the description of the historical site refer to the individual listings later in this book).

WWII sites in the Bay Area:

✓	Museum or historical site	Date Visited
	1. Salinas Valley Memorial Hospital Museum of Medical History: WWII-era hospital equipment. #179	
	2. Japanese American Museum of San Jose: Japanese-American relocation artifacts, photos, and reconstructed buildings. #94	
	3. The Museum of Art & History at the McPherson Center-Santa Cruz: civil defense, coastal patrols, and other aspects of WWII in the area. #203	
	4. Oakland Aviation Museum: WWII era aircraft, historic missions that departed from the airport, including the Doolittle Raid. #146	
	5. *S.S. Jeremiah O'Brien*-San Francisco: an actual WWII transport ship. #196	
	6. *USS Pampanito* - San Francisco Maritime National Park: an actual WWII submarine. #212	
	7. Oakland Museum of California: WWII on the homefront and domestic life. #147	
	8. Vallejo Naval and Historical Museum: historic naval vessels from WWII and many other interesting artifacts from the war. #216	

	9. Alameda Museum: WWII on the homefront, historic shipyards, etc. #5	
	10. Marin headlands gun emplacements at Forts Baker, Barry, and Cronkhite: the remnants of the great gun emplacements. #71	
	11. Hiller Museum-San Carlos: WWII era aircraft. #87	
	12. The Mothball Fleet-Martinez: a few transports and oilers that were used in WWII. #129	
	13. *U.S.S. Hornet*-Alameda: an aircraft carrier that conducted several important campaigns in the Pacific in WWII. #211	
	14. The Blackhawk Museum-Danville: historic automobiles from the era. #25	
	15. Richmond Museum of History: WWII on the homefront, historic shipyards, etc. #175	
	16. Alcatraz Island: some WWII era defenses are identified, the famous historic prison. #6	
	17. The Presidio Visitor's Center and The Officers' Club - San Francisco: historic photos of the base, historic buildings, training areas, Letterman Hospital, WWII era artillery pieces, etc. #169	
	18. San Francisco Fire Dept. Fire Museum: WWII era equipment, harbor fires. #191	
	19. San Francisco Maritime National Historic Park: home of the *Pampanito, O'Brien*, and historic ferries. #190	
	20. Museum of American Heritage-Palo Alto: WWII-era electronics and domestic items are often displayed. #125	
	21. Hamilton Field Museum-Novato: historic photos, uniforms, and other WWII items. #80	
	22. Capitola Historical Museum: beach resort items and wartime beach restrictions. #35	
	23. Rosie the Riveter-WWII Home Front National Historical Park-Richmond: oral histories, posters related to women, labor, rationing, farms, etc. Some WWII-era artifacts such as uniforms, shipbuilding equipment, ration coupons, etc. #178	
	24. *Red Oak* Victory Ship-Richmond: an actual WWII transport ship. #173	
	25. The Niles Depot Model Railroads and Museum: historic railcars and other railroad items. #143	
	26. *U.S.S. Potomac*-Oakland: personal items belonging to F.D.R. #213	
	27. Hoover Institute-Stanford: WWII propaganda posters and other historic documents. #89	
	28. The South Bay Historical Railroad Society-Santa Clara: an historic railcar and other railroad items. #199	
	29. Contra Costa County History Center-Martinez: artifacts from the	

	Port Chicago disaster, historic photos of historic shipyards, and other WWII items. #49	
	30. Angel Island: WWII defenses, troop housing, and immigration items. #9	
	31. African American Museum & Library-Oakland: historic shipyards, army bases, and other aspects of WWII. #1	
	32. Agnews Historic Cemetery and Museum-Santa Clara: historic mental hospital artifacts and photos. #2	
	33. Moffett Field Historical Museum-Mountain View: WWII aircraft-related items, combat missions, blimps, and coastal defenses. #126	
	34. Wings of History Museum-San Martin: WWII aircraft and equipment. #224	
	35. Travis Air Force Base Heritage Center-Fairfield: WWII aircraft and equipment. #208	
	36. Watsonville Fire Museum: WWII-era fire-fighting equipment. #217	
	37. Crockett Historical Museum-Crockett: wartime industries, domestic items, and servicemen from the area. #52	
	38. South San Francisco Historical Society Museum: historical photos of shipbuilding in WWII. #200	
	39. Hayward Area Historical Museum: a nice collection of WWII items such as rationing coupons, a v-mail packet, victory garden handbooks, and civil defense equipment. #83	
	40. Military Intelligence Service Historic Learning Center-San Francisco: primary sources accounts of Japanese-American translators who served in the US armed forces in WWII. #115	
	41. Colma Historical Society: WWII display. #47	
	42. Point Pinos Lighthouse: wartime coastal patrols. #166	
	43. The San Francisco History Museum: WWII exhibit. #192	
	44. The Museum of San Carlos History: the expansion of the railroads and the building boom following WWII. #204	

I certify that _____ has visited all of the above sites and has done his or her part for the war effort.

X _____ (museum staff member).

Red Oak Victory Ship- Richmond

52

The Cold War and the Postwar Boom

After being released from the service after WWII, many servicemen decided that the Bay Area seemed like a nice place to live, so they settled down there to start a family. This led to explosive growth of the cities and suburbs. Many veterans with engineering and aeronautics experience found jobs in the region's burgeoning technology industries. As the Soviet Union turned from being a wartime ally to a Cold War rival, an arms race ensued. California's defense industry became an increasingly important part of keeping ahead of the Soviets on new weapons technology. Aerospace became one of the most important industries in the region, which led to many new spin-off industries in electronics and communication.

As the Cold War conflicts began to shift from Europe to Asia in the 1950s, California once again became the staging ground for American forces being sent to the Korean and Vietnam Wars. Many other forces passed through the region on their way to postings in the Philippines, Hawaii, Guam, and other Pacific defensive positions. While most of the commercial shipbuilding moved out of the area to larger facilities in Southern California and elsewhere, many of the region's naval bases and shipyards continued to play active roles in the outfitting and transportation of troops. Increasingly, troops and sometimes supplies were airlifted to Asia, Latin America, and later the Middle East. Travis and Hamilton Air Force bases have excellent museums explaining how they changed from fighter and bomber bases to transport, rescue, and logistical support.

Coastal artillery batteries were phased out and replaced, first with bomber defenses and then NIKE surface-to-air missiles. A particularly well-preserved NIKE launch site is located at Fort Barry in Marin. Fortunately, these were never used. The basic strategy was to destroy incoming nuclear missiles with our own in the atmosphere above our cities. The fallout and radiation on the civilian populace would still have been considerable, although not as bad as if a missile had made a direct hit. Items like undersea listening devices and daily sub chaser planes out of Moffett Field were dedicated to detecting and intercepting Soviet submarines carrying nuclear missiles. They even caught them sneaking into the San Francisco Bay a few times! Related photos can be viewed at the Moffett Field museum.

As in the years following WWII, many servicemen passing through the Bay Area on their way to Korea, Vietnam, and other Cold War postings were attracted to the pleasant weather and job opportunities of the Bay Area and decided to settle down and start families there after they returned to civilian life. Interestingly, a reverse flow of population began to occur as refugees from Korea, Communist China, Vietnam, Laos, and Cambodia came to California to escape Communism and explore greater economic opportunities. Other Asians followed in large numbers to seek jobs and better educational opportunities for their families. Mexican and other Latin American immigrants also came in large numbers to escape poverty or oppressive revolutionary regimes or dictators.

By the 1960s, due to ongoing Cold War conflicts, one fifth of government spending was going to California. Several factors led to this development. San Francisco had developed into the banking and business capital of the West. The

Federal Reserve further aided banks by locating its western office in San Francisco. Many large companies and banks established their headquarters in the Bay Area. This meant that capital was ready for investors who wanted to pioneer new inventions. California would eventually lead the world in new patents. The wartime industries of WWII at first scaled down considerably, but they later resumed production to create weapons for the Cold War. After WWII, there was a shift in emphasis from naval to air warfare, but the availability of abundant skilled workers made the transition go smoothly.

The Bay Area also had the benefit of a highly educated workforce. Many men took advantage of the GI Bill to go to college after WWII. Major universities, such as Stanford, UC Berkeley, and others, increased in size and scope in the postwar years. California led the nation in the establishment of affordable higher education for its citizens. A first-rate, inexpensive system of state subsidized colleges was established and expanded. Financial aid made education available to far more women, minorities, and underprivileged students than ever before. Community colleges sprang up around the Bay Area to make education in trades and technical skills even more accessible. Throughout the region, public elementary and secondary schools were built almost as fast as the tract homes. Even though they were very overcrowded and often had to run double sessions until new schools could be built in adjacent neighborhoods, they provided some of the best education in the nation. Today, California has the highest percentage of the population with advanced degrees of any region in the world.

California's educational researchers encouraged reforms and experimental educational practices. Teachers were encouraged to use innovative curriculum and teaching methods (some of which worked and some of which had unintended negative consequences). The rest of the nation began to look to California for the lead in textbooks, assessment, and curriculum design. Education was greatly improved for special needs students and the children of immigrants and migrant workers. Educational funding was much more plentiful than today. Following the embarrassing revelation that the Soviets launched the first artificial satellite, Sputnik, ahead of the U.S., science and math were given top funding priority. This is still true, but unlike today, abundant funding for the arts, libraries, field trips, and sports were also commonplace. Many consider this to have been the Golden Age of education in California and long for similar days to return.

During WWII, Dwight Eisenhower took a road trip across the U.S. to assess our defenses and war readiness. The trip took him weeks and he was appalled at our poor road conditions. He knew that if troops were to be mobilized and transported quickly, our roads would have to be improved. While fighting in Europe during the war, he marveled at the speed and efficiency of Hitler's new autobahn system. When he became president in 1952, he asked Congress to pass the Highway Act to begin a national network of modern highways that would allow for inexpensive and seamless travel from coast to coast. The state of California followed his lead, and particularly under Governor Pat Brown, built a system of reliable and toll free highways that would become a model for the nation, indeed the world. He was also instrumental in developing a water management system that included many new dams, aqueducts, and canals to redistribute water from the northern part of the state where it was plentiful to the thirsty cities of the Bay Area and Southern California. To understand how this works, visit the Bay Model in Sausalito.

In the years following WWII, still more bridges were built to span rivers and cross the bay. Ferries and commuter train lines were expanded to help workers commute from the suburbs to the major cities. Major new international airports were established in San Francisco, Oakland, and San Jose. Many smaller airports were built around the bay as well. An experimental electric train system called the Bay Area Rapid Transit began to connect San Francisco to outlying areas, although it still today hasn't lived up to early promises that it would someday circle the entire Bay Area. Nonetheless, the fast and efficient trains were copied by many other cities nationwide. Countless new county and city roads were paved so quickly that coming up for names for them was quite a challenge. Instead of following traditional north-south, east-west grids and numbering systems like those used on the East Coast, Bay Area communities experimented with odd street shapes and named them for artists, national parks, trees, flowers, Spanish and Indian names, local pioneers, WWII heroes, and anything else they could imagine.

Migrants came into the area from around the nation and immigration soared. The Bay Area became a mixture of cultures and language such as the world has never seen. By the 1960s, the majority of California residents had been born outside the state. New cities grew up in places that had previously only been farming communities. Suburbia became commonplace in the Bay Area and established cities soon spread out to connect with each other. Annexation wars ensued as each Bay Area community gobbled up smaller neighboring communities and unincorporated areas. Cities rivaled others to become the largest and most prominent in the Bay Area. They aggressively marketed their communities as ideal residences to potential settlers. This uncontrolled growth sometimes led to some pretty poor planning as urban sprawl trumped practicality at times. Inefficient traffic flow and infrastructure support led to headaches that Bay area urban planners are still trying to resolve. Traditional downtown areas declined because they could not compete with the modern buildings, shopping, and easy parking of the suburbs. Many local community museums have displays about how their region was changed by this population explosion, but it is perhaps best illustrated at the San Mateo County History Museum in Redwood City.

Tragically, many wildlife habitats and historic buildings were destroyed to make way for development. Landfill became a common practice along the shores of the San Francisco Bay. Garbage dumps were also built along the bay and considerable illegal dumping into the bay itself took place as well. It took on a strange odor due to stagnation and urban and industrial pollutants. There were oil spills and wildlife die-offs. Fish from the bay were no longer safe to eat. At first, it seemed to make sense to level useless hills and turn them into attractive waterfront property, but the bay continued to shrink and no one was keeping track of the environmental cost. There were even outrageous plans laid forth to fill in most of the bay until it was just a series of canals and lakes. Finally in the 1960s, a group of university professors' wives founded a group called Save the Bay that began to halt and even eventually somewhat reverse the process. Had this not been done, the bay would have become an environmental disaster area due to inadequate water circulation and pollution.

After this first successful environmental movement, many others would follow. Californians would become leaders in the Environmental Movement. California communities would lead the world in improved waste management programs, recycling, and cleanup efforts. They would establish clean air and water districts, coastal protection, and marine wildlife preserves. They would create water districts to protect clean drinking water, mitigate droughts, improve irrigation, and regulate fair distribution of this precious resource. Californians would also create many new state and county parks, as well as wildlife preserves and open space districts.

Oil has always been very important to California's economy in the 20th century. Huge refineries were built in the Richmond and Martinez areas that helped fuel the economic engine of the region. By the 1970s, as California's oil reserves began to decline, however, more and more oil was imported. California therefore began to lead the world in research for alternative energy sources. Solar and geothermal power were developed extensively in the region. California has also led the way in atomic particle research. At first it turned to nuclear reactors as an inexpensive energy source, but when the public began to fear the occurrence of a nuclear accident due to reactors being built on fault lines or too close to urban areas, protest movements forced them to halt or cancel construction of new facilities. Research began into fusion or other energy sources at facilities in the Bay Area, such as the Stanford Linear Accelerator and the Berkeley and Livermore Labs. These facilities have tours for visitors to learn about their important history and research.

(The numbers after the description of the historical site refer to the individual listings later in this book).

Cold War historical sites:

✓	Museum or historical site	Date Visited
	1. Oakland Museum of California: postwar boom and Cold War artifacts. #147	
	2. Sunnyvale Heritage Park Museum: urbanization, electronics, Moffett Field, NASA, and the US Naval Air Station. #202	
	3. NASA Ames-Sunnyvale: tours of experimental wind tunnels and other aeronautics research facilities. #140	
	4. Lawrence Livermore National Laboratory: research on nuclear and other forms of energy; many interesting Cold War and energy research artifacts and displays. #101	
	5. *U.S.S Hornet*-Alameda: an aircraft carrier that was deployed to many Cold War conflicts, and also picked up returning astronauts. #211	
	6. Oakland Aviation Museum: civilian and military aviation; development of airlines and airports. #146	

	7. Lawrence Berkeley National Laboratory: atomic research and other forms of energy; artifacts from pioneers in the field. #100	
	8. Hoover Institute-Stanford: a conflict studies institute. Fascinating displays on the Cold War, dictatorships, and other challenges to peace and freedom. #89	
	9. Napa Valley Museum-Yountville: naval history and the postwar boom. #139	
	10. Fort Barry-Marin: coastal and nuclear defenses. #71	
	11. African American Museum & Library-Oakland: the postwar boom. #1	
	12. Angel Island: coastal and nuclear defenses; immigration. #9	
	13. Moffett Field Historical Museum-Mountain View: coastal and nuclear defenses. #126	
	14. Hamilton Field Museum-Novato: Cold War air deployment. #80	
	15. Wings of History Museum-San Martin: aviation history and Bay Area airports. #224	
	16. Travis Air Force Base Heritage Center: Cold War air deployment. #208	
	17. Crockett Historical Museum: bridges, oil, and industry. #52	
	18. Federal Reserve -San Francisco: banking and finance. #67	
	19. Blackhawk Museum-Danville: expertly restored historic automobiles. #25	
	20. San Francisco Maritime National Historic Park: historic ferries and ship models. #190	
	21. Richmond Museum of History: oil refineries, naval history, and the postwar boom. #175	
	22. Vallejo Naval and Historical Museum: Cold War-era ships and naval facilities at Mare Island. #216	
	23. Quail Hollow Ranch County Park-Felton home of Sunset magazine founder. #171	
	24. The San Francisco History Museum: celebrities and politicians from this era, local landmarks, beatniks, and hippies #192	

I certify that _____ has visited all of the above sites and has survived the Cold War.

X _____ (museum staff member).

Travis Air Force Base Heritage Center-Fairfield

From the Counter Culture to Silicon Valley and Beyond

While most people supported the efforts to contain communism during the Cold War, it was not without its critics. From the beginning of the Cold War, there were those who disagreed with the motives, methods, and monetary costs of fighting communism. The degree of conformity among Americans in the 1950's has often been vastly overstated, but there was a degree of acceptance of common values by those who emerged from the Second World War. The generation that had grown up in the Great Depression understandably valued frugality, self-sacrifice, and selfless devotion to a cause. When the deprivations of the Depression and the Second World War were finally over, the lucky survivors naturally felt entitled to relieve their pent up demand. They married, got better jobs, purchased new homes and cars, and had children. To them, the threat of communism seemed to be just the latest threat to the American way of life. They had defeated the Depression, totalitarianism, and Japanese imperialism, why should they not be able to stop communism as well? No amount of sacrifice seemed unreasonable to stop a threat that was made even more immediate by the specter of nuclear annihilation.

There had long been a tiny portion of the American populace that had been attracted to leftist politics. The Old Left was splintered into small parties that quarreled with each other over whether true revolution was necessary or merely better rights for workers. Their endless infighting meant that they were hopelessly ineffective in bringing about any real change. Most Americans had long been suspicious of any leftist movement and casually lumped socialists, Communists, and anarchists together as dangerous radicals that should be suppressed. After WWII, when anyone criticized the war effort, the development of the atomic bomb, or the status of the USSR as an enemy, they were quickly denounced as un-American and as one who was sympathetic to communism or was a "pinko".

Matters especially came to a head when the USSR developed its own nuclear bomb. Most people assumed that the backward Soviets could not have done this without the help of American spies. While there were some Americans that revealed strategic secrets to the USSR, they had not necessarily done so because they were Communists. In their own testimony, they often said they did so because they feared what might happen to the US if it maintained a nuclear monopoly. The collaborators naively felt that aiding the USSR would create a nuclear balance that would make anyone too afraid to actually use the terrifying new war technology. What started out as legitimate investigations to root out spies grew into the excesses of McCarthyism, where many people in the Army, the State Department, and even President Eisenhower had their loyalty called into question. When McCarthy criticized the beloved Ike with his typical tactic of accusing anyone who opposed him of being secretly sympathetic towards Communism, the public turned on McCarthy and the hearings were finally brought to a halt.

The first postwar protest movement to take shape was the beatniks. They were into improvised poetry, jazz, and marijuana use. They rejected postwar materialism and conformity. They wore unconventional clothing and used a strange lingo all of their own. They stressed pacifism and strong individualism. The movement started in New York and then moved to San Francisco. From there it spread across the nation. Alan Ginsburg, Jack Kerouac, and other authors wrote books that challenged the existing social mores and philosophies in shocking ways. The movement never had a great following, but it was very influential in later non-conformist movements. There was once a beat museum in San Francisco, but it is, unfortunately, gone. A small exhibit in the Museum of San Francisco and some items at the Oakland Museum of California are all that are currently available for the public to see.

A much tamer social movement was the surfer craze. Although Texas, Hawaii, and other locations are also popular for surfing, the beach culture really had its heart in California. All you have to do is listen to the lyrics of the Beach Boys' song, "Surfin' USA" to hear how many places in California were important surf spots. The beach bums did not advocate much for social causes, except for equal access for women in the sport. They helped popularize shaggy haircuts, shorts, sandals, VW buses, and hot rod cars. The music challenged the 1950's doo-wop music with its energetic rhythms and positive lyrics. "California Girls" became the standard of beauty for the nation. Everyone wanted to go to there to see the beautiful beaches and try surfing. The history of the sport from its Hawaiian origins to today is immortalized in the Santa Cruz Surfing Museum. The image of the laid-back bleach blonde or suntanned movie star has become as much of an icon in American culture as the cowboy.

Hollywood also showed an interest in the Bay Area. Because of its many varied types of architecture and scenery, it is no wonder that many movies and TV shows have been shot in the Bay Area. Some of the more famous ones include: *The Birds, Bullitt, American Graffiti, Mrs. Doubtfire*, and some of the *Indiana Jones, Star Trek*, and *Planet of the Apes* movies. The Bay Area has been home to many leaders in the film industry, such as George Lucas, Steven Spielberg, and others. Locations used by Lucas in his films are highlighted in the San Enselmo Museum. TV shows set in the Bay Area include *The Streets of San Francisco, Ironsides, Mythbusters, Dharma and Greg, Full House*, and many others. Many actors also have chosen to make it their home. The Walt Disney Family Museum in the Presidio in San Francisco tells the story of his life and remarkable accomplishments. Another great location to learn about the history of film is the Berkeley Art Museum and Pacific Film Archive.

Other forms of entertainment, such as cartoons, were also developed in the Bay Area, including *Peanuts, Doonesbury*, and others. You can see great examples of original artwork at The Charles M. Schulz Museum and Research Center in Santa Rosa and The Cartoon Art Museum in San Francisco. Many groundbreaking amusement parks have also been built in the Bay Area, including such lost treasures as Marine World, Frontier Village, Santa's Village, and Neptune Park. The local museums that are near the former location of these parks sometimes have exhibits about them. One of the early amusement parks that is still open is the Santa Cruz Beach Boardwalk. They have a small museum called Santa Cruz Boardwalk Historium, which tells about the park's little-known role in the development of beauty pageants and it former prominence as a concert and dance venue in the big band era. More recently opened parks, such as Great America and Six Flags, sometimes have displays about their history as well. As the population of the Bay

Area grew, it also attracted the attention of major league sports. Eastern teams took the opportunity to relocate to the area, such as the San Francisco Giants (from New York), the Oakland A's (originally from Philadelphia, then Kansas City), and the San Francisco/Golden State Warriors (from Philadelphia). New expansion teams were also added, like the Oakland Raiders, San Francisco Forty Niners, and San Jose Sharks.

Meanwhile, protest movements continued to evolve, including one of the milder forms, the folk music movement. It started out as an alternative to the hard driving rhythm of rock and roll. It was an effort to rescue traditional American songs from a simpler past that were in danger of being forgotten. As the movement progressed, however, elements of anti-war and pro-civil rights movement sympathies were sneaked past the censors through the use of oblique lyrics. Eventually, artists like Bob Dylan and Joan Baez dropped the pretense and began to address their favorite causes more directly. This movement also had many key players from the Bay Area. Local clubs and radio stations were more amenable to playing the songs than in most other regions of the country. DJ's were given considerably more autonomy than they are today and they used it to advance their pet causes. This became the music that motivated a generation that wanted to change the world, enveloping a wide range of individuals, such as environmentalists, civil rights workers, and even technology evangelists like Steve Jobs.

Eventually, folk music was eclipsed by edgier rock and roll music as it moved away from doo-wop and pop music to harder forms of rock, including acid rock and psychedelic music. These types of music embraced elements of Eastern religion and the drug culture, which greatly alienated many of the young people's parents. This widened the existing 'generation gap' even further. Many key artists in the 1960s started in the Bay Area, like Jefferson Airplane, Santana, and others. Inexplicably, there is no central rock museum in the region, unlike other parts of the country. For now, we have to content ourselves with small exhibits here and there in local museums.

The largest social movement that had its origins in the Bay Area was the Hippie movement. This movement was inspired by the Beatniks, but it had a much larger and more influential following. The Hippies advocated free love, drug use, and turning away from commercialism and materialism. Many rejected traditional Judeo-Christian values and turned instead to astrology, Buddhism, East Indian gurus, and newly fabricated religions like EST and transcendental meditation. Some joined a new movement of Christianity called The Jesus People, which emphasized less formal dress and contemporary music and worship. It was a more personal, experiential religion with less doctrine and traditional practices than in mainline churches. It is impossible to think about the Hippies without thinking of the Bay Area, as the song "Are You Going to San Francisco?" attests. Many key events happened there: the Berkeley Free Speech Movement, the Summer of Love, the Haight-Ashbury District, the free concerts in Golden Gate Park, the communes, and the campus protests. There were also many famous rock and roll firsts in legendary theaters like the Fillmore and others.

Many important social changes grew out of the Hippie movement. On the positive side, changes included the environmental movement, the civil rights movement, and equality for women and minorities. On the negative side, there is a lasting legacy of drug abuse and many unforeseen tragic consequences of the sexual revolution, as well as the weakening of the concept of the traditional family unit and traditional American values. Many of the loftier goals, like world peace, a simpler and less materialistic life, brotherhood, and love for all, remained elusive, but there is no doubt that their goal of changing the world was accomplished. Every aspect of society was influenced by this movement, and many of their reforms were first instituted in California.

Many ethnic groups sought greater equality during this era. On Alcatraz Island, one of the most important demonstrations for Native American rights took place when various tribes occupied the island from 1969-1970. In the 1960s and 1970s, Cesar Chavez also led demonstrations and boycotts to improve the lot of migrant farm workers in the Bay Area. The Black Power movement had its center in the Oakland area. This and other aspects of the Civil Rights Movement can be seen and researched at The African American Museum & Library in Oakland. Many other groups have subsequently adopted the tactics of the activists of the 1960s.

One of the ways in which the Hippies expressed their nonconformity was through casual dress. The most enduring icon of this era in fashion was blue jeans. They went from being working-man's clothes to the symbol of a generation. No respectable teen was without them for decades. Later, they became a fashion statement and prices soared. An interesting museum captures the story of these legendary American products from their early role in the Gold Rush to today. This is the Levi's Plaza Store and Historical Archives in San Francisco.

However, the most lasting social revolution that started in the Bay Area was the tech revolution, which grew out of the postwar aerospace and electronics industries. There was never any shortage of engineers and electronic parts in the Bay Area. Local universities and electronics stores had meetings where hobbyists could assemble circuit boards and other gizmos for fun and to impress others. Out of these clubs came Steve Jobs, Steve Wosniak, Bill Gates, and many lesser-known tech innovators. They saw themselves as revolutionaries who wanted to take the power of the computer out of the hands of big corporations and give it to the common man. The personal computer, the internet, smart phones, desktop publishing, and many other technologies had some of their most important advancements developed in the Bay Area, leading to the Santa Clara Valley and surrounding areas being given the nickname "Silicon Valley". A long list of tech giants like Apple, HP, IBM, Oracle, Intel, and many other influential companies that lead the world, started in Silicon Valley and surrounding communities. The best places to see the history of the technical revolution are The Tech Museum in San Jose, the Computer History Museum in Mountain View, The Intel Museum in Santa Clara, The Sunnyvale Heritage Park Museum, San Mateo County Museum and the Lawrence Hall of Science in Berkeley. In recent years, the Bay Area has also been a leader in solar, biotech, and medical research as well.

The end of the Cold War had a major impact on the Bay Area. Economic problems led to military base closures and massive cuts in the military and the space program. Many former military bases have been declared obsolete and converted to civilian purposes. One has to wonder if California would be adequately protected in the event of a future attack. If there were to be another big conflict like WWII, there is no longer enough open cheap land to stage another major buildup in the Bay Area like America did in those days. Even the computer industry underwent big changes in the 1990s, as programming, manufacturing, and even tech support jobs were moved overseas to cut costs. This led to major disruptions as many people were forced to move out of the area when they lost their jobs and could no longer afford to live there.

Things got really bad in 2000 when over-rated stock prices for startup internet-based companies crashed and unwise mortgage lending practices led to a collapse of house prices and massive foreclosures in the first decade of the new century (the so-called "dotcom bubble"). There were massive layoffs and closures. Tech buildings and homes sat empty and a ripple effect went through the area as other businesses suffered or were closed. As a result, the tax base shrunk. Bay Area communities were critically short of money for their schools, parks, libraries, police, and infrastructure.

Silicon Valley has proved to be amazingly resilient, however, and they still manage to produce the "next big thing" every couple of years. This gives the economy a shot in the arm and creates new jobs. There is hope for the future because products and services made in the Bay Area are now in daily use by people around the globe.

(The numbers after the description of the historical site refer to the individual listings later in this book).

Museums and Historic Sites for the Counter Culture and Silicon Valley:

✓	Museum or historic site	Date Visited
	1. Santa Cruz Surfing Museum: historic surfboards and photos of surfers. #188	
	2. Los Altos History Museum: tech history. #104	
	3. African American Museum & Library-Oakland: Civil rights documents, photos, etc. #1	
	4. Museum on Main-Pleasanton: technology growth, especially Lawrence Livermore Labs. #163	
	5. San Mateo County History Museum-Redwood City: tech companies, urban housing boom. #185	
	6. Blackhawk Museum-Danville: historic automobiles. #25	
	7. Richmond Museum of History: Civil Rights movement, African American history. #175	
	8. Hayward Area Historical Museum: postwar growth and change. #83	
	9. Alcatraz Island: the Indian Occupation is shown in photos and historic graffiti. #6	

	10. Marin County Civic Center-San Rafael: architectural innovations of Frank Lloyd Wright that inspired many other Bay Area buildings, especially tech companies.	
	11. Federal Reserve -San Francisco: economic history, banking and business. #67	
	12. Levi's Plaza Store and Historical Archives-San Francisco: historic blue jeans collection and the impact that they had on pop culture. #102	
	13. The Cartoon Art Museum-San Francisco: original artwork from cartoon artists. #36	
	14. Berkeley Art Museum and Pacific Film Archive: historic film clips from many genres. No listing.	
	15. Agnews Historic Cemetery and Museum: the history of mental health care. #2	
	16. Lawrence Livermore National Laboratory: displays on research on nuclear particles, physics, alternate energy, seismology, advanced weaponry, and many other disciplines. #101	
	17. Santa Cruz Boardwalk Historium- Santa Cruz: historic photos of the Boardwalk. #186	
	18. Wings of History Museum-San Martin: historic aircraft and photos of Bay Area airports. #224	
	19. Oakland Aviation Museum: historic aircraft and photos of Bay Area airports. #146	
	20. The Charles M. Schulz Museum and Research Center-Santa Rosa: Schultz's den, many of his personal effects, original artwork, etc. #40	
	21. Computer History Museum-Mountain View: examples of historic computers going back centuries. Some vary rare items as well as things you will remember using in your lifetime. #48	
	22. The HP Garage-Palo Alto: The house where Hewlett-Packard began. #90	
	23. Apple Headquarters-Cupertino contains no public museum at present. No listing.	
	24. The Tech Museum-San Jose: technology of every kind. Displays are rotated, but sometimes include gadgets from Silicon Valley pioneers. #204	
	25. Intel Museum-Santa Clara: historic computer chips and displays on how they are made today. #91	
	26. The San Francisco History Museum: a complete hippie's bedroom. #192	
	27. Berkeley Historical Society: historical photos and documents related to the Free Speech Movement and hippies. #22	
	28. The Walt Disney Family Museum-San Francisco: original Disney artwork, videos, and a huge model of Disneyland. #169	

I certify that _____ has visited all of the above sites and is a certified hippie and/ or technology nerd.

X _____ (museum staff member).

Lockheed Engineer's desk at the Sunnyvale Heritage Park Museum

64

Museums and Historical Sites Listed by Category

Museums and Historical sites Listed by County:

(The numbers next to name of the historical site refer to the individual listings later in this book).

Monterey County:
Point Pinos Lighthouse-Pacific Grove #166
Tor House-Carmel #206
Boronda Adobe History Center-Salinas #127
The National Steinbeck Center-Salinas #141
Point Lobos Whaling Station #165
Presidio Museum of Monterey #168
Museum of Monterey #136
Monterey State Historic Park #128

Royal Presidio Chapel- Monterey #128
Mission Carmel #116
Mission Soledad #122
The Pacific House in Monterey #128
California Rodeo Heritage Museum (only open during the Salinas Rodeo) #31
Salinas Valley Memorial Hospital Museum of Medical History #179
Monterey County Agricultural & Rural Life Museum-King City #123

Santa Cruz County:
Aptos History Museum #11
Agricultural History Project Center and Museum-Watsonville #3
Pajaro Valley Historical Association-Watsonville #152
Santa Cruz Surfing Museum #188
Capitola Historical Museum #35
The Museum of Art & History at the McPherson Center-Santa Cruz #203
Wilder Ranch State Park-Santa Cruz #222
Mission Santa Cruz #121
Santa Cruz Natural History Museum #187
The San Lorenzo Valley Museum-Boulder Creek #184
Soquel Pioneer and Historical Association #198
Quail Hollow Ranch County Park-Felton #171
Cowell Lime Works Historic District- Santa Cruz #50
Santa Cruz Boardwalk Historium- Santa Cruz #186
Watsonville Fire Museum #218

Santa Clara County:
Ulistac Natural Area-Santa Clara #209
The California History Center-De Anza College #30
Hoover Institute-Stanford #89
Hoover Tower #89
Egyptian Museum-San Jose-#64
Cantor Arts Center –Stanford #34
Computer History Museum-Mountain View #48
The HP Garage-Palo Alto #90
Apple-Cupertino (no listing)
The Tech Museum of Innovation-San Jose #204
Intel Museum-Santa Clara #91
Japanese American Museum of San Jose #94
Los Altos Historical Museum #104
Sunnyvale Heritage Park Museum #202
NASA Ames-Sunnyvale #140
The South Bay Historical Railroad Society-Santa Clara #199
Lick Observatory-Mt. Hamilton #131
Moffett Field Historical Museum-Mountain View #126
Museum of American Heritage-Palo Alto #125
Pine Ridge Museum-Henry Coe State Park-east of Morgan Hill #161

Gilroy Hot Springs #76
Hayes Mansion-San Jose #82
Fallon House-San Jose #157
Ainsley House-Campbell #4
Campbell Historical Museum #32
Cupertino Historical Museum #53
The Gilroy Museum #75
Harris-Lass House Museum-Santa Clara #81
New Museum Los Gatos #105
The Headen-Inman House-Santa Clara #84
Saratoga Historical Park & Museum #189
Prusch Farm-San Jose #170
Winchester Mystery House-San Jose #223
Rengstorff House-Mountain View #174
Montalvo Arts Center –Saratoga #217
Hakone Gardens- Saratoga #79
Peralta Adobe and Fallon House #157
History San Jose #88
The Headen-Inman House-Santa Clara #84
Berryessa Adobe-Santa Clara #23
Mission Santa Clara #120
The deSaisset Museum at Santa Clara University #58
Deer Hollow Farm in Rancho San Antonio County Park-Cupertino #56
Chitactac-Adams Heritage County Park-Gilroy #43
New Almaden Quicksilver Mining Museum -San Jose #142
San Jose Fire Museum #181
Agnews Historic Cemetery and Museum #2
Evergreen Valley College Library's Heritage Room-San Jose #66
Wings of History Museum-San Martin #224
Villa Mira Monte #227

San Mateo County:
The Woodside Store #225
Filoli-Woodside #68
Sanchez Adobe-Pacifica #182
The Museum of San Carlos History #204
The Daly City History Museum #54
South San Francisco Historical Museum #200
Lathrop House-Redwood City #99
San Mateo County History Museum-Redwood City #185
Hiller Museum-San Carlos #87
Kohl Mansion-Burlingame (open for special events only) no listing
Colma Historical Society #47
Burlingame Hillsborough History Museum #27
Millbrae History Museum #113
Millbrae Train Museum #114

The Woodside Community Museum #226

San Francisco County:
Mission Dolores-San Francisco #117
Presidio Visitor's Center and The Officers' Club -San Francisco #169
Levi's Plaza Store and Historical Archives-San Francisco #102
Cable Car Museum San Francisco #28
Haas-Lilienthal House-San Francisco #78
California Historical Society-San Francisco #29
Palace of the Legion of Honor-San Francisco #153
San Francisco Fire Dept. Fire Museum #191
San Francisco Maritime National Historical Park #190
Musee Mecanique-San Francisco #133
S.S. Jeremiah O'Brien-San Francisco #196
USS Pampanito - San Francisco Maritime National Park #212
Federal Reserve -San Francisco #67
deYoung Museum- San Francisco #59
Asian Art Museum-San Francisco #13
Chinese Historical Society of America Museum-San Francisco #42
Museum of the African Diaspora-San Francisco #124
Pacific Heritage Museum-San Francisco #151
The San Francisco History Museum #192
Octagon House-San Francisco #149
Fort Point #72
Golden Gate Bridge #77
Alcatraz Island #6
Wells Fargo History Museum- San Francisco #219
The Cartoon Art Museum-San Francisco #36
Military Intelligence Service Historic Learning Center-San Francisco #115
The Walt Disney Family Museum-San Francisco: #169

Marin County:
Olompali State Historic Park-north of Novato #148
The Museum of the American Indian-Novato #137
Fort Ross-Jenner #73
Mission San Rafael Arcangel #119
Angel Island immigration museum #9
Falkirk Cultural Center-San Rafael (open for special events only) no listing
Marin History Museum-San Rafael #109
China Camp Historic District-San Rafael #41
Point Bonita Light House #164
Forts Baker, Barry, and Cronkhite Marin County Headlands #71
Point Reyes Light Station District #167
Hamilton Field Museum-Novato #80
Railroad & Ferry Museum-Tiburon #18
China Cabin-Belvedere #18

Bolinas Museum #26
Novato History Museum #145
Bear Valley Visitor Center, Kule Loklo, Pierce Point Ranch #17
San Anselmo Historical Museum #180
Tomales Regional History Center-Tomales #206
Jack Mason Museum of West Marin History-Inverness #93

Sonoma County:
Petaluma Adobe State Historic Park #158
Sonoma State Historic Park:(General Vallejo Home, Mission San Francisco de Solano, the Blue Wing Inn, Sonoma Barracks, the Toscano Hotel, the Servants Quarters (the remains of La Casa Grande)-Sonoma #197
Jack London State Historic Park-Glen Ellen #92
Luther Burbank Home & Gardens-Santa Rosa #107
Cloverdale Historical Society Museum #45
Petaluma Historical Library and Museum #159
Healdsburg Museum #85
Jesse Peter Native American Art Museum-Santa Rosa #95
Luther Burbank Gold Ridge Experimental Farm-Sebastopol #106
Western Sonoma County Historical Society West County Museum- Sebastopol #221
Depot Park Museum-Sonoma #57
The General Joseph Hooker House-Sonoma #74
The Charles M. Schulz Museum and Research Center-Santa Rosa #40
Fort Ross #73

Napa County:
Napa Valley Museum-Yountville #139
Bale Grist Mill-St. Helena #15
Sharpsteen Museum-Calistoga #194
Napa Firefighters Museum #138
The Robert Louis Stevenson Museum-St. Helena #177
Robert Louis Stevenson State Park-Calistoga #177

Solano County:
Rio Vista Museum #176
Western Railway Museum-Suisun City #220
Travis Air Force Base Heritage Center #208
The Vacaville Museum #214
Vallejo Naval and Historical Museum #216
Benicia Capitol State Historic Park #19
Benicia Historical Museum #21
Fischer-Hanlon House-Benicia #19
Benicia Fire Museum #20
The Pena Adobe-Vacaville #155

Contra Costa County:
Black Diamond Mines –Antioch #24
Clayton Historical Society Museum #44
East Contra Costa Historical Society Museum-Brentwood #63
John Muir National Historic Site-Martinez #96
Martinez Museum #111
Pittsburg Historical Society #162
Richmond Museum of History #175
Rosie the Riveter-WWII Home Front National Historical Park-Richmond #178
Crockett Historical Museum #52
Martinez Adobe-Martinez #96
Contra Costa County History Center-Martinez #49
Orinda Historical Society #150
Lafayette Historical Society #98
Blackhawk Museum-Danville #25
Eugene O'Neill National Historic Site-Danville #65
The David and Eliza Glass House Museum-San Ramon #70
Mount Diablo State Park #130
Shadelands Ranch Historical Museum-Walnut Creek #193
Museum of the San Ramon Valley-Danville #135
Antioch Historical Museum #10
Mothball Fleet-Martinez #129
The Alvarado Adobe, Blume House and Bunk House- San Pablo #7

Alameda County:
The Phoebe A. Hearst Museum of Anthropology-Berkeley #160
Bancroft Library-Berkeley #16
The Berkeley Historical Society #22
Judah L. Magnes Museum-University of California, Berkeley #108
Lawrence Berkeley National Laboratory #100
The Oakland Museum of California #147
African American Museum & Library-Oakland #1
Dunsmuir House & Gardens-Oakland #62
Cohen-Bray House-Oakland #46
Pardee Home Museum-Oakland #154
Camron-Stanford House-Oakland #33
U.S.S. Potomac-Oakland #213
Alameda Museum #5
U.S.S. Hornet-Alameda #211
McConaghy House- Hayward #112
The C.E. Smith Museum of Anthropology-Hayward #39
Hayward Area Historical Museum #83
Union City Historical Museum #210
Coyote Hills Regional Park -Fremont #51
Mission San Jose-Fremont #118
The Higuera Adobe-Fremont #86

70

Vallejo Adobe-Fremont #215
Shinn Historic Park & Arboretum-Fremont #195
Ardenwood Historic Farm- Fremont #12
Niles Essanay Silent Film Museum-Fremont #144
Niles Depot-Fremont #143
The Museum of Local History-Fremont #134
Museum on Main-Pleasanton #163
Dublin Heritage Park & Museums #61
Lawrence Livermore National Laboratory #101
Ravenswood Historical Site-Livermore #172
Murrietta's Well-Livermore #132
Centennial Light Bulb-Livermore #38
Alviso Adobe- Pleasanton #8
Badè Museum of Biblical Archaeology-Berkeley #14
The Livermore Heritage Guild #103
The Peralta House Museum of History-Oakland #156
Oakland Aviation Museum #146
Duarte Garage-Livermore #60

The David and Eliza Glass House Museum-San Ramon

Museums Listed by Other Categories

World History sites:
Phoebe Apperson Hearst Museum of Anthropology-Berkeley #160
Cantor Arts Center –Stanford #34
Egyptian Museum-San Jose #64
Palace of the Legion of Honor-San Francisco #153
Oakland Museum of California #147
deYoung Museum- San Francisco #59
Asian Art Museum-San Francisco #13
Chinese Historical Society of America Museum-San Francisco #42
Museum of the African Diaspora-San Francisco #124
Pacific Heritage Museum-San Francisco #151
Judah L. Magnes Museum-University of California, Berkeley #108
Badè Museum of Biblical Archaeology- Berkeley #14
The C.E. Smith Museum of Anthropology-Hayward #39
Hoover Institute-Stanford #89
Hakone Gardens-Saratoga #79

Famous Literary figures:
The Charles M. Schulz Museum and Research Center-Santa Rosa #40
African American Museum & Library-Oakland #1
The Cartoon Art Museum-San Francisco #36
John Muir National Historic Site-Martinez #96
Robert Louis Stevenson State Park-Calistoga #177
Montalvo Arts Center-Saratoga #216
The National Steinbeck Center-Salinas #141
Eugene O'Neill National Historic Site-Danville #65
Jack London State Historic Park-Glen Ellen #92
The San Francisco History Museum #192
Tor House-Carmel #206
Hakone Gardens-Saratoga #79
Robert Louis Stevenson House-Monterey #128
The Walt Disney Family Museum-San Francisco: #169

Business tycoons:
The HP Garage-Palo Alto #90
Computer History Museum-Mountain View #48
Levi's Plaza Store and Historical Archives-San Francisco #102
Lathrop House-Redwood City #99
Winchester Mystery House-San Jose #223
Pardee Home Museum-Oakland #154
Camron-Stanford House-Oakland #33
Ainsley House-Campbell #4
Haas-Lilienthal House-San Francisco #78
Filoli-Woodside #68

Wells Fargo History Museum-San Francisco #219
Crockett Historical Museum #52

Trains:
The South Bay Historical Railroad Society-Santa Clara #199
Railroad & Ferry Museum-Tiburon #18
Western Railway Museum-Suisun City #220
Golden Gate Railroad Museum-Sunol (not an actual physical museum; they are historic train rides on the Niles Canyon Railway. See http://ggrm.org/ for information). No listing.
The Niles Depot Model Railroads and Museum-Niles #143
Colma Historical Society #47
Millbrae Train Museum #114
Burlingame Hillsborough History Museum #27
The Depot Park Museum-Sonoma #57
Clayton Historical Society Museum #44
Museum of the San Ramon Valley-Danville #135
The Museum of San Carlos History #204

Agriculture:
Dublin Heritage Park & Museums #61
The National Steinbeck Center-Salinas #141
Orinda Historical Society #150
Vacaville Museum #214
The Livermore Heritage Guild #103
Antioch Historical Museum #10
Monterey County Agricultural & Rural Life Museum-King City #123
Agricultural History Project Center and Museum- Watsonville #3
Museum of American Heritage-Palo Alto #125
Saratoga Historical Park & Museum #189
Prusch Farm-San Jose #170
Luther Burbank Gold Ridge Experimental Farm-Sebastopol #106
Shinn Historic Park & Arboretum-Fremont #195
California Rodeo Heritage Museum (only open during the Salinas Rodeo) #31
Ardenwood Historic Farm- Fremont #12
Forest Home Farms Historic Park: The David and Eliza Glass House Museum-San Ramon #70
Sunnyvale Heritage Park Museum #202
Boronda Adobe History Center-Salinas #127
General Vallejo Home-Sonoma #197
History San Jose #88
Oakland Museum of California #147
Los Altos History Museum #104
San Mateo County History Museum-Redwood City #185
Contra Costa County History Center-Martinez #49
Napa Valley Museum-Yountville #139

Ulistac Natural Area-Santa Clara #209
Evergreen Valley College Library's Heritage Room-San Jose #66
Petaluma Historical Library and Museum #159
Museum of the San Ramon Valley-Danville #135
Oakland Museum of California #147
Filoli-Woodside #68
Bale Grist Mill-St. Helena #15
Fischer-Hanlon House-Benicia #19
Sharpsteen Museum-Calistoga #194
The Museum of Art & History at the McPherson Center-Santa Cruz #203
Ygnacio Peralta Home-San Leandro (no listing)
Union City Historical Museum #210
The Daly City History Museum #54
Aptos History Museum #11
Rengstorff House-Mountain View #174
Montalvo Arts Center-Saratoga #216
Alameda Museum #5
Museum on Main-Pleasanton #163
Clayton Historical Society Museum #44
East Contra Costa Historical Society Museum-Brentwood #63
John Muir National Historic Site-Martinez #96
Martinez Museum #111
Pittsburg Historical Society #162
Richmond Museum of History #175
Shadelands Ranch Historical Museum-Walnut Creek #193
Ainsley House-Campbell #4
Cupertino Historical Museum #53
The Gilroy Museum #75
Harris-Lass House Museum-Santa Clara #81
New Museum Los Gatos #105
The Headen-Inman House-Santa Clara #84
Saratoga Historical Park & Museum #189
Marin History Museum-San Rafael #109
Wilder Ranch State Park-Santa Cruz #222
Pajaro Valley Historical Association-Watsonville #152
Novato History Museum #145
The Berkeley Historical Society #22
The Woodside Store #225
Pine Ridge Museum-Henry Coe State Park #161
The Museum of Local History-Fremont #134
Contra Costa County History Center-Martinez #49
Lafayette Historical Society #98
Chinese Historical Society of America Museum-San Francisco #42
Japanese American Museum of San Jose #94
Campbell Historical Museum #32
Villa Mira Monte #227

Ships:
China Camp Historic District-San Rafael #41
Point Bonita Light House #164
Point Reyes Light Station District #167
Point Pinos Lighthouse-Pacific Grove #166
The National Steinbeck Center-Salinas #141
Point Lobos Whaling Station #165
Museum of Monterey #136
Richmond Museum of History #175
Vallejo Naval and Historical Museum #216
S.S. Jeremiah O'Brien -San Francisco #196
USS Pampanito - San Francisco Maritime National Park #212
Mothball Fleet-Martinez #129
U.S.S. Hornet-Alameda #211
Rosie the Riveter-WWII Home Front National Historical Park-Richmond #178
Red Oak Victory Ship-Richmond #173
U.S.S. Potomac-Oakland #213
San Francisco Maritime National Historic Park #190
China Cabin-Belvedere #18

Scientific Discoveries:
Computer History Museum-Mountain View #48
The HP Garage-Palo Alto #90
Apple-Cupertino (no listing)
The Tech Museum of Innovation-San Jose #204
Intel Museum-Santa Clara #91
Sunnyvale Heritage Park Museum #202
NASA Ames-Sunnyvale #140
Lawrence Livermore National Laboratory #101
Oakland Aviation Museum #146
Lawrence Berkeley National Laboratory #100
Museum of American Heritage-Palo Alto #125
Lick Observatory-Mt. Hamilton #131
History San Jose #88
Luther Burbank Home & Gardens-Santa Rosa #107
Luther Burbank Gold Ridge Experimental Farm-Sebastopol #106
The Phoebe A. Hearst Museum of Anthropology Berkeley #160
Judah L. Magnes Museum-University of California, Berkeley #108
Lawrence Berkeley National Laboratory #100
The Oakland Museum California #147
San Mateo County History Museum-Redwood City #185

Mines:
Black Diamond Mines –Antioch #24
New Almaden Quicksilver Mining Museum -San Jose #142
Filoli-Woodside #68

Firefighters:
Napa Firefighters Museum #138
San Jose Fire Museum #181
San Francisco Fire Dept. Fire Museum #191
Watsonville Fire Museum #218
Colma Historical Society #47
Daly City History Museum #54
The Museum of San Carlos History #204
Benicia Fire Museum #20

Historic homes:
Dublin Heritage Park & Museums #61
Ravenswood Historical Site-Livermore #172
Falkirk Cultural Center-San Rafael no listing
Fischer-Hanlon House-Benicia #19
The General Joseph Hooker House-Sonoma #74
Octagon House-San Francisco #149
Haas-Lilienthal House-San Francisco #78
Kohl Mansion-Burlingame (open for special events only) no listing
Lathrop House-Redwood City #99
Rengstorff House-Mountain View #174
Winchester Mystery House-San Jose #223
Hayes Mansion-San Jose #82
Fallon House-San Jose #157
Ainsley House-Campbell #4
The Headen-Inman House-Santa Clara #84
Harris-Lass House Museum-Santa Clara #81
Ainsley House-Campbell #4
Hayes Mansion-San Jose #82
Fallon House-San Jose #157
Mission Santa Cruz #121
Tor House-Carmel #206
Boronda Adobe History Center Salinas #127
Martinez Adobe-Martinez #96
Eugene O'Neill National Historic Site-Danville #65
The David and Eliza Glass House Museum-San Ramon #70
Camron-Stanford House-Oakland #33
Dunsmuir House & Gardens-Oakland #62
Cohen-Bray House-Oakland #46
Pardee Home Museum-Oakland #154
McConaghy House- Hayward #112
The Higuera Adobe-Fremont #86
Shinn Historic Park & Arboretum-Fremont #195
Shadelands Ranch Historical Museum-Walnut Creek #193
Pajaro Valley Historical Association-Watsonville #152
The Peralta House Museum of History-Oakland #156

The J. Gilbert Smith House-Los Altos #104
Rodgers House-Watsonville #3
The Alvarado Adobe, Blume House and Bunk House-San Pablo #7
The Meyers House and Gardens-Alameda #5
The General Joseph Hooker House-Sonoma #74
Villa Mira Monte #227

Historic sites:
Travis Air Force Base Heritage Center #208
Mission San Rafael Arcangel #119
Golden Gate Bridge #77
Chinatown- San Francisco
Mission Dolores-San Francisco #117
Mission Santa Clara #120
Hakone Gardens- Saratoga #79
Montalvo Arts Center-Saratoga #216
Gilroy Hot Springs #76
Moffett Field Historical Museum -Sunnyvale #126
Lick Observatory-Mt. Hamilton #131
The HP Garage-Palo Alto #90
Apple-Cupertino (no listing)
Hoover Tower-Stanford #89
Mission Carmel #116
Mission Soledad #122
Mothball Fleet-Martinez #129
Lawrence Berkeley National Laboratory #100
U.S.S. Potomac-Oakland #213
U.S.S. Hornet-Alameda #211
Mission San Jose-Fremont #118

Private museums:
Military Intelligence Service Historic Learning Center-San Francisco #115
Cowell Lime Works Historic District- Santa Cruz #50
Salinas Valley Memorial Hospital Museum of Medical History #179
Hiller Museum-San Carlos #87
Filoli-Woodside #68
Benicia Fire Museum #20
Western Railway Museum-Suisun City #220
Sharpsteen Museum-Calistoga #194
Napa Firefighters Museum #138
Jesse Peter Native American Art Museum-Santa Rosa #95
The Museum of the American Indian-Novato #137
The San Francisco History Museum #192
Pacific Heritage Museum-San Francisco #151
Chinese Historical Society of America Museum-San Francisco #42
The South Bay Historical Railroad Society-Santa Clara #199

Asian Art Museum-San Francisco #13
deYoung Museum- San Francisco #59
Museum of the African Diaspora-San Francisco #124
Musee Mecanique-San Francisco #133
San Francisco Fire Dept. Fire Museum #191
Palace of the Legion of Honor-San Francisco #153
California Historical Society-San Francisco #29
Cable Car Museum San Francisco #28
Levi's Plaza Store and Historical Archives-San Francisco #102
The deSaisset Museum at Santa Clara University #58
San Jose Fire Museum #181
Museum of American Heritage-Palo Alto #125
The Tech Museum of Innovation-San Jose #204
Intel Museum-Santa Clara #91
Japanese American Museum of San Jose #94
Computer History Museum-Mountain View #48
The California History Center-De Anza College #30
Hoover Institute-Stanford #89
Egyptian Museum-San Jose #64
Cantor Arts Center –Stanford #34
The National Steinbeck Center-Salinas #141
Point Pinos Lighthouse-Pacific Grove #166
Blackhawk Museum-Danville #25
The Phoebe A. Hearst Museum of Anthropology Berkeley #160
Bancroft Library-Berkeley #16
Judah L. Magnes Museum-University of California, Berkeley #108
The C.E. Smith Museum of Anthropology-Hayward #39
Niles Essanay Silent Film Museum-Fremont #144
The Robert Louis Stevenson Museum-St. Helena #177
Wells Fargo History Museum- San Francisco #219
Murrietta's Well-Livermore #132
Wings of History Museum-San Martin #222
The Pena Adobe-Vacaville #155
The Charles M. Schulz Museum and Research Center-Santa Rosa #40
The Walt Disney Family Museum-San Francisco: #169

Local or City Museums:
The Alvarado Adobe, Blume House and Bunk House-San Pablo #7
The Peralta House Museum of History-Oakland #156
The Livermore Heritage Guild #103
Agricultural History Project Center and Museum-Watsonville #3
Pajaro Valley Historical Association-Watsonville #152
The San Lorenzo Valley Museum-Boulder Creek #184
Tomales Regional History Center-Tomales #206
Benicia Historical Museum #21
Vallejo Naval and Historical Museum #216

Rio Vista Museum #176

Depot Park Museum-Sonoma #57

Healdsburg Museum #85

Cloverdale Historical Society Museum #45

Petaluma Historical Library and Museum #159

Luther Burbank Home & Gardens-Santa Rosa #107

San Anselmo Historical Museum #180

Novato History Museum #145

Bolinas Museum #26

China Cabin-Belvedere #18

Railroad & Ferry Museum-Tiburon #18

South San Francisco Historical Museum #200

The Museum of San Carlos History #204

The Daly City History Museum #54

Peralta Adobe #157

History San Jose #88

The Headen-Inman House-Santa Clara #84

Berryessa Adobe-Santa Clara #23

Sunnyvale Heritage Park Museum #202

Saratoga Historical Park & Museum #189

Prusch Farm-San Jose #170

Los Altos History Museum #104

New Museum Los Gatos #105

Cupertino Historical Museum #53

The Gilroy Museum #75

Los Altos Historical Museum #104

Sunnyvale Heritage Park Museum #202

Santa Cruz Natural History Museum #187

Aptos History Museum #11

The Museum of Art & History at the McPherson Center-Santa Cruz #203

Capitola Historical Museum #35

Pajaro Valley Historical Association-Watsonville #152

Martinez Museum #111

Orinda Historical Society #150

Lafayette Historical Society #98

The Berkeley Historical Society #22

The Oakland Museum California #147

African American Museum & Library-Oakland #1

Alameda Museum #5

Hayward Area Historical Museum-Hayward #83

Union City Historical Museum #210

The Museum of Local History-Fremont #134

Museum on Main-Pleasanton #163

Dublin Heritage Park & Museums #61

Agnews Historic Cemetery and Museum-Santa Clara #2

Ulistac Natural Area-Santa Clara #209

Evergreen Valley College Library's Heritage Room #66
Museum of the San Ramon Valley-Danville #135
Alviso Adobe- Pleasanton #8
Centennial Light Bulb-Livermore #38
Soquel Pioneer and Historical Association #198
Watsonville Fire Museum #218
The General Joseph Hooker House-Sonoma #74
Depot Park Museum-Sonoma #57
Colma Historical Society #47
Campbell Historical Museum #32
Villa Mira Monte #227

County Museums:
Napa Valley Museum-Yountville #139
Western Sonoma County Historical Society West County Museum- Sebastopol #221
Luther Burbank Gold Ridge Experimental Farm-Sebastopol #106
Marin History Museum-San Rafael #109
San Mateo County History Museum-Redwood City #185
The Woodside Store #225
Sanchez Adobe-Pacifica #182
New Almaden Quicksilver Mining Museum -San Jose #142
Deer Hollow Farm in Rancho San Antonio County Park-Cupertino #56
Chitactac-Adams Heritage County Park-Gilroy #43
Contra Costa County History Center-Martinez #49
East Contra Costa Historical Society Museum-Brentwood #63
Coyote Hills Park-Fremont #51
Ardenwood Historic Farm- Fremont #12
Jack Mason Museum of West Marin History #93
Quail Hollow Ranch County Park-Felton #171
Monterey County Agricultural & Rural Life Museum-King City #123

State Historic Parks:
Benicia Capitol State Historic Park #19
Bale Grist Mill-St. Helena #15
Robert Louis Stevenson State Park-Calistoga #177
Jack London State Historic Park-Glen Ellen #92
Sonoma State Historic Park #197
Petaluma Adobe State Historic Park #158
China Camp Historic District-San Rafael #41
Angel Island State Park #9
Fort Ross-Jenner #73
Olompali State Historic Park #148
Pine Ridge Museum-Henry Coe State Park #161
Wilder Ranch State Park-Santa Cruz #222
Monterey State Historic Park #128
Point Lobos State Preserve #165

Mount Diablo State Park #130
Mission Santa Cruz #121

National Parks or Historic sites:
Point Reyes National Seashore #17 and #167
Hamilton Field Museum-Novato #80
Alcatraz Island #6
Fort Point #72
Federal Reserve -San Francisco #67
USS Pampanito - San Francisco Maritime National Park #212
S.S. Jeremiah O'Brien-San Francisco #196
San Francisco Maritime National Historic Park #190
Presidio Visitor's Center and The Officers' Club -San Francisco #169
NASA Ames-Sunnyvale #140
Rosie the Riveter-WWII Home Front National Historical Park-Richmond #178
John Muir National Historic Site-Martinez #96
Eugene O'Neill National Historic Site-Danville #65
Lawrence Livermore National Laboratory #101
Moffett Field Historical Museum #126

Travis Air Force Base Heritage Center

Individual Museum Listings

1. **African American Museum & Library-Oakland**
2. Location: 659 14th Street, Oakland, CA. 94612.
3. Website: http://www.oaklandlibrary.org/locations/african-american-museum-library-oakland
4. Phone number: (510) 637-0200.
5. E-mail: eanswers@oaklandlibrary.org
6. Hours of operation: Tuesday- Saturday: 12:00p.m. - 5:30p.m.
7. Cost: free.
8. Permanent Exhibits: African-American general store, business pioneers, WWII, the Civil Rights Movement, Black Panthers, music, churches, journalism, writers, etc.
9. Special Exhibits: rotating exhibits.
10. Historical era that is featured the best: 1800s-1900s.
11. Targeted age groups: all ages.
12. Special activities for children: available for field trips.
13. Guided tours: guided tours are available upon request.
14. Hands-on activities: many of the displays have interactive components.
15. The best-kept secrets at the museum: the archives hold many important historical documents. Some of these are on display at the museum.
16. Hidden treasures at the museum: the general store on the ground floor has many interesting artifacts.
17. What is unique about the museum that can't be found anywhere else: it is dedicated to the discovery, preservation, interpretation, and sharing of historical and cultural experiences of African Americans in California and the West for present and future generations.
18. The most important things about local, state, or American history that can be learned at the museum: this is the best collection on black history available in the Bay Area. The community is outlined from its origins to the present.
19. Annual events held at the site or elsewhere in the community: There are many events throughout the year (see website for details).
20. Research facilities or archives at the site: Aa.m.LO's archival collection is a unique resource on the history of African Americans in Northern California and the Bay Area. The over 160 collections in the archives contain the diaries of prominent families, pioneers, churches, social and political organizations. *Freedom's Journal, the Liberator, California Voice, Sun Reporter, Muhammed Speakers*, and the Black Panther newspapers are available on microfilm.

Using Aa.m.LO's oral history collection, researchers can listen to interviews with local civil rights activists, educators, writers, and musicians. Aa.m.LO is home to the Eternal Voices video library containing more than 80 years of African American East Bay history and Susheel Bibb's Meet Mary Pleasant DVD (scholarly interviews, key issues and documents).

The microfilm collection includes primary research information on African American enslavement, military service, California census records 1910-1930, Marcus Garvey's Universal Negro Improvement Association, W.E.B. Dubois,

Benjamin Banneker, Mary Church Terrell, Paul Robeson and others. The archives department is open from 12-4 p.m. To make an appointment, call (510) 637-0198.
21. Type of gift shop and what is for sale: postcards and African American dolls are for sale.

1. **Agnews Historic Cemetery and Museum- Santa Clara**

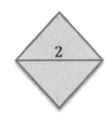

2. Location: 1250 Hope Drive, Santa Clara, CA. 95054.
3. Website: http://santaclaraca.gov/index.aspx?page=1411
4. Phone number: (408) 615-3790.
5. E-mail: Cemetery@santaclaraca.gov
6. Hours of operation: Fridays only between 10 a.m. and 2 p.m.
7. Cost: free.
8. Permanent Exhibits: displays of hospital and pharmacy equipment, items belonging to the staff and patients, historic photos, and documents. There is a display on the impact of the 1906 earthquake on the site.
9. Special Exhibits: none.
10. Historical era that is featured the best: 1888-2009.
11. Targeted age groups: all ages.
12. Special activities for children: none.
13. Guided tours: available from docents during open hours.
14. Hands-on activities: none.
15. The best-kept secrets at the museum: the human skullcap in the men's bathroom!
16. Hidden treasures at the museum: the hospital director's desk, the bell, "muscle stimulator", and many other interesting items.
17. What is unique about the museum that can't be found anywhere else: where else can you find a museum about a mental hospital?
18. The most important things about local, state, or American history that can be learned at the museum: the site has had many different names and roles over the years from Insane Asylum to Agnews State Hospital and later Agnews Developmental Center. The hospital was a self-sufficient community with its own farms, police, and fire departments. More people were killed on this site than any other in the 1906 earthquake because so many of its brick buildings were destroyed.
19. Annual events held at the site or elsewhere in the community: none.
20. Research facilities or archives at the site: none.
21. Type of gift shop and what is for sale: a DVD about the history of Agnews is for sale.

1. **Agricultural History Project Center and Museum- Watsonville**

2. Location: 2601 East Lake Avenue, Watsonville, California, CA. 95076.
3. Website: http://www.aghistoryproject.org/
4. Phone number: (831) 724-5898.
5. E-mail: postmaster@aghistoryproject.org
6. Hours of operation: Thursday – Sunday: Noon - 4 p.m.
7. Cost: free.

8. Permanent Exhibits: The Codiga Center & Museum: AHP's two story California style barn is home to exhibits, research center, archives, and the "Country Corner" gift shop. Exhibits include "When Apples Were King," the story of the once flourishing apple industry; "Pick Now, Eat Later," food preservation methods for our bountiful production; and "Legacy of the Vaqueros," cattle from the Mission days to current times. There are also extensive fruit jar, milk bottle, dairy artifact, and hand tools displays. The Porter Implement Shed has a collection of restored horse drawn equipment including plows, binders, reapers and planters. The Snyder Building includes a restoration shop and storage for restored equipment. An Illinois Central Caboose was donated to AHP to represent the importance of train transportation in moving agricultural products to market.

9. Special Exhibits: rotating exhibits in the Codiga Center.

10. Historical era that is featured the best: 1800s-present.

11. Targeted age groups: all ages.

12. Special activities for children: the entire place is very kid-friendly. You can play a game to identify apples, milk a mechanical cow, run a freezer conveyor belt, and do many other engaging activities.

13. Guided tours: available upon request.

14. Hands-on activities: there are many interactive displays, both indoors and outdoors. This is one of the best I have seen in this category.

15. The best-kept secrets at the museum: milk bottle collection, canning displays, vintage cowboy equipment, and more!

16. Hidden treasures at the museum: this place is amazing. It has hundreds of farm tools, vehicles, and equipment in every model imaginable, all restored to their original condition.

17. What is unique about the museum that can't be found anywhere else: this is one of the best agricultural museums in the area. It is very comprehensive, modern, and lovingly maintained. The sheer scale of the place dwarfs most other agricultural museums in comparison.

18. The most important things about local, state, or American history that can be learned at the museum: one of the best places around to appreciate just how important agriculture has been to the region.

19. Annual events held at the site or elsewhere in the community: Second Saturday on the Farm, Santa Cruz County Fair, and many other events (see website for details).

20. Research facilities or archives at the site: the upstairs Santa Cruz County Room archive houses a non-circulating collection of agricultural related books, photos, and an extensive collection of USDA and UC Extension Service pamphlets. Research is available by appointment only.

21. Type of gift shop and what is for sale: a charming collection of farm-related items and toys.

1. **Ainsley House-Campbell**
2. Location: 300 Grant Street, Campbell, CA. 95008.
3. Website: http://campbellmuseums.org/ainsley-house
4. Phone number: (408) 866-2758.

5. E-mail: kerryp@cityofcampbell.com

6. Hours of operation: Thursday - Sunday   12:00 p.m. to 4:00 p.m.   (last tour leaves at 3:30p.m.).

7. Cost: $6.00 adults, $4.00 seniors, $2.50 youth (7-17),   under 7 years free.

8. Permanent Exhibits: The historic Ainsley House is an example of the English Tudor Revival style popular in the South San Francisco Bay Area during the 1920s. The home was built in 1925 as the third home for Campbell canning pioneer John Colpitts Ainsley and his wife Alcinda.

9. Special Exhibits: the carriage house, now the Morgan Gallery, offers free exhibits and videos detailing the history of Campbell.

10. Historical era that is featured the best: early 1900s.

11. Targeted age groups: all ages.

12. Special activities for children: school tours.

13. Guided tours: all entrances include guided tours. Group tours are available by arrangement.

14. Hands-on activities: none.

15. The best-kept secrets at the museum: the architecture of the house is quite original and attractive. It incorporates Tudor and Arts and Crafts design elements.

16. Hidden treasures at the museum: The 15 rooms are furnished with much of the original furniture from the era when the house was one of the grand homes in the Santa Clara Valley.

17. What is unique about the museum that can't be found anywhere else: The house was moved from another location about a mile away.

18. The most important things about local, state, or American history that can be learned at the museum: Ainsley was a very important leader in the fruit packing industry.

19. Annual events held at the site or elsewhere in the community: The Spirit of Campbell Photography Exhibit, Holiday Fair; the house is a frequent wedding venue (see website for details).

20. Research facilities or archives at the site: none.

21. Type of gift shop and what is for sale: local history, craft and gift items are for sale.

1. **Alameda Museum**

2. Location: 2324 Alameda Avenue, Alameda, CA. 94501.

3. Website: http://www.alamedamuseum.org/

4. Phone number: (510) 521-1233.

5. E-mail: damsel_d@pacbell.net

6. Hours of operation: Wednesday-Sunday: 1:30-4 p.m.

7. Cost: free

8. Permanent Exhibits: Ohlone Indian artifacts, ships, navigation, a barbershop, kitchen, toys, dolls, and a complete lady's bedroom featuring dolls, sewing, and clothing. Local businesses and schools are also featured.

9. Special Exhibits: an art gallery with periodic shows, with many items also for sale.

10. Historical era that is featured the best: 1800-1900s.

11. Targeted age groups: all ages.

12. Special activities for children: none

13. Guided tours: available upon request.

14. Hands-on activities: none.

15. The best-kept secrets at the museum: one of the largest collections of Ohlone artifacts in the Bay Area.

16. Hidden treasures at the museum: a Phyllis Diller display.

17. What is unique about the museum that can't be found anywhere else: a display about Neptune Beach, the "Coney Island of the West", a large amusement park that used to exist in the area.

18. The most important things about local, state, or American history that can be learned at the museum: Alameda's unique role in the development of the Bay Area.

19. Annual events held at the site or elsewhere in the community: Legacy Home Tour and the Lecture Series.

20. Research facilities or archives at the site: none, but the website has links to County Historical Society and City library resources.

21. Type of gift shop and what is for sale: the gift shop is the major operating funds raiser for the museum and features an eclectic mix of merchandise, furniture, dishes, bric-a-brac, linens, jewelry, and memorabilia. This large gift shop is more like an antique store/thrift shop. Lots of historical books are for sale.

22. Additional information: The museum also operates the Meyers House, erected in 1897, an example of Colonial Revival architecture. It is open for tours on the 2nd & 4th Sat. of each month from1 p.m. – 4 p.m.; admission: $5.

1. Alcatraz Island

2. Location: the only way to get to Alcatraz is by a ferry operated by Alcatraz Cruises, LLC. They are located on The Embarcadero near the intersection of Bay Street - just a bit southeast of Fisherman's Wharf.

3. Website: http://www.nps.gov/alca/index.htm and http://www.alcatrazcruises.com/

4. Phone number: (415) 561-4900.

5. E-mail: use the contact form on the NPS website.

6. Hours of operation: 8:45-9:30 (summer); 8:45-4:30 (winter).

7. Cost: Ferry prices are $30 and up depending upon the time of day and the age of the passenger. See http://www.alcatrazcruises.com/ for details.

8. Permanent Exhibits: the federal penitentiary and other historic buildings.

9. Special Exhibits: rotating art exhibits.

10. Historical era that is featured the best: 1850s to the present.

11. Targeted age groups: all ages.

12. Special activities for children: materials are available for educators.

13. Guided tours: Ranger-led talks and self-guided tours are available. Admission includes an audio tour of the cellblock narrated by former inmates and guards.

14. Hands-on activities: on some tours, the rangers will lock you in a cellblock for a few moments to get the feel of what is was like to be a prisoner there.

15. The best-kept secrets at the museum: the period of Indian occupation from November 1969-June 1971. Only a few traces remain from this protest period. Also,

the historic gardens have been restored and nesting sea birds are protected on a portion of the island.

16. Hidden treasures at the museum: the site of the most famous escape attempt in 1962 by the Anglin brothers has been preserved.

17. What is unique about the museum that can't be found anywhere else: it is the most isolated prison on the West Coast. Many famous inmates stayed there, such as Al Capone and the Birdman of Alcatraz.

18. The most important things about local, state, or American history that can be learned at the museum: the history of Alcatraz is surprising to those that only know the Hollywood version. It has been a Civil War fortress, an infamous federal prison, a bird sanctuary, the first lighthouse on the West Coast, and the birthplace of the American Indian Red Power movement.

19. Annual events held at the site or elsewhere in the community: see the NPS website for details.

20. Research facilities or archives at the site: none.

21. Type of gift shop and what is for sale: a bookstore with souvenirs, books, films, and many other items is located on the island.

22. Additional information: The weather can be unpredictable, so dress in layers. The ferry company has a monopoly on travel to the island, so the prices are pretty steep. This is one of the most popular tourist attractions in the Bay Area, so tickets often sell out weeks in advance. Try to go on a weekday or plan accordingly. There is no other way off of the island besides the ferry, so don't miss the last one!

1. **The Alvarado Adobe, The Blume House, and The Bunk House- San Pablo**

2. Location: 5 Church Lane, San Pablo, CA. 94806.

3. Website: http://www.ci.san-pablo.ca.us/index.aspx?NID=966

4. Phone number: (510) 215-3092.

5. E-mail: none.

6. Hours of operation: both museums are open the 2nd and 4th Sundays of each month from 12 – 4p.m.

7. Cost: free.

8. Permanent Exhibits: the Alvarado Adobe is the former home of Juan Alvarado, the governor of Mexican Alta California. The Blume House and "Bunk House" adjacent to it are just a short walk from the Alvarado Adobe. Built in 1905, the Blume House is a great example of agricultural era living in the Bay Area.

9. Special Exhibits: none.

10. Historical era that is featured the best: 1800s-1900s.

11. Targeted age groups: all ages.

12. Special activities for children: school tours. Traveling historical trunk.

13. Guided tours: docent-led tours during visiting hours.

14. Hands-on activities: Kids can dress up in some of the articles of clothing at the Blume House. Some of the replica Ohlone Indian items at the Alvarado Adobe can be used by visitors.

15. The best-kept secrets at the museum: many of the items in the houses actually belonged to the respective families.

16. Hidden treasures at the museum: Ohlone Indian artifacts, bricks from the original adobe, an antique piano, and period furniture.

17. What is unique about the museum that can't be found anywhere else: the original building was torn down in the 1970s. The current adobe building was rebuilt nearby.

18. The most important things about local, state, or American history that can be learned at the museum: the buildings represent two distinct periods in California history. The adobe is from the Mexican period and is a good representation of the home of an important governor. The Blume House is from the early 20th Century, when Germans and other Europeans migrated to the Bay Area because of its rich farmland.

19. Annual events held at the site or elsewhere in the community: none.

20. Research facilities or archives at the site: the San Pablo Historical Society has some records available upon request at the Blume House.

21. Type of gift shop and what is for sale: there are books and gift items reflective of each time period at both houses.

1. **Alviso Adobe- Pleasanton**

2. Location: Old Foothill Road and Foothill Road, on the west side of Highway 680, Pleasanton, CA. 94588.

3. Website: http://www.cityofpleasantonca.gov/services/recreation/alviso-adobe.html

4. Phone number: (925) 931-3483.

5. E-mail: enicholas@cityofpleasantonca.gov

6. Hours of operation: Wednesday through Sunday from 10:00 a.m. to 4:00 p.m.

7. Cost: free.

8. Permanent Exhibits: the Alviso Adobe, the first adobe building in the Amador Valley, is the physical and interpretive centerpiece of the park. A re-creation of the historic Meadowlark Dairy milking barn and bunkhouse contain many interesting displays about how the use of the land has changed over time.

9. Special Exhibits: tour temporary displays are rotated annually in the Milk Barn.

10. Historical era that is featured the best: 1800s-1900s.

11. Targeted age groups: all ages.

12. Special activities for children: the entire site is very child-friendly. There is a classroom in the dairy barn that has many interesting activities for children, such as identifying artifacts, identifying wildlife and milking a mechanical cow. There are many replicas of animals, Native American artifacts, and dairy items that can be handled.

13. Guided tours: self-guided tours; school tours are available with reservations.

14. Hands-on activities: adobe brick making, rope making, acorn crushing, cattle roping, ice cream making, native plant use, and many other state-of-the-art interactive displays and activities are available at the site during field trips and special events.

15. The best-kept secrets at the museum: it has one of the best collections of Ohlone Indian replica artifacts in the Bay Area.

16. Hidden treasures at the museum: many interesting dairy items; a bedrock mortar used by the Indians that is in its original location along the creek.

17. What is unique about the museum that can't be found anywhere else: It is one of the best local museums around in terms of being kid-friendly.

18. The most important things about local, state, or American history that can be learned at the museum: a comprehensive overview of local history from the Native American through the Spanish, Mexican, and American periods.

19. Annual events held at the site or elsewhere in the community: contact the city of Pleasanton for details.

20. Research facilities or archives at the site: the park shares research information as requested and conducts ongoing collections and archeological field research in conjunction with local universities.

21. Type of gift shop: none.

1. **Angel Island State Park**

2. Location: near Tiburon, California.

3. Website: http://www.parks.ca.gov/?page_id=468

4. Phone number: (415) 435-5390.

5. E-mail: daryl.woodward@parks.ca.gov

6. Hours of operation: 8 a.m. to sunset. Immigration Station Museum hours: open 7 days a week from 11:00 a.m. to 3:00 p.m.

7. Cost: Entry to the park is free, but there are fees at the Immigration Station Museum: Adults (18 & over) $5.00 Youth (6-17 Years) $3.00 Children (5 & under) free.

8. Permanent Exhibits: Angel Island is truly a walk through time! Beginning with the earliest inhabitants, the Coast Miwok, Angel Island was a seasonal hunting and gathering location for the local native tribes. Later, it was a safe refuge and supply stop for Spanish explorers like Juan Manuel de Ayala, one of the first to map the San Francisco Bay. From 1910 to 1940, the U.S. Immigration Station processed hundreds of thousands of immigrants, the majority from China. During World War II, Japanese and German POWs were detained at the station before being sent to facilities farther inland. The island has also been a cattle ranch. The island has over 100 years of military history beginning with the Civil War at Camp Reynolds. With the outbreaks of WWI and WWII, thousands of troops, both embarking for and returning from conflicts around the world, were processed through Angel Island. In the '50s and '60s, the island saw its last military service as a home to a Nike missile base.

9. Special Exhibits: there are both permanent and special exhibits in the park's visitor's center at Ayala Cove.

10. Historical era that is featured the best: 1800s-1900s.

11. Targeted age groups: all ages.

12. Special activities for children: camping, school tours, ranger talks, and other events.

13. Guided tours: park staff and volunteers provide interpretive programs and conduct tours for schools, clubs and other groups. For tour schedules and reservations, call (415) 435-5537 or email: tours.angelisland@parks.ca.gov.

14. Hands-on activities: currently none, but plans are underway at the museum.

15. The best-kept secrets at the museum: the barracks, chapel, and guardhouse museums are only open at select times when a ranger leads a guided tour of them (see website for details)

16. Hidden treasures at the museum: Civil War artifacts and buildings are found on the island. The park rangers even fire off a cannon from time to time!

17. What is unique about the museum that can't be found anywhere else: The island has unique flora and fauna. It also has spectacular views of the San Francisco Bay and its famous landmarks.

18. The most important things about local, state, or American history that can be learned at the museum: a comprehensive history of the island can be seen, from the time of Native American settlements up to the Cold War. The many uses of the island as a quarantine area, immigration processing center, and various military facilities throughout time can be viewed. The island has played a role in every major U.S. conflict since the Civil War. The most impressive facility on the island is the Immigration Station. Thousands of immigrants from Asia and other parts of the world were detained here for long periods while awaiting permission to settle in the United States. The poems that they inscribed on the walls, expressing their loneliness and despair while going through extensive interrogation and medical exams, are heart-breaking.

19. Annual events held at the site or elsewhere in the community: seasonal in nature (see website for details).

20. Research facilities or archives at the site: none.

21. Type of gift shop and what is for sale: there are park souvenirs at the Angel Island Store and a few books related to the immigrants at the Immigration Station Museum.

22. Additional information: In order to get to the island, it is necessary to take a ferry from Tiburon, San Francisco, or Alameda. See the website for links to the ferry companies. Scheduling your stay must be coordinated very carefully with ferry arrival and departure times because they only travel to and from the island a few times a day. Once on the island, transportation must be made by shuttle, tram, bicycles, Segways, or on foot. No cars are allowed on the island. Rental facilities are available for transportation on the island. Food and restroom facilities are limited.

1. **Antioch Historical Museum**
2. Location: 1500 W. Fourth Street, Antioch, CA. 94509.
3. Website: http://www.art4antioch.org/ahs.asp
4. Phone number: (925) 325 9897.
5. E-mail: antiochhistoricalsociety@comcast.net
6. Hours of operation: Wednesdays & Saturdays, 1-4 p.m. (or by appointment).
7. Cost: free.
8. Permanent Exhibits: sports legends, bridal room, children and toys, military, local businesses, the bay and bridges, nature and wildlife, movies and theaters, lady's bedroom, cameras, saloon, businesses, industry, government offices, Miwok Indian artifacts, parlor and music, historic mural, and more.
9. Special Exhibits: The Cook House and rotating exhibits.

10. Historical era that is featured the best: 1800-1900s.
11. Targeted age groups: all ages
12. Special activities for children: none.
13. Guided tours: available upon request.
14. Hands-on activities: none.
15. The best-kept secrets at the museum: a vintage movie theater and a giant wheel from a Gold Rush era steamboat.
16. Hidden treasures at the museum: a Civil War drum and many other interesting items.
17. What is unique about the museum that can't be found anywhere else: it has an emphasis on the Bay and Delta region. There are many interesting artifacts that are well displayed.
18. The most important things about local, state, or American history that can be learned at the museum: how the region was settled and its important role as a crossroads for the state.
19. Annual events held at the site or elsewhere in the community: a fashion show, car show, concerts, art exhibits, etc. (see website for details).
20. Research facilities or archives at the site: there is a fairly large archive in the basement. Contact the museum for information regarding use of the facility.
21. Type of gift shop and what is for sale: antique and replica gift items reflective of the turn of the century.
22. Additional information: It is a very well organized and well-labeled collection. There are several rooms and each room has a theme.

1. **Aptos History Museum**
2. Location: 7605-B Old Dominion Ct. Aptos, CA. 95003.
3. Website: http://www.aptoshistory.org/
4. Phone number: (831) 688-9514.

5. E-mail: aptoshistory@yahoo.com
6. Hours of operation: Monday – Friday: 9:00 a.m. - 4:00 p.m.
7. Cost: free.
8. Permanent Exhibits: Ohlone Indians, Spanish and Mexican ranches, pioneer families, Spreckels the "Sugar King", the coming of the railroad, Asian immigration, the lumber industry, apples, flight pioneer John Montgomery, resort building in the 20's and 30's, Blue Angels founder Butch Voris, the founding of Cabrillo College, the Loma Prieta Earthquake, and more.
9. Special Exhibits: rotating exhibits.
10. Historical era that is featured the best: 1800s-1900s.
11. Targeted age groups: all ages.
12. Special activities for children: 3rd grade tours and school visits.
13. Guided tours: available with reservations.
14. Hands-on activities: none.
15. The best-kept secrets at the museum: it has quite a large Ohlone exhibit for such a small museum.
16. Hidden treasures at the museum: the logging and Spreckels exhibits are the best.

17. What is unique about the museum that can't be found anywhere else: It is just minutes from the beach and the redwoods.

18. The most important things about local, state, or American history that can be learned at the museum: this small town has been an Indian village, Mexican rancho, a millionaire's thoroughbred ranch, and then an American resort town. It has also had many different industries.

19. Annual events held at the site or elsewhere in the community: Dining for History presentations; "A Night to Rally" professional tennis and auction fundraiser; historic home tours, beach tours; etc. (see website for details).

20. Research facilities or archives at the site: by reservation only.

21. Type of gift shop and what is for sale: books and note cards.

1. **Ardenwood Historic Farm- Fremont**

2. Location: 34600 Ardenwood Blvd. Fremont, CA. 94555.

3. Website: http://www.ebparks.org/parks/ardenwood

4. Phone number: (510) 544-2797.

5. E-mail: awvisit@ebparks.org

6. Hours of operation: 10 a.m. to 4 p.m. Tuesdays through Sundays, year round, including Labor Day and Memorial Day; closed Thanksgiving and Christmas Day. The Patterson House, the train and blacksmith shop are closed from mid-November to April.

7. Cost: Summer entry fees: Tues., Wed., & Sat.--$3/adults (18+ years), $3/seniors (62+ years), $2/children (4-17 years), under 4 years - free.
Thurs., Fri. and Sun.--$6/adults (18+ years), $5/seniors (62+ year), $4/children (4-17 years), under 4 years - free.
Winter entry fees: Tuesday-Sunday--$3 adults, $2 children (4-17 years), under 4 years - free.

8. Permanent Exhibits: the farm still grows the same kind of produce that was grown in the region over the last 100 years, utilizing agricultural practices from the 1870s to the present, demonstrating the transition from horse-powered to horsepower farming. The interpretive staff and volunteers, attired in Victorian clothing, guide guests through the Victorian house, demonstrate farm chores, and explain what life was like in the early 1900s. Other exhibits include The Victorian Gardens and Patterson House Museum, an animal farm, a blacksmith shop, and equipment sheds.

9. Special Exhibits: none.

10. Historical era that is featured the best: 1850s-1900.

11. Targeted age groups: all ages.

12. Special activities for children: there is a horse drawn train and an animal farm. Through Ardenwood's educational programs, visitors can see and participate in many activities common to a turn-of-last-century farm. Weekdays, naturalists provide programs for school classes and other groups by reservation. Lots of great teacher materials are available on the website and on location.

13. Guided tours: available upon request.

14. Hands-on activities: weekend programs include the planting, tending and harvesting of Ardenwood's organic crops, farm chore demonstrations, and hands-on experiences for the whole family.

15. The best-kept secrets at the museum: the historic interpreters are among the best in the Bay Area.

16. Hidden treasures at the museum: the Patterson House has many interesting furnishings from the time period.

17. What is unique about the museum that can't be found anywhere else: this is probably the best site in the Bay Area to experience farm life in the past. It is a great place to take kids.

18. The most important things about local, state, or American history that can be learned at the museum: agriculture's contribution to the Bay Area's history.

19. Annual events held at the site or elsewhere in the community: see website for details.

20. Research facilities or archives at the site: none.

21. Type of gift shop and what is for sale: farm produce and prepared food are available.

1. **Asian Art Museum- San Francisco**

2. Location: 200 Larkin Street, San Francisco, CA. 94102.

3. Website: http://www.asianart.org/

4. Phone number: (415) 581-3500.

5. E-mail: use the online contact form.

6. Hours of operation: Tuesday-Sunday 10 a.m.-5 p.m. Thursday: 10 a.m-9 p.m.

7. Cost: Adults $12, seniors, university students, and youths (13–17) $8, children 12 & under are free.

8. Permanent Exhibits: spanning cultures from Turkey to India and China to the Philippines through 6,000 years, the collection provides a panorama of Asian art and culture. Included are over 18,000 objects ranging from tiny jades to monumental sculptures. Superb paintings, porcelains, arms and armor, furniture, textiles, and bronzes are featured.

9. Special Exhibits: rotating special exhibits, such as the terracotta warriors from the China.

10. Historical era that is featured the best: all eras.

11. Targeted age groups: all ages.

12. Special activities for children: school visits and lesson plans for teachers.

13. Guided tours: docent-led tours are available with reservations.

14. Hands-on activities: Some exhibits have interactive displays. Some have activities for use with QR readers on cell phones and tablets. Restoration artists also give workshops demonstrating their work.

15. The best-kept secrets at the museum: The museum draws top-notch traveling exhibits. They are some of the best in California.

16.Hidden treasures at the museum: countless priceless treasures are held at the museum. Many are from areas of the world that usually do not get much attention in other museums.

13

17.What is unique about the museum that can't be found anywhere else: the museum has one of the largest comprehensive collections of Asian art in the world.

18.The most important things about local, state, or American history that can be learned at the museum: the museum emphasizes that Asia includes all of Asia and not just East Asia as in some other museums. A special display explores the topic of what Asia is. Western, Central, and Southern Asia are also well represented. Asian art has had a big influence on America.

19.Annual events held at the site or elsewhere in the community: there are many public events throughout the year, such as storytelling, lectures, performances, films, workshops, etc. (see website for details).

20. Research facilities or archives at the site: none.

21. Type of gift shop and what is for sale: the museum has a first class gift shop containing a wide range of artwork, books, and souvenirs.

1. **Badè Museum of Biblical Archaeology- Berkeley**

2. Location: 1798 Scenic Avenue, Berkeley, CA. 94709.

3. Website: http://www.psr.edu/bade/

4. Phone number: (510) 849-8200.

5. E-mail: bade@psr.edu

6. Hours of operation: Tues, Thurs, Fri: 10:00a.m.-3:00p.m.

7. Cost: free.

8. Permanent Exhibits: artifacts from the excavations of William F. Bade of Tell en-Nasbeh, located northwest of Jerusalem (1926, 1927, 1929, 1932, and 1935). These include pottery, jewelry, coins, lamps, weapons, and burial items.

9. Special Exhibits: The Doug Adams Gallery has rotating exhibits of modern art.

10. Historical era that is featured the best: Ancient Israel from the Bronze Age to the Iron Age.

11. Targeted age groups: primarily adults, but some tours can be tailored for children.

12. Special activities for children: none.

13. Guided tours: by special arrangement only.

14. Hands-on activities: none

15. The best-kept secrets at the museum: a coin from Pontius Pilate's era.

16. Hidden treasures at the museum: small statues of Canaanite goddesses, sling stones, large collection of hand lamps.

17. What is unique about the museum that can't be found anywhere else: it is rare to find this kind of collection outside of Israel.

18. The most important things about local, state, or American history that can be learned at the museum: UC Berkeley's role in the study of ancient archeology.

19. Annual events held at the site or elsewhere in the community: the Annual Fall Lecture featuring a scholar of the archaeology or religion of the ancient world.

20. Research facilities or archives at the site: the collection is open to archeology and religious studies researchers.

21. Type of gift shop: none.

22. Additional information: some of the artifacts can be included in traveling exhibits for educational institutions.

1. **Bale Grist Mill**
2. Location: three miles north of St. Helena (3369 N St.) on Highway 29.
3. Website: http://www.parks.ca.gov/?page_id=482
4. Phone number: (707) 942-4575.
5. E-mail: info@parks.ca.gov and http://napavalleystateparks.org
6. Hours of operation: Saturday and Sunday: 10a.m.-5p.m.
7. Cost: Adults $5.00. Children 6 to 17: $2.00. Children under 6 are free.
8. Permanent Exhibits: the park is the site of a water-powered gristmill that was built in 1846. It was once the center of social activity as Napa Valley settlers gathered to have their corn and wheat ground into meal or flour. The owner of the mill was Dr. Edward Turner Bale. He received the property in a land grant from the Mexican government and lived near the site until his death in 1849. The mill remained in use until the early 1900s. The mill and its 36-foot water wheel are protected as a state historic landmark and have been partially restored. A trail connects the historic park to Bothe-Napa Valley State Park. Additionally, the park includes the site of the first church in the Napa Valley, as well as the Pioneer Cemetery.
9. Special Exhibits: none.
10. Historical era that is featured the best: 1846-1900.
11. Targeted age groups: all ages.
12. Special activities for children: school tours are available by reservations (Tuesdays only); nature camps.
13. Guided tours: milling demonstrations and historic tours are offered on weekends.
14. Hands-on activities: none.
15. The best-kept secrets at the museum: delicious, fresh baked bread made from grain milled at the site is available on occasion.
16. Hidden treasures at the museum: When the water wheel is in operation, it is an impressive sight.
17. What is unique about the museum that can't be found anywhere else: it is one of the few working gristmills left in the state.
18. The most important things about local, state, or American history that can be learned at the museum: the importance of milling to local communities is demonstrated.
19. Annual events held at the site or elsewhere in the community: concerts; running events; Earth Day, nature camps; Harvest Dinner; Old Mill Days; Bothe-Napa Sawyers and Antique Machinery Get-Together; Pioneer Christmas. See http://napavalleystateparks.org/our-special-events/ for details.
20. Research facilities or archives at the site: none.
21. Type of gift shop and what is for sale: delicious homemade bread and locally ground flour is available for sale, along with other gift items.

1. **Bancroft Library-Berkeley**
2. Location: The Bancroft Library, University of California, Berkeley, CA. 94720-6000.
3. Website: http://bancroft.berkeley.edu/

4. Phone number: (510) 642-3781.

5. E-mail: bancroft@library.berkeley.edu

6. Hours of operation: M-F: 10-5.

7. Cost: free.

8. Permanent Exhibits: none

9. Special Exhibits: a few historical documents are on display on a rotating basis.

10. Historical era that is featured the best: 1700s to present.

11. Targeted age groups: adults.

12. Special activities for children: none.

13. Guided tours: not available.

14. Hands-on activities: none.

15. The best-kept secrets at the museum: many original historical documents that cannot be found anywhere else.

16. Hidden treasures at the museum: extensive online resources.

17. What is unique about the museum that can't be found anywhere else: thousands of important and priceless historical documents, books, and photographs.

18. The most important things about local, state, or American history that can be learned at the museum: this is one of the premier sites for research in California history.

19. Annual events held at the site or elsewhere in the community: book talks, guest speakers, and special exhibits (see website for details).

20. Research facilities or archives at the site: this is the primary function of this facility. There are many rare books, documents, and photographs available.

21. Type of gift shop: none.

1. **Bear Valley Visitor's Center-Olema**

2. Location: 1 Bear Valley Rd, Point Reyes Station, CA. 94956.

3. Website: http://www.nps.gov/pore/planyourvisit/visitorcenters.htm

4. Phone number: (415) 464-5100.

5. E-mail: use the online contact form.

6. Hours of operation: Summer hours: weekdays from 10 am to 5 pm; weekends and holidays: from 9 am to 5 pm. Fall-winter-spring seasons: weekdays from 10 am to 4:30 pm.; weekends and holidays from 9 am to 4:30 pm. Hours are subject to change, so call ahead or check the website.

7. Cost: free.

8. Permanent Exhibits: Visitor's Center, Kule Loklo Miwok Indian Village, Morgan Horse Corral, Earthquake Trail.

9. Special Exhibits: films and special displays are at the Visitor's Center in the auditorium.

10. Historical era that is featured the best: prehistory-present.

11. Targeted age groups: all ages.

12. Special activities for children: there are many. See the calendar on the website for details.

13. Guided tours: the visitor's center is self-guided. Rangers and docents are available on site for information about the trails, beaches, and other facilities of the park. Field trips may be scheduled with reservations.

14. Hands-on activities: some of the displays at the visitor's center are interactive.

15. The best-kept secrets at the museum: The Earthquake Trail is not to be missed. One section of a ranch fence along the trail shifted twenty feet apart from the original line of the fence!

16. Hidden treasures at the museum: the Kule Loklo Miwok Indian Village has replica homes, mortars and a native plant garden. It is often the location of cultural events.

17. What is unique about the museum that can't be found anywhere else: there are so many different historical sites in one location. The historic horse ranch, the Indian village, and visible damage from the 1906 earthquake are all within walking distance of the visitor's center.

18. The most important things about local, state, or American history that can be learned at the museum: this is the heart of the park. The many uses of the land over time are explained at the visitor's center.

19. Annual events held at the site or elsewhere in the community: There are many. See the calendar on the website for details.

20. Research facilities or archives at the site: none.

21. Type of gift shop and what is for sale: many fine gifts related to the natural beauty and history of the park and region such as films, posters, books and more.

22. Additional information: At nearby Drakes Beach, the Kenneth C. Patrick Visitor Center contains exhibits that focus on Francis Drake's explorations, marine fossils, and marine environments. A minke whale skeleton is suspended from the ceiling. The bookstore has nature books, cards, and posters for sale. Allow 20–30 minutes to view the exhibits. The visitor's center is currently only open in the summer time and weekends.

1. **Belvedere-Tiburon Landmarks Society**

2. Location: Railroad and Ferry Museum -1920 Paradise Drive, Tiburon, CA. 94920; Old St. Hilary's Church - 201 Esperanza Street, Tiburon, CA 94920; The China Cabin -52 Beach Road, Belvedere, CA, 94920.

3. Website: http://www.landmarks-society.org/

4. Phone number: (415) 435-1853.

5. E-mail: use the contact form on the website.

6. Hours of operation: April thru October: 1p.m. – 4pm.
Railroad & Ferry Depot Museum - Wednesday thru Sunday; Old St. Hilary- Sundays only; China Cabin - Saturday & Sunday.

7. Cost: free.

8. Permanent Exhibits: The Railroad and Ferry Museum includes the stationmaster's house upstairs, with a living room, child's bedroom, kitchen, and dining room. The downstairs is an area dedicated to the railroads and ferries of the Tiburon area. The Old St. Hilary's Church is a Carpenter Gothic style building from the 1880's set on a scenic hilltop amidst wildflowers. The China Cabin is an elegant dining hall made from a saloon, which was removed from the PS China steamship that was built in 1866.

9. Special Exhibits: none.

10. Historical era that is featured the best: 1800s-1900s.

11. Targeted age groups: all ages

12. Special activities for children: school tours.

13. Guided tours: available upon request.

14. Hands-on activities: video tours of Northwestern Pacific Railroad and the Stationmaster's Home.

15. The best-kept secrets at the museum: a large, detailed model of the ferry and rail depot; a 1931 Philco radio that is totally original and in working condition.

16. Hidden treasures at the museum: interesting rail and ferry items, maps, and other items of historical interest.

17. What is unique about the museum that can't be found anywhere else: it is the only remaining combination rail and ferry depot in the West.

18. The most important things about local, state, or American history that can be learned at the museum: Tiburon's role as an important transit area for the Bay Area is well explained.

19. Annual events held at the site or elsewhere in the community: concerts; golf tournament; Mad-hatter party; Holiday Art & Craft Sale; and Walk Your History (see website for details).

20. Research facilities or archives at the site: the Landmarks History Collections are located at 1550 Tiburon Blvd. in the Boardwalk Shopping Center. It contains records, artifacts, fine art, photographs, and ephemera, which chronicle the history of the Marin County area.

21. Type of gift shop and what is for sale: local history books, artwork, and note cards.

1. **Benicia Capitol State Historic Park**

2. Location: 115 West G Street Benicia, CA. 94510

3. Website: http://www.parks.ca.gov/?page_id=475

4. Phone number: (707) 745-3385.

5. E-mail: info@parks.ca.gov

6. Hours of operation: Thursday: Noon - 4p.m., Friday, Saturday & Sunday: 10 a.m. – 5 p.m.

7. Cost: Adults: $3. Children: $2. Free to all military personnel with I.D.

8. Permanent Exhibits: Benicia Capitol State Historic Park is the site of California's third seat of government (1853-54). It is the only pre-Sacramento capitol that survives. The original building has been restored with reconstructed period furnishings and exhibits. The interior includes a board-for-board reconstruction of the building's original floor with ponderosa pine. The desks, three of which are originals from the Benicia period or earlier, are furnished with a candlestick, a 19th century newspaper, a quill pen, and a top hat.

9. Special Exhibits: rotating exhibits related to California history.

10. Historical era that is featured the best: 1853-54.

11. Targeted age groups: all ages.

12. Special activities for children: school tours are available.

13. Guided tours: docent on duty for tours. Group tours are available with reservations.

14. Hands-on activities: none.

15. The best-kept secrets at the museum: the original furnishings are quite nice.
16. Hidden treasures at the museum: There are many interesting displays about statehood, the Gold Rush and other topics.
17. What is unique about the museum that can't be found anywhere else: none of the other early state capitols have survived. It is so well furnished that it looks like the legislature just stepped out for lunch a few minutes ago.
18. The most important things about local, state, or American history that can be learned at the museum: It explains why the state capitol moved so many times in the early years of the state. It also demonstrates how the struggle over whether California would be admitted to the Union as a free or slave state affected the adoption of the state's constitution.
19. Annual events held at the site or elsewhere in the community: none.
20. Research facilities or archives at the site: On the website, there is an extensive online archives collection and an historic map of Benicia.
21. Type of gift shop: none.
22. While you are there, visit the historic Fischer-Hanlon house next door. Tours are available monthly on the first Sunday and the third Saturday and Sunday. Tour times are 1 p.m., 2 p.m., and 3 p.m. Tours are led by docents dressed in period attire. Admission is $3 for adults and $2 for children ages 6-17.

1. **The Benicia Fire Museum**
2. Location: 900 East Second Street, Benicia, CA. 94510.
3. Website: http://www.beniciafiremuseum.org/
4. Phone number: (707) 745-1688.
5. E-mail: Benicia-firemuseum@pacbell.net
6. Hours of operation: the first three Sundays of the month, from 1p.m. to 4pm.
7. Cost: free.
8. Permanent Exhibits: antique firefighting equipment, uniforms, fire extinguishers, hoses, fire nets, fire engines, etc.
9. Special Exhibits: none.
10. Historical era that is featured the best: 1820s to the present.
11. Targeted age groups: all ages.
12. Special activities for children: school tours; dressing up like a fireman; fireman related toys and advertising.
13. Guided tours: Special tours are frequently conducted for groups, schools, and even individuals. Call the museum to make arrangements.
14. Hands-on activities: During school visits.
15. The best-kept secrets at the museum: See the wooden pipes that firemen would tap into and then plug. This is the origin of the term "fireplug" for a hydrant.
16. Hidden treasures at the museum: a fine collection of antique firebombs, which were used before fire extinguishers were invented.
17. What is unique about the museum that can't be found anywhere else: the Phoenix Engine was originally owned by the Pacific Steam Mail Co. It is believed to be the first fire engine to arrive in California, built by Roger & Son in the 1820s.
18. The most important things about local, state, or American history that can be learned at the museum: It provides a glimpse into how firefighting techniques have

changed over time. The Benicia Volunteer Firemen Incorporated was founded in 1847 and is the oldest continuous volunteer fire service in California. Benicia has faced the challenge of fires both on land and on the water.

19. Annual events held at the site or elsewhere in the community: the fire engines are sometimes featured in civic parades and other functions. Call for information.

20. Research facilities or archives at the site: none.

21. Type of gift shop and what is for sale: fire-related toys and gifts.

1. **The Benicia Historical Museum**

2. Location: 2060 Camel Road, Benicia, CA. 94510.

3. Website: http://beniciahistoricalmuseum.org/

4. Phone number: (707) 745-5435.

5. E-mail: info@beniciahistoricalmuseum.org

6. Hours of operation: Wednesdays through Sundays, 1:00 p.m. to 4:00 pm.

7. Cost: $5. Free on first Wednesday of the month.

8. Permanent Exhibits: California's Great Inland Port, industrial exhibit and military exhibit at the Powder Magazine.

9. Special Exhibits: 2-3 rotating exhibits per year.

10. Historical era that is featured the best: 1800s-1900s.

11. Targeted age groups: all ages

12. Special activities for children: school tours, traveling trunks, and many kid-friendly displays.

13. Guided tours: available with reservations.

14. Hands-on activities: daily chores of the 1800's, sailor's knot tying, playing Indian music, etc.

15. The best-kept secrets at the museum: there is a display on the many flags of California. You will be surprised how many nations have claimed it.

16. Hidden treasures at the museum: the famous camel collection, many interesting historical artifacts.

17. What is unique about the museum that can't be found anywhere else: the history of The Camel Corps.

18. The most important things about local, state, or American history that can be learned at the museum: Benicia was an important crossroads. Many important events took place in Benicia including its brief time as the state's capital. See how many historic firsts that took place in Benicia you can find while touring the museum. You will be astonished how many there were. Benicia had a role in many major events in California's history, including the Mexican War, the Gold Rush, The Civil War, The Pony Express and Transcontinental Railroad, right up until WWII.

19. Annual events held at the site or elsewhere in the community: concerts, Christmas tree sales, opening days for special exhibits.

20. Research facilities or archives at the site: contact the museum's curator for arrangements.

21. Type of gift shop and what is for sale: local history books and souvenirs.

1. **Berkeley Historical Society**

2. Location: 1931 Center Street, Berkeley, CA. 94704.

3. Website: http://www.berkeleyhistoricalsociety.org/

4. Phone number: (510) 848-0181.

5. E-mail: Use the online contact form.

6. Hours of operation: Thursdays, Fridays, and Saturdays from 1 to 4 p.m.

7. Cost: free.

8. Permanent Exhibits: none

9. Special Exhibits: rotating exhibits featuring local history.

10. Historical era that is featured the best: 1800s-present

11. Targeted age groups: all ages.

12. Special activities for children: none.

13. Guided tours: available during visiting hours; historic walking tours are held in the spring and fall seasons. Details are available on the website.

14. Hands-on activities: none.

15. The best-kept secrets at the museum: its publications and community events.

16. Hidden treasures at the museum: historical maps and photos.

17. What is unique about the museum that can't be found anywhere else: its emphasis on local history.

18. The most important things about local, state, or American history that can be learned at the museum: how Berkeley was founded and how its name was chosen; how the community has changed over the years; its historic role in education, the free speech movement, and the arts.

19. Annual events held at the site or elsewhere in the community: events vary each year. Consult the website for details.

20. Research facilities or archives at the site: a small library is available for research. The library has an extensive video library as well as many oral histories.

21. Type of gift shop and what is for sale: some local history books are for sale.

1. **Berryessa Adobe-Santa Clara**

2. Location: 373 Jefferson Street, Santa Clara, CA. 95054.

3. Website: http://santaclaraca.gov/index.aspx?page=2086

4. Phone number: (408) 615-2488.

5. E-mail: BerryessaAdobe@santaclaraca.gov

6. Hours of operation: Thursdays and Saturdays, 12 noon to 2 p.m., or by arrangement.

7. Cost: free.

8. Permanent Exhibits: displays on the history of the house and the families that lived there; information about the de Anza Expedition.

9. Special Exhibits: food that was made in the house; an historic garden.

10. Historical era that is featured the best: 1840's–present.

11. Targeted age groups: all ages.

12. Special activities for children: activity on foods that your family eats.

13. Guided tours: group tours may also be arranged.

14. Hands-on activities: none.

15. The best-kept secrets at the museum: a cut-away reveals the original adobe walls.

16. Hidden treasures at the museum: clothing and other items belonging to the Berryessa family.

17. What is unique about the museum that can't be found anywhere else: the Berryessa Adobe is one of the last adobes in the Santa Clara Valley and is an interpretive site on the Juan Bautista de Anza National Historic Trail.

18. The most important things about local, state, or American history that can be learned at the museum: In the 1840s, this simple adobe dwelling was constructed about a mile west of Mission Santa Clara. The house was lived in by generations of families who immigrated to Santa Clara to labor in the fields and factories, and to make new lives for themselves.

19. Annual events held at the site or elsewhere in the community: none.

20. Research facilities or archives at the site: none.

21. Type of gift shop and what is for sale: a book on Santa Clara history is for sale.

1. **Black Diamond Mines Regional Preserve-Antioch**

2. Location: 5175 Somersville Road, Antioch, CA. 94509.

3. Website: http://www.ebparks.org/parks/black_diamond

4. Phone number: (510) 544-2750.

5. E-mail: bdvisit@ebparks.org

6. Hours of operation: Sidney Flat Visitor Center: weekends 10:00 a.m. – 4:30 p.m. Open December – February; call ahead for hours at other times of year. Greathouse Visitor Center: weekends 10 a.m. - 4:30 p.m. from March - November.

7. Cost: $5 parking fee.

8. Permanent Exhibits: mining equipment, photographs, glass items made from sand from the mine, tombstones, school bell, and other artifacts from the mine towns.

9. Special Exhibits: the Hazel-Atlas mine is open for tours on weekends.

10. Historical era that is featured the best: late 1800s and early 1900s.

11. Targeted age groups: all ages.

12. Special activities for children: field trips by advance reservation.

13. Guided tours: the Hazel-Atlas mine is open for tours on weekends.

14. Hands-on activities: none.

15. The best-kept secrets at the museum: coal mining photographs.

16. Hidden treasures at the museum: a huge Chinese pickle jar.

17. What is unique about the museum that can't be found anywhere else: Long used for ranching, this site was once part of the largest coal-mining region in California and was later home to a silica sand mine.

18. The most important things about local, state, or American history that can be learned at the museum: coal mined here helped fuel the industrial revolution in California.   In their time, communities of the Mt. Diablo Coalfield were among the most populous regions within Contra Costa County.

19. Annual events held at the site or elsewhere in the community: Mine open houses are offered periodically. Naturalists in the park also have events seasonally. See the website for information.

20. Research facilities or archives at the site: naturalists may be able to assist with research on residents of the Mt. Diablo Coalfield.

21. Type of gift shop and what is for sale: some books, t-shirts, coal samples, and other items are available at the visitor's center.

1. **Blackhawk Museum-Danville**

2. Location: 3700 Blackhawk Plaza Circle, Danville, CA. 94506.

3. Website: http://www.blackhawkmuseum.org/

4. Phone number: (925) 736-2280.

5. E-mail: museum@blackhawkmuseum.org

6. Hours of operation: Wednesday–Sunday, 10 a.m.–5 p.m.

7. Cost: adults: 18-64 years of age $10; students: 7-17 years of age $7; seniors: 65+ years and older: $7.

8. Permanent Exhibits: an impressive collection of classic and specialty cars restored to mint condition.

9. Special Exhibits: available on a rotating basis.

10. Historical era that is featured the best: 1880-1900s.

11. Targeted age groups: all ages.

12. Special activities for children: school tours and family programs. The Children's Education & Transportation Fund makes reimbursement available for the transportation costs to the museum.

13. Guided tours: docent-led tours of the automobile and changing exhibitions are conducted at 2 p.m. every weekend. Each tour lasts about an hour and is included free with admission.

14. Hands-on activities: none.

15. The best-kept secrets at the museum: cars belonging to presidents and movie stars.

16. Hidden treasures at the museum: many rare and prototype vehicles.

17. What is unique about the museum that can't be found anywhere else: The collection features some of the best-restored historic cars available in California.

18. The most important things about local, state, or American history that can be learned at the museum: the role that autos played in the development of California.

19. Annual events held at the site or elsewhere in the community: see website for details.

20. Research facilities or archives at the site: research library available.

21. Type of gift shop and what is for sale: an extensive selection of car models, books, and other automobile–related items are sold.

1. **Bolinas Museum**

2. Location: 48 Wharf Road, P.O. Box 450, Bolinas, CA. 94924.

3. Website: http://www.bolinasmuseum.org/

4. Phone number: (415) 868-0330.

5. E-mail: info@bolinasmuseum.org

6. Hours of operation: Friday 1:00 - 5:00 p.m., Saturday & Sunday 12:00 - 5:00 p.m.

7. Cost: free.

8. Permanent Exhibits: the museum is composed of five galleries as well as the Wintersteen Courtyard. The Main Gallery offers exhibitions of contemporary art and history. The Helene Sturdivant Mayne Photography Gallery presents

exhibitions of diverse fine art photography. Regional artists are featured in the Coastal Marin Artists Gallery. The Margaret Duncan Greene Gallery hosts selections from the permanent art collection from the 1800s to the present. The Floyd Russell Family History Room details the history of the area with photographs, documents, and objects from the extensive collections in the museum's archive.

9. Special Exhibits: rotating art and photography exhibits.

10. Historical era that is featured the best: 1800s-present.

11. Targeted age groups: all ages.

12. Special activities for children: none.

13. Guided tours: available for some special events.

14. Hands-on activities: some of the art exhibits are interactive.

15. The best-kept secrets at the museum: it has a nice collection of local Indian artifacts. It also has interesting displays on the geology and nature of the region.

16. Hidden treasures at the museum: historical photos, maps, local history artifacts, and plans for property developments that were, fortunately, never put into effect.

17. What is unique about the museum that can't be found anywhere else: it is a combination of a history and fine arts museum.

18. The most important things about local, state, or American history that can be learned at the museum: the ways in which the area has changed over time; how development nearly spoiled the natural beauty of the area.

19. Annual events held at the site or elsewhere in the community: Art Auction; the annual Holiday Mini Show; Historic Walking Tour; and the 100th Anniversary of Marconi and the radio.

20. Research facilities or archives at the site: there is an archive available to researchers by arrangement.

21. Type of gift shop and what is for sale: historical books cards and posters.

1. **Burlingame Hillsborough History Museum**

2. Location: Burlingame Train Station, 290 California Drive @ Burlingame Ave. Burlingame, CA. 94011.

3. Website: http://burlingamehistory.org/

4. Phone number: (650) 340-9960.

5. E-mail: bgamehistory@gmail.com

6. Hours of operation: first Sunday of each month (except July), 1:00–4:00 p.m.

7. Cost: free.

8. Permanent Exhibits: Peninsula Royalty: The Founding Families; historic trees; dairies; fire department; Pacific City "Coney Island of the West"; and Anson Burlingame.

9. Special Exhibits: none.

10. Historical era that is featured the best: 1800s-1900s.

11. Targeted age groups: all ages.

12. Special activities for children: The society offers historical educational programs for adults and children.

13. Guided tours: group tours available with reservations; a self-guided tour of the town's historic buildings is also available.

14. Hands-on activities: there is a virtual museum on the website.

27

15. The best-kept secrets at the museum: local school memorabilia, a vintage El Camino landmark bell.

16. Hidden treasures at the museum: historic photos, train items, and an antique fire engine.

17. What is unique about the museum that can't be found anywhere else: It is located in an historic train station. There is also information about the trolley line that used to run to Millbrae from there.

18. The most important things about local, state, or American history that can be learned at the museum: The town has been the location of several historic mansions belonging to wealthy San Franciscans seeking a country home. It later became the home of many refuges whose homes had been destroyed in the 1906 San Francisco earthquake.

19. Annual events held at the site or elsewhere in the community: classes on Burlingame's art, architecture, and history.

20. Research facilities or archives at the site: The Burlingame Historical Society maintains an extensive archive of historic memorabilia from Hillsborough and Burlingame's past.

21. Type of gift shop and what is for sale: a book on the history of the town.

1. **Cable Car Museum-San Francisco**

2. Location: Cable Car Museum, 1201 Mason Street, San Francisco, CA. 94108.

3. Website: http://www.cablecarmuseum.org/

4. Phone number: (415) 474-1887.

5. E-mail: shop@cablecarmuseum.org

6. Hours of operation: 10 a.m. - 6 p.m., April 1 thru September 30;

10 a.m. - 5 p.m. October 1 thru March 31; open every day except New Year's Day, Easter Sunday, Thanksgiving, and Christmas.

7. Cost: free.

8. Permanent Exhibits: Located in the historic Washington/Mason cable car barn and powerhouse, the museum deck overlooks the huge engines and winding wheels that pull the cables. Downstairs is a viewing area of the large sheaves and cable line entering the building through the channel under the street. On display are various mechanical devices such as grips, track, cable, brake mechanisms, tools, detailed models, and a large collection of historic photographs. The museum houses three antique cable cars from the 1870s: The Sutter Street Railway No. 46 grip car, No. 54 trailer (the only surviving car from the first cable car company), and the Clay Street Hill Railroad No. 8 grip car.

9. Special Exhibits: none.

10. Historical era that is featured the best: 1870s-present.

11. Targeted age groups: all ages.

12. Special activities for children: none.

13. Guided tours: none.

14. Hands-on activities: none.

15. The best-kept secrets at the museum: You can see the actual cable that pulls the cars running through the museum!

16. Hidden treasures at the museum: You can smell the burning sawdust while the wooden brakes are in operation!

17. What is unique about the museum that can't be found anywhere else: San Francisco has one of the few historic cable car systems still in operation in the world.

18. The most important things about local, state, or American history that can be learned at the museum: Learn everything about this unique form of transportation.

19. Annual events held at the site or elsewhere in the community: the annual Bell Ringing Competition.

20. Research facilities or archives at the site: none.

21. Type of gift shop and what is for sale: The museum store offers a variety of cable car memorabilia, books, clothing, cards, and even genuine cable car bells!

1. California Historical Society-San Francisco

2. Location: 678 Mission Street, San Francisco, CA. 94105.

3. Website: http://www.californiahistoricalsociety.org/

4. Phone number: (415) 357-1848.

5. E-mail: info@calhist.org

6. Hours of operation: Gallery and Store: Tuesday – Sunday 12:00p.m. to 5:00p.m. North Baker Research Library: Wednesday-Friday, 12:00p.m.-5:00p.m.

7. Cost: $5 general admission; free admission to CHS members.

8. Permanent Exhibits: none.

9. Special Exhibits: rotating exhibits with various themes related to California history

10. Historical era that is featured the best: 1700s-present.

11. Targeted age groups: adults.

12. Special activities for children: History for Half-Pints.

13. Guided tours: available with reservations at 415-357-1848 x222.

14. Hands-on activities: The History Speaks and Ten Lions Talks lecture and panel discussion series host conversations about the relevance of history presently and in the future. The San Francisco Time Travel Project and Night with the Archivists encourage personal experiences with the collections. With entertaining and participatory activities, History for Half-Pints reaches across generations.

15. The best-kept secrets at the museum: Displays are constantly changing, so a visitor will see different things every time he or she visits.

16. Hidden treasures at the museum: many unique documents, paintings, prints, etc.

17. What is unique about the museum that can't be found anywhere else: primary source books, maps, documents, and artwork related to California history.

18. The most important things about local, state, or American history that can be learned at the museum: A wide array of subjects is included in the archives. It is an excellent research facility on California history.

19. Annual events held at the site or elsewhere in the community: there are weekly programs open to the public. See www.californiahistoricalsociety.com. Additional events are offered to members and donors by invitation.

20. Research facilities or archives at the site: The North Baker Research Library is a top-notch research facility with online resources as well.

21. Type of gift shop and what is for sale: The Ten Lions Bookstore, a partnership between the California Historical Society and Heyday Books, features key Heyday titles that focus on California's myriad stories and locally crafted items from Bay Area artisans, as well as hosting curated events and discussions.

1. **The California History Center-De Anza College**

2. Location: in the 1895 Petit Trianon on the De Anza College campus. 21250 Stevens Creek Blvd., Cupertino, CA. 95014.

3. Website: http://www.calhistory.org/

4. Phone number: (408) 864-8987.

5. E-mail: izutom@deanza.edu

6. Hours of operation: Tuesday - Thursday, 9:30-noon, 1:00-4:00, and Friday by appointment. The center is closed during July and August.

7. Cost: free.

8. Permanent Exhibits: none.

9. Special Exhibits: rotating exhibits on California history themes.

10. Historical era that is featured the best: 1700s-present.

11. Targeted age groups: adults.

12. Special activities for children: none.

13. Guided tours: none.

14. Hands-on activities: none.

15. The best-kept secrets at the museum: a great collection of local history materials.

16. Hidden treasures at the museum: oral histories and local history documents.

17. What is unique about the museum that can't be found anywhere else: many original documents that cannot be found anywhere else.

18. The most important things about local, state, or American history that can be learned at the museum: it is a research center for California history, so there are great resources for local history.

19. Annual events held at the site or elsewhere in the community: see the De Anza College website.

20. Research facilities or archives at the site: The Louis E. Stocklmeir Regional History Library and Archives includes student research papers, oral histories on audio and video tape, photographs, maps, prints, postcards, ephemera, a clipping and pamphlet file, periodicals, and books.

21. Type of gift shop: none.

22. Additional information: Call ahead since the display room is not open all year. The library is open most of the school year, however.

1. **California Rodeo Heritage Museum-Salinas**

2. Location: 1034 North Main Street in Salinas (on the California Rodeo Grounds).

3. Website: http://www.carodeo.com/events_detail.aspx?id=64

4. Phone number: (831) 775-3100.

5. E-mail: none.

6. Hours of operation: (open only during the Salinas Rodeo in July) Thursday and Friday from 4 p.m. into the evening, and Saturday and Sunday from 11a.m. It is also open by special appointment throughout the year.

7. Cost: free with admission to the rodeo. Ticket prices vary (see website for details).

8. Permanent Exhibits: memorabilia relative to the rodeo, including attractive displays of vintage Miss California Rodeo outfits, rodeo clown costumes, and cowboy attire from some of the California Rodeo's most famous alumni; saddles, cowboy hats, and tack donated by those families connected to the rodeo's founding directors and participants.

9. Special Exhibits: none.

10. Historical era that is featured the best: 1872-present.

11. Targeted age groups: all ages.

12. Special activities for children: interactive learning activities.

13. Guided tours: none.

14. Hands-on activities: some displays are interactive.

15. The best-kept secrets at the museum: most people do not realize that rodeos have been held in the area for so long.

16. Hidden treasures at the museum: a real Wells Fargo stagecoach.

17. What is unique about the museum that can't be found anywhere else: the Salinas Rodeo is one of the oldest and largest rodeos in the West. People come to this event from around the world.

18. The most important things about local, state, or American history that can be learned at the museum: The California Rodeo Heritage Museum celebrates the history of the California Rodeo from its days of being a semi-annual round-up to its modern day adaptations.

19. Annual events held at the site or elsewhere in the community: none.

20. Research facilities or archives at the site: none.

21. Type of gift shop and what is for sale: there are cowboy related items for sale at the concession stands.

1. **Campbell Historical Museum**

2. Location: 51 North Central Ave. Campbell, CA. 95008.

3. Website: http://campbellmuseums.org/history

4. Phone number: (408) 866-2119.

5. E-mail: kerryp@cityofcampbell.com

6. Hours of operation: Thursday - Sunday   12:00 p.m. to 4:00 p.m.

7. Cost: $2.00 adults, $2.00 seniors, $2.00 youth (7-17)   under 7 years free .

8. Permanent Exhibits: a "General Store" that served as the community center; an early parlor; examples of "Decorative Arts" in early Campbell; the roots of Campbell's agricultural past; hometown music and drama as early forms of recreation.

9. Special Exhibits: rotating exhibits.

10. Historical era that is featured the best: early 1900s.

11. Targeted age groups: all ages.

12. Special activities for children: school tours, school trunk rentals.

32

13. Guided tours: group tours available by arrangement; walking tours of downtown businesses and homes.

14. Hands-on activities: many items are labeled "please touch".

15. The best-kept secrets at the museum: The agricultural related items are some of the best available in the area.

16. Hidden treasures at the museum: the schoolhouse items are fun for kids.

17. What is unique about the museum that can't be found anywhere else: it is located in an old firehouse.

18. The most important things about local, state, or American history that can be learned at the museum: Campbell was important in the fruit packing industry.

19. Annual events held at the site or elsewhere in the community: The Spirit of Campbell Photography Exhibit, holiday fair, etc. (see website for details).

20. Research facilities or archives at the site: none.

21. Type of gift shop and what is for sale: local history items, books, and toys are for sale.

1. **Camron-Stanford House-Oakland**

2. Location: 1418 Lakeside Drive on the banks of Lake Merritt, Oakland, CA. 94612-4307.

3. Website: http://www.cshouse.org/

4. Phone number: (510) 874-7802.

5. E-mail: nmehler@cshouse.org

6. Hours of operation: Sunday tours at 1, 2 and 3 p.m. and by special appointment (call 510-874-7802).

7. Cost: adults: $5.00, seniors: $4.00, children: free.

8. Permanent Exhibits: the museum houses a small but exquisite collection of American decorative arts and furniture, which reflect the Victorian Era (1875-1885). Special emphasis is placed on women's needle and craftwork and the practice of art collecting in the 19th century, as exemplified by David Hewes' art collection listed in his 1886 published catalog. The house also has a small photographic collection of 19th century interiors and a small teaching collection of 19th century household items.

9. Special Exhibits: there is a room dedicated to the years that the house was the Oakland Museum. Some of the original displays are still there.

10. Historical era that is featured the best: 1800s to early 1900s.

11. Targeted age groups: all ages.

12. Special activities for children: none.

13. Guided tours: docent led tours only, no self-guided tours; private tours are available with reservations; some tours are available with a tea or lunch (see website for details).

14. Hands-on activities: none.

15. The best-kept secrets at the museum: the house has the only working gas-lit chandelier in Oakland.

16. Hidden treasures at the museum: Many original furnishings, artwork and personal items from the families that lived there are on display. In typical Victorian

fashion, the house is crammed with artwork from the many countries the owners visited while on their grand tours of Europe.

17. What is unique about the museum that can't be found anywhere else: the Camron-Stanford House is the last of the beautiful 19th century mansions that once surrounded Lake Merritt. In its long life, the house was the private residence of five families instrumental in the development of the City of Oakland and the State of California. In the early 20th century, it became the first museum in the City of Oakland.

18. The most important things about local, state, or American history that can be learned at the museum: the house was owned or rented by several prominent Oakland families, including the Camrons, Heweses, Stanfords, and Wrights. The Camrons were active in state and local government, the Heweses helped to build San Francisco, the Stanfords built the Transcontinental Railroad, and the Wrights established a shipping company.

19. Annual events held at the site or elsewhere in the community: May Day Crafts for Kids, Mother's Day teas, and other events (see website for details).

20. Research facilities or archives at the site: none.

21. Type of gift shop: none.

22. Additional information: The site is a popular wedding venue.

1. Cantor Arts Center-Stanford

2. Location: at the intersection of Museum Way and Lomita Drive on the Stanford campus, northwest of The Oval and the Main Quad; just one block from Palm Drive, facing the Bing Concert Hall.

3. Website: https://museum.stanford.edu/

4. Phone number: (650) 723-4177.

5. E-mail: abryan1@stanford.edu

6. Hours of operation: Wednesday – Sunday: 11 a.m. – 5 p.m. Thursday: 11 a.m. – 8 p.m.

7. Cost: free.

8. Permanent Exhibits: art from Europe & America, Asia, Africa, Oceania, Native Americas; Modern Art; prints, drawings and photographs; items reflecting the history of the Stanford family; and an outdoor sculpture garden.

9. Special Exhibits: rotating exhibits (see website for details).

10. Historical era that is featured the best: ancient times-present.

11. Targeted age groups: all ages.

12. Special activities for children: educators' guide, school tours, and art classes (see website for details).

13. Guided tours: docent-guided tours free to schools and not-for-profit groups.

14. Hands-on activities: only during art classes.

15. The best-kept secrets at the museum: the Rodin collection is exceptional.

16. Hidden treasures at the museum: many, many art treasures from around the world.

17. What is unique about the museum that can't be found anywhere else: This is one of the few places in the Bay Area where you can see ancient to renaissance art. It is one of the few comprehensive world art museums in the Bay Area.

110

18. The most important things about local, state, or American history that can be learned at the museum: one of the best collections on the Stanford family, as well as American and Native American art.

19. Annual events held at the site or elsewhere in the community: there are many events on the calendar on the website.

20. Research facilities or archives at the site: research opportunities for university students, researchers, and others (contact the center for information). The center also has publications that it publishes.

21. Type of gift shop and what is for sale: there is a café, but no gift shop.

1. **Capitola Historical Museum**
2. Location: 410 Capitola Ave, Capitola, CA. 95010.
3. Website: http://www.capitolamuseum.org
4. Phone number: 831-464-0322.
5. E-mail: capitolamuseum@gmail.com
6. Hours of operation: Wednesdays, Fridays, Saturdays, and Sundays: 12-4. Sometimes closed in winter for exhibit changes.
7. Cost: free.
8. Permanent Exhibits: history of the town and resorts; museum grounds include a reconstructed cottage and washhouse from the beach resort era of the early 20th century.
9. Special Exhibits: change annually (see website for details).
10. Historical era that is featured the best: 1800s-1900s.
11. Targeted age groups: all ages.
12. Special activities for children: some.
13. Guided tours: walking tours of historic Capitola.
14. Hands-on activities: some.
15. The best-kept secrets at the museum: the beach-related items are fun.
16. Hidden treasures at the museum: items from local resorts and beach attractions.
17. What is unique about the museum that can't be found anywhere else: The museum capitalizes on Capitola's importance as a beach and vacation community.
18. The most important things about local, state, or American history that can be learned at the museum: Capitola is the oldest seaside resort on the West Coast. It was established as "Camp Capitola" in 1874.
19. Annual events held at the site or elsewhere in the community: see website for details.
20. Research facilities or archives at the site: available by appointment.
21. Type of gift shop and what is for sale: gift items, books, videos, etc.

1. **Cartoon Art Museum- San Francisco**
2. Location: 655 Mission St. San Francisco, CA. 94105.
3. Website: http://cartoonart.org/
4. Phone number: 415-CAR-TOON, (415) 227-8666.
5. E-mail: office@cartoonart.org
6. Hours of operation: Tuesday to Sunday, 11a.m. – 5p.m.
7. Cost: $8 – Adults, $6 – Students & Seniors, $4 – Children (ages 6 – 12), free –

Children (age 5 & under). The first Tuesday of every calendar month is "Pay What You Wish Day."

8. Permanent Exhibits: pieces that represent the history, contemporary development, creators, design, and processes underlying the art forms of cartoons, comics, digital animation, illustration, and videogames.

9. Special Exhibits: rotating special exhibits.

10. Historical era that is featured the best: 20th century-present.

11. Targeted age groups: all ages.

12. Special activities for children: educational outreach programs, classes, and workshops are available.

13. Guided tours: available with reservations.

14. Hands-on activities: they vary based on the exhibitions. Past activities included the opportunity to create your own cartoons.

15. The best-kept secrets at the museum: many original pieces of cartoon art or developmental sketches or works signed by the artists.

16. Hidden treasures at the museum: a few rare old cartoons from the 1700-1800s.

17. What is unique about the museum that can't be found anywhere else: A comprehensive history of this art form.

18. The most important things about local, state, or American history that can be learned at the museum: the role that this form of entertainment has in our culture and how it has changed over time.

19. Annual events held at the site or elsewhere in the community: dozens of events throughout the year, including book signings, creator appearances, lectures and workshops.

20. Research facilities or archives at the site: none.

21. Type of gift shop and what is for sale: a cartoon bookstore with a large variety of comics, books, and action figures.

1. **Casa Peralta-San Leandro**

2. Location: 384 West Estudillo Avenue, San Leandro, CA. 94577.

3. Website: https://www.sanleandro.org/depts/library/about_us/history/casa.asp

4. Phone number: (510) 577-3474.

5. E-mail: pmallari@sanleandro.org

6. Hours of operation: Saturday and Sunday 11:00 a.m. - 3:00 p.m.

7. Cost: free.

8. Permanent Exhibits: dining room, kitchen, parlor, music room, sunroom, bedrooms, bathroom, a beautiful garden with an historic fountain.

9. Special Exhibits: wooden and clay models of local historical buildings.

10. Historical era that is featured the best: 1800s-1900s.

11. Targeted age groups: all ages.

12. Special activities for children: school tours.

13. Guided tours: docent-led tours during visiting hours.

14. Hands-on activities: none.

15. The best-kept secrets at the museum: historic maps, photos, paintings, and personal effects of the Peralta family.

37

16. Hidden treasures at the museum: historic clock that belonged to the family.

17. What is unique about the museum that can't be found anywhere else: It was remodeled in the 1920s to resemble a Spanish villa. It has numerous hand-made tiles from Spain depicting the life of Don Quixote.

18. The most important things about local, state, or American history that can be learned at the museum: it is the home of Ignacio Peralta, one of the original Spanish settlers of the area. Three descendants of the original land grant of Rancho San Antonio (ranging from the San Leandro Creek to the current-day city of El Cerrito) lived in the Casa.

19. Annual events held at the site or elsewhere in the community: Cherry Festival. See the city website for details.

20. Research facilities or archives at the site: none.

21. Type of gift shop: none.

1. **Centennial Light Bulb-Livermore**

2. Location: Fire Station #6, 4550 East Ave., Livermore, CA. 94550.

3. Website: http://www.centennialbulb.org/

4. Phone number: (925) 454-2361.

5. E-mail: centennialbulb@hotmail.com

6. Hours of Operation: open during regular firehouse daylight hours.

7. Cost: free.

8. Permanent Exhibits: the Centennial Bulb, the longest burning light bulb in history. It is in its 114th year of illumination.

9. Special Exhibits: Many awards, papers, and historical photos related to the bulb are on display. A permanent flat screen television runs a continuous slide show about the bulb and it's times. There is also a display case with fire fighters tools, an antique light bulb display, including a Shelby bulb.

10. Historical era that is featured the best: 1900s-present.

11. Targeted age groups: all ages.

12. Special activities for children: Sometimes, after the tour of the station, the firefighters let the kids use the fire hose.

13. Guided tours: just ring the doorbell at the fire station and a firefighter will let you in.

14. Hands-on activities: If you ask the firefighters, they may let you hold the Shelby bulb.

15. The best-kept secrets at the museum: the light bulb has been featured in *Ripley's Believe it or Not*, *The Guiness Book of World Records*, "Mythbusters" and "California's Gold", two documentary films, and two children's books.

16. Hidden treasures at the museum: there is a webcam that shows the light at all times. If you stand in the front of the station in the line of site of the "Bulbcam" your image can be captured as a souvenir photo.

17. What is unique about the museum that can't be found anywhere else: this bulb has never burned out since being installed in 1901. It is also the only bulb seen all around the world on a bulbcam. People also sang happy birthday to it!

18. The most important things about local, state or American history that can be learned at the museum: Books and films have been made about the history of the

bulb and speculating why all bulbs can't be made to last this long. A Shelby Bulb is being studied at Sandia National Laboratories. You can read about the study at: http://www.centennialbulb.org/sandia-test.htm

19. Annual events held at the site or elsewhere in the community: periodic anniversary celebrations are held at the fire station; the last one was in 2015 for the 1 millionth hour anniversary of the bulb shining.

20. Research facilities or archives at the site: none.

21. Type of gift shop and what is for sale: Many items are for sale at the fire station to support the Fire Fighters Association including books, films, postcards, bookmarkers, t-shirts, hats, glasses, and mugs.

22. Additional information: More can be learned about the history of Livermore at the Heritage Guild at livermorehistory.com, and about the bulb's origins at the Shelby Ohio History Museum at http://www.rootsweb.ancestry.com/~ohsmh/. Also a new Fire Department History site is in the development stage.

1. **The C.E. Smith Museum of Anthropology- Hayward**

2. Location: The museum's exhibit hall is located in MI 4047, fourth floor of Meiklejohn Hall, at the southwest corner of the CSUEB Hayward campus.

3. Website: http://class.csueastbay.edu/anthropologymuseum/Home_Page.php

4. Phone number: (510) 885-7414.

5. E-mail: Use the form on the webpage.

6. Hours of operation: Monday through Friday, 11 a.m. to 4 p.m. only during the exhibition season.

7. Cost: free.

8. Permanent Exhibits: none.

9. Special Exhibits: there are rotating exhibits created by university students and staff. Past themes have included women in history, magic lanterns, collections, trains, the Chinese in the Bay Area, Hopi Indians, and many other topics.

10. Historical era that is featured the best: varies by exhibit.

11. Targeted age groups: adults.

12. Special activities for children: none.

13. Guided tours: none.

14. Hands-on activities: There is a pretty extensive virtual museum on the website featuring local archeological digs and items from around the world that are not currently on display.

15. The best-kept secrets at the museum: the items on display are different every time you visit. Only a small portion of them is on display at any given time.

16. Hidden treasures at the museum: there are interesting artifacts from many different cultures around the globe, some historical and some contemporary.

17. What is unique about the museum that can't be found anywhere else: It is one of the few anthropological museums in the Bay Area. It is small, but always has interesting exhibits.

18. The most important things about local, state, or American history that can be learned at the museum: there are frequently items of local historical interest included in the displays, particularly Native American items. There is also

information about an excavation of a Gold Rush era shipwreck and of a Chinese settlement.

19. Annual events held at the site or elsewhere in the community: there is usually an event associated with the opening of a new exhibit (see website for details).

20. Research facilities or archives at the site: contact the university for information.

21. Type of gift shop: none.

22. Additional information: Note: This museum is very seasonal. Typically exhibits are only open in the spring during university hours. Always check the website or call before visiting.

1. **The Charles M. Schulz Museum and Research Center-Santa Rosa**

40

2. Location: 2301 Hardies Lane, Santa Rosa, CA. 95403.

3. Website: https://schulzmuseum.org/

4. Phone number: (707) 579-4452.

5. E-mail: tours@schulzmuseum.org

6. Hours of operation: From Labor Day (the first Monday in September) through Memorial Day (the last Monday in May): Weekdays 11 a.m. to 5 p.m. — except Tuesdays, Weekends 10 a.m. to 5 p.m. From Memorial Day (the last Monday in May) through Labor Day (the first Monday in September): Weekdays 11 a.m. to 5 p.m. Weekends 10 a.m. to 5 p.m.

7. Cost: Adults: $10, Seniors (62 and over with ID): $5, Youth/Students (4–18 or with valid student ID): $5, Museum Members & Youth 3 and under are free.

8. Permanent Exhibits: Schulz's re-created studio, Wrapped Snoopy House, Snoopy Labyrinth, "Peanuts" Tile Mural, Nursery Wall, Morphing Snoopy Wood Sculpture, and The Museum Theatre. The Collections feature archival documents about the artist, his personal effects, non-cartoon art he created, a library of his books, a multimedia collection including music, films and other media, a collection of original comic strips, "Peanuts"-related merchandise, photography, and tributes by other artists.

9. Special Exhibits: rotating exhibits on Schulz and his artwork. There are also traveling exhibitions featuring Charles Schulz that tour the world.

10. Historical era that is featured the best: 20th century.

11. Targeted age groups: all ages.

12. Special activities for children: Become a cartoonist yourself. Draw, animate, learn, discover! The hands-on Education Room is a place for visitors of all ages to practice cartooning, color "Peanuts" characters, fold Snoopy's doghouse out of origami, create your own hand-drawn animation for their giant zoetropes, learn more about the exhibitions, and enjoy other activities as scheduled. The Education Room is free with price of Museum Admission. It is open during regular museum operating hours (except special events or rentals). There are many classes and camps on the calendar on the website.

13. Guided tours: group tours are available with reservations.

14. Hands-on activities: see Education Room above.

15. The best-kept secrets at the museum: the original artwork is most impressive, but there are many interesting personal effects of Schulz's that are also fascinating.

16. Hidden treasures at the museum: There are many interesting art forms incorporated into the building itself that reflect the "Peanuts" theme.

17. What is unique about the museum that can't be found anywhere else: it is the only museum dedicated exclusively to Charles Schulz.

18. The most important things about local, state, or American history that can be learned at the museum: Schulz was very influential worldwide, but Santa Rosa was his home. His works have been translated into many languages. His animated cartoons have become American classics. His images and names even made it into space as a part of the Apollo program.

19. Annual events held at the site or elsewhere in the community: visitors have opportunities to meet professional cartoonists, view some of Schulz's favorite movies, create hands-on crafts, learn about different cartooning techniques, and attend nembers-only parties (see website for details).

20. Research facilities or archives at the site: the Research Center is a place to study and explore the life and career of Charles M. Schulz.

21. Type of gift shop and what is for sale: there is a vast gift shop with every kind of Peanuts merchandise imaginable.

22. Additional information: there is also an ice arena called Snoopy's Home Ice that has skating, hockey, birthday parties and other events. It includes the Warm Puppy Café.

1. **China Camp Historic District-San Rafael**

2. Location: San Rafael, CA. 94901. Four miles east of San Rafael on the shore of San Pablo Bay. From Highway 101, go east on North San Pedro Road for five miles until it enters the park.

3. Website: http://www.parks.ca.gov/?page_id=466 and http://www.friendsofchinacamp.org/

4. Phone number: (415) 488-5161.

5. E-mail: friendsofchinacamp@gmail.com

6. Hours of operation: 8:00 a.m. to sunset daily.

7. Cost: $5 day use fee.

8. Permanent Exhibits: a museum describing an early Chinese settlement. A Chinese shrimp-fishing village thrived on this site in the 1880s. Nearly 500 people, originally from Canton, China, lived in the village. In its heyday, there were three general stores, a marine supply store, and a barbershop. Fishermen by trade in their native country, they gravitated to the work they knew best. Over 90% of the shrimp they netted were dried and shipped to China or Chinese communities throughout the US. The museum at China Camp Village helps tell the story of these hardy shrimp fishermen.

9. Special Exhibits: none.

10. Historical era that is featured the best: 1880s.

11. Targeted age groups: all ages.

12. Special activities for children: Junior Ranger Program.

13. Guided tours: if you are interested in scheduling a group tour please contact the China Camp Ranger Office at (415) 456-0766. Docents are available to give China Camp history programs.

14. Hands-on activities: there are some hands-on demonstrations at the visitor's center.

15. The best-kept secrets at the museum: some of the original buildings are still standing.

16. Hidden treasures at the museum: fishing equipment, boats, historic pictures and documents that detail the lives of the fishermen.

17. What is unique about the museum that can't be found anywhere else: This is the only Chinese fishing village in the Bay Area that is still in existence.

18. The most important things about local, state, or American history that can be learned at the museum: the difficulties encountered by Chinese settlers in the U.S. during the 1800s.

19. Annual events held at the site or elsewhere in the community: Heritage Day and other events. See the Friends of China Camp website.

20. Research facilities or archives at the site: digital records of the history of China Camp, including photographs, academic studies, videos, and newspaper articles are available for review on request.

21. Type of gift shop and what is for sale: the Quan Brothers snack shop at China Camp Village is open on weekends. Food, beverages, and ice cream are available. You can meet the long-time resident and shrimp fisherman Frank Quan here. There is some merchandise available for purchase on the weekends in both the museum and cafe.

22. Additional information: on weekends, between 11a.m. and 4p.m. there is generally a docent in the museum to help with interpretation and answer questions. Both the Huell Howser China Camp video and the "Bay Fishery" chapter of KQED's Saving the Bay are run in the museum during those times. From June through end of October, the replica Chinese shrimping junk, the *Grace Quan*, is docked at the China Camp pier.

1. **Chinese Historical Society of America-San Francisco**
2. Location: 965 Clay St. San Francisco, CA. 94108.
3. Website: http://www.chsa.org/
4. Phone number: (415) 391-1188 x101.
5. E-mail: info@chsa.org

6. Hours of operation: Tuesday-Friday 12-5 p.m. Saturdays 11 a.m.–4 p.m. Closed Sunday, Monday, and holidays.
7. Cost: Adults: $5, College Students (with ID) and Seniors: $3, Children 6-17: $2, Free for CHSA members and children 5 and under. Free to the public on the first Thursday of every month.
8. Permanent Exhibits: Chinese in America.
9. Special Exhibits: Creative Spaces, rotating exhibits.
10. Historical era that is featured the best: late 1800s.
11. Targeted age groups: all ages.
12. Special activities for children: Chinese storytelling for grade K-3.
13. Guided tours: docent-led tours of museum and walking tours of Chinatown.
14. Hands-on activities: "History Alive" performance.

15. The best-kept secrets at the museum: the display on anti-Chinese racism in America.

16. Hidden treasures at the museum: the only surviving historic junk ship from the Bay Area.

17. What is unique about the museum that can't be found anywhere else: Chinatown miniatures, Jake Lee paintings, and a James Leong mural.

18.The most important things about local, state, or American history that can be learned at the museum: the detailed history of the Chinese in America from the Gold Rush to the present. Many types of jobs that Chinese have done, how they lived, and the challenges they faced.

19. Annual events held at the site or elsewhere in the community: Traveling exhibits such as the 1906 earthquake and Chinatown, Voice and Vision Gala.

20. Research facilities or archives at the site: available upon request.

21.Type of gift shop and what is for sale: academic books and journals

22. Additional information: online exhibits and publications available.

1. **Chitactac-Adams Heritage County Park- Watsonville**

2. Location: Chitactac-Adams   10001 Watsonville Rd. Gilroy, CA. 95020.

3. Website: http://www.sccgov.org/sites/parks/parkfinder/Pages/Chitactac-Adams.aspx

4. Phone number: (408) 323-0107.

5. E-mail: parkinfo@prk.sccgov.org

6. Hours of operation: open year round   8:00 a.m.–sunset.

7. Cost: free.

8. Permanent Exhibits: the park features the beautiful Uvas Creek and a wealth of cultural artifacts including bedrock mortars and petroglyphs left by the Ohlone Indians. The park includes a self-guided interpretive walk and an interpretive shelter focusing on Ohlone Indian culture and the Adams schoolhouse which was sited on this property from the 1850s until 1956. A self-guided interpretive walk around the site, including eight stations with interpretive panels, is supplemented by an interpretive shelter with seven additional panels and displays. The trail panels include photographs and original art covering the Adams School, Ohlone village life, Ohlone buildings, petroglyphs (rock art), Ohlone food processing, natural history of Uvas Creek, Spanish, California and Ohlone culture and petroglyphs and their preservation.

9. Special Exhibits: none.

10. Historical era that is featured the best: prehistory-1900s.

11. Targeted age groups: all ages.

12. Special activities for children: guided school tours and interpretive programs are offered by staff and volunteer docents. Call (408) 918-7772 for information and schedules. Teachers' packets are available online and materials are available for classroom loan.

13. Guided tours: staff-led programs and group tours are available by appointment for groups of 10 or more.

14. Hands-on activities: none.

15. The best-kept secrets at the museum: the petroglyphs are some of the oldest art forms in the country. This is like the Bay Area's Stonehenge.

16. Hidden treasures at the museum: the bedrock mortars where the Ohlone people pounded acorns and other seeds are numerous and well preserved.

17. What is unique about the museum that can't be found anywhere else: most other sites with Ohlone art and mortars are in very remote or hidden areas. This is one of the most accessible sites available to the public.

18. The most important things about local, state, or American history that can be learned at the museum: the site has had many uses over the years as it passed into Spanish, Mexican and then American hands. It was rescued and restored after heavy vandalism in recent years. It is a beautiful site with a rich history.

19. Annual events held at the site or elsewhere in the community: there are occasional Ohlone cultural activities, nature and historical walks held by park docents (see website for details).

20. Research facilities or archives at the site: none.

21. Type of gift shop: none.

1. **Clayton Historical Society Museum**

2. Location: 6101 Main Street, P.O. Box 94, Clayton, CA. 94517-1201.

3. Website: http://www.claytonhistory.org/Pages/default.aspx

4. Phone number: (925) 672-0240.

5. E-mail: Use the online contact form.

6. Hours of operation: Wednesdays and Sundays, 2:00 - 4:00 p.m.

7. Cost: free.

8. Permanent Exhibits: Native American artifacts, mining, farming, pioneer and vintage clothing, furniture, musical instruments, kitchen, bedrooms, schools, jailhouse, outhouse, etc.

9. Special Exhibits: railroads of the Clayton and Diablo Valleys and Beyond and other rotating exhibits.

10. Historical era that is featured the best: 1800s to the present.

11. Targeted age groups: all ages.

12. Special activities for children: Kids' Corner.

13. Guided tours: available during visiting hours.

14. Hands-on activities: hands-on corner for children.

15. The best-kept secrets at the museum: Joaquin Muiretta historical marker.

16. Hidden treasures at the museum: vintage clothing, mining equipment, and pioneer artifacts.

17. What is unique about the museum that can't be found anywhere else: it explains Clayton's role as an important regional crossroads.

18. The most important things about local, state, or American history that can be learned at the museum: the role that mining, farming, the railroads, and oil industry played in the development of the area.

19. Annual events held at the site or elsewhere in the community: Railroad Day and many other events each year. See the webpage for details.

20. Research facilities or archives at the site: local history records are available for research.

21. Type of gift shop and what is for sale: local history books, gifts, and railroad related items.

1. **Cloverdale Historical Society Museum**
2. Location: 215 N. Cloverdale Blvd. CA. 95425.
3. Website: http://www.cloverdalehistory.org/
4. Phone number: (707) 894-2067.
5. E-mail: office@cloverdalehistory.org
6. Hours of operation: Thursday 10:00 a.m. - 4:00 p.m. Friday 10:00 a.m.-2:00 p.m. Saturday 10:00 a.m. - 4:00 p.m. Sunday 12:00 p.m. - 4:00 p.m.
7. Cost: free.
8. Permanent Exhibits: the Victorian-style Gould-Shaw House, is decorated as it would have been at the turn of the 20th Century. Pomo artistry and artifacts, showcasing examples of basket making, grinding stones and flake tools. Timeline Wall highlighting key episodes in the history of the town and vicinity. The Citrus Fair: a Cloverdale tradition since 1892. A vintage mud wagon, tools, equipment, and machinery. The Bank of Cloverdale's curious cannonball safe
9. Special Exhibits: appear in the Adler Exhibit Hall, the Trump Library, and Cooley Community Room. Special exhibits have included Quilts of the Clover Quilters and Service, Support, & Sacrifice: Wartime Collections and Recollections.
10. Historical era that is featured the best: 1800s-1900s.
11. Targeted age groups: all ages.
12. Special activities for children: essay contest. School tours available upon request.
13. Guided tours: available upon request.
14. Hands-on activities: none.
15. The best-kept secrets at the museum: Native American artifacts.
16. Hidden treasures at the museum: the cannonball safe.
17. What is unique about the museum that can't be found anywhere else: Cloverdale is a crossroads of Northern California. It has an important agricultural legacy.
18. The most important things about local, state, or American history that can be learned at the museum: the greater Cloverdale area is the home to farms, geysers, and much natural beauty. It has attracted farmers and tourists from further south for many years.
19. Annual events held at the site or elsewhere in the community: check out the calendar on the website for programs and events of the historical society.
20. Research facilities or archives at the site: the Cloverdale Historical Society offers an extensive library and research center for both the casual and the serious researcher. The library includes public documents, photographs, books, and more.
21. Type of gift shop and what is for sale: local history books, postcards, note cards, and candy.

1. **Cohen-Bray House-Oakland**
2. Location: 1440 29th Avenue, Oakland, CA. 94601.
3. Website: http://www.cohenbrayhouse.info/
4. Phone number: (510) 536-1703.
5. E-mail: Use online form.

6. Hours of operation: 2:00 p.m. on the fourth Sunday of each month. Call first for reservations.

7. Cost: $5.

8. Permanent Exhibits: The house was built in 1882-1884 by Julia Moses and Watson A. Bray, for their daughter, Emma, upon her marriage to Alfred H. Cohen, attorney, on February 28, 1884.

9. Special Exhibits: none.

10. Historical era that is featured the best: 1880s-1960s.

11. Targeted age groups: all ages.

12. Special activities for children: school tours.

13. Guided tours: special tours for interested groups including school children are welcomed and can be arranged by calling in advance to arrange reservations, times, fees. (510) 527-5209.

14. Hands-on activities: none.

15. The best-kept secrets at the museum: it has never been restored. Everything you see in the house is completely original and belonged to the family.

16. Hidden treasures at the museum: stained glass windows, grandfather clock, a women's suffrage outfit, fine artwork, and many interesting personal items that belonged to the family.

17. What is unique about the museum that can't be found anywhere else: visitors standing today in its halls, parlors, and bedrooms can see a period home with original wallpaper, woodwork, accessories, even heat sources (fireplaces only) as they were for the honeymooners in 1884. This is due in large part to the fact that the house has never been sold outside of the family.

18. The most important things about local, state, or American history that can be learned at the museum: the house typifies the Stick style of architecture of the 1880's and still contains many examples of its original furnishings in the Aesthetic style of Charles Eastlake. The original interior decoration of the house also remains a quintessential example of the Anglo-Japanese design craze that so caught the fancy of both American and British tastes in the 1880s.

19. Annual events held at the site or elsewhere in the community: the Annual Mother's Day Tea and Explore the Paranormal at the historic Cohen Bray House.

20. Research facilities or archives at the site: none.

21. Type of gift shop and what is for sale: there are some greeting cards created by Emmelita Cohen herself, and a book about historic homes in the Bay Area.

1. Colma Historical Society

2. Location: 1500 Hillside Blvd. Colma, CA. 94014.

3. Website: http://www.colmahistory.org/

4. Phone number: (650) 757-1676.

5. E-mail: colmahist@sbcglobal.net

6. Hours of operation: Tuesday to Sunday 10:00a.m. to 3:00p.m. Closed Mondays and holidays.

7. Cost: free.

8. Permanent Exhibits: Ohlone Indians, immigrant groups in Colma, an early twentieth century kitchen, cemetery room, funerary items, world wars, business

47

machines, police and fire departments. A railroad station dating to 1863 fully stocked with tickets, maps, schedules, and railroad equipment; a blacksmith shop; a freight station with baggage, scales, a model of the city and train station; and information about local business.

9. Special Exhibits: Rotating displays with such themes as Father's Day, boxing and the 90th anniversary of the city. WWI and WWII displays, typewriters, and Victorian hair artwork.

10. Historical era that is featured the best: 1800s-1900s.

11. Targeted age groups: all ages.

12. Special activities for children: school tours.

13. Guided tours: guided tours of all four buildings. Cemetery tours are available on Tuesdays-Sundays with reservations.

14. Hands-on activities: this is a hands-on, please touch museum.

15. The best-kept secrets at the museum: one of the oldest railroad stations in California. The museum also has Ohlone Indian arrowheads, a portable stretcher for burials dating to 1886, an unmarked monument dug up by BART when they were building tracks through Colma, and many other fascinating items.

16. Hidden treasures at the museum: information about the curious burial of Wyatt Earp of Shootout at the OK Corral fame. His wife wanted him to be buried in the Jewish cemetery because she was Jewish. Her father said the only way he would allow him to be buried there was if he were cremated. Vandals have stolen the tombstone twice, but a third one now marks the grave.

17. What is unique about the museum that can't be found anywhere else: it has tons of information about local cemeteries and the famous people who are buried in them, such as Levi Strauss, Joe DiMaggio, Emperor Norton, William Randolph Hearst, and Governor Pat Brown. Colma is known as the "City of Souls" because it has over one and a half million residents under ground and only about one thousand five hundred above ground!

18. The most important things about local, state, or American history that can be learned at the museum: San Francisco passed an ordinance in 1900 stating that there would be no more cemeteries allowed in San Francisco. Bodies were dug up and headstones moved out of town because of high land values, vandalism and health risks. Colma was the only place near the city with enough open land to accommodate them, especially after the numerous deaths in the 1906 earthquake. There are cemeteries for many different nationalities and even one for pets.

19. Annual events held at the site or elsewhere in the community: Victorian Day Walk, Tea of Many Themes, garage sale, and an Annual Fundraising Dinner.

20. Research facilities or archives at the site: there is a small research library available to patrons during regular hours or by appointment. It contains local and county books and school yearbooks. Copies of documents made upon request.

21. Type of gift shop and what is for sale: local history books, t-shirts, caps, tapes, and other gift items. Free brochures on local history.

1. **Computer History Museum-Mountain View**
2. Location: 1401 N. Shoreline Blvd. Mountain View, CA. 94043.
3. Website: http://www.computerhistory.org/.

48

4. Phone number: (650) 810-1010.

5. E-mail: Use the online contact form.

6. Hours of operation: Wednesday-Sunday: 10-5.

7. Cost: $15, children under 12 are free.

8. Permanent Exhibits: the Computer History Museum offers a wide variety of information, exhibits, research, and a rich library of multimedia content garnered from some of the most influential people of the computing era.

9. Special Exhibits: Rotating special exhibits (see website for details).

10. Historical era that is featured the best: 20th century-present.

11. Targeted age groups: all ages.

12. Special activities for children: school programs for all ages, workshops, and field trip materials for educators.

13. Guided tours: self-guided tours are available for groups of 10 or more by making a reservation at least 10 days prior to arrival. Docent–led tours are available for groups of 10 or more by making a reservation at least 45 days prior to arrival.

14. Hands-on activities: in keeping with the tech-oriented theme of the museum, there are many interactive displays.

15. The best-kept secrets at the museum: there are early progenitors to the modern computer going back to the 1700s.

16. Hidden treasures at the museum: The first coin-operated video game, calculators and countless computers of every kind, including rare Russian models.

17. What is unique about the museum that can't be found anywhere else: it is one of the largest computer museums in the world. It is located in Silicon Valley where so many important innovations were developed.

18. The most important things about local, state, or American history that can be learned at the museum: the computer has changed the world in many ways. No other museum does a better job of documenting this than this one.

19. Annual events held at the site or elsewhere in the community: guest speakers on computer history and innovations, awards, and other special events (see website for details).

20. Research facilities or archives at the site: Catalog Search is a powerful resource for researchers, students, and history enthusiasts. The museum's collection encompasses hardware, ephemera, photographs, moving images, software, and documents of computer history. Oral histories, and articles related to computers are also available.

21. Type of gift shop and what is for sale: computer-related items including, books, t-shirts, mugs, videos, scientific toys, etc.

1. **Contra Costa County History Center** (maintained by the Contra Costa County Historical Society)

2. Location: 724 Escobar Street, Martinez, CA. 94553-1114.

3. Website: http://www.cocohistory.com/

4. Phone number: (925) 229-1042.

5. E-mail: info@cocohistory.com

6. Hours of operation: Tuesdays 9:00 a.m. to 4:00 p.m., Wednesdays 9:00 a.m. to

4:00 p.m., Thursdays 9:00 a.m. to 4:00 p.m. In addition, the History Center is open on the third Saturday of each month from 10:00 a.m. to 2:00 p.m.

7. Cost: free.

8. Permanent Exhibits: a permanent exhibit recently mounted features the contents of the History Center's archives. A small lobby display on Contra Costa County history contains Native American items, the Spanish-Mexican period, the Gold Rush, farmers and ranchers, oil industry and the Port Chicago explosion in WWII. Archives include a map room, court records, genealogy, tax records, extensive clippings files, periodicals, and more.

9. Special Exhibits: vary from time to time

10. Historical era that is featured the best: 1800-1940s.

11. Targeted age groups: all ages.

12. Special activities for children: none.

13. Guided tours: on request.

14. Hands-on activities: Public Access Computer Terminal (PACT) gives access to indexes, oldest newspapers (1880s), and photos by town.

15. The best-kept secrets at the museum: an extensive collection on the family of Sheriff Veale, county sheriff for 40 years (1879-1939).

16. Hidden treasures at the archives: family history resources and maps.

17. What is unique about the archives that can't be found anywhere else: a large collection of records related to county history.

18. The most important things about local, state, or American history that can be learned at the museum: research opportunities on the history of the county and the State of California

19. Annual events held at the site or elsewhere in the community: none at this time.

20. Research facilities or archives at the site: this is the primary function of the site.

21. Type of gift shop and what is for sale: a good–sized bookstore with many gifts and books related to Contra Costa County history.

22. Additional information: The Society maintains a very large number of unique historical records documenting the county's history from the 1800s onward.

1. **Cowell Lime Works Historic District- Santa Cruz**

2. Location: UC Santa Cruz, 1156 High Street, Santa Cruz, CA. 95064.

3. Website: http://limeworks.ucsc.edu/

50

4. Phone number: (831) 459-1254.

5. E-mail: none.

6. Hours of operation: daylight hours.

7. Cost: daily parking permit ($6.00).

8. Permanent Exhibits: the District includes four limekilns, the cooperage (where barrels were made), the hay barn, cookhouse, lime worker cabins, the Cardiff house, and many other historic structures.

9. Special Exhibits: none.

10. Historical era that is featured the best: 1850s-1920s.

11. Targeted age groups: all ages.

12. Special activities for children: none.

13. Guided tours: self-guided walking tour. A brochure can be downloaded from the website.

14. Hands-on activities: you may download a kit from the website to make a paper model of historic Cabin B.

15. The best-kept secrets at the museum: equipment used for cutting trees, firing the furnaces, and storing the lime for shipment.

16. Hidden treasures at the museum: Tithe kilns themselves are quite an impressive sight.

17. What is unique about the museum that can't be found anywhere else: it is on the UC Santa Cruz campus. Some of the buildings are still used by the university.

18. The most important things about local, state, or American history that can be learned at the museum: The firm of Davis and Jordan began making lime there in 1853. Within a few years, they became the largest lime manufacturer in California and were a major supplier of lime to San Francisco after the Gold Rush.

19. Annual events held at the site or elsewhere in the community: Restoration projects, archeological digs, etc. (see website for details).

20. Research facilities or archives at the site: none.

21. Type of gift shop: none.

1. **Coyote Hills Regional Park- Fremont**

2. Location: 8000 Patterson Ranch Road, Fremont, CA. 94555.

3. Website: http://www.ebparks.org/parks/coyote_hills

4. Phone number: 888-EBPARKS (888) 327-2757, option 3, extension 4519.

5. E-mail: use the contact form on the website.

6. Hours of operation: Wed. - Sun. 10 a.m. - 4p.m. Closed on Thanksgiving and Christmas Day.

7. Cost: Parking fee of $5 per vehicle; $4 per trailered vehicle. Buses: $25/per bus.

8. Permanent Exhibits: Visitor's Center, Coyote Hills Visitor Center contains educational displays and exhibits, as well as the Possum's Pocket Nature Store. The exhibits portray the Ohlone way of life, and include a tule reed boat constructed by park staff and volunteers using Native American methods. Other exhibits cover the park's natural history and wildlife. Trails lead to a recreated historic Ohlone village and salt marshes.

9. Special Exhibits: none.

10. Historical era that is featured the best: prehistoric times-the present.

11. Targeted age groups: all ages.

12. Special activities for children: school tours, camps, etc.

13. Guided tours: naturalist guided tours and group tours available.

14. Hands-on activities: none.

15. The best-kept secrets at the museum: the shell mounds in the area were used by the Native Americans for thousands of years.

16. Hidden treasures at the museum: there are many interesting Indian artifacts in the visitor's center.

17. What is unique about the museum that can't be found anywhere else: there is a fine mural of an Ohlone village.

18. The most important things about local, state, or American history that can be learned at the museum: this is one of the best-preserved Ohlone sites.

19. Annual events held at the site or elsewhere in the community: the annual Ohlone Tribal Gathering is not to be missed. There are many interesting hands-on activities, guest speakers, dancers, and native crafts.

20. Research facilities or archives at the site: none.

21. Type of gift shop and what is for sale: there are some historical books and nature related items in this well-stocked bookstore.

1. **Crockett Historical Society and Museum**

2. Location: 900 Loring Avenue, Crockett, CA. 94525.

3. Website: http://crockettmuseum.org/

4. Phone number: (510) 787-2178.

5. E-mail: use the contact form on the website.

6. Hours of operation: Wednesdays and Saturdays to the public, from 10a.m. – 3p.m.

7. Cost: free.

8. Permanent Exhibits: military items, local sports, the town founders, the building of the Benicia Bridge, telephones and communication, toys and games, hardware store, and the C & H Sugar Company.

9. Special Exhibits: local veterans and celebrities.

10. Historical era that is featured the best: 1800s-present.

11. Targeted age groups: all ages.

12. Special activities for children: none.

13. Guided tours: none.

14. Hands-on activities: none.

15. The best-kept secrets at the museum: if you look around hard enough you can see relics from every war going back to the Civil War.

16. Hidden treasures at the museum: the museum has a wide variety of items from interesting antiques to campy hunting trophies.

17. What is unique about the museum that can't be found anywhere else: they have everything including the kitchen sink here, so you have to take your time to see it all. It's easy to miss some of the treasures in the clutter.

18. The most important things about local, state, or American history that can be learned at the museum: The museum is built in the former train station, so you will hear trains going by the whole time you are there. It is also very near the Benicia Bridge, so naturally transportation is a major theme of the museum. The museum is in the shadow of the giant C & H sugar refinery, so the huge impact that the sugar industry had on the development of California and Hawaii is well documented.

19. Annual events held at the site or elsewhere in the community: see website for details.

20. Research facilities or archives at the site: the historical society has documents and photographs available for researchers by appointment.

21. Type of gift shop and what is for sale: local history books, t-shirts, and other gift items.

1. **Cupertino Historical Society & Museum**
2. Location: Quinlan Community Center, 10185 N. Stelling Road, Cupertino, CA. 95014.
3. Website: http://www.cupertinohistoricalsociety.org/
4. Phone number: (408) 973-1495.
5. E-mail: cuphistsociety@sbcglobal.net
6. Hours of operation: Wednesday through Saturday from 10 a.m.–4 p.m. depending on the availability of museum volunteers. Please call (408) 973-1495 to make sure the museum is open.
7. Cost: Admission is free.
8. Permanent Exhibits: the de Anza expedition, Spanish and Mexican settlers, founders such as Stephens and Doyle, a Japanese family orchard, the Montgomery house, and a general store display.
9. Special Exhibits: there are rotating exhibits throughout the year.
10. Historical era that is featured the best: 1800s-1900s.
11. Targeted age groups: all ages.
12. Special activities for children: traveling trunks that go to schools.
13. Guided tours: available upon request.
14. Hands-on activities: none.
15. The best-kept secrets at the museum: the general store display is the best. Hundreds of antique items are on display.
16. Hidden treasures at the museum: the museum has over 3000 artifacts, but only a tiny fraction of them are display at one time. Exhibits change often.
17. What is unique about the museum that can't be found anywhere else: it is housed in the community center in a beautiful modern building.
18. The most important things about local, state, or American history that can be learned at the museum: Cupertino has seen many changes over time as it grew from an orchard area to the center of Silicon Valley electronics.
19. Annual events held at the site or elsewhere in the community: guest speakers and other events (see website for details).
20. Research facilities or archives at the site: a small research library is on site.
21. Type of gift shop and what is for sale: a small gift shop sells books, blanket, t-shirts, etc.

1. **Daly City History Museum**
2. Location: 6351 Mission Street, Daly City, CA. 94014.
3. Website: www.dalycityhistorymuseum.org
4. Phone number: (650) 757-7177.
5. E-mail: info@dalycityhistorymuseum.org
6. Hours of operation: Tuesdays and Saturdays from noon to 3 p.m., and by special appointment.
7. Cost: free.
8. Permanent Exhibits: a framed and captioned photo gallery of historic images of Daly City, the Fire Department collection including the 1907 hand-pulled chemical cart, a timeline exhibit "A Walk Through Time" featuring 12,000 years of local history with photos and images.

9. Special Exhibits: Coming soon.

10. Historical era that is featured the best: 1900s to the present.

11. Targeted age groups: all ages.

12. Special activities for children: none.

13. Guided tours: the volunteer staff is available to lead tours, including showing a historical documentary film, during our public open hours and by special appointment.

14. Hands-on activities: none.

15. The best-kept secrets at the museum: when San Francisco began banning boxing, gambling, etc., the outlawed activities that were known in the wild days of the San Francisco Barbary Coast just moved south over the San Mateo County border to the area that became Daly City. Daly City had a very colorful history long before it became a suburban bedroom community for San Francisco.

16. Hidden treasures at the museum: The area and thus its history has some interesting stories to tell about boxing in the early 1900s, the "wet" side of prohibition in the 1920s and 1930s, and one of the most famous post-war suburban developments in the nation, Westlake. The story of Daly City is a unique example of a town that has experienced enormous change physically and culturally.

17. What is unique about the museum that can't be found anywhere else: It has the most complete information available on the famous Broderick-Terry duel, which was an important showdown over whether California would enter the Union as a free or slave-owning state.

18. The most important things about local, state, or American history that can be learned at the museum: Starting with the Spanish road to the Presidio and Mission Dolores that passed through the area that became Daly City, the San Francisco Earthquake and fire that resulted in the area becoming settled by refugees soon after created Daly City, to post-war suburban culture and rapid foreign immigration, Daly City is an example of how a place is connected to the larger stage of history. Daly City was a small, closely-knit agricultural community before World War II. Rapid post-war suburban and freeway development radically changed the area in a short amount of time. Later, beginning in the 1960s, new federal immigration laws brought an influx of immigration, primarily from the Philippines. Outside of Honolulu, Daly City is now the largest city in the United States with a majority Asian population and over 53% of the population is foreign born.

19. Annual events held at the site or elsewhere in the community: five times a year there is a free general meeting open to the public featuring a history lecture and social time with refreshments at the Doelger Senior Center where there is ample free parking. There are also occasional walking tours or special events such as a historical re-enactment of the Broderick-Terry duel.

20. Research facilities or archives at the site: an archive of news clippings, first-person historical accounts, photos and other documents are available to researchers.

21. Type of gift shop and what is for sale: books on local history, documentary CDs, and a small assortment of collectibles.

128

1. **Davenport Jail Museum**
2. Location: 2 Davenport Avenue, Davenport, CA. 95017.
3. Website: http://www.santacruzmah.org/our-exhibition-philosophy/historic-sites/
4. Phone number: (831) 429-1964.
5. E-mail: none.
6. Hours of operation: 11 a.m.- 4 p.m. on the 1st Sunday of every month in the summer season.
7. Cost: free.
8. Permanent Exhibits: aspects of the North Coast history such as native settlements, the natural environment, major industries, early families, and community life.
9. Special Exhibits: none.
10. Historical era that is featured the best: early 1900s.
11. Targeted age groups: all ages.
12. Special activities for children: none.
13. Guided tours: none.
14. Hands-on activities: none.
15. The best-kept secrets at the museum: you can pretend you have been locked up in one of the cells!
16. Hidden treasures at the museum: historic photos and relics from the communities past.
17. What is unique about the museum that can't be found anywhere else: Built in 1914, this two-cell county jail was used only once before being abandoned in 1936.
18. The most important things about local, state, or American history that can be learned at the museum: The rural, coastal lifestyle of the region is highlighted. Even though it is near many large population centers, the area has a small town atmosphere. Logging, farming, cement, whaling, and other industries contributed to the region's development.
19. Annual events held at the site or elsewhere in the community: none.
20. Research facilities or archives at the site: none.
21. Type of gift shop and what is for sale: local history books and other gift items.
22. Additional information: The museum is administered by the Santa Cruz Museum of Art & History at the McPherson Center on 705 Front Street, Santa Cruz, CA 95060 (831) 429-1964. Contact them for any information regarding special events, etc.

1. **Deer Hollow Farm- Cupertino**
2. Location: Rancho San Antonio County Park, Rancho San Antonio,   22500 Cristo Rey Drive, Cupertino, CA. 95014.
3. Websites:
http://www.sccgov.org/sites/parks/parkfinder/Pages/RanchoSanAntonio.aspx and
http://www.mountainview.gov/city_hall/comm_services/recreation_programs_and_services/deer_hollow_farm.asp or http://www.fodhf.org/
4. Phone number: (650) 903-6430 or (650) 691-1200.
5. E-mail: parkinfo@prk.sccgov.org

6. Hours of operation: open year round   8:00 a.m. – sunset. Deer Hollow Farm is closed on Mondays.

7. Cost: free. Seasonal parking rates may be charged.

8. Permanent Exhibits: the 150 year-old farm is an educational center where the public, school classes, and community groups can observe and participate in a historic working farm. In the tradition of a working homestead, the farm produces food on-site, such as fresh eggs and seasonal orchard produce, which are for sale when available. Nearby is a replica Ohlone Village.

9. Special Exhibits: none.

10. Historical era that is featured the best: 1800s.

11. Targeted age groups: all ages.

12. Special activities for children: nearly 5,500 elementary students (K-5th grade) participate in the farm's environmental education program each school year. Volunteer teaching docents lead small groups of students through the farm and garden, the surrounding wilderness preserve, and a replica Ohlone Village.

13. Guided tours: only on special event days.

14. Hands-on activities: the farm animals are very friendly.

15. The best-kept secrets at the museum: the Ohlone village replica is a bit off the main path, so you have to hunt for it. Get a park map and watch for small signage.

16. Hidden treasures at the museum: the historic farm buildings are original.

17. What is unique about the museum that can't be found anywhere else: it is a working farm within minutes of the city.

18. The most important things about local, state, or American history that can be learned at the museum: the valley's lost farm heritage can be appreciated. Ohlone Indian use of the area is interpreted.

19. Annual events held at the site or elsewhere in the community: a variety of environmental and agricultural education programs are conducted here throughout the year.

20. Research facilities or archives at the site: none.

21. Type of gift shop: none.

1. **Depot Park Museum-Sonoma**

2. Location: 270 1st Street West, Sonoma, CA. 95476.

3. Website: http://depotparkmuseum.org/

4. Phone number: (707) 938-1762.

5. E-mail: depotparkmuseum@comcast.net

6. Hours of operation: Fri. - Sun. 1-4 p.m.

7. Cost: free.

8. Permanent Exhibits: Railroads, Pomo Indians, Victorian Kitchen, the Vallejo Family, Raising of the Bear Flag, One Room School House, The Pianoforte, Union Hall Stage "Drop Curtain", and Early Business around the Plaza.

9. Special Exhibits: Rotating exhibits such as the Women of Sonoma. There is also a railroad caboose behind the museum.

10. Historical era that is featured the best: 1800s-1900s.

11. Targeted age groups: all ages.

57

12. Special activities for children: school tours, which include a visit inside the caboose. Summer camps such as the Mapping Sonoma Surveying Camp and Archaeology Camp are offered.

13. Guided tours: Available upon request.

14. Hands-on activities: there is a costume area and a few other "please touch" items.

15. The best-kept secrets at the museum: Pomo Indian arrowheads, baskets, etc.

16. Hidden treasures at the museum: railroad items, personal effects of the Vallejo family, and a pair of boots made from grizzly bear feet reportedly worn by U.S. Grant.

17. What is unique about the museum that can't be found anywhere else: it is in an old rail depot.

18. The most important things about local, state, or American history that can be learned at the museum: it has a broad cross section of Sonoma Valley history. Sonoma was the northernmost Spanish settlement. It was built to halt the expansion of Russia into Northern California. Important events took place in the mission and the plaza, such as the Bear Flag Revolt. The importance of railroads and local agriculture is highlighted at the museum as well.

19. Annual events held at the site or elsewhere in the community: guest speakers and other events (see website for details).

20. Research facilities or archives at the site: there are some local history books and records available for researches upon request.

21. Type of gift shop and what is for sale: a CD of music from the turn-of-the-century music box, railroad items, local history books, jewelry, and other gift items.

1. **The deSaisset Museum at Santa Clara University**

2. Location: 500 El Camino Real Santa Clara, CA. 95053.

3. Website: http://www.scu.edu/deSaisset/

4. Phone number: (408) 554-4528.

5. E-mail: deSaissetMuseum@scu.edu

6. Hours of operation: Tuesday-Sunday 11 a.m. - 4 p.m.

7. Cost: free.

58

8. Permanent Exhibits: history collections including many items from the Santa Clara Mission, Ohlone Indians, Spanish, Mexican, and American settlers and the history of the university. There is also a sizeable art collection.

9. Special Exhibits: Rotating exhibits.

10. Historical era that is featured the best: 1700s-1920s.

11. Targeted age groups: all ages.

12. Special activities for children: 4th grade California history tours, a teacher's curriculum guide, and Classroom Connection programs.

13. Guided tours: available for groups with a reservation.

14. Hands-on activities: the free ibook *Moving Forward: Santa Clara's Story of Transformation* can be downloaded at the itunes store.

15. The best-kept secrets at the museum: a nearly full-sized replica of an Ohlone dwelling.

16. Hidden treasures at the museum: many priceless treasures from the mission such as vestments, relics, and the cornerstone from the third mission building on the site.

17. What is unique about the museum that can't be found anywhere else: it is a much larger collection than most mission museums. The collection is well maintained and the items are clearly identified. It is the only mission that still has an active university around it.

18. The most important things about local, state, or American history that can be learned at the museum: the mission is the nucleus of Santa Clara Valley. All further Spanish, Mexican and American development radiated from there.

19. Annual events held at the site or elsewhere in the community: Members' Reception, Exhibit Reception, College Night, guest lectures, etc. (see website for details).

20. Research facilities or archives at the site: research is primarily done through the university. Contact the museum for details.

21. Type of gift shop and what is for sale: none.

1. de Young Museum- San Francisco

2. Location: Golden Gate Park, 50 Hagiwara Tea Garden Drive, San Francisco, CA. 94118.

3. Website: http://deyoungmuseum.org/

4. Phone number: (415) 750-3600.

5. E-mail: use the contact form on the website.

6. Hours of operation: Tuesdays through Sundays: 9:30 a.m. to 5:15 p.m. Open for extended hours on Fridays from March –November: 9:30 a.m. to 8:45 p.m.

7. Cost: General admission: Adults: $10, Seniors 65+$7, Youths 13–17 and College students: $6, Children 12 and under: Free. Free on the first Tuesday of the month.

8. Permanent Exhibits: American painting, sculpture, and decorative arts from the 17th to the 21st centuries; art from Africa, Oceania, and the Americas; costume and textile arts; and international modern and contemporary art.

9. Special Exhibits: Rotating exhibits (see website for details).

10. Historical era that is featured the best: ancient times to the present.

11. Targeted age groups: all ages.

12. Special activities for children: Summer Art Camp, school programs, art classes and educator materials.

13. Guided tours: audio tours available. Regularly scheduled docent tours are available Tuesdays through Sundays. Tours are free with museum admission, with no reservations required.

14. Hands-on activities: sometimes available with special exhibits such as interactive elements for mobile devices.

15. The best-kept secrets at the museum: there are thousands of fascinating objects that are constantly rotated.

16. Hidden treasures at the museum: there are many priceless objects that can be seen nowhere else.

17. What is unique about the museum that can't be found anywhere else: it has a large selection of non-European art. The size and quality of its collection make it one of the best museums on the West Coast.

18. The most important things about local, state, or American history that can be learned at the museum: there is a large collection of American paintings, graphic and decorative art. The scope of American art can be seen here better than almost any other Californian museum.

19. Annual events held at the site or elsewhere in the community: there are many different events held at the museum year round (see website for details).

20. Research facilities or archives at the site: none.

21. Type of gift shop and what is for sale: a state of the art gift shop contains many interesting items at every price level from common souvenirs to fine art.

1. **The Duarte Garage & Lincoln Highway Museum-Livermore**
2. Location: Portola Ave. at L St. in Livermore, CA. 94551.
3. Website: http://www.livermorehistory.com/Duarte%20Garage /Duarte%20Garage.html
4. Phone number: (925) 449-9927.
5. E-mail: jkaskey@yahoo.com
6. Hours of operation: 3rd Sunday of each month, 10 a.m.-2 p.m.
7. Cost: free.
8. Permanent Exhibits: Antique Livermore fire engines, highway garage workshop, signage, oilcans, gas pumps and repair equipment.
9. Special Exhibits: an authentic Lincoln Highway marker, and a temporary exhibit on local one-room schools.
10. Historical era that is featured the best: 1915-1930s.
11. Targeted age groups: all ages.
12. Special activities for children: none.
13. Guided tours: none, but docents are on hand to explain the site, and if you have a group (scouts, car clubs, etc.), the museum can arrange to open the garage on other days.
14. Hands-on activities: kids of all ages enjoy sitting and having their picture taken in one of the restored fire trucks.
15. The best-kept secrets at the museum: historic photographs and car collectables.
16. Hidden treasures at the museum: antique Coke sign, the grease pit, and 1920 Seagrave fire engine with amazing hand-work on the restored gold leaf.
17. What is unique about the museum that can't be found anywhere else: the garage was built on the original Lincoln Highway, the first transcontinental U.S. Highway. It was also a car dealership.
18. The most important things about local, state, or American history that can be learned at the museum: this was the age when cars were becoming more commonplace and began to replace earlier forms of transportation.
19. Annual events held at the site or elsewhere in the community: The Annual Heritage Guild Dinner and Auction, and various car club events.
20. Research facilities or archives at the site: none.

60

21. Type of gift shop and what is for sale: Lincoln Highway t-shirts, hats, and other pieces are for sale.
22. Additional information: check the website for times when the museum is closed.

1. **Dublin Heritage Park & Museums**
2. Location: 6600 Donlon Way, Dublin, CA. 94568.
3. Website: http://dublinca.gov/index.aspx?NID=269
4. Phone number: (925) 452-2100.
5. E-mail: elizabeth.isles@dublin.ca.gov for museum matters and stephanie.mein@dublin.ca.gov for rental, tour and business matters.
6. Hours of operation: Wednesday – Sunday 1:00 p.m. - 4:00 p.m.
7. Cost: free during hours of operation.
8. Permanent Exhibits: a ten-acre park with historic buildings, lawns, an historic cemetery, and picnic areas. The park is open to the public during daylight hours. There are two museums on site: the Murray Schoolhouse, which houses a permanent exhibit on Dublin's history; and the Kolb House, an historic house museum.
9. Special Exhibits: the "Little Classroom Gallery" regularly hosts local history exhibits.
10. Historical era that is featured the best: 1850s-1950.
11. Targeted age groups: all ages.
12. Special activities for children: the cemetery has a lively scavenger hunt. The Heritage Park is home to a variety of classes, camps, events, and tours. There is a gold panning rig for hands-on fun and a vintage tractor for wagon rides. There is a play area behind the Sunday School Barn with a play kitchen and checker and chess tables. Within the Murray Schoolhouse Museum is a little pioneer playhouse for young children to pretend that they are living on the frontier.
13. Guided tours: available upon request. Group tours are $3.50 -$5.00.
14. Hands-on activities: some of the displays have hands-on elements.
15. The best-kept secrets at the museum: the museum is formed around the primary source account of one of Dublin's early settlers.
16. Hidden treasures at the museum: most of the items in The Kolb house belonged to the family and are in their original placement as the family used them.
17. What is unique about the museum that can't be found anywhere else: it has colorful and modern displays. It is very appealing to children.
18. The most important things about local, state, or American history that can be learned at the museum: Dublin was first settled by Irish immigrants in 1846 and a second wave from Denmark and Germany in the late 1800's. Dublin remained an agricultural town with just a school, church, two hotels, blacksmith and general store through the 1950s. Beginning in 1960, Dublin grew from just a couple of hundred residents to several thousand. It's population has now grown to 50,000.
19. Annual events held at the site or elsewhere in the community: The Harvest Faire in October, Holiday Tea in December, and The Spring Faire in May. Call for information

20. Research facilities or archives at the site: there is an archive of local history that is accessible only staff and specialized volunteers. Assistance for researchers is available by calling (925) 452-2100.

21. Type of gift shop and what is for sale: a few books and souvenirs are available at the museum.

1. Dunsmuir Hellman Historic Estate- Oakland

2. Location: 2960 Peralta Oaks Court, Oakland, CA. 94605.

3. Website: http://dunsmuir-hellman.com/

4. Phone number: (510) 615-5555.

5. E-mail: DCooper@oaklandnet.com

6. Hours of operation: the estate grounds are open to the public Tuesdays thru Fridays 10 a.m. to 4p.m. Mansion tours are only available April thru September on Wednesdays at 11a.m.

7. Cost: Adults $5, Seniors $4, Children $4.

8. Permanent Exhibits: the Dunsmuir House was built by Alexander Dunsmuir, who came to the Bay Area in 1878. The son of Robert Dunsmuir, a wealthy coal baron from Victoria, British Columbia, Alexander oversaw the family business in San Francisco. In 1906, the estate was purchased by I.W. Hellman Jr., who worked for Wells Fargo Bank in San Francisco, as a summer home for his family. There are many bedrooms, a parlour, game room, dining room, kitchen, laundry room, etc., to visit. All are elegantly furnished.

9. Special Exhibits: none.

10. Historical era that is featured the best: late 1800s to early 1900s.

11. Targeted age groups: all ages.

12. Special activities for children: only during special events.

13. Guided tours: all tours are guided by docents. Purchase tickets at the smaller house near the entrance at least 15 minutes before the tour.

14. Hands-on activities: none.

15. The best-kept secrets at the museum: former domestic members at the house offered their insights into how the house was decorated and operated. Historic photographs have been used to guide restoration.

16. Hidden treasures at the museum: the rooms have been lovingly decorated to look as if the families still live there. Many of their original possessions and furnishings have been restored to the home.

17. What is unique about the museum that can't be found anywhere else: this is one of the largest historic mansions in the Bay Area. The extensive gardens and grounds have also been preserved. It has been featured in numerous films and TV shows.

18. The most important things about local, state, or American history that can be learned at the museum: this house is a fine example of the architecture of the times. It was owned by wealthy capitalists who had an important role in the development of the Bay Area.

19. Annual events held at the site or elsewhere in the community: Great Egg Hunt, Mother's Day High Tea, Dads and Jazz, A Holiday Tradition, and other events (see website for details).

20. Research facilities or archives at the site: none.

21. Type of gift shop and what is for sale: a large collection of gift items. The Christmas tree decorations are especially nice.
22. Additional information: The house is a popular site for weddings and other events.

1. East Contra Costa Historical Society Museum- Brentwood

2. Location: 3890 Sellers Ave. Brentwood, CA. 94513.
3. Website: http://www.eastcontracostahistory.org/
4. Phone number: (925) 516-7484.
5. E-mail: see the contact page on the website.
6. Hours of operation: 2:00 p.m. - 4:00 p.m., every Saturday & every third Sunday of the month from April - October.
7. Cost: free.
8. Permanent Exhibits: a parlor, children's room, men's room, women's room, kitchen, the office, and farm equipment.
9. Special Exhibits: Exhibit on John Marsh.
10. Historical era that is featured the best: 1800s-1900s.
11. Targeted age groups: all ages.
12. Special activities for children: school tours. A teacher's guide can be downloaded from the website.
13. Guided tours: docent-led tours available with reservations.
14. Hands-on activities: none.
15. The best-kept secrets at the museum: information about pioneers and founders, law enforcement, schools, farms, historic buildings, photos and maps.
16. Hidden treasures at the museum: antique farm equipment and household items.
17. What is unique about the museum that can't be found anywhere else: Brentwood is one of the easternmost communities in the Bay Area. As such, it serves as a gateway to the Sacramento Delta Region.
18. The most important things about local, state, or American history that can be learned at the museum: the history of the city is intimately tied into the fortunes of the Delta. It is an important transportation hub for the state.
19. Annual events held at the site or elsewhere in the community: Festival of the Trees and other events (see website for details).
20. Research facilities or archives at the site: there are archival resources available to researchers.
21. Type of gift shop: none.

1. Egyptian Museum-San Jose

2. Location: 1660 Park Avenue, San Jose, CA. 95191.
3. Website: http://www.egyptianmuseum.org/
4. Phone number: 408-947-3635.
5. E-mail: use online contact form.
6. Hours of operation: W - F: 9:00a.m. - 5:00p.m., Sun: 10:00a.m. - 6:00p.m.
7. Cost: $9.00 general admission, $7.00 seniors 55 and older, $7.00 students with I.D., $5.00 children ages 5 – 10, free children under 5.

8. Permanent Exhibits: architecturally inspired by the Temple of Amon at Karnak, it houses the largest collection of Egyptian artifacts on exhibit in western North America including objects from pre-dynastic times through Egypt's early Islamic era.

9. Special Exhibits: special rotating exhibits. There is also a planetarium on campus that has regular shows about astronomy and the universe (see website for details).

10. Historical era that is featured the best: ancient times-the Middle Ages.

11. Targeted age groups: all ages.

12. Special activities for children: a Junior Archaeologists program including workshops, guided tomb tours, an artifact quest, a Night in the Afterlife "sleepover"! An educator's curriculum guide is available for fieldtrips.

13. Guided tours: Tomb Tours: Wed. 3:00p.m., Thurs. – Fri. 2:30p.m. Sat. – Sun. 1:30p.m. and 4:30p.m. Go inside of a reproduction of an ancient Egyptian tomb. It is very well decorated and feels like you are in the real thing.

14. Hands-on activities: an MP3 audio tour is now available for download.

15. The best-kept secrets at the museum: some of the larger items are reproductions, but many of the smaller artifacts are genuine.

16. Hidden treasures at the museum: mummies! There are very few other places in California to see real ones.

17. What is unique about the museum that can't be found anywhere else: the grounds contain faithful reproductions of ancient fountains, statuary and temples. The museum's collections are large and well maintained.

18. The most important things about world history that can be learned at the museum: the collections include items from all over the Ancient Near East. It is one of the best places to see these items on the West Coast, particularly if you have a student in the 6th grade who is studying ancient history.

19. Annual events held at the site or elsewhere in the community: see website for details.

20. Research facilities or archives at the site: for Rosicrucian Order members only.

21. Type of gift shop and what is for sale: the gift shop once contained a large variety of fascinating gift items related to Ancient Egypt, but it has been closed temporarily. Political instability in Egypt has made it very difficult to obtain souvenirs from the region, but there a few items for sale at the front desk of the lobby.

1. **Eugene O'Neill National Historic Site- Danville**
2. Location: 1000 Kuss Rd, Danville, CA. 94526.
3. Website: http://www.nps.gov/euon/index.htm
4. Phone number: (925) 838-0249.
5. E-mail: Use the online contact form.
6. Hours of operation: ranger-led guided tours are available by reservation only at either 10 a.m. or 2 p.m. on Wed., Thurs, Fri., and Sundays. On Saturdays reservations are not required for self-guided tours. The Saturday shuttle leaves from 205 Railroad Ave., in front of the Museum of the San Ramon Valley at 10:15 a.m., 12:15 p.m. and 2:15 p.m. on a first-come, first-served basis. Please allow 1¾ hours for your visit.
7. Cost: free.

65

8. Permanent Exhibits: O'Neill's final residence. It combined a Spanish exterior and Chinese interior.

9. Special Exhibits: rotating exhibits.

10. Historical era that is featured the best: 20th century.

11. Targeted age groups: adults.

12. Special activities for children: bird watching and nature trails.

13. Guided tours: See above.

14. Hands-on activities: none.

15. The best-kept secrets at the museum: historic photos and personal effects of the author. O'Neill's private study containing many of his books.

16. Hidden treasures at the museum: antique oriental furnishings and theatrical masks.

17. What is unique about the museum that can't be found anywhere else: it is one of the few sites dedicated to this prolific and influential playwright.

18. The most important things about local, state, or American history that can be learned at the museum: of all the places Eugene O'Neill called home during his restless life, Tao House was the one that held him longest, the refuge where he wrote his last plays. O'Neill's works were an important turning point in the development of modern drama. Some of his most important works were written here.

19. Annual events held at the site or elsewhere in the community: Eugene O'Neill Festival, Playwright Theater, Student Days, and Artist Days (see website for details).

20. Research facilities or archives at the site: none.

21. Type of gift shop and what is for sale: there is a bookstore with works related to O'Neill.

22. Additional information: Eugene O'Neill National Historic Site is only accessible by National Park Service Shuttle. Visitors are not permitted to drive their personal/private vehicles to the site.

1. **Evergreen Valley College Library's Heritage Room- San Jose**

2. Location: Evergreen Valley Community College, 3095 Yerba Buena Rd, San Jose, CA. 95135. In the library on the third floor, room number: LE 304.

3. Website: http://www.evc.edu/library/heritage/index.htm

4. Phone number: call the library's circulation desk at (408) 270-6433 to arrange access to the room.

5. E-mail: evc.circdesk@evc.edu

6. Hours of operation: Monday-Thursday 8a.m.-8p.m., Friday 9-3, Saturday 10-2.

7. Cost: free.

8. Permanent Exhibits: the Heritage Collection includes over 100 copies of photographs from Evergreen history, the village, schools, mining, agriculture, families from the 1800s and early 1900s, and the contributions from Ohlone Indians, Mexican Americans, and others to the area's diverse heritage. Maps, newspaper articles, artwork, and memorabilia are also included in the collection.

9. Special Exhibits: none.

10. Historical era that is featured the best: prehistory-early 1900s.

11. Targeted age groups: adults.

66

12. Special activities for children: none
13. Guided tours: none.
14. Hands-on activities: none.
15. The best-kept secrets at the museum: the local family history records are exceptional.
16. Hidden treasures at the museum: maps and historic photos of the area. Of particular interest is a collection of documents related to the famous fatal flight of John J. Montgomery at Evergreen. Montgomery made some of world's first non-powered flights in his gliders.
17. What is unique about the museum that can't be found anywhere else: it is the best collection of items on the Evergreen Valley available.
18. The most important things about local, state, or American history that can be learned at the museum: the many uses of the valley over time are well documented.
19. Annual events held at the site or elsewhere in the community: none.
20. Research facilities or archives at the site: the site is primarily for research.
21. Type of gift shop: none.
22. Additional information: many of the historic photos are available on the website.

1. **Federal Reserve Bank-San Francisco**
2. Location: 101 Market Street, San Francisco, CA. 94105.
3. Website: http://www.frbsf.org/education/teacher-resources/american-currency-exhibit
4. Phone number: (800) 227-4133, option 2.
5. E-mail: none.
6. Hours of operation: Monday – Friday, 8:00 a.m. – 5:00 p.m.
7. Cost: free.
8. Permanent Exhibits: the American Currency collection has one of the best collections of American forms of money from the beginning of the Republic to today.
9. Special Exhibits: none.
10. Historical era that is featured the best: 1770s-today.
11. Targeted age groups: not recommended for young children. This facility will be appreciated best by middle school students and up. Ideal for high school business, economics, or U.S. History classes.
12. Special activities for children: online simulations and bank tours. Many free educational products are available.
13. Guided tours: available with reservations. See the website for special requirements.
14. Hands-on activities: there are some interactive displays in the lobby area.
15. The best-kept secrets at the museum: there are elaborate security measures to get into the bank. The sight of millions of dollars being cleaned, sorted, and either destroyed or reshipped is a once-in-a-lifetime experience!
16. Hidden treasures at the museum: many of the currency items on display are very rare or one of a kind.
17. What is unique about the museum that can't be found anywhere else: where else can you see this much money in one place? Displays explain how money is made and how it is distributed by the Federal Reserve.

 67

18. The most important things about local, state, or American history that can be learned at the museum: the unique role of the Fed in banking and many other areas of our economy is well-documented.

19. Annual events held at the site or elsewhere in the community: there are many financial information seminars and other activities for adults offered for free (see website for details).

20. Research facilities or archives at the site: economic articles are published by The Fed in its various publications.

21. Type of gift shop and what is for sale: shredded money and other fun, money-related souvenirs.

22. Additional information: It can be tough to get in during school months, but group tours are much easier to arrange during summer months.

1. **Filoli-Woodside**

2. Location: 86 Cañada Road, Woodside, CA. 94062.

3. Website: http://www.filoli.org/

4. Phone number: (650) 364-8300, ext. 507.

5. E-mail: visitorservices@filoli.org

6. Hours of operation: Tuesday - Saturday: 10:00 a.m.–3:30 p.m. (last admission 2:30 p.m.) Sunday: 11:00 am–3:30 pm (last admission 2:30 pm).

7. Cost: Adults $20 / Seniors $17 (65 years and older) / Students $10 / Children 4 years and younger are free / K–12 educators with employee ID from adjoining counties (San Francisco, Contra Costa, San Mateo, Santa Clara and Alameda) and National Trust for Historic Preservation members $10.

8. Permanent Exhibits: Recognized as one of the finest remaining country estates of the early 20th century, Filoli welcomes the public to this remarkable 654–acre property, including the 36,000 square foot Georgian country house and spectacular 16–acre English Renaissance garden.

9. Special Exhibits: none.

10. Historical era that is featured the best: early 20th century.

11. Targeted age groups: all ages.

12. Special activities for children: school programs, gardening classes, art discovery, nature hikes, etc. (see website for details).

13. Guided tours: all tours are free with the price of admission. Prepaid advanced reservations are recommended, especially during April and May. House and garden tours and guided nature hikes. Online tours are available.

14. Hands-on activities: classes include hands-on activities.

15. The best-kept secrets at the museum: the historic house was used as a location in dozens of movies.

16. Hidden treasures at the museum: fine artwork and beautiful gardens make this a beautiful outing.

17. What is unique about the museum that can't be found anywhere else: it is one of the best preserved of the Peninsula houses built by wealthy San Franciscans to escape the crowding of the city.

18. The most important things about local, state, or American history that can be learned at the museum: the builder of this estate, William Bowers Bourn II, made his

money from the Empire Mine in Grass Valley, the richest gold mine in California. A later owner, William P. Roth, made his money pioneering shipping lines to Hawaii.

19. Annual events held at the site or elsewhere in the community: flower shows, teas, Fall Festival, concerts, artist access, and many other events (see website for details).

20. Research facilities or archives at the site: none.

21. Type of gift shop and what is for sale: plants, gardening items, refreshments, and souvenirs.

1. Folger Estate Stable Carriage Room Museum- Woodside

2. Location: 4040 Woodside Rd., Woodside, CA. 94062.

3. Website: http://www.huddartwunderlichfriends.org/index.php/the-park/wunderlich-park/folger-stable-history

4. Phone number: (650) 851-2660.

5. E-mail: Friends@HuddartWunderlichFriends.org

6. Hours of operation: the Carriage Room Museum is open every Saturday from 10:00a.m.-4:00p.m.

7. Cost: free.

8. Permanent Exhibits: the main stable building, the carriage house, the stone walls lining the roads on the grounds, the blacksmith barn, and the dairy house.

9. Special Exhibits: the stable building has a fascinating special display on the history of horses.

10. Historical era that is featured the best: 1870s-1950s.

11. Targeted age groups: all ages.

12. Special activities for children: none.

13. Guided tours: docents are available during visiting hours.

14. Hands-on activities: some interactive displays.

15. The best-kept secrets at the museum: the stables are some of the most luxurious I have ever seen. They are not open to the public, but you can peek inside from the Carriage Room Museum.

16. Hidden treasures at the museum: an incredible video of San Francisco one week before the 1906 earthquake. Horses can be seen haphazardly avoiding the pedestrians and newfangled streetcars and automobiles. A week later, many of them would be gone forever.

17. What is unique about the museum that can't be found anywhere else: it details the many owners of the property, including the Folger family, of coffee fame.

18. The most important things about local, state, or American history that can be learned at the museum: it chronicles the history of the area from Ohlone Indian settlements to modern times.

19. Annual events held at the site or elsewhere in the community: equestrian and other park events (see website for details).

20. Research facilities or archives at the site: none.

21. Type of gift shop: none.

1. Forest Home Farms Historic Park-San Ramon

2. Location: 19953 San Ramon Valley Blvd., San Ramon, CA. 94583.

3. Website: http://www.sanramon.ca.gov/Parks/programs/historic.htm and the San Ramon Historic Foundation at: http://www.srhf.org/tours/

4. Phone number: (925) 973-3284.

5. E-mail: parks@sanramon.ca.gov

6. Hours of operation: Tours are typically scheduled for the Second Saturday of each month, from 10a.m. to 2p.m., but other times are available by appointment.
Glass House Tours: 10 a.m., 11 a.m., Noon & 1 p.m. "Fun on the Farm" days on the second Saturday of each month also offer free themed activities appropriate for families.

7. Cost: $5 per person for Glass House tours.

8. Permanent Exhibits: Forest Home Farms Historic Park is a 16-acre park with 21 structures, including 2 historic houses and a Tractor Museum.

9. Special Exhibits: objects belonging to the family that owned this farm are on display in the Welcome Center (in the same building as the gift shop). There is also a film about some of the interesting innovations for the way work was done on the farm that were first tried there.

10. Historical era that is featured the best: mid 1880s-mid 1900s.

11. Targeted age groups: all ages.

12. Special activities for children: "Fun on the Farm" second Saturdays, and group tours by appointment including: All About the Farm, Fun with Farm Animals, Dig in and Grow, and Preschool Fun at the Farm.

13. Guided tours: group tours are offered weekdays, by appointment only. See above for individual tours. Tours of the Glass House Museum can also be scheduled for adults, families or youth groups ages 5 and up.

14. Hands-on activities: many of the farm activities have fun hands-on elements and the school tours include dressing up and other participatory activities.

15. The best-kept secrets at the museum: the Glass House is not made of glass. It is named for the family that built it. It has many exquisite Victorian artifacts.

16. Hidden treasures at the museum: there is a huge amount of tractors in the tractor museum. They are being restored to very fine condition.

17. What is unique about the museum that can't be found anywhere else: there are sheep herding demonstrations, and it has a large number of structures related to agriculture, ranging from a furnished Victorian farm house to an equipment shed housing a large collection of restored antique tractors.

18. The most important things about local, state, or American history that can be learned at the museum: the museum shows how farming changed over time including important improvements and innovations in agriculture, some of which were first tried at this farm.

19. Annual events held at the site or elsewhere in the community: Oktoberfest, Sheep Shearing Day, Holiday on the Farm every December, and other events (see website for details).

20. Research facilities or archives at the site: none.

21. Type of gift shop and what is for sale: books, candy, old-fashioned toys and gifts.

22. Additional information: This is a great place to take children. There are many fun activities on events days like games, contests, food, and farm demonstrations.

1. Forts Baker, Cronkhite, and the Marin Headlands Visitor Center at Fort Barry

2. Location: The Marin Headlands Visitor Center, accessible from the Alexander Ave. exit of Hwy. 101 north. Follow signs for the visitor center--turn left onto Bunker Rd., proceed two miles to Field Rd.

3. Website: http://www.nps.gov/goga/marin-headlands.htm

4. Phone number: (415) 331-1540.

5. E-mail: use the contact form on the website.

6. Hours of operation: the Visitor Center is open daily from 9:30-4:30, closed Thanksgiving and Christmas.

7. Cost: free.

8. Permanent Exhibits: Forts Baker, Barry, and Cronkhite are excellent examples of 20th century coastal defense structures. These lands, located at the southern tip of Marin County, command strategically important positions overlooking the Golden Gate straits. The fortifications constructed here augmented those at the Presidio of San Francisco, to prevent successful passage of hostile ships through the Golden Gate into the San Francisco Bay. During World War II, Fort Baker was designated Mine Command Headquarters, responsible for laying protective minefields across the Golden Gate. Fort Barry's first battery, Battery Mendell (1901-1943), featured two 12-inch breech-loading rifles capable of firing 1,100-pound projectiles over eight miles. Batteries Samuel Rathbone and James McIndoe (1904-1946) defended the minefields outside the Golden Gate during World War II. Many empty gun emplacements are accessible to the public and provide spectacular views of the rugged shoreline. However, Fort Barry's most visited attraction is Nike Missile site SF-88 — the nation's only completely restored Nike launch site. Fort Cronkhite's trademark beachside barracks were completed in 1941, typical of tens of thousands of wartime barracks once found from coast to coast. Battery Townsley (1940-1948) is located just uphill from the barracks, its two massive 16-inch rifles capable of hurling 2,100-pound shells 25 miles out to sea.

9. Special Exhibits: none.

10. Historical era that is featured the best: WWI to WWII.

11. Targeted age groups: all ages.

12. Special activities for children: viewing the abandoned gunnery platforms up close is great fun for kids with good imaginations. The exhibits inside the Visitor Center are kid-friendly as well.

13. Guided tours: rangers answer questions and lead scheduled interpretive walks and programs.

14. Hands-on activities: there is an interactive display on the Miwok at the Visitor's center.

15. The best-kept secrets at the museum: the Nike missile site at Fort Barry is an important Cold War relic.

16. Hidden treasures at the museum: there are all sorts of old military facilities tucked in between the hills and mountains of the Marin Headlands. Driving the winding roads and seeing the surprises is an adventure in itself.

17. What is unique about the museum that can't be found anywhere else: the views of the Pacific Ocean are spectacular.

18. The most important things about local, state, or American history that can be learned at the museum: the important role of coastal defense in the WWII era is best understood by visiting these sites. The visitor's center also has exhibits on the Vaqueros, local dairy farmers, and the 1855 Point Bonita Lighthouse. The story of the planned development called Marincello is also told. Had this actually been built, it would have drastically altered the balance of people versus natural areas in the region.

19. Annual events held at the site or elsewhere in the community: please check the website for upcoming special events: www.nps.gov/goga

20. Research facilities or archives at the site: see the Park Archives building in the Presidio.

21. Type of gift shop and what is for sale: a shop at the visitor's center, which is managed by the Parks Conservancy, carries a good selection of books and field guides about the area.

1. **Fort Point- San Francisco**

2. Location: under the Golden Gate Bridge at the end of Marine Drive on the Presidio of San Francisco.

3. Website: http://www.nps.gov/fopo/index.htm

4. Phone number: (415) 556-1693.

5. E-mail: Use the contact form on the website.

6. Hours of operation: Friday through Sunday -10 a.m. to 5 p.m.

7. Cost: free.

8. Permanent Exhibits: a Civil War era fort built to guard the Golden Gate; Fort Point, Guardian of the Golden Gate - an award-winning 30-minute video program about the history of Fort Point, from 1776 through World War II; Building the Golden Gate Bridge - the construction of this national civil engineering landmark.

9. Special Exhibits: Ready & Forward - Equality for the Buffalo Soldiers was always an issue. These brave men fought for the same beliefs as others did, but usually didn't receive the same kind of respect.

The Lights of Fort Point - Over the centuries, three lighthouses have stood at Fort Point. Learn how sailors depended on these beacons to guide their way into the bay and about the lives of the keepers and their families at this once remote site.

Gatekeepers - Andy Freeberg's photographs capture the bridge's human side with individual portraits of engineers, painters, toll takers, and others responsible for the daily care and safety of the bridge.

Bridging the Golden Gate - This exhibit depicts the men and the processes involved in constructing the bridge, while using Fort Point as the base headquarters.

10. Historical era that is featured the best: 1850s- 1900.

11. Targeted age groups: all ages.

12. Special activities for children: interactive games available at the website. Teacher-led interactive programs at the site include: Sensible Habitats, Point of Inquiry, and Artillery, Bricks & Co.

13. Guided tours: available upon request.

14. Hands-on activities: Cannon Loading Demonstration: Learn how soldiers were taught to load and fire a Napoleon 12-pounder cannon during a Civil War artillery drill. They often ask for volunteers!

15. The best-kept secrets at the museum: The cannons!

16. Hidden treasures at the museum: The fort is under the bridge and often overlooked by visitors.

17. What is unique about the museum that can't be found anywhere else: one of the few West Coast forts that is still intact.

18. The most important things about local, state, or American history that can be learned at the museum: how the defenses for the Bay Area were arranged in the days before aircraft and missiles. The fort played a little-known role in the Civil War.

19. Annual events held at the site or elsewhere in the community: see website for details.

20. Research facilities or archives at the site: none.

21. Type of gift shop and what is for sale: a small bookstore is located inside Fort Point.

1. **Fort Ross**

2. Location: Fort Ross State Historic Park is located on California's Sonoma County Coast, eleven miles north of the town of Jenner on Highway One.

3. Website: http://www.fortross.org/

73

4. Phone number: (707) 847-3437 or (707) 847-3286.

5. E-mail: info@fortross.org

6. Hours of operation: varies with the seasons. Winter days are usually Fridays through Mondays. Summer season has more open days. Please see the website for specific days. Hours are 10a.m.- 4:30p.m.

7. Cost: Gate fee is $8 per car, or $7 with senior. Special events can cost more. See the website: www.fortross.org.

8. Permanent Exhibits: the Rotchev House is an original Russian-era structure and a National Landmark Structure. The fort compound, historic orchard, and Russian cemetery are interesting historic sites. The Fort Ross Visitor Center includes a museum, gift shop, and auditorium. During normal business hours, you can view an 18-minute documentary on the history of Fort Ross. The Call House Museum, an early California ranch era house, is open for guided tours the first weekend of each month from 1 p.m.-4 p.m.

9. Special Exhibits: various displays at the visitor's center.

10. Historical era that is featured the best: 1700s-1800s.

11. Targeted age groups: all ages.

12. Special activities for children: events throughout the year highlighting historic crafts and activities.

13. Guided tours: custom, private tours (in Russian or English) available upon request. Free 1-hour interpretive talks available twice a day on weekends.

14. Hands-on activities: Only during festival days.

15. The best-kept secrets at the museum: the cannons are always a crowd-pleaser.

16. Hidden treasures at the museum: the chapel furnishings are some of the few examples of Russian churches in California.

17. What is unique about the museum that can't be found anywhere else: this is the last and southernmost settlement of the Russian presence in California.

18. The most important things about local, state, or American history that can be learned at the museum: this outpost was critical to supplying Russia's colonies in Alaska. The cultural interaction between the local Indians and the Russians and the settlers brought from Alaska was quite different than any other settlement in California. As a result of this settlement, the Spanish began to make further missions and settlements in Northern California to fortify their claim.

19. Annual events held at the site or elsewhere in the community: Wintersongs Eastern European singing, Harvest Festival, Fort Ross Festival, Fort Ross Seaview Grand Wine Tasting and Luncheon (October); historic windmill turning, nature hikes, and potlucks. See www.fortross.org for details.

20. Research facilities or archives at the site: Fort Ross Conservancy library offers a strong selection of natural and cultural books and archival photographs relating to the Kashaya, Alaska Native, Russian, and American Ranch periods as well as the natural history of the Sonoma Coast. Online digital library is at www.fortross.org/lib.htm.

21. Type of gift shop and what is for sale: The Fort Ross Conservancy gift shop sells a fantastic variety of interpretive items relating to Fort Ross's natural and cultural history. They stock a fine selection of books related to the park, in particular field guides and historical nonfiction, and the children's book section has stories that center around both the Russian and Kashaya people. In addition to specialty books, it carries a wide variety of Fort Ross memorabilia, pre-packaged snacks, bottled water, and sweatshirts.

22. Additional information: see www.fortross.org

1. **The General Joseph Hooker House- Sonoma**

2. Location: 414, 1st St E, Sonoma, CA. 95476.

3. Website: http://sonomaleague.org/historic-hooker-house-sonoma.html

4. Phone number: (707) 938-0169.

5. E-mail: info@sonomaleague.org

6. Hours of operation: Saturdays, Sundays, and Mondays, 1 p.m. - 4 p.m.

7. Cost: free.

8. Permanent Exhibits: a timeline of Joseph Hooker's life and the town of Sonoma, historic photographs and documents.

9. Special Exhibits: Civil War photos and other rotating exhibits such as Sonoma at Work, Transit and Tourism in Sonoma, The History of the Plaza, and The Sonoma Women's Club.

10. Historical era that is featured the best: just before and after the Civil War.

11. Targeted age groups: all ages.

12. Special activities for children: none.

13. Guided tours: self-guided tours.

14. Hands-on activities: the timeline is also available on the website.

15. The best-kept secrets at the museum: a copy of a letter from Abraham Lincoln that gives Hooker command of the Army of the Potomac. It is quick to point out his

weaknesses and warns him not to allow others to criticize their superiors as he had done!

16. Hidden treasures at the museum: historic furnishings in the upstairs rooms, a stereopticon, a piece of redwood pipe from Mariano Vallejo's water company, and an adobe brick from the mission.

17. What is unique about the museum that can't be found anywhere else: it is the only home in California that was owned by a famous Civil War general.

18. The most important things about local, state, or American history that can be learned at the museum: "Fighting Joe" Hooker was one of the generals that Lincoln hired and fired before settling on U.S. Grant to lead the army. At first, Lincoln liked him because he fought well at The Battle of Williamsburg and made necessary military reforms, but when Robert Lee defeated him at Chancellorsville, he was demoted.

19. Annual events held at the site or elsewhere in the community: on the second Saturday in December, Christmas at the Mission is celebrated.

20. Research facilities or archives at the site: none.

21. Type of gift shop and what is for sale: a few books and postcards are for sale.

22. Additional information: The house is in an alleyway just off of Sonoma Plaza. You can gain entry to El Paseo through a walkway on East Spain Street or First Street East. It is a good idea to ask for directions at the Visitor's Center at the Plaza or another nearby historical museum because it can be a bit difficult to locate.

1. **The Gilroy Museum**

2. Location: 195 Fifth Street, Gilroy, CA. 95020.

3. Website:http://www.cityofgilroy.org/cityofgilroy/community/museum/default.aspx

75

4. Phone number: (408) 846-0446.

5. E-mail: gilroy.museum@ci.gilroy.ca.us

6. Hours of operation: Tuesday and Thursday10:00 a.m. - 5:00 p.m. Winter Hours (Nov - Jan) 10:00 a.m. - 4:00 p.m. First Saturday of the Month10:00 a.m. - 2:00 p.m. (except holiday weekends).

7. Cost: free.

8. Permanent Exhibits: Ohlone Indians, Spanish explorers & settlers, Mexican period, American pioneers, local businesses, resources, schools, women & children.

9. Special Exhibits: none.

10. Historical era that is featured the best: it is a comprehensive museum, but the American period of settlement is best represented.

11. Targeted age groups: all ages.

12. Special activities for children: the museum has compiled trunks filled with duplicate museum artifacts, replicas, and reproductions along two themes: Kids in the 1890's and Ohlone Indians. They're available free of charge to schools and community groups.

13.Guided tours: Walking Tours through Gilroy's historic districts. Tours are given on the first Saturday of each month from 10a.m. to noon. Reservations are recommended but not required.

14. Hands-on activities: none.

15. The best-kept secrets at the museum: the Andrew Carnegie display.
16. Hidden treasures at the museum: displays on the Gilroy Hot Springs and the Ohlone artifacts collection.
17. What is unique about the museum that can't be found anywhere else: it focuses on the Gilroy area.
18. The most important things about local, state, or American history that can be learned at the museum: the importance of Gilroy to the region and the waves of settlement that came to the area.
19. Annual events held at the site or elsewhere in the community: the garlic festival.
20. Research facilities or archives at the site: archive materials are available for research by appointment only; please call and make reservations.
21. Type of gift shop and what is for sale: books, toys, and other gifts.

1. **Gilroy Yamato Hot Springs**
2. Location: Henry W. Coe State Park.
3. Website: http://GilroyYamatoHotSprings.org/
4. Phone number: (408) 314-7185.
5. E-mail: info@GilroyYamatoHotSprings.org

6. Hours of operation: GYHS is currently only open for guided tours or special events (see website for details).
7. Cost: varies by event (see website for details).
8. Permanent Exhibits: ruins of a once popular resort built in the 1860s to take advantage of the warm spring waters that were felt to be beneficial to one's health. Many changes were made to the property over the years, including its 1939 transformation into a Japanese-style bathing resort.
9. Special Exhibits: listed on the National Register of Historic Places: NPS-95000906, California State Historical Landmark #1017.
10. Historical era that is featured the best: late 1860s to 1940s.
11. Targeted age groups: all ages.
12. Special activities for children: the special events often include children's activities.
13. Guided tours: guided tours continue monthly, the 2nd and 4th Saturdays, subject to public demand and availability of docents. May include hiking or other activities.
14. Hands-on activities: vary by event, age, and purpose.
15. The best-kept secrets at the museum: its existence. Most people do not know that this facility existed or that it is open to the public once again.
16. Hidden treasures at the museum: the remnants of the bathhouses and cabins dating back to the 1860s and the Shinto shrine from the 1939 World's Fair at Treasure Island, San Francisco.
17. What is unique about the museum that can't be found anywhere else: it is the only historic site that combines cultural diversity at a warm mineral water resort. It was the only Japanese-owned mineral water resort in California, still housing the oldest existing Shinto shrine in California, originally part of the 1939 World's Fair Japan Pavilion at Treasure Island, San Francisco.

18. The most important things about local, state, or American history that can be learned at the museum: established in 1865, this once-thriving resort included a 5-star hotel and restaurants that drew visitors from around the world.

19. Annual events held at the site or elsewhere in the community: semi-annual all-day public tours and other fundraising events including guided tours, picnics, group meetings, campouts, and volunteer work days (see website for details).

20. Research facilities or archives at the site: none on site at the time of this printing. Collaborative collections are held by The Gilroy Museum and the Monterey District, California State Parks. Long-term restoration plans include an on-site museum and archive.

21. Type of gift shop and what is for sale: some gift items are available at events, and at the Henry W. Coe State Park's visitor's center.

22. Additional information: Several items from the site and a complete description of its history can be seen at The Gilroy Museum at 195 Fifth Street, Gilroy, CA 95020.

1. **Golden Gate Bridge- San Francisco**

2. Location: Near Fort Point, San Francisco, CA.

3. Website: http://www.nps.gov/prsf/planyourvisit/golden-gate-bridge.htm and http://goldengatebridge.org/

4. Phone number: (415) 561-3000.

5. E-mail: tellmemore@parksconservancy.org

6. Hours of operation: The first on-site center dedicated to telling the stories of the Golden Gate Bridge is now open Monday-Friday from 9 a.m.–6 p.m. and Saturday-Sunday from 9 a.m.–7 p.m. (except Thanksgiving and Christmas).

7. Cost: free.

8. Permanent Exhibits: Golden Gate Bridge Pavilion.

9. Special Exhibits: none.

10. Historical era that is featured the best: 1900s.

11. Targeted age groups: all ages.

12. Special activities for children: none.

13. Guided tours: the Golden Gate Bridge Tours and Photo Program have closed for business. Although the Parks Conservancy's Golden Gate Bridge walking tours have ceased operations, if you are interested in the history of the Golden Gate Bridge, it is highly recommended to attend the twice-weekly free bridge walks offered by City Guides, a non-profit organization associated with the San Francisco Public Library. For more information and a schedule of their walks, please see www.sfcityguides.org

14. Hands-on activities: none.

15. The best-kept secrets at the museum: there is a virtual tour of the Bridge Exhibition at the Golden Gate Bridge Visitor Area near the south tower. They allow visitors the opportunity to learn more about the engineering and history of the Golden Gate Bridge.

16. Hidden treasures at the museum: see a section of the cable used to make the bridge and many other interesting photos and items at the visitor area.

17. What is unique about the museum that can't be found anywhere else: the bridge is a world-class landmark with an interesting history of its own.

18. The most important things about local, state, or American history that can be learned at the museum: see how transportation in the region improved dramatically with the bridge's completion. Learn the story of its construction, use, and maintenance.

19. Annual events held at the site or elsewhere in the community: see website for details.

20. Research facilities or archives at the site: none.

21. Type of gift shop and what is for sale: high-quality commemorative and interpretive merchandise of San Francisco and the bridge are available at the Pavilion.

22. Additional information: If you plan to walk across the bridge, be advised that the distance is longer than most people realize, especially if you walk both ways. The weather and traffic can also be unpredictable. Please plan accordingly.

1. **Haas-Lilienthal House-San Francisco**
2. Location: 2007 Franklin Street, San Francisco, CA. 94109.
3. Website: http://www.sfheritage.org/haas-lilienthal-house/tours/
4. Phone number: (415) 441-3000.
5. E-mail: use the online contact form.
6. Hours of operation: Wednesdays and Saturdays (noon – 3 p.m.), and Sundays (11 a.m. – 4 p.m.).
7. Cost: General admission is $8, and admission for seniors and children under twelve is $5.
8. Permanent Exhibits: The Haas-Lilienthal House was designed by Peter R. Schmidt in 1886. Built in the Queen Anne style, the house features prominent open gables, varied styles of shingles and siding, and a turreted corner tower topped by a "witches cap" roof.
9. Special Exhibits: a history of the house and the families that lived in it is displayed in the downstairs supper-room.
10. Historical era that is featured the best: 1886-1920s.
11. Targeted age groups: all ages.
12. Special activities for children: none.
13. Guided tours: all tours are guided. Private group tours can be arranged on days other than the regular public hours.
14. Hands-on activities: none.
15. The best-kept secrets at the museum: most of the exquisite furnishings and artwork belonged to the families that lived there.
16. Hidden treasures at the museum: a portion of the antique train set owned by the family has been restored and is currently running. The large trains follow elaborate track layouts and even light up in the dark.
17. What is unique about the museum that can't be found anywhere else: as the only period era home open to the public in San Francisco, the house beautifully exemplifies upper-middle class life in the Victorian Era.
18. The most important things about local, state, or American history that can be learned at the museum: this is one of the last of its kind in the city. Most similar homes were destroyed in the 1906 Earthquake or subsequently demolished.

78

19. Annual events held at the site or elsewhere in the community: The house is available for rental for special events.

20. Research facilities or archives at the site: none.

21. Type of gift shop and what is for sale: there are a few books and pictures for sale related to San Francisco history, architecture, and the Victorian Era.

1. **Hakone Gardens- Saratoga**

2. Location: Hakone Estate and Gardens, 21000 Big Basin Way, Saratoga, CA. 95070.

79

3. Website: http://www.hakone.com/main.html

4. Phone number: (408) 741-4994.

5. E-mail: giftshop@hakone.com

6. Hours of operation: Weekdays: 10:00 a.m. - 5:00 p.m. Weekends: 11:00 a.m. - 5:00 p.m. Closed only on Christmas Day and New Year's Day.

7. Cost: $8.00 per person, $6 for seniors (65 +) and students 5-17 with valid ID, Children 4 and under free.

8. Permanent Exhibits: one of the National Trust for Historic Preservation's premier sites and nearly a century old, Hakone is the oldest Japanese and Asian estate, retreat and gardens in the Western Hemisphere: 18 acres of magnificent beauty nestled in the verdant hills of Saratoga overlooking Silicon Valley.

9. Special Exhibits: there are frequently special exhibits in the historic houses on the property.

10. Historical era that is featured the best: 1900s-present.

11. Targeted age groups: all ages.

12. Special activities for children: a wide variety of art, music, and cultural classes (see website for details).

13. Guided tours: docent-led tours and traditional tea ceremonies.

14. Hands-on activities: none.

15. The best-kept secrets at the museum: many people do not expect to see a traditional Japanese garden amidst the redwoods of Saratoga, but it is a beautiful and peaceful site.

16. Hidden treasures at the museum: authentic reproductions of East Asian sculpture, architecture, and landscaping elements.

17. What is unique about the museum that can't be found anywhere else: it has remained largely unchanged since it was built by the Stine family.

18. The most important things about local, state, or American history that can be learned at the museum: the garden is a faithful reproduction of historic gardens in Japan.

19. Annual events held at the site or elsewhere in the community: they also offer many annual cultural festivals which showcase ancient civilizations from throughout Asia. As one of the premier art and cultural retreats on the West Coast, the gardens offer a unique experience to those who visit.

20. Research facilities or archives at the site: some cultural research is done on site. Contact the staff for information.

21. Type of gift shop and what is for sale: there is a gift shop featuring Japanese, garden, and nature-related items.

1. **Hamilton Field Museum- Novato**
2. Location: 555 Hangar Ave. Novato, CA. 94949.
3. Website: http://www.cityofnovato.org/Index.aspx?page=387
4. Phone number: (415) 382-8614.
5. E-mail: PRCS@novato.org
6. Hours of operation: Wednesday, Thursday, and Saturday: 12p.m.-4p.m., or by appointment.
7. Cost: free.
8. Permanent Exhibits: a model of Hamilton Air Force base, historic photos and film. Uniforms, aeronautical equipment, and models of aircraft used at the base.
9. Special Exhibits: a display on the namesake of the base and its key leaders such as "Hap" Arnold, a U-2 Exhibit.
10. Historical era that is featured the best: 1938-1980.
11. Targeted age groups: all ages.
12. Special activities for children: a flight simulator and an aircraft drawing station. 3rd grade tours are available for Novato schools.
13. Guided tours: docents are available during visiting hours.
14. Hands-on activities: some of the instruments can be manipulated. There is a link trainer that was used by pilots that visitors can try out with assistance.
15. The best-kept secrets at the museum: the collection of model planes is quite extensive.
16. Hidden treasures at the museum: artifacts recovered from a nearby plane crash are displayed.
17. What is unique about the museum that can't be found anywhere else: the entire history of the base is laid out. Most of the items in the museum are actually from the base.
18. The most important things about local, state, or American history that can be learned at the museum: the base's changing roles in local air defense is outlined. The support that the base provided for conflicts during WWII and the Cold War is well covered.
19. Annual events held at the site or elsewhere in the community: there are many veterans' memorials, monthly military history guest speakers, and other events. The Novato Historical Guild meets in September. Contact the museum for details.
20. Research facilities or archives at the site: contact the museum to arrange for a visit.
21. Type of gift shop and what is for sale: books, videos, and other aeronautical items and souvenirs are available for purchase.

1. **Harris - Lass House Museum- Santa Clara**
2. Location: 1889 Market Street in Santa Clara, CA. 95050.
3. Website: http://www.harrislass.org/
4. Phone number: (408) 249-7905.
5. E-mail: info@harrislass.org
6. Hours of operation: Saturdays and Sundays, 12 noon to 3:30.
The weekends that the museum is open vary from month-to-month, so call to

confirm before visiting. Open hours are also listed on the web site.

7. Cost: Adults: $3.00, Seniors (60+): $2.00, Children (6-12): $1.00.

8. Permanent Exhibits: the museum consists of the house, a classic California barn, summer kitchen, a tank house, and landscaped gardens. Commercial canneries in Santa Clara Valley and home canning. There is a video presentation about the museum and the Lass family, "The Final Harvest: The Story of the Harris-Lass House".

9. Special Exhibits: ladies' hats and clothing, aprons and quilts, household antiques.

10. Historical era that is featured the best: 1910-1930s. Farming in the 1920's and 30's.

11. Targeted age groups: all ages.

12. Special activities for children: an onsite classroom, school tours, and teacher's guides. Graded readers about the house are also available.

13. Guided tours: During museum hours. Tours during the week and/or group tours can be arranged by calling the message line at 408 -249-7905 and requesting a tour.

14. Hands-on activities: some are available in the classroom.

15. The best-kept secrets at the museum: the two basement rooms with the family vault. Vintage clothing from early 1900's in the bedroom closets. Horse drawn carriage in the barn.

16. Hidden treasures at the museum: many antique record players, canning items, and other interesting artifacts. The displays are very well organized. 90% of items in the house actually belonged to the family. The 1865 house is still on its original site. The owners had a 13 acre prune orchard nearby that is now gone.

17. What is unique about the museum that can't be found anywhere else: the house survived the 1906 earthquake. It is the last surviving farm site in Santa Clara. Only two families have lived in the house and the majority of the items in the house are from the Lass family, the second family to live there.

18. The most important things about local, state, or American history that can be learned at the museum: the site is the last farm site in Santa Clara. It is a good place to learn about farm life in an orchard.

19. Annual events held at the site or elsewhere in the community: the Yard Sale & Flea Market, movie nights, tea and vintage fashion show, and the antique appraisal luncheon.

20. Research facilities or archives at the site: none.

21. Type of gift shop and what is for sale: replicas of antiques and boutique gift items, home décor, jewelry, and toys.

22. Additional information: The museum is managed for the City of Santa Clara by the Historic Preservation Society of Santa Clara (HPSSC). Member of the Bay Area Historic House Museums (http>//www.bahhm.org), which issues a quarterly newsletter called "The Meteor", named after the flagship of Captain Christian Lass.

1. **Hayes Mansion-San Jose**
2. Location: 200 Edenvale Avenue, San Jose, CA. 95136.
3. Website: http://www.hayesmansion.com/
4. Phone number: (408) 226-3200.
5. E-mail: info_hayesmansion@dolce.com

6. Hours of operation: the exhibits are available whenever the hotel is open.

7. Cost: free. Guest rooms and amenities are extra.

8. Permanent Exhibits: Once a lavish private estate, the Hayes Mansion stands as one of the South Bay's most impressive and distinctive historical structures. Surrounded by lush, emerald green lawns, accented with gardens of vibrant, colorful flowers and guarded by towering palm trees, the 100-year old estate has been refurbished, upgraded and transformed into a luxurious hotel, conference center, resort and spa.

9. Special Exhibits: there is a display about the Hayes family and the history of the mansion in the lobby.

10. Historical era that is featured the best: Early 1900s.

11. Targeted age groups: all ages.

12. Special activities for children: none.

13. Guided tours: none. Self-guided tours are available.

14. Hands-on activities: none.

15. The best-kept secrets at the museum: there are some items that belonged to the family on display.

16. Hidden treasures at the museum: photographs, furnishings, and artwork belonging to the Hayes family.

17. What is unique about the museum that can't be found anywhere else: it is an operating luxury hotel.

18. The most important things about local, state, or American history that can be learned at the museum: the Hayes family was one of prominence and influence, producing mayors and other prominent community members in San Jose.

19. Annual events held at the site or elsewhere in the community: it is a frequent venue for weddings and other events.

20. Research facilities or archives at the site: none.

21. Type of gift shop and what is for sale: there is a small gift shop near the lobby, which has some souvenirs of historical interest.

1. **Hayward Area Historical Museum**

2. Location: HAHS Center for History & Culture, 22380 Foothill Boulevard, Hayward, CA. 94541.

3. Website: http://www.haywardareahistory.org/

4. Phone number: (510) 581-0223.

5. E-mail: info@haywardareahistory.org

6. Hours of operation: Wednesday, Friday, Saturday, Sunday: 11:00 a.m. – 4:00 p.m. Thursday: 11:00 a.m. – 7:00 p.m.

7. Cost: Adults: $8, Students and Seniors: $5, Free for children 4 and under.

8. Permanent Exhibits: local industries, homes, School Days, Japanese American Internment, Making a Community Function, Playing Around, Protecting the Community, Fruitful Land, Cow Culture, Row Crops, Movie Theaters, Eggs, and a WWII display.

9. Special Exhibits: rotating exhibits such as such as photos of historic cars.

10. Historical era that is featured the best: 1800s-1900s.

11. Targeted age groups: all ages.

12. Special activities for children: school tours, discovery kits, and teacher resources. The Children's Gallery has great interactive displays where kids may can fruit, run a general store or a historic hotel. You can even push a button and smell which food is being canned that day!

13. Guided tours: available with reservations.

14. Hands-on activities: see the children's section above. This is one of the best museums for this category.

15. The best-kept secrets at the museum: there are a lot of fun everyday household items, even from fairly recent times, like Atari video games and Trivial Pursuit!

16. Hidden treasures at the museum: it has nice collection of WWII items such as rationing coupons, a v-mail packet, victory garden handbooks, and civil defense equipment.

17. What is unique about the museum that can't be found anywhere else: it is brand new so it has state-of-the–art displays. There are local oral history excerpts throughout the museum, for example.

18. The most important things about local, state, or American history that can be learned at the museum: it has a nice overview of how the community has changed over time.

19. Annual events held at the site or elsewhere in the community: see the online calendar for information. Visitors can rent the space for special events and meetings.

20. Research facilities or archives at the site: the archive includes magazines, maps, newspapers, oral histories, photographs, yearbooks, scrapbooks, telephone books, reference books and more. Call for an appointment.

21. Type of gift shop and what is for sale: local history books, t-shirts, HAHS merchandise such as key chains, water bottles, and glasses. The Cannery Café is in the same building as the museum.

22. Additional information: The museum is brand new, so it is actively seeking objects to expand its collection.

1. **The Headen-Inman House** (Santa Clara Arts and Historical Consortium)

2. Location: 1509 Warburton Avenue, Santa Clara, CA. 95051.

3. Website: http://santaclaraca.gov/index.aspx?page=1159

84

4. Phone number: (408) 248-2787.

5. E-mail: jimnarveson@earthlink.net

6. Hours of operation: Sundays, 1 to 4 p.m. except holidays or during December.

7. Cost: free.

8. Permanent Exhibits: Dr. Warburton's study, bedroom, Los Fundadores (The Founders of Santa Clara), and the Pioneers of Santa Clara.

9. Special Exhibits: Sister Cities of Santa Clara, a display of porcelain artwork, and a doll collection.

10. Historical era that is featured the best: 1700s to early 1900s.

11. Targeted age groups: all ages

12. Special activities for children: none.

13. Guided tours: walking tour of Santa Clara.

14. Hands-on activities: none.

15. The best-kept secrets at the museum: an original drawing of the little known Battle of Santa Clara. Family trees and genealogical information on early California families.

16. Hidden treasures at the museum: a bayonet from the battle and early Californio objects. This is from one of the handful of recorded battles to ever take place in the Bay Area.

17. What is unique about the museum that can't be found anywhere else: Dr. Warburton's items.

18. The most important things about local, state, or American history that can be learned at the museum: Santa Clara's pivotal role in the development of the county. Records of early Santa Clara settlers.

19. Annual events held at the site or elsewhere in the community: none

20. Research facilities or archives at the site: a few documents, periodicals, and books are available.

21. Type of gift shop and what is for sale: some books and postcards are available.

1. **Healdsburg Museum**

2. Location: 221 Matheson Street, Healdsburg, CA. 95448.

3. Website: http://www.healdsburgmuseum.org/

4. Phone number: (707) 431-3325.

5. E-mail: info@healdsburgmuseum.org

6. Hours of operation: Wednesday – Sunday: 11 a.m. – 4 p.m.

7. Cost: free.

85

8. Permanent Exhibits: The Healdsburg Museum & Historical Society collection of artifacts, documents, and photographs related to northern Sonoma County history comprises one of the finest regional collections in California. Pomo & Wappo Indian artifacts, textiles, paintings and framed photographs, tools, armament, household furnishings and implements, leisure time items, architectural remnants, and business furnishings.

9. Special Exhibits: Rotating special exhibits such as Farm to Table and the Moviestars Next Door (see website for details).

10. Historical era that is featured the best: 1880s-1900.

11. Targeted age groups: all ages.

12. Special activities for children: school tours are available.

13. Guided tours: available upon request.

14. Hands-on activities: The Healdsburg Museum has been a leader in its use of learning enhancements. A touch-screen computer station in the gallery allows visitors to explore architectural aspects of Healdsburg, review photos, examine artifacts, learn about historic figures, enjoy film clips of the city from 1939 and 1951, and take an animated 3-D tour of the historic plaza. Hand-held audio devices, available for self-guided tours, provide additional content and context to visitors experiencing the gallery's exhibits.

15. The best-kept secrets at the museum: Native American and pioneer items.

16. Hidden treasures at the museum: the weapons collection is quite large.

17. What is unique about the museum that can't be found anywhere else: It is the best of its kind in the region.

18. The most important things about local, state, or American history that can be learned at the museum: Healdsburg is an important agricultural region and crossroads for California trade.

19. Annual events held at the site or elsewhere in the community: Christmas on the Ranch, The Antique Fair, Georgetown Tour and BBQ (see website for details).

20. Research facilities or archives at the site: The Roberta Iversen Smith Alexander Research Center holds the museum's extensive collection of local history books, genealogical publications, historical photographs, oral histories, maps, building records, and city records documenting Healdsburg and Sonoma County. It maintains an archive of over 16,000 historical photographs. The Research Center also contains burial records, voting and census records, city and county directories, microfilms of local newspapers and a detailed newspaper index dating from 1858.

21. Type of gift shop and what is for sale: visitors will find an eclectic selection of items including postcards of historical clothing, books on local history, local artwork, souvenirs, and unique gift options.

1. **The Higuera Adobe-Fremont**

2. Location: 47300 Rancho Higuera Rd. Fremont, CA. 94539.

3. Website: http://www.fremont.gov/BusinessDirectoryII.aspx?lngBusinessCategoryID=26

4. Phone number: (510) 623-7907.

5. E-mail: info@museumoflocalhistory.org

6. Hours of operation: by appointment only. Contact The Museum of Local History in Fremont at (510) 623-7907 for tour information.

7. Cost: free.

8. Permanent Exhibits: Higuera Adobe, located at the foot of Mission Peak in the Warm Springs area of Fremont, is the last of seven adobes built in 1840 on Fulgencio Higuera's ranch. The structure consists of a large main room, two small bedrooms with dirt floors, and a stable. The adobe has been restored and furnished with handcrafted redwood furniture. It is available for visits to view the exterior only.

9. Special Exhibits: none.

10. Historical era that is featured the best: 1840s.

11. Targeted age groups: all ages.

12. Special activities for children: none.

13. Guided tours: none.

14. Hands-on activities: none.

15. The best-kept secrets at the museum: none.

16. Hidden treasures at the museum: none.

17. What is unique about the museum that can't be found anywhere else: it is one of the few original structures left from the Mexican Era in the Bay Area.

18. The most important things about local, state, or American history that can be learned at the museum: the Rancho era was an important step in the development of the area. A few large land grants were given to a select few. These later fell into dispute as American settlers challenged their claims.

19. Annual events held at the site or elsewhere in the community: occasional events are held at the site (see website for details).
20. Research facilities or archives at the site: none.
21. Type of gift shop: none.

1. **Hiller Aviation Museum-San Carlos**
2. Location: 601 Skyway Road, San Carlos, CA. 94070.
3. Website: http://www.hiller.org/
4. Phone number: (650) 654-0200.
5. E-mail: museum@hiller.org
6. Hours of operation: 10a.m.-5p.m., 7 days a week. Closed Easter, Thanksgiving, and Christmas Day.
7. Cost: adult: $14, seniors: $9, youth: $9, children under 4: free.
8. Permanent Exhibits: Dedicated to the dreams of flight, the museum chronicles over a century of aviation history and provides a glimpse into air transportation's future. Two large display areas contain the majority of the museum exhibits. Vintage and futuristic aircraft, prototypes, photographic displays, and models are on display. In the museum's main gallery, aircraft, and exhibits showcase aviation history as far back as 1869. The 27,600 square foot main gallery contains over forty aircraft, exhibits, and many interactive displays.
9. Special Exhibits: rotating special exhibits (see website for details).
10. Historical era that is featured the best: 1869-present.
11. Targeted age groups: all ages.
12. Special activities for children: educational programs, scouting activities, Aviation Camp, and field trips.
13. Guided tours: discounted pricing is available for groups of 12 or more visiting the museum together. Advance reservations must be requested.
14. Hands-on activities: the Flight Sim Zone and various interactive displays are available throughout the museum.
15. The best-kept secrets at the museum: local aviation treasures such as the Montgomery gliders and other pioneer aircraft. There is also a replica of the Wright Brothers' plane.
16. Hidden treasures at the museum: hovercraft and early helicopters that the Hiller Corporation made.
17. What is unique about the museum that can't be found anywhere else: it is one of the best air museums in the state. It is spacious and has a wide variety of aircraft.
18. The most important things about local, state, or American history that can be learned at the museum: a comprehensive overview of the development of manned flight is outlined. The reasons why the Bay Area was so important as a development and test flight area are explained.
19. Annual events held at the site or elsewhere in the community: various events throughout the year, including one-of-a-kind seasonal events, lectures and book signings by aviation celebrities, and displays of unique visiting aircraft (see website for details).

20. Research facilities or archives at the site: The Michael King Smith Research Library contains more than 5,400 published aviation-related books and a large and varied collection of aviation magazines. The library's collection is open to both researchers and the general public.

21. Type of gift shop and what is for sale: a wide variety of aviation related items are for sale including books, videos, toys, and many interesting gift items.

1. **History Park- San Jose**
2. Location: Kelly Park, 635 Phelan Avenue, San Jose, CA 95112
3. Website: http://www.historysanjose.org
4. Phone number: (408) 287-2290.
5. E-mail: mpowers@historysanjose.org
6. Hours of operation: programs & events: Sat. & Sun. 11a.m to 5p.m.
7. Cost: City parking is available for $6.
8. Permanent Exhibits: 32 historic and replica buildings and historic vehicles in History Park recreating the streets of a small town. It features a bank, a fire station, dentist office, gas station, blacksmith, stable, print shop, fruit barn, schoolhouse, and a trolley barn with running historic trolleys. There is even a large replica of an electric light tower that once adorned downtown San Jose.
9. Special Exhibits: special rotating exhibits year round.
10. Historical era that is featured the best: 1800s-1900s.
11. Targeted age groups: all ages.
12. Special activities for children: school programs are offered during the school year. Check the website for weekend programs and events.
13. Guided tours: available through reservation.
14. Hands-on activities: check website for Friends & Family Day Series.
15. The best-kept secrets at the museum: there is a Collection Center with a full research library and archive with more than 500,000 artifacts. Research appointments are available through the website.
16. Hidden treasures at the museum: the historic buildings at History Park are full of artifacts from the time period and culture represented by the building.
17. What is unique about the museum that can't be found anywhere else: this site is the queen of all Bay Area historical parks. It is the largest and most comprehensive site of its kind in Northern California. It is rivaled only by historical parks in Sacramento and the Gold Country.
18. The most important things about local, state, or American history that can be learned at the museum: the mission of History San José is to collect, preserve, and celebrate the diversity and innovation of San Jose and the Santa Clara Valley. Each historic building is themed to tell the story of the family or business that used it.
19. Annual events held at the site or elsewhere in the community: They have one of the busiest activity calendars of any Bay Area museum. There is always something fun and interesting going on. Most are very family friendly (see website for details).
20. Research facilities or archives at the site: There is a full Research Library and Archive Research; appointments are available through the website.
21. Type of gift shop and what is for sale: The gift shop is under renovation; however, the historic O'Brien's Ice Cream and Candy Store is open weekends year

round and weekdays during the summer. It features turn-of-the-century candy and fountain treats. Check the website for hours.

22. Additional information: It is not uncommon for communities to move an historic home to another location so that it can be better preserved, but San Jose has done this with an astonishing number of houses. It has also rebuilt lost buildings of historic fame. Thus, History Park is a one-stop location to see many historic buildings and vehicles in once place.

1. **Hoover Tower and The Hoover Institution- Stanford**

2. Location: Get directions and parking instructions from the Stanford Visitor Center, 295 Galvez Street, Stanford, CA. 94305-6104.

3. Website: http://www.stanford.edu/dept/visitorinfo/plan/guides/hoover.html

4. Phone number: (650) 723-2560.

5. E-mail: visitorinfo@stanford.edu

6. Hours of operation: Tuesday –Saturday from 11a.m.–4p.m. The observation deck and exhibits close at 4:00p.m. The last tickets are sold at 3:50p.m. Tower closures may occur due to limited staff availability during academic breaks.

7. Cost: Adults: $2.00, Seniors (65 and older): $1.00, Children (12 and under): $1.00.

8. Permanent Exhibits: see the Stanford campus from the top of the Hoover Tower Observation Platform. Completed in 1941 to celebrate the University's 50th anniversary, the 285-foot tower is a landmark for students, alumni, and the local community.

9. Special Exhibits: the lobby of the tower houses the Herbert Hoover and Lou Henry Hoover exhibits, which feature memorabilia from the careers and lives of the thirty-first U.S. President and his wife, both of whom were Stanford alumni.

The Herbert Hoover Memorial Exhibit Pavilion has exhibits open to the public and is located next to Hoover Tower.

10. Historical era that is featured the best: early 20th Century.

11. Targeted age groups: all ages. Use caution with young children. Please note that strollers, skateboards, and backpacks or large bags are not allowed on the platform, and cannot be stored in the Hoover Tower lobby.

12. Special activities for children: none.

13. Guided tours: the observation platform is located on the fourteenth story of Hoover Tower. When you step off the elevator you will be welcomed by a tour guide who is available to point out Stanford University landmarks and, on a clear day, sights around the San Francisco Bay Area.

14. Hands-on activities: none.

15. The best-kept secrets at the museum: the view from the top is one of the most spectacular in the South Bay region.

16. Hidden treasures at the museum: at the top of the tower, visitors can see a carillon of 48 bells cast in Tournai, Belgium, a gift of the Belgian-American Education Foundation. The largest bell is inscribed, "For Peace Alone Do I Ring."

17. What is unique about the museum that can't be found anywhere else: It is one of the few tributes to the president who usually is unfairly blamed for the Great Depression.

18. The most important things about local, state, or American history that can be learned at the museum: Hoover's many humanitarian and other positive accomplishments are emphasized.

19. Annual events held at the site or elsewhere in the community: see the university website for information. The Hoover Institution has some top-rate guest speakers including world-famous scholars and former national policy makers.

20. Research facilities or archives at the site: Hoover Tower is part of the Hoover Institution on War, Revolution, and Peace, a Stanford-affiliated public policy research center founded by Herbert Hoover, a member of the University's pioneer class of 1895 and the 31st President of the United States. The Institution has fascinating rotating exhibits on the 20th century wars and peacemaking efforts. It has a special emphasis on fascism, communism, and other challenges to democracy.

21. Type of gift shop and what is for sale: there are some books and publications available for sale at the Hoover Institution.

22. Additional information: Visit on a clear day, if possible. You can see landmarks and scenery for many miles.

1. **The HP Garage-Palo Alto**

2. Location: 367 Addison Avenue, Palo Alto, CA. 94309.

3. Website: http://www8.hp.com/us/en/hp-information/about-hp/history/hp-garage/hp-garage.html

4. Phone number: none.

5. E-mail: use the online contact form on HP's website.

6. Hours of operation: daylight hours.

7. Cost: free.

8. Permanent Exhibits: From 1938 through 1939, 367 Addison Avenue served as home, think-tank, lab, office, and production department for Bill Hewlett and Dave Packard. They chose the home because of the garage. They developed the 200A and 200B audio oscillators, HP's first products, there.

9. Special Exhibits: none.

10. Historical era that is featured the best: 20th century.

11. Targeted age groups: all ages.

12. Special activities for children: none.

13. Guided tours: while the HP Garage is not open for public tours, visitors may view and photograph the property and landmark from the sidewalk.

14. Hands-on activities: none.

15. The best-kept secrets at the museum: its existence. Many people do not know the significance of this site.

16. Hidden treasures at the museum: some mysterious household items belonging to prior residents were discovered during the restoration of the home.

17. What is unique about the museum that can't be found anywhere else: It is one of the few sites from early technology developers that has been preserved. Many Silicon Valley companies began in garages, but the buildings are gone or are in private hands.

18. The most important things about local, state, or American history that can be learned at the museum: The Garage is generally regarded by historians, engineers

and others to be one of the most significant artifacts of the early days of the electronics industry remaining in Silicon Valley today.

19. Annual events held at the site or elsewhere in the community: none.

20. Research facilities or archives at the site: none.

21. Type of gift shop: none.

1. **Intel Museum- Santa Clara**

2. Location: 2200 Mission College Boulevard, Santa Clara, CA. 95054.

3. Website: http://www.intel.com/content/www/us/en/company-overview/intel-museum.html

4. Phone number: (408) 765-5050.

5. E-mail: museum@intel.com

6. Hours of operation: Monday-Friday: 9:00 a.m. to 6:00 p.m., Saturday: 10:00 a.m. to 5:00 p.m.

7. Cost: free.

8. Permanent Exhibits: the design and manufacture of computer chips; the history of Intel and Silicon Valley in general.

9. Special Exhibits: occasional special exhibits.

10. Historical era that is featured the best: the post-war technology boom.

11. Targeted age groups: all ages.

12. Special activities for children: school tours with hands-on experiences in the Learning Lab.

13. Guided tours: available with reservations.

14. Hands-on activities: Trying on a bunny suit, clean room FAQ's, digital rain, Artie the robot, and many other interactive displays are available throughout the museum.

15. The best-kept secrets at the museum: Moore's Law and Robert Noyce's legacy are explained rather nicely.

16. Hidden treasures at the museum: historical computers, components, and circuit boards.

17. What is unique about the museum that can't be found anywhere else: a comprehensive history of electronics from transistors to microchips.

18. The most important things about local, state, or American history that can be learned at the museum: Intel's role in the development of computers and other devices. Unfortunately, other chipmakers and Apple computers are not mentioned, even though they were also very influential in the development of computers.

19. Annual events held at the site or elsewhere in the community: none.

20. Research facilities or archives at the site: none.

21. Type of gift shop and what is for sale: Intel and computer-related items.

1. **Jack London State Historic Park-Glen Ellen**

2. Location: 2400 London Ranch Road in Glen Ellen, CA. 95442.

3. Website: http://www.parks.ca.gov/?page_id=478 and http://www.jacklondonpark.com/

4. Phone number: (707) 938-5216.

5. E-mail: info@parks.ca.gov

6. Hours of operation: 9:30a.m. to 5p.m. May 1 through October 31: open every day; November 1 through April 30: open Thursday - Monday (closed Tuesday and Wednesday).

7. Cost: $10 park entry, plus $4 extra for admission to London's cottage.

8. Permanent Exhibits: Jack London State Historic Park is a memorial to writer and adventurer Jack London, who made his home at the site from 1905 until his death in 1916. The park was once part of the famous writer's Beauty Ranch. There is a museum in "The House of Happy Walls" which Mrs. London built in a redwood grove. You can find park information, exhibits, and a small sales area there. A nearby trail leads to Jack London's grave and to the remains of "Wolf House", London's dream house which was destroyed by fire in 1913. The park also contains the cottage residence where he wrote books, short stories, articles, and letters while he oversaw various agricultural enterprises. The historic structures of the ranch include the innovative "Pig Palace", where you can discover how Jack's new approaches to farming are still relevant today.

9. Special Exhibits: There are special exhibits in the museum that vary from time to time.

10. Historical era that is featured the best: 1905-1916.

11. Targeted age groups: all ages.

12. Special activities for children: none.

13. Guided tours: docent-led tours and special events may be available, visit the website or call park for details.

14. Hands-on activities: none.

15. The best-kept secrets at the museum: many personal items from London's life and career, including his library.

16. Hidden treasures at the museum: Polynesian treasures London brought home from his travels.

17. What is unique about the museum that can't be found anywhere else: The many jobs and adventures that London had in his short life are well described and exhibited.

18. The most important things about local, state, or American history that can be learned at the museum: the legacy of this important writer is well documented.

19. Annual events held at the site or elsewhere in the community: Broadway Under the Stars, Plowing Day, concerts, picnics, and more (see website for details).

20. Research facilities or archives at the site: none.

21. Type of gift shop and what is for sale: London's books and other gift items are available at the museum.

1. **Jack Mason Museum of West Marin History-Inverness**

2. Location: in the Inverness Library, 15 Park Avenue, Inverness, CA. 94937.

3. Website: http://www.jackmasonmuseum.org/

4. Phone number: (415) 669-1099.

5. E-mail: info@ jackmasonmuseum.org

6. Hours of operation: Mon. 3-6 and 7-9, Tues. & Wed. 10-1 and 2-6, Friday 3-6, and Sat.10-1.

7. Cost: free.

93

8. Permanent Exhibits: The Gables, an historic house.

9. Special Exhibits: rotating photographic exhibits on West Marin history.

10. Historical era that is featured the best: 1800s-1900s.

11. Targeted age groups: all ages.

12. Special activities for children: none.

13. Guided tours: none.

14. Hands-on activities: none.

15. The best-kept secrets at the museum: historical documents about the landing of Sir Francis Drake, the Shafter family, and important historical events; maps and historic artwork. These materials are in the archives and available only by appointment.

16. Hidden treasures at the museum: thousands of historic photographs of the area are in the archives and available only by appointment.

17. What is unique about the museum that can't be found anywhere else: it is a tribute to one historian's life's work to establish this collection.

18. The most important things about local, state, or American history that can be learned at the museum: Jack Mason (1911-1986) was a newspaper editor from Inverness. He wrote eight books and a quarterly history journal. He donated his extensive local history collection to the Inverness Foundation upon his death. For the past 30 years, volunteers have continued to collect additional material and organize the collection.

19. Annual events held at the site or elsewhere in the community: check the library and museum web pages.

20. Research facilities or archives at the site: Baily's cottage contains the archives. Call for an appointment to do research.

21. Type of gift shop and what is for sale: an e-book bookstore will soon be available on the website.

22. Additional information: Jack Mason donated his home and museum collection to the Inverness Foundation. The home, The Gables, is now the Inverness Branch of the Marin County Free Library. The reading room of the library also serves as the exhibit space for the museum.

1. **Japanese American Museum of San Jose**

2. Location: 535 North 5th St., San Jose, CA. 95112.

3. Website: http://www.jamsj.org/

4. Phone number: (408) 294-3138.

5. E-mail: mail@jamsj.org

6. Hours of operation: Thursday through Sunday, 12 - 4 p.m.

7. Cost: Adults $5, Seniors (65 and older with valid ID): $3, Students (with valid ID): $3, Children (under 12): Free.

8. Permanent Exhibits: an agricultural exhibit, Pioneers of San Jose, Japantown, WWII: Assembly Centers and Internment Camps, 100th Infantry Battalion and 442nd Regimental Combat Team, WWII: Military Intelligence Service, Post WWII: Resettlement, and Sports in the Japanese American Community.

9. Special Exhibits: rotating exhibits such as "Jack's Show: His Life and Sketches" showcasing the work of Japanese American cartoonist Jack Matsuoka.

94

10. Historical era that is featured the best: WWII.

11. Targeted age groups: all ages

12. Special activities for children: school outreach programs for grades 8 and up.

13. Guided tours: available for groups upon request. Walking tours of Japantown.

14. Hands-on activities: a wall of tags that identified each interred family, nature activities.

15. The best-kept secrets at the museum: a replica of a typical cabin used at the internment camps during WWII.

16. Hidden treasures at the museum: hand-made items made by camp internees.

17. What is unique about the museum that can't be found anywhere else: it is located in one of the last intact Japan towns in America. It has the largest internment display outside of the camps themselves.

18. The most important things about local, state, or American history that can be learned at the museum: the role of the Japanese in the development of San Jose.

19. Annual events held at the site or elsewhere in the community: guest speakers, film series, and a book club.

20. Research facilities or archives at the site: an oral history project. Educator resources are also available.

21. Type of gift shop and what is for sale: Japanese gifts and an impressive collection of books and films.

1. **Jesse Peter Native American Art Museum-Santa Rosa**

2. Location: Bussman Hall, Santa Rosa Junior College, 1501 Mendocino Ave., Santa Rosa, CA. 95401.

3. Website: http://www.santarosa.edu/museum/index.html

4. Phone number: (707) 527-4479.

5. E-mail: none.

6. Hours of operation: Monday-Thursday: 9-12 & 1-4:30. Friday: 9-12 & 1-3:00. Closed for the summer and on school holidays.

7. Cost: free.

8. Permanent Exhibits: The SRJC Museum houses collections of ethnographic art from throughout the Americas and parts of Africa, Asia, and the Pacific. Pomo basketry, Plains and Plateau Indians, Pueblo pottery, and Kachina figures.

9. Special Exhibits: Online exhibits. Rotating exhibits on special themes.

10. Historical era that is featured the best: 1800s –present.

11. Targeted age groups: adult students.

12. Special activities for children: school tours.

13. Guided tours: available with reservations.

14. Hands-on activities: online exhibits.

15. The best-kept secrets at the museum: It is a surprisingly large collection for a junior college. The exhibits are always different every time you visit.

16. Hidden treasures at the museum: the Pomo basketry collection is very fine.

17. What is unique about the museum that can't be found anywhere else: It is located on a college campus. It has items from a wide variety of cultures.

18. The most important things about local, state, or American history that can be learned at the museum: it is a good place to study the Indian cultures of Northern Sonoma County.

19. Annual events held at the site or elsewhere in the community: contact the college for information.

20. Research facilities or archives at the site: college students may conduct research with their classes.

21. Type of gift shop: none.

1. **John Muir National Historic Site-Martinez**

2. Location: 4202 Alhambra Ave., Martinez, CA. 94553.

3. Website: http://www.nps.gov/jomu/index.htm

4. Phone number: (925) 228-8860.

5. E-mail: Use the online contact form.

6. Hours of operation: 10a.m.-5p.m. Wednesday through Sunday.

7. Cost: free.

8. Permanent Exhibits: the visitor center, the Strentzel-Muir House and the Martinez Adobe.

9. Special Exhibits: de Anza Expedition display at the Martinez Adobe.

10. Historical era that is featured the best: 1700-1914.

11. Targeted age groups: all ages.

12. Special activities for children: a Junior Ranger program.

13. Guided tours: cell phone and ranger-guided tours of the house and orchards are available on site. Walks to Mt. Wanda.

14. Hands-on activities: Family Days and the Father of the National Parks exhibit.

15. The best-kept secrets at the museum: the de Anza Expedition exhibit.
Also, the film on Muir's life at the visitor's center, "A Glorious Journey", is exceptional.

16. Hidden treasures at the museum: originals of Muir's books, paintings, etc.

17. What is unique about the museum that can't be found anywhere else: Muir's legacy of founding the national parks, also his lesser-known importance as a local farmer.

18. The most important things about local, state, or American history that can be learned at the museum: Muir's considerable influence on the environmental movement.

19. Annual events held at the site or elsewhere in the community: campfire programs featuring songs, stories, and skits. Full Moon Walks to Mt. Wanda.

20. Research facilities or archives at the site: none.

21. Type of gift shop and what is for sale: a large gift shop with National Park Service gifts, including nature and Muir related items.

1. **Johnston House-Half Moon Bay**

2. Location: The Johnston House is located just south of the city of Half Moon Bay on the east side of Highway 1 at Higgins-Purisima Road.

3. Website: http://www.johnstonhouse.org/

4. Phone number: (650) 726-0329.

5. E-mail: events@johnstonhouse.org

6. Hours of operation: The third Saturday of each month from 11 a.m. to 3 p.m. It is closed October, November, and December.

7. Cost: free.

8. Permanent Exhibits: The classic New England saltbox (two stories in front, one in back) was built by '49er pioneer James Johnston between 1853-1855 for his Californiano bride, Petra Maria de Jara.

9. Special Exhibits: none.

10. Historical era that is featured the best: 1850s-1900.

11. Targeted age groups: all ages.

12. Special activities for children: school tours.

13. Guided tours: available with reservations.

14. Hands-on activities: none.

15. The best-kept secrets at the museum: it is known as the White House of Half Moon Bay because of its striking appearance and stellar coastal views.

16. Hidden treasures at the museum: the family's private shrine. Some of the furnishings belonged to the family.

17. What is unique about the museum that can't be found anywhere else: It is one of the few examples of saltbox houses on the West Coast.

18. The most important things about local, state, or American history that can be learned at the museum: it is one of the best-restored historical homes on the San Mateo County coast. The Johnstons were important local pioneers. He was a real estate investor and helped Mexican residents to protect their property rights after California became part of the United States.

19. Annual events held at the site or elsewhere in the community: The Half Moon Bay Art & Pumpkin Festival and the Johnston Holiday Boutique.

20. Research facilities or archives at the site: there are some records available to researchers.

21. Type of gift shop and what is for sale: books, posters, and other gift items.

1. **Lafayette Historical Society**

2. Location: Lafayette Library & Learning Center, enter on Golden Gate Way 133 Lafayette, CA. 94549.

98

3. Website: http://www.lafayettehistory.org/wp/

4. Phone number: (925) 283-1848.

5. E-mail: use the online contact form.

6. Hours of operation: Tuesdays, Thursdays and Saturdays, 10 a.m.–2 p.m.

7. Cost: free.

8. Permanent Exhibits: historical photos, Ohlone arrowheads, historical clothing, tools, a blacksmith's anvil, and other artifacts.

9. Special Exhibits: Items from the collections are rotated on a regular basis.

10. Historical era that is featured the best: 1800s-1900s.

11. Targeted age groups: all ages.

12. Special activities for children: none.

13. Guided tours: cemetery tours with historical interpreters, walking tour of historical areas of the town.

14. Hands-on activities: the historical walking tour has an app that can be downloaded for the iphone.

15. The best-kept secrets at the museum: many interesting items are stored in the cabinet drawers. Open and explore!

16. Hidden treasures at the museum: a lantern that came to California with the Donner Party.

17. What is unique about the museum that can't be found anywhere else: it is part of the library, but it is located in a separate building.

18. The most important things about local, state, or American history that can be learned at the museum: the town started as a Mexican land grant, then grew to a sleepy little American town, and then suddenly became a busy crossroads connecting the East Bay to the San Ramon and Diablo Valleys.

19. Annual events held at the site or elsewhere in the community: the guest speaker series.

20. Research facilities or archives at the site: there is an archive with historic photos and an oral history collection.

21. Type of gift shop and what is for sale: books about Lafayette and historic photos.

1. **Lathrop House-Redwood City**

2. Location: 627 Hamilton Street (County Center), Redwood City, CA. 94063.

3. Website: http://www.lathrophouse.org/index.htm

4. Phone number: (650) 365-5564.

5. E-mail: none.

6. Hours of operation: first 4 Wednesdays, 3rd Saturday every month, 11a.m.-3p.m. Closed in August.

7. Cost: free.

8. Permanent Exhibits: the Lathrop House is one of the Peninsula's oldest mansions. It was built in 1863 by San Mateo County's first assessor-clerk-recorder, who was also chairman of the Board of Supervisors. He later helped found the Southern Pacific Railroad and was the owner of a large tract of land in the Menlo Park area.

9. Special Exhibits: none.

10. Historical era that is featured the best: 1860s-1880s.

11. Targeted age groups: all ages.

12. Special activities for children: none.

13. Guided tours: available upon request.

14. Hands-on activities: none.

15. The best-kept secrets at the museum: Steamboat Gothic style of architecture.

16. Hidden treasures at the museum: Many interesting antiques and furnishings are found in the home. The house is furnished with period pieces and even has a few items from its original occupants It's filled with interesting artifacts from that era: furniture, kitchen implements, clothing, papers, and so on.

17. What is unique about the museum that can't be found anywhere else: it is the best house of its kind in San Mateo County.

18. The most important things about local, state, or American history that can be learned at the museum: the role of local pioneers in the area.

19. Annual events held at the site or elsewhere in the community: July 4 Open House

20. Research facilities or archives at the site: none.

21. Type of gift shop and what is for sale: the shop is called "Tarnished Doorknobs Antiques". It sells mostly small, one-of-a-kind antique decorative items, but also has postcards, jewelry, china, and some other items.

22. Additional information: Be sure to call ahead because the museum is not always open during published hours. Ring the doorbell to alert the staff that you have arrived because they may be upstairs and unable to hear you.

1. **Lawrence Berkeley National Laboratory**

2. Location: 1 Cyclotron Road, Berkeley, CA. 94720.

3. Website: http://www.lbl.gov/

4. Phone number: (510) 486-4000.

5. E-mail: tours@lbl.gov

6. Hours of operation: 10 a.m.-1 p.m. one Friday per month. See the calendar on the website.

7. Cost: free.

8. Permanent Exhibits: historic equipment for atomic particle research and other energy technologies.

9. Special Exhibits: current research is carried on in many fields. Hands-on activities are done for visiting students and teachers.

10. Historical era that is featured the best: 20th Century.

11. Targeted age groups: 16 and up.

12. Special activities for children: tours, workshops, and long-term internships are available for students. See the website for more info for student visits - http://education.lbl.gov/.

13. Guided tours: guided tours occur monthly. Go to the website to sign up ahead of time - http://www.lbl.gov/community/tours-faq/tours/ (see website for details).

14. Hands-on activities: current research and lab techniques are demonstrated both on site and at Bay Area schools.

15. The best-kept secrets at the museum: it is a working research facility as well as a site that preserves some of its past scientific accomplishments.

16. Hidden treasures at the museum: the original atom-splitting cyclotrons used by Lawrence and other scientists.

17. What is unique about the museum that can't be found anywhere else: this is one of the most important birthplaces of the atomic age.

18. The most important things about local, state, or American history that can be learned at the museum: the Cold War would not have been the same without this place. Some of the most important developments in atomic particle research started here.

19. Annual events held at the site or elsewhere in the community: see website for details.

20. Research facilities or archives at the site: it is primarily a scientific research facility. For historical records, visit other UC Berkeley campus facilities.

21. Type of gift shop: none.

1. **Lawrence Livermore National Laboratory Discovery Center**
2. Location: located off Greenville Road on Eastgate Drive, Livermore, CA. 94550.
3. Website: https://www.llnl.gov/about/discoverycenter.html
4. Phone number: (925) 423-3272.
5. E-mail: use the contact form on the website.
6. Hours of operation: Tuesday-Friday from 1-4 p.m.
7. Cost: free.
8. Permanent Exhibits: the history of the laboratory and its important founders, nuclear weapons, fusion energy research, Homeland Security and the War on Terrorism, Science and Technology in the National Interest, and Biomedical research.
9. Special Exhibits: energy bikes.
10. Historical era that is featured the best: 1930s-present.
11. Targeted age groups: middle school and up.
12. Special activities for children: a science activities lab, school tours available.
13. Guided tours: available upon request. More in-depth tours of the facilities themselves are available on Tuesdays only. Make reservations far in advance because they book up quickly.
14. Hands-on activities: there are many interactive elements to the displays.
15. The best-kept secrets at the museum: most people do not know how many different kinds of research are done at the facility and think that is not open to the public.
16. Hidden treasures at the museum: a nose cone from a multiple-warhead nuclear missile that was developed at the site is on display.
17. What is unique about the museum that can't be found anywhere else: it is one of the most important research facilities in the nation. Important energy research that is conducted may lead to major breakthroughs in fusion power any day now.
18. The most important things about local, state, or American history that can be learned at the museum: the Atomic Age could not have happened without this facility. Many major weapons and energy developments were discovered at this site.
19. Annual events held at the site or elsewhere in the community: There are talks and demonstrations given in downtown Livermore by scientists from the various labs and facilities on site. See llnl.gov for information.
20. Research facilities or archives at the site: there are no public historical archives, but some facilities are made available to visiting scientists and dignitaries by special arrangement.
21. Type of gift shop and what is for sale: there are some science-related gift items available in the lobby area.

1. **Levi's Plaza Store and Historical Archives-San Francisco**
2. Location: 1155 Battery Street, San Francisco, CA. 94111.
3. Websites: http://www.sanfrancisco.travel/partnerships/levistrauss.html and http://www.levistrauss.com/about/heritage
4. Phone number: (415) 501-6000.

5. E-mail: none.

6. Hours of operation: 9 a.m. – 6 p.m. Monday – Friday; 12 p.m. – 5 p.m. Saturday & Sunday.

7. Cost: free.

8. Permanent Exhibits: historic pants and other garments made by Levi's. A brief overview of the history of jeans and Levi's in general.

9. Special Exhibits: rotating exhibits such as the film on how designers still use legacy garments to inspire today's designs.

10. Historical era that is featured the best: the Gold Rush-present.

11. Targeted age groups: all ages.

12. Special activities for children: none.

13. Guided tours: none.

14. Hands-on activities: none.

15. The best-kept secrets at the museum: some of the jeans are very old. They are preserved because of their historical value, even if they are in rough shape.

16. Hidden treasures at the museum: one pair was found in a mine in Nevada! No one knows what happened to its owner.

17. What is unique about the museum that can't be found anywhere else: it is the only one of its kind.

18. The most important things about local, state, or American history that can be learned at the museum: The changing role of Levi's and what they meant to pop culture, including miners, loggers, the military, industrial workers, hippies, and Hollywood.

19. Annual events held at the site or elsewhere in the community: see website for details.

20. Research facilities or archives at the site: there is an archive of historic fabrics for clothing designers, but it is only open by invitation.

21. Type of gift shop and what is for sale: there is a Levi's store with replica legacy clothing and contemporary styles right next to the museum.

1. The Livermore Heritage Guild

2. Location: The History Center in the Carnegie Building - 2155 Third Street (at 3rd and K Streets) in Livermore, CA. 94551.

3. Website: http://www.livermorehistory.com/

4. Phone number: (925) 449-9927.

5. E-mail: jkaskey@yahoo.com

6. Hours of operation: Wednesday through Sunday from 11:30 a.m. to 4:00 p.m

7. Cost: free.

8. Permanent Exhibits: apothecary shop, historic photos, historic clothing, tools, the Livermore family.

9. Special Exhibits: rotating art exhibits.

10. Historical era that is featured the best: 1800s-1900s.

11. Targeted age groups: all ages.

12. Special activities for children: the Historymobile, created by members Tillie Calhoun and Barry Schrader, is available to all third grade classes in Livermore.

13. Guided tours: docents are available during visiting hours.

103

14. Hands-on activities: none.

15. The best-kept secrets at the museum: it doubles as a historical museum and an art gallery.

16. Hidden treasures at the museum: miniature dioramas of vintage stores and businesses in the area.

17. What is unique about the museum that can't be found anywhere else: it is located in a former Carnegie Library.

18. The most important things about local, state, or American history that can be learned at the museum: the growth of Livermore and its changing roles over the years.

19. Annual events held at the site or elsewhere in the community: History Talks, the Historymobile, and an annual auction. The Historymobile is a regular attraction at the Harvest Celebration held at the Concannon Winery and at the annual Ice Cream Social at Ravenswood.

20. Research facilities or archives at the site: a small collection of local history books and oral histories is available for researchers.

21. Type of gift shop and what is for sale: original works of art, local history books and commemorative mugs.

1. **Los Altos History Museum**

2. Location: 51 So. San Antonio Road, Los Altos, CA. 94022.

3. Website: http://www.losaltoshistory.org/index.html

4. Phone number: (650) 948-9427.

5. E-mail: lbajuk@losaltoshistory.org

6. Hours of operation: Thursday-Sunday: noon-4 p.m.

7. Cost: free.

8. Permanent Exhibits: the J. Gilbert Smith History House is located on one of the last active apricot orchards in the Santa Clara Valley. This 1905 shingled farmhouse was built with many Craftsman-style features. Visitors are welcome to stroll through the historic gardens filled with towering oaks and the active apricot orchard that surrounds the museum complex. A refurbished 1915 tank house, antique farm equipment, walnut hullers, and tools for cutting, sulfuring, and drying apricots.

9. Special Exhibits: the changing exhibit gallery features up to four different exhibits a year. These exhibits are designed to reflect historical content and local artifacts relevant to this area.

10. Historical era that is featured the best: 1800s-1900s.

11. Targeted age groups: all ages.

12. Special activities for children: the trains in the model town are a big hit with kids. Education Curriculum tours for 3rd and 4th grade. The Margaret Thompson Essay Contest.

13. Guided tours: Self-guided and docent tours available: Explore the main museum on your own or opt for a docent-guided tour at no additional charge. The J. Gilbert Smith House requires a docent guide. A free audio tour is available at the museum store for the upper level permanent exhibit. Special tours may be scheduled for groups of ten or more.

14. Hands-on activities: an audio tour of the museum is available. Some displays are interactive.

15. The best-kept secrets at the museum: the Ohlone and Mexican rancho items are exceptionally fine. There are many interesting farm implements on display as well.

16. Hidden treasures at the museum: a replica of downtown Los Altos in 1932 that features a model railroad and many of the sights and sounds of that era.

17. What is unique about the museum that can't be found anywhere else: the diorama of downtown Los Altos is one of the biggest in the South Bay Area. It has many moving parts and is very entertaining to watch. The combination of a historic home and a comprehensive history museum allows for more display space than other sites.

18. The most important things about local, state, or American history that can be learned at the museum: the orchard park gives visitors a good feel for the agricultural heritage of the area. The museum gives a good overview of the growth of Los Altos from a small farming town to a modern city.

19. Annual events held at the site or elsewhere in the community: guest speakers, art shows, First Day of Spring Reception, and other events (see website for details).

20. Research facilities or archives at the site: the museum's lower level is the repository of the archive and object collections, including artifacts, maps, photos, manuscripts, clippings, oral histories and memorabilia. Available by appointment.

21. Type of gift shop and what is for sale: the museum store features a wide array of unique items for sale, including cards, toys, books, commemorative objects, and one-of-a-kind gifts that appeal to all ages.

1. **New Museum Los Gatos**

2. Location: 110 E. Main Street, Los Gatos, CA 95030.

3. Website: http://www.museumsoflosgatos.org/site/history-museum/

4. Phone number: (408) 354-2646.

5. e-mail: operations@museumsoflosgatos.org

6. Hours of Operation: Tues.-Sun 11 a.m.-5p.m.; Thurs. 11a.m.-8p.m. NUMU will open in 2 phases: the first floor on May 20, 2015, the Museum Association's 50th Anniversary, and the lower floor in September of 2015.

7. Cost: Adults (to be determined), youth and children under 18 are free.

8. Permanent Exhibits: an interactive permanent Los Gatos History exhibit, Bay Area history, art, and the innovation of our times.

9. Special Exhibits: Dynamic, interactive, and frequently changing exhibitions. 18 rotating exhibitions annually.

10. Historical era that is featured the best: 1800s-1900s.

11. Targeted age groups: all ages.

12. Special activities for children: a rigorous education program for all ages.

13. Guided tours: available with reservations. 50 docent-led walks annually.

14. Hands-on activities: constantly changing state-of-the-art interactive displays.

15. The best-kept secrets at the museum: more information will be available upon the opening of the museum.

16. Hidden treasures at the museum: more information will be available upon the opening of the museum.

17. What is unique about the museum that can't be found anywhere else? The new museum will be much larger than its predecessor and have a more regional focus. It will engage community at the intersection of art, history, and education through innovative, locally connected, and globally relevant exhibits, programs and experiences. Its goal is to consistently show how the past influences what we define as new.

18. The most important things about local, state or American history that can be learned at the museum: Los Gatos has transformed from an agricultural area to a thriving Silicon Valley town. It has survived earthquakes, urbanization, and many other challenges. It is the link to the Santa Clara Valley for many Santa Cruz Mountains dwellers.

19. Annual events held at the site or elsewhere in the community: 12 family art days, youth programs and lectures annually (see the website for details).

20. Research facilities or archives at the site: none.

21. Type of gift shop and what is for sale: history books, art, and other and gifts will be available for sale.

1. **Luther Burbank Gold Ridge Experiment Farm-Sebastopol**

2. Location: 7777 Bodega Ave., Sebastopol, CA. 95472.

3. Website: http://www.wschsgrf.org/luther-burbank-gold-ridge-experiment-farm or http://www.sebastopol-farm-museum.org

4. Phone number: (707) 829-6711.

5. E-mail: use the online contact form.

6. Hours of operation: open 7 days a week for self-guided tours.

7. Cost: free for self-guided tour.

8. Permanent Exhibits: experimental gardens and cottage.

9. Special Exhibits: outdoor plant laboratory for plant experiments.

10. Historical era that is featured the best: 1885-1926.

11. Targeted age groups: all ages.

12. Special activities for children: school tours.

13. Guided tours: docent led tours are by appointment, call (707) 829-6711.

14. Hands-on activities: gardening classes.

15. The best-kept secrets at the museum: the farm cottage was placed on the National Register of Historic Places in 1978. Some of the original Burbank plants are still living at the farm.

16. Hidden treasures at the museum: pictures of famous visitors Helen Keller, Thomas Edison, and Henry Ford.

17. What is unique about the museum that can't be found anywhere else: local historians and volunteers saved and restored the farm that most certainly would not have survived without their vision. It is a work in progress, as many of Burbank's experiments were never finished.

18. The most important things about local, state, or American history that can be learned at the museum: Over 800 plant varieties and hybrids were developed by Burbank, including the Shasta daisy, Russet potatoes and Santa Rosa plums.

19. Annual events held at the site or elsewhere in the community: Spring and Fall Open House at the Farm with exhibits and plant sales, October Cemetery Walk with

historical re-enactors, Mother's Day Tea, and Volunteer Work Days (see website for details).

20. Research facilities or archives at the site: records of Burbank's life and research.

21. Type of gift shop and what is for sale: gardening items, T-shirts, gardening books, and pamphlets. Plant sales are on Wednesdays from 9-12.

1. **Luther Burbank Home & Gardens-Santa Rosa**
2. Location: 204 Santa Rosa Avenue, Santa Rosa, CA. 95404.
3. Website: http://www.lutherburbank.org/
4. Phone number: (707) 524-5445.
5. E-mail: burbankhome@lutherburbank.org
6. Hours of operation: the Carriage House Gift Shop and Museum is open and walk-in docent-led tours are available April through October. The grounds are open daily from 8:00 a.m. to dusk year-round for self-guided tours and reserved group and children's tours.

7. Cost: free.
8. Permanent Exhibits: the famed horticulturist made his home in Santa Rosa for more than 50 years, and it was at the farm that he conducted plant-breeding experiments that brought him world fame.
9. Special Exhibits: rotating exhibits are in the museum at various times.
10. Historical era that is featured the best: Late 1880s to early 1900s.
11. Targeted age groups: all ages.
12. Special activities for children: school tours and teacher resources are available.
13. Guided tours: available upon request.
14. Hands-on activities: gardening demonstrations and volunteer opportunities.
15. The best-kept secrets at the museum: Specialty gardens, such as edible or medicinal plants, spineless cacti, and wildlife habitats.
16. Hidden treasures at the museum: photos of Burbank with Henry Ford and other famous visitors.
17. What is unique about the museum that can't be found anywhere else: the amazing creativity of this great inventor is displayed. Many of his projects were still unfinished at the time of his death.
18. The most important things about local, state, or American history that can be learned at the museum: during his career, Burbank introduced more than 800 new varieties of plants - including over 200 varieties of fruits, many vegetables, nuts and grains, and hundreds of ornamental flowers.
19. Annual events held at the site or elsewhere in the community: lectures, plant sales, dinners, and a holiday open house (see website for details).
20. Research facilities or archives at the site: none.
21. Type of gift shop and what is for sale: gardening items, t-shirts, apparel, books, prints, postcards, and many items related to the Shasta daisy.

1. **The Magnes Collection of Jewish Art and Life-Berkeley**
2. Location: 2121 Allston Way, Berkeley, CA. 93710.
3. Website: http://www.magnes.org/
4. Phone number: (510) 643-2526.

5. E-mail: use the online contact form.

6. Hours of operation: Wed.-Sun. 12–4 p.m.; Thurs. until 7 p.m.

7. Cost: free.

8. Permanent Exhibits: none.

9. Special Exhibits: rotating exhibits of Jewish life from around the world. Twice a year, the Main Gallery presents collaborative projects with artists-in-residence as well as exhibitions that enhance teaching at UC Berkeley.

10. Historical era that is featured the best: all eras.

11. Targeted age groups: all ages.

12. Special activities for children: none.

13. Guided tours: available with reservations.

14. Hands-on activities: none.

15. The best-kept secrets at the museum: many of the objects in the vault can still be seen because it has glass walls.

16. Hidden treasures at the museum: art, artifacts, and documents from around the world.

17. What is unique about the museum that can't be found anywhere else: It has a large collection of Jewish items.

18. The most important things about local, state, or American history that can be learned at the museum: The experience of Jews in America is also portrayed at the museum.

19. Annual events held at the site or elsewhere in the community: The Magnes's educational and public programs include tours, lectures, artist talks, and scholarly symposia, as well as collaborations with local cultural and performing arts institutions

20. Research facilities or archives at the site: a large collection of documents is available to researchers.

21. Type of gift shop: none.

1. **Marin History Museum**

2. Location: 1125 B Street, San Rafael, CA. 94901.

3. Website: http://www.marinhistory.org/index.php

4. Phone number: (415) 454-8538.

5. E-mail: info@marinhistory.org

6. Hours of operation: Tuesday & Wednesday: 11a.m.–4p.m., Thursday: 11a.m.–8p.m., Friday & Saturday: 11a.m.–4p.m.

7. Cost: free

8. Permanent Exhibits: the range of the collection includes utilitarian items to fine arts. Examples include maps, paintings, furniture, tools, household objects, and clothing. Although there is a strong emphasis on 19th and 20th century history, the museum holds items related to the age of the Miwoks, the Spanish Mission period, and the Mexican Land Grants era. The museum collection also has contemporary pieces related to modern-day Marin. The collection features objects from the 1906 Earthquake, two World Fairs, the construction of the Golden Gate Bridge, Marinship, Hamilton Field, Northwest Pacific Railroad & Ferry Company, San Quentin Prison, and personal effects of arctic explorer Louise Boyd.   Some unique items in the

109

collection include a 17th century Spanish sword, the Verdenal pioneer journal, Louise Boyd's expedition snowshoes, and artwork made by San Quentin inmates.

9. Special Exhibits: rotating special exhibitions on local history.

10. Historical era that is featured the best: 19th and 20th century history.

11. Targeted age groups: all ages.

12. Special activities for children: history trunks on dairies and railroads for schools and Wee History programs.

13. Guided tours: available upon request.

14. Hands-on activities: a children's area has some objects they can touch and play with.

15. The best-kept secrets at the museum: the exhibit about the Arctic explorer and adventurer Louise Arner Boyd.

16. Hidden treasures at the museum: a Johnny Cash poster from his famous concert at San Quentin Prison and other interesting prison artifacts.

17. What is unique about the museum that can't be found anywhere else: it has a good cross section of the entire county's history.

18. The most important things about local, state, or American history that can be learned at the museum: Marin County has had a long and varied history. Marin is more than just a suburb of San Francisco. It has a rich history of its own.

19. Annual events held at the site or elsewhere in the community: Museum by Moonlight, Annual Antique & Appraisal Day, and MHM's Annual Garden Party.

20. Research facilities or archives at the site: a research library, archives, and oral history collection.

21. Type of gift shop and what is for sale: a small gift shop with items of local historical interest.

22. Additional information: every Thursday, the Boyd Gate House stays open until 8 pm. You can visit the museum and see the beauty of the Boyd at night.

1. **Marin Civic Center**

2. Location: Civic Center, 3501 Civic Center Drive, San Rafael, CA. 94903-4176.

3. Website: http://www.marincounty.org/depts/cu/visitor-services

4. Phone number: (415) 473-3762.

5. E-mail: use the contact form on the website.

6. Hours of operation: 8:30-5 weekdays.

7. Cost: free.

8. Permanent Exhibits: the buildings, including the library, offices, and a famous spire designed by Frank Lloyd Wright.

9. Special Exhibits: posters telling the history and design of the center and a model of the facility are available on the first and second floor corridors near the library.

10. Historical era that is featured the best: 1950s.

11. Targeted age groups: all ages.

12. Special activities for children: none.

13. Guided tours: self-guided tour brochure and virtual tours available on website. Docent-led tours are available. See the calendar on the website for details.

14. Hands-on activities: none.

110

15. The best-kept secrets at the museum: the spire was originally designed as a radio tower.

16. Hidden treasures at the museum: the architectural elements within the building are indicative of Wright's unique style.

17. What is unique about the museum that can't be found anywhere else: this is the last building designed by Wright and one of the few government buildings that he created that is still functional.

18. The most important things about local, state, or American history that can be learned at the museum: the role of this very influential architect in Western design and the political controversies regarding the building of the center.

19. Annual events held at the site or elsewhere in the community: there are numerous events at the cultural center (see website for details)

20. Research facilities or archives at the site: none.

21. Type of gift shop: none.

1. **Martinez Museum**

2. Location: 1005 Escobar Street, Martinez, CA. 94553.

3. Website: http://www.martinezhistory.org/

4. Phone number: (925) 228-8160.

5. E-mail: webmaster@martinezhistory.org

6. Hours of operation: Tuesday and Thursday 11:30 a.m.- 3:00p.m. and the first four Sundays 1:00 p.m.- 4:00p.m.

7. Cost: free.

8. Permanent Exhibits: the 2-story Borland house. Displays on local history, sports teams, navigation items, tools, oil refinery, the Port Chicago explosion, building of the Carquinez Bridge, barbershop, historical kitchen, toys, local businesses, Sheriff Veale, and a chest and clothing from the Martinez family.

9. Special Exhibits: rotating displays.

10. Historical era that is featured the best: 1800-1900s.

11. Targeted age groups: all ages.

12. Special activities for children: none.

13. Guided tours: museum tour, cemetery tour, and a walking tour of Martinez.

14. Hands-on activities: none.

15. The best-kept secrets at the museum: there are many interesting artifacts crammed into this small museum. The displays about the oil refineries and bridges are the best.

16. Hidden treasures at the museum: clothing and articles belonging to the Martinez family.

17. What is unique about the museum that can't be found anywhere else: see above.

18. The most important things about local, state, or American history that can be learned at the museum: the strategic role Martinez has had as a crossroads for the Bay Area and Delta regions.

19. Annual events held at the site or elsewhere in the community: call for information.

20. Research facilities or archives at the site: none.

21. Type of gift shop and what is for sale: there is a small area selling books and postcards related to the history of the area.

1. The McConaghy House-Hayward

2. Location: 18701 Hesperian Boulevard, Hayward, CA, 94541 (next to Kennedy Park).
3. Website: http://www.haywardareahistory.org/
4. Phone number: (510) 581-0223.
5. E-mail: info@haywardareahistory.org
6. Hours of operation: third Sunday of each month, 1 – 4 p.m.
7. Cost: $5.00 adults, $3.00 Students/ Seniors (over 65), free for children 10 and under, free for Hayward Area Historical Society members.
8. Permanent Exhibits: the McConaghy family built their 12-room farmhouse, tank house, and carriage house in 1886. There is a parlor, family room, dining room, kitchen, and upstairs bedrooms and bathroom.
9. Special Exhibits: none.
10. Historical era that is featured the best: 1880s to early 1900s.
11. Targeted age groups: all ages.
12. Special activities for children: school visits. There is also a special room called Archie's Playroom with old-fashioned toys and other hands-on activities for kids.
13. Guided tours: group and school tours available Tuesday through Friday by appointment. Please contact the Education Department to schedule your tour at (510) 581-0223.
14. Hands-on activities: Archie's Playroom.
15. The best-kept secrets at the museum: some of the family's original belongings and furniture are in the house.
16. Hidden treasures at the museum: several original pieces of artwork by family members are found in the house.
17. What is unique about the museum that can't be found anywhere else: tours of the house offer visitors a fun and informative environment to learn more about what life was like for farming families during the Victorian Period.
18. The most important things about local, state, or American history that can be learned at the museum: this was an important pioneer family in the region. It offers a glimpse of how middle class families lived in the Victorian Era.
19. Annual events held at the site or elsewhere in the community: Christmas at The McConaghy House (see website for details).
20. Research facilities or archives at the site: none.
21. Type of gift shop and what is for sale: the McConaghy House Boutique features Victorian gifts and books for purchase to commemorate your visit.

1. Millbrae History Museum

2. Location: Millbrae History Museum 450 Poplar Avenue, Millbrae, CA. 94030.
3. Website: http://www.millbraehs.org/millbrae-history-museum.html
4. Phone number: (650) 692-5786.
5. E-mail: use the online contact form.
6. Hours of operation: Saturdays 12 noon to 4:00 p.m.

7. Cost: Suggested donation $2.

8. Permanent Exhibits: inside the history museum are a set of well-organized displays depicting the history of Millbrae and the surrounding area. Numerous photos, artifacts, period furniture, and historical documents are stored within the 1895-built house.

9. Special Exhibits: none.

10. Historical era that is featured the best: 1800s-1900s.

11. Targeted age groups: all ages.

12. Special activities for children: school tours.

13. Guided tours: the Historical Walk.

14. Hands-on activities: none.

15. The best-kept secrets at the museum: information about the fire that destroyed the historic Mills Mansion. There are historic photos that show the once vast Hills estate, and how land was moved to build the San Francisco Airport.

16. Hidden treasures at the museum: a wide range of interesting antique clothing, household items, a vintage piano, a record player, and an historic kitchen.

17. What is unique about the museum that can't be found anywhere else: the main museum is located in the 1895 Spring Valley Water Company manager's house.

18. The most important things about local, state, or American history that can be learned at the museum: the town has always been an important transportation center with the trolley line, railroads, the Bayshore Highway, and airports. It has also been the home of historic mansions for wealthy San Franciscans seeking country homes.

19. Annual events held at the site or elsewhere in the community: Annual Yard Sale and Millbrae Night at the Movies.

20. Research facilities or archives at the site: there are some historic records available at the Millbrae History Museum.

21. Type of gift shop and what is for sale: local history books.

1. **Millbrae Train Museum**

2. Location: California Drive at Murchison Drive, Millbrae, CA. 94030.

3. Website: http://www.millbraehs.org/millbrae-history-museum.html

114

4. Phone number: (650) 333-1136.

5. E-mail: use the online contact form.

6. Hours of operation: Saturdays 10:00 a.m. to 2:00 p.m.

7. Cost: suggested donation $2.

8. Permanent Exhibits: the rail museum has train station furnishings, rail schedules, historic photos and models.

9. Special Exhibits: a luxury rail car, *The Civic Center*, from *The City of San Francisco*, a transcontinental liner made by the Pullman Company.

10. Historical era that is featured the best: 1800s-1900s.

11. Targeted age groups: all ages.

12. Special activities for children: the train museum has a kiddies' train ride machine.

13. Guided tours: available upon request.

14. Hands-on activities: there are some items at the train museum that can be handled.

15. The best-kept secrets at the museum: historic photos of the "Big Four" rail magnates and local historic railroads.

16. Hidden treasures at the museum: rail schedules, models, lamps, and many other railroad items.

17. What is unique about the museum that can't be found anywhere else: the train museum is in the historic 1907 train station.

18. The most important things about local, state, or American history that can be learned at the museum: the town has always been an important transportation center with the trolley line, railroads, the Bayshore Highway, and airports.

19. Annual events held at the site or elsewhere in the community: Annual Yard Sale and Millbrae Night at the Movies.

20. Research facilities or archives at the site: there are some train books and videos available to the public.

21. Type of gift shop and what is for sale: train videos, books, and collectables.

1. **Military Intelligence Service Historic Learning Center-San Francisco**

2. Location: (Bldg. 640) Presidio of San Francisco (Crissy Field) 640 Mason Street, San Francisco, CA. 94115.

3. Website: http://njahs.org/640/exhibits/

4. Phone number: (415) 921-5007.

5. E-mail: njahs@njahs.org

6. Hours of operation: Sat. and Sun. 12 – 5 p.m.

7. Cost: general admission: $10, NJAHS members, veterans and children under 12 years old: Free.

8. Permanent Exhibits: Introduction, Japanese-American History, Development of MIS at Building 640, Pearl Harbor and Executive Order 9066, MIS in MN. , Internment, Winning the War, Winning the Peace, MIS Classroom, MIS Honor Wall, and Epilogue.

9. Special Exhibits: rotating exhibits.

10. Historical era that is featured the best: WWII.

11. Targeted age groups: all ages.

12. Special activities for children: the MIS Classroom and school tours. Curriculum is under development.

13. Guided tours: contact the museum staff for information.

14. Hands-on activities: there are several state-of-the-art interactive exhibits.

15. The best-kept secrets at the museum: it's location. It is brand new.

16. Hidden treasures at the museum: oral histories that come alive through interactive displays.

17. What is unique about the museum that can't be found anywhere else: this is the only museum of its kind.

18. The most important things about local, state, or American history that can be learned at the museum: the Pacific Theater campaign could not have been won without these Japanese-American translators. They faced discrimination at home

and on the battlefield. They had to do their work while their families were being held in internment camps.

19. Annual events held at the site or elsewhere in the community: the facility is available for events.

20. Research facilities or archives at the site: contact the museum staff for information.

21. Type of gift shop: none.

1. **Mission Carmel**

2. Location: 3080 Rio Road, Carmel, CA. 93923.

3. Website: http://www.carmelmission.org/

4. Phone number: (831) 624-1271.

5. E-mail: store@carmelmission.org

6. Hours of operation: 9:30 a.m. to 5:00 p.m. Monday through Saturday and 10:30 a.m. to 5:00 p.m. on Sunday. The mission is closed Easter Sunday and Monday, Thanksgiving, and over the Christmas holidays from Dec. 24 through Dec. 26.

7. Cost: $6.50 for adults, $4.00 for seniors, $2.00 for children ages 7 and up (free for children under 6).

8. Permanent Exhibits: the Basilica Church, a registered National Historic Landmark, is the centerpiece of the mission. Upon entering, visitors are usually struck by its catenary ceiling, thirty-foot reredos, and 5-foot-thick walls. The mission's fine collection of Spanish Colonial Liturgical Art and Artifacts are displayed through the church. The Harry Downie Museum, located in the forecourt to the basilica, houses interpretive displays and artifacts devoted to telling the restoration story of the mission and the significance of Harry Downie's efforts in the restoration. Behind the basilica, in the Munrás Courtyard, one will find the Munrás Family Heritage Museum. It displays the treasured keepsakes of one prominent Monterey family. Adjacent to the basilica, the Jo Mora Chapel Gallery houses the elaborate Serra Memorial Cenotaph, sculpted in 1924 by Jo Mora, of travertine marble and bronze. In the Convento Museum, the cell used by Junipero Serra is found. He died there in 1784.

9. Special Exhibits: the Jo Mora Chapel Gallery museum is also the home to an art exhibit, which changes periodically. There is also a large display commemorating the visit of Pope John Paul II.

10. Historical era that is featured the best: 1770s-1800s.

11. Targeted age groups: all ages.

12. Special activities for children: there is a special section of the webpage dedicated to 4th graders studying the missions. School tours.

13. Guided tours: self-guided and docent led tours. Reservations required for group tours.

14. Hands-on activities: There is a podcast and 3-D model of the mission and its history available for download on the website.

15. The best-kept secrets at the museum: The burial site of Father Serra, founder of the missions.

16. Hidden treasures at the museum: the mission and its gardens are among the most beautiful in California. Visitors can see rare books, furnishings, artwork, and religious items belonging to the padres.

17. What is unique about the museum that can't be found anywhere else: the Carmel Mission still functions as a thriving parish and school. It contains what is thought to be California's first library, as well as the famous Serra Monument and a statue that was on the altar when the mission first opened its doors.

18. The most important things about local, state, or American history that can be learned at the museum: this is one of the key missions in California. It was the scene of many important historical events. The buildings and grounds have been very well preserved. Unfortunately, however, not much attention is given in the exhibits or gift shop to the Indians who helped build the mission.

19. Annual events held at the site or elsewhere in the community: concerts, Carmel Mission Classic and other events (see website for details).

20. Research facilities or archives at the site: none.

21. Type of gift shop and what is for sale: mission-related books and souvenirs, religious items, etc.

1. **Mission Dolores-San Francisco**

2. Location: 3321 Sixteenth Street, San Francisco, CA. 94114.

3. Website: http://missiondolores.org/old-mission/visitor.html

117

4. Phone number: (415) 621-8203.

5. E-mail: parish@missiondolores.org

6. Hours of operation: open daily except Thanksgiving, Christmas, Easter, & New Year's Day. 9 a.m.-4:30 p.m. May 1-Oct. 31; 9 a.m.-4 p.m. Nov. 1-Apr. 30; 9 a.m.-noon Good Friday; 9 a.m.-4 p.m., Holy Saturday; closed Easter Sunday.

7. Cost: Suggested Donation   - Adult $5, Senior Citizen $3, Student $3.

8. Permanent Exhibits: the basilica and mission grounds, which include a historic cemetery and garden. There are a few rooms dedicated to displaying Indian and mission artifacts.

9. Special Exhibits: rotating exhibits.

10. Historical era that is featured the best: 1800s.

11. Targeted age groups: all ages.

12. Special activities for children: school tours available.

13. Guided tours: by reservation only.

14. Hands-on activities: none.

15. The best-kept secrets at the museum: thousands of Indians and many notable San Francisco pioneers are buried in the cemetery.

16. Hidden treasures at the museum: there is a replica of a native dwelling in the cemetery.

17. What is unique about the museum that can't be found anywhere else: it is the only mission building that has been in continuous use since its construction. It has survived numerous earthquakes and fires.

18. The most important things about local, state, or American history that can be learned at the museum: this building was the nucleus around which San Francisco grew. Many different Native American groups were settled there and intermarried.

Spanish, Mexican, and later, American settlers developed the land around it until the sleepy village of Yerba Buena transformed into the Gold Rush city of San Francisco.

19. Annual events held at the site or elsewhere in the community: concerts, organ recitals, and religious observances (see website for details).

20. Research facilities or archives at the site: none.

21. Type of gift shop and what is for sale: the mission has religious trinkets, mission souvenirs, and books. The selection of books on Native Americans is very limited compared to most missions, however.

1. **Mission San Jose-Fremont**

2. Location: 43300 Mission Blvd, Fremont, CA. 94539.

3. Website: http://www.missionsanjose.org/

4. Phone number: 510-657-1797, x100.

5. E-mail: none.

6. Hours of operation: Daily 10-5 except holidays.

7. Cost: free.

8. Permanent Exhibits: the mission grounds and chapel, numerous items belonging to the priests and the church, and Ohlone Indian artifacts.

9. Special Exhibits: none.

10. Historical era that is featured the best: 1800s.

11. Targeted age groups: all ages.

12. Special activities for children: a special packet is available for the 4th grade missions project done in local schools.

13. Guided tours: available with reservations.

14. Hands-on activities: none.

15. The best-kept secrets at the museum: it has some of the best displays on the Ohlone Indians that are available anywhere.

16. Hidden treasures at the museum: priceless art objects from Mexico and Spain.

17. What is unique about the museum that can't be found anywhere else: it is one of the best-restored missions around. The cemetery is well preserved and contains the tombstones of many local historical figures.

18. The most important things about local, state, or American history that can be learned at the museum: this is one of the most important historical buildings in the area. It was the nucleus of all the settlement in the region.

19. Annual events held at the site or elsewhere in the community: St. Joseph Parish International Festival, Las Posadas, concerts, and other events (see website for details).

20. Research facilities or archives at the site: genealogy records of mission inhabitants are available upon request.

21. Type of gift shop and what is for sale: historical books, mission souvenirs, and religious items.

1. **Mission San Rafael Arcangel**

2. Location: 1104 Fifth Avenue, San Rafael, CA. 94901.

3. Website: http://saintraphael.com/mission-san-rafael-arcangel/

4. Phone number: (415) 454-8141.

5. E-mail: hbernardoni@saintraphael.com

6. Hours of operation: daily from 6:30a.m. – 6:30 p.m.

7. Cost: free.

8. Permanent Exhibits: the replica chapel built in 1949 on the site of the original mission. The mission museum contains artifacts, paintings, and other objects for public viewing, including three of the original bells from Mission San Rafael Arcangel.

9. Special Exhibits: none.

10. Historical era that is featured the best: 1800s.

11. Targeted age groups: all ages.

12. Special activities for children: none.

13. Guided tours: tours of the mission and museum are available for groups of 10 or more with advance reservations.

14. Hands-on activities: none.

15. The best-kept secrets at the museum: the original mission bells.

16. Hidden treasures at the museum: the historic paintings are of interest.

17. What is unique about the museum that can't be found anywhere else: this is one of the last missions built. It only served as a mission for 12 years.

18. The most important things about local, state, or American history that can be learned at the museum: Mission San Rafael Arcangel, the 20th of the California missions, was established as a helper, or asistencia, to Mission Dolores in December 1817. It was then that over 200 Indians and four Franciscan friars, Sarria, Abella, Duran, and Taboada, traveled across the bay to found a hospital mission whose patron, Arcangel Rafael, is God's healing messenger. The mission became Marin County's first hospital, first church, first school, and first justice court. It laid the groundwork for the diverse culture to follow. It was the first mission to be secularized in 1834.

19. Annual events held at the site or elsewhere in the community: see website for details.

20. Research facilities or archives at the site: none.

21. Type of gift shop and what is for sale: the Mission Gift Shop features items related to the California missions, as well as a variety of religious items, such as crosses, rosaries, Bibles, statues, jewelry, trinkets, and much more.

1. **Mission Santa Clara**

2. Location: Santa Clara University, 500 El Camino Real, Santa Clara, CA. 95053.

3. Website: https://www.scu.edu/mission/

4. Phone number: (408) 554-4000.

5. E-mail: use the online contact form.

6. Hours of operation: open daily 8 a.m. to 6 p.m.

7. Cost: free.

8. Permanent Exhibits: the restored mission church. It contains historic statues, paintings, and other items of interest.

9. Special Exhibits: none.

10. Historical era that is featured the best: 1700s-present.

120

11. Targeted age groups: all ages.

12. Special activities for children: school group tours are available.

13. Guided tours: there are self-guided tours and docent-led tours available with a reservation.

14. Hands-on activities: none on site, but there is a virtual tour on the website.

15. The best-kept secrets at the museum: don't forget to visit the mission gardens just outside the church. There are many interesting mission related architectural elements scattered throughout it. Follow the signs.

16. Hidden treasures at the museum: there are many hidden ruins of earlier mission buildings around the university campus. Sometimes they are just the fragment of a wall or even a trace of pavement on the street showing the outline of a lost building.

17. What is unique about the museum that can't be found anywhere else: Santa Clara University, the oldest college in California, is also the only college in the state to be the successor of a Spanish mission.

18. The most important things about local, state, or American history that can be learned at the museum: this was the nucleus for the growth of Santa Clara Valley. Many important events occurred at or near the mission.

19. Annual events held at the site or elsewhere in the community: this is a very popular site for weddings, concerts, and other events (see website for details). It is best to not plan your visit during weekend hours, as you may not be able to see inside the church.

20. Research facilities or archives at the site: not available to the public. Contact the university for research requests.

21. Type of gift shop: none.

22. Additional information: parking is limited. Get a visitor's pass at the gatehouse at the main entrance and follow the directions closely to avoid being cited. Don't miss the nearby deSaisset museum. It has many of the mission's surviving relics and many other interesting historical items.

1. **Mission Santa Cruz**

2. Location: 144 School Street, Santa Cruz, CA. 95060.

3. Website: http://www.parks.ca.gov/?page_id=548

4. Phone number: (831) 425-5849 and 831-426-5686.

5. E-mail: use the online contact form for the State Historic Park. For the mission, write to blpedrazzi@sbcglobal.net

6. Hours of operation: State Historic Park: Thursday, Friday, Saturday, and Monday from 10:00 a.m. - 4:00p.m.
Holy Cross Church and Galleria, Mission Santa Cruz and the Galleria store are open to the public: Tuesday - Saturday: 10:00 a.m. to 4:00 p.m. and Sunday: 10:00 a.m. to 2:00 p.m.

7. Cost: free.

8. Permanent Exhibits: new exhibits and a wall-sized movie projection tell the story of the Ohlone and Yokuts Indian experience at the Santa Cruz Mission. This portion of the adobe, built in the early 1800's, is the only surviving building from Mission Santa Cruz. Archeological excavations in the 1980's revealed that this had been Indian family housing, the only example of its kind still standing in California today.

121

A 7-room building that also includes information about the California Indian experience in the mission, archeological excavations, and Neary-Rodriguez family history. The Mission Museum, next to the church, houses a fine collection of Mission Era vestments from the original mission. There are also sacred vessels used in the Catholic mass and silver candlesticks on display.

9. Special Exhibits: occasional rotating exhibits.

10. Historical era that is featured the best: 1800s.

11. Targeted age groups: all ages.

12. Special activities for children: school group programs on Mondays, Thursdays, and Fridays.

13. Guided tours: the park offers guided tours, living history demonstrations, and Family Drop-In Crafts throughout the year. Click on Events and Activities on the website for more information.

14. Hands-on activities: during special events.

15. The best-kept secrets at the museum: some of the original mission housing is still standing. This is the only mission that still has these buildings intact. They show how Indian families transitioned into mission life.

16. Hidden treasures at the museum: many original mission and Ohlone Indian Items. There are a few ruins of the original walls behind the church.

17. What is unique about the museum that can't be found anywhere else: the state historic park is run completely separately from the church itself.

18. The most important things about local, state, or American history that can be learned at the museum: this is the core of the development for the Santa Cruz area. The mission was destroyed by natural disasters and rebuilt several times. The current church is fairly modern.

19. Annual events held at the site or elsewhere in the community: there are many cultural demonstrations, tours, etc. (see website for details).

20. Research facilities or archives at the site: none.

21. Type of gift shop and what is for sale: there are actually two separate gift shops, one for the church and one for the state historic park. Visit both because they have different items. These include mission books, natural history, religious trinkets, and videos. There are also some historic items from the mission in the one run by the church. They are within walking distance of one another, but have different hours and are separately administered.

1. **Mission Soledad**

2. Location: 36641 Fort Romie Road, Soledad, CA, 93960.

3. Website: http://missionsoledad.com/

4. Phone number: (831) 678 2586.

5. E-mail: none.

6. Hours of operation: 10:00 to 4:00 daily except for Christmas, Thanksgiving, New Year's, Easter, and July 4th.

7. Cost: free.

8. Permanent Exhibits: the mission church and grounds.

9. Special Exhibits: there are some displays related to the archaeological digs.

10. Historical era that is featured the best: 1791-1800s.

122

11. Targeted age groups: all ages.

12. Special activities for children: school tours.

13. Guided tours: tours are self-guided.

14. Hands-on activities: none.

15. The best-kept secrets at the museum: mission art, relics, and furnishings.

16. Hidden treasures at the museum: archeologists unearthed a tile floor in a room in the south wing and the original tile floor in the church. They also were able to determine where a smaller church foundation and a very large foundation met the south wing. Previous digs have found other remnants of the original mission and its walls. Soon there will be "viewing boxes" in order for the public to see the archaeology and avoid covering the discoveries.

17. What is unique about the museum that can't be found anywhere else: this mission has not yet undergone the major restoration that many other missions have had (though plans are under way). This allows the unique opportunity to see the original buildings in a state of decay. It can be difficult in some of the other missions to distinguish between original components of the architecture and the restored portions. Some of these restorations were conducted using controversial methods. Here you can see a mission in its original glory.

18. The most important things about local, state, or American history that can be learned at the museum: this was intended to be the start of a second string of missions to colonize the interior of California, but the rest of the missions were never completed. How different Spanish settlement of California could have been or what would have happened if the Spanish had made it to the Sierra Nevada Mountains and discovered gold first is a matter of fascinating speculation.

19. Annual events held at the site or elsewhere in the community: call the mission for information.

20. Research facilities or archives at the site: information about the archaeological digs on the site is available from the mission.

21. Type of gift shop and what is for sale: mission-related books and souvenirs, religious items, etc.

1. **Monterey County Agricultural & Rural Life Museum-King City**

2. Location: located within San Lorenzo County Park, 1160 Broadway, King City, CA. 93930.

3. Website: http://www.mcarlm.org/

4. Phone number: (831) 386-0965.

5. E-mail: mctic@earthlink.net

6. Hours of operation: the Main Exhibit Barn is open 10:00a.m. to 4:00p.m., Tuesday thru Friday, closed Christmas Eve, Christmas Day, New Year's Eve, New Years Day, Thanksgiving Day and the day after. The Spreckels House, Schoolhouse, Train Depot, and Olson Blacksmith Shop are open Friday 12:00 noon to 4:00 p.m. and Saturdays and Sundays from 11:00 a.m. to 4:00 p.m. with tour guides available to help you. The History of Irrigation Museum is also open for viewing on weekends, but it is recommended that you call ahead if you wish to wish to view the entire facility and see the movie.

123

7. Cost: there is no fee to enter the museum. There is a day use fee for the park of $6 per car Monday through Friday, $8 Saturday and Sunday.

8. Permanent Exhibits: the museum complex has 6 buildings: the Exhibit Barn, Olson Blacksmith Shop, and the History of Irrigation Museum; plus the historic Spreckels House (1898), La Gloria Schoolhouse (1887), and the King City Train Depot (1903). There are outdoor exhibits of antique farm equipment dating from the late 1800s into the 1940s. The Main Exhibit Barn features displays following the development of Salinas Valley agriculture and rural life from the late 1700s to 1940.

9. Special Exhibits: the Common Ground Educational Garden.

10. Historical era that is featured the best: the last quarter of the 19th century through World War II.

11. Targeted age groups: all ages.

12. Special activities for children: the artifact-rich exhibits and hands-on interactive materials made available during school tours provide a fun and memorable educational experience for students.

13. Guided tours: available with reservations.

14. Hands-on activities: some of the displays have interactive elements. Special events and school tours feature hands-on activities.

15. The best-kept secrets at the museum: the buildings have connections to such notables as Claus Spreckels of the Spreckels Sugar Company, lumber magnate Charles H. King, and railroad tycoon Collis P. Huntington.

16. Hidden treasures at the museum: a large collection of farm tools and vehicles dating back to the 1700s.

17. What is unique about the museum that can't be found anywhere else: it is a unique collection of agricultural buildings that are very comprehensive in nature.

18. The most important things about local, state, or American history that can be learned at the museum: the importance of agriculture to the region is well documented.

19. Annual events held at the site or elsewhere in the community: Clam Chowder Dinner, 4th of July in the Park and Car Show, The Ag Tour, and other events (see website for details).

20. Research facilities or archives at the site: the archives contain the museum's records and the complete collection of the San Antonio Valley Historical Association is available by appointment.

21. Type of gift shop and what is for sale: homemade wooden toys, books, and farm-related items.

1. **Museum of the African Diaspora- San Francisco**
2. Location: 685 Mission Street (at Third), San Francisco, CA. 94105.
3. Website: http://www.moadsf.org/
4. Phone number: (415) 358-7200.
5. E-mail: use the online contact form.
6. Hours of operation: Wed.-Sat. 11 a.m.-6 p.m.; Sun. 12 a.m.-5 p.m.
7. Cost: Adults: $10; seniors (65 and over) and students (full-time with current ID): $5; children (12 and under): free.

124

8. Permanent Exhibits: The Origins of the African Diaspora, Celebrations: Ritual and Ceremony, Adornment, Music of the Diaspora, Culinary Traditions, and Slavery Passages.

9. Special Exhibits: rotating exhibits on African Diaspora themes.

10. Historical era that is featured the best: all eras.

11. Targeted age groups: all ages.

12. Special activities for children: school tours, workshops, and many educational outreach programs (see website for details).

13. Guided tours: available with reservations.

14. Hands-on activities: MoAD uses traditional and innovative delivery methods — computer, multi-media images, projection screens, "talking walls," interactive tables, programmed lighting and music, and other sensory stimuli — in presenting and examining the art, culture, and history of the African Diaspora and the communities of people of African descent worldwide.

15. The best-kept secrets at the museum: there is a sizeable collection of films that can be viewed on demand for free in the Freedom Theater.

16. Hidden treasures at the museum: the slave narratives are very compelling.

17. What is unique about the museum that can't be found anywhere else: you won't find many artifacts in this museum. It is a non-traditional, experiential institution.

18. The most important things about local, state, or American history that can be learned at the museum: African culture and people have had a worldwide influence.

19. Annual events held at the site or elsewhere in the community: there are many events throughout the year (see website for details).

20. Research facilities or archives at the site: there is a research area. Contact the museum for details.

21. Type of gift shop and what is for sale: there is a wide variety of interesting books, music, and artwork from which to choose.

1. **Museum of American Heritage-Palo Alto**

2. Location: 351 Homer Avenue, Palo Alto, CA. 94302-1731.

3. Website: http://www.moah.org/

4. Phone number: (650) 321-1004.

5. E-mail: mail@maoh.org

6. Hours of operation: 11 a.m. to 4 p.m., Friday, Saturday, and Sunday.

7. Cost: free.

8. Permanent Exhibits: the exhibits present inventions and technology of the 19th and 20th century in a series of settings typical of the era: An Early 20th Century Kitchen, 1920s General Store, The Ruth Bell Lane Memorial Gardens, a 1920s-40s replica of an auto-repair garage with vintage car, and the Print Shop.

9. Special Exhibits: exhibits rotate twice a year. Exhibits focus on the history of mechanical and electrical technologies. Special exhibits change several times a year and highlight artifacts from toys to typewriters to toasters. In cooperation with other local organizations and institutions, MOAH has established satellite exhibits of interesting objects selected from the museum's collection. These "Mini-MOAH" exhibits are changed periodically and circulate between sites.

125

10. Historical era that is featured the best: the museum generally targets the pre-transistor era. The collections and exhibits highlight inventions and technologies from 1750 to 1950.

11. Targeted age groups: all ages

12. Special activities for children: special workshops and classes for children. There is a dedicated "Children's Room" where children are encouraged to try using an old typewriter, adding machine and rotary telephone. The museum caters portions of each exhibit towards children. They also offer science and technology based workshops, science samplers for school groups, and exhibit tours.

13. Guided tours: docent-led tours for groups and schools for a donation of $3 per person during regular museum hours. Special tours can be arranged at other times with a donation of $5 per person. Group tours are available by appointment.

14. Hands-on activities: The Children's Discovery Room. Activities vary for the main exhibits, according to the current exhibit.

15. The best-kept secrets at the museum: only a small portion of the artifacts in the museum's collection are kept at the house at any time. Rotating exhibits bring items out of storage on a regular basis, so you will not see the same thing if you return a few months later. The collection of over 5,000 mechanical and electrical artifacts, which are located in an offsite warehouse are the best-kept secret.

16. Hidden treasures at the museum: the historic doctor's office of Thomas Williams, a print shop, and a fully stocked general store. A Model-A Ford in an historic repair shop.

17. What is unique about the museum that can't be found anywhere else: the collection of over 5,000 electrical and mechanical artifacts from 1750-1950 is unique, especially in the Bay Area. There is an emphasis on technology and ordinary domestic items.

18. The most important things about local, state, or American history that can be learned at the museum: how technology changed life in America. The museum helps the younger generations develop an appreciation for American inventions of the past and sparks a sense of nostalgia in more senior audiences. As the museum is located in a historic Palo Alto home built for the family of Dr. Williams in 1907, visitors are invited to get a taste of local history through learning about the family that built and lived in the home. The historic gardens are also exemplary of an early 20th century California garden and inspire an interest in plants and horticulture of the past.

19. Annual events held at the site or elsewhere in the community: Vintage Vehicles and Family Festival, which features a wide range of unique vintage cars, an open house featuring Meccano models, hands-on science demonstrations, Annual Holiday LEGO display, a lecture series, classes and workshops, and other family friendly activities.

20. Research facilities or archives at the site: none

21. Type of gift shop: none.

22. Additional information: in the future, the Palo Alto Historical Museum will open across the street.

1. **Moffett Field Historical Museum**

2. Location: Severyns Ave., Building 126, P.O. Box 16, Moffett Field, CA. 94035-0016.

3. Website: http://www.moffettfieldmuseum.org/moffett.html

4. Phone number: (650) 964-4024.

5. E-mail: moffettmuseum@sbcglobal.net

6. Hours of operation: Wednesday-Saturday, 10-2 p.m.

7. Cost: $8 adults, $3 youth, children under 12 free, senior and disabled $5, active military free.

8. Permanent Exhibits: the opening of the base, William Moffett, USS Macon, Army Air Corps, WWII blimps, Fighter/Attack Plane Era, Cold War Patrol, Transport Squads, NASA, Memorial Area, navigational equipment, event room, uniforms, aircraft/cockpits, electronic warfare, and aircrew rescue.

9. Special Exhibits: none.

10. Historical era that is featured the best: 1930s-1990s.

11. Targeted age groups: all ages.

12. Special activities for children: school group visits are available with reservations.

13. Guided tours: docent-led tours are available.

14. Hands-on activities: a cockpit simulator is available for visitors with docent assistance.

15. The best-kept secrets at the museum: it contains a wide variety of aeronautical equipment, uniforms, and historic photos and documents.

16. Hidden treasures at the museum: captured Japanese military gear from WWII, USS Macon artifacts, a U2 flight suit, sub chaser photos and many other interesting items.

17. What is unique about the museum that can't be found anywhere else: it is right beside historic Hangar One. This is as close as you can get to the humongous structure that can be seen from most of the southern Bay Area. It is so big that the Titanic could have fit inside of it!

18. The most important things about local, state, or American history that can be learned at the museum: the base has played many different roles throughout the years. It has played a major role in many twentieth century wars. It is one of the few remaining historic blimp hangars in the world.

19. Annual events held at the site or elsewhere in the community: guest speakers and other special events (see website for details).

20. Research facilities or archives at the site: The MFHS Library has an extensive collection with a wealth of information about Moffett Field and its associated military and other uses, including general material about aviation and NASA.

21. Type of gift shop and what is for sale: a large variety of Moffett Field, NASA, and aeronautical gift items are for sale.

22. Additional information: there are a few historic aircraft outside the museum with more to come in the future.

1. **Monterey County Historical Society-Salinas**

2. Location: Boronda Adobe History Center, 333 Boronda Road, Salinas, CA. 93907.

3. Website: http://mchsmuseum.com/salinas/

4. Phone number: (831) 757-8085.

5. E-mail: use the online contact form.

6. Hours of operation: Office Hours: Monday-Friday, 9 a.m.-3 p.m.
Adobe Tours: Monday-Friday, 10 a.m.-2 p.m.

7. Cost: free.

8. Permanent Exhibits: The Weeks Home, The Jose Eusebio Boronda Adobe, The Bataan Memorial, The Lagunita Schoolhouse, and The Filipino Bunkhouse.

9. Special Exhibits: coming soon.

10. Historical era that is featured the best: 1800s

11. Targeted age groups: all ages.

12. Special activities for children: school tours are available.

13. Guided tours: available upon request.

14. Hands-on activities: none.

15. The best-kept secrets at the museum: the one room schoolhouse has some historical quilts and Indian objects as well.

16. Hidden treasures at the museum: many items from the rancho era are on display at the adobe.

17. What is unique about the museum that can't be found anywhere else: it has an interesting mix of historical buildings and monuments from different historical eras.

18. The most important things about local, state, or American history that can be learned at the museum: Monterey and the surrounding communities have played a pivotal role in California becoming a state. It has an important marine commerce and agricultural role as well.

19. Annual events held at the site or elsewhere in the community: see website for details.

20. Research facilities or archives at the site: the Robert B. Johnston Archival Vault has thousands of historical documents, photographs, and archeological artifacts. Researchers are welcome. Appointments may be made by calling the Monterey County Historical Society at (831) 757-8085.

21. Type of gift shop and what is for sale: local history books and postcards.

22. Additional information: the Monterey County Historical Society is in the process of building a 12,400 square foot agricultural museum and research center. Construction is ongoing on the 5-acre parcel at the Boronda History Center.

1. **Monterey State Historic Park**

2. Location: within walking distance of Fisherman's Wharf. Download the map from the website for specific locations.

3. Websites: http://www.parks.ca.gov/?page_id=575 and http://www.mshpa.org/

4. Phone number: (831) 649-7111.

5. E-mail: mshpa@att.net

6. Hours of operation: start your tour at the Custom House or Pacific House. They are open from 10 a.m. to 4 p.m. Friday, Saturday, Sunday, and Monday Holidays.

7. Cost: the ticket you buy at the Custom House or Pacific House will gain you admission to most of the other buildings. Adults (13 and over) $3.00, kids (12 and under) free when accompanied by paying adult.

8. Permanent Exhibits: there are several historic buildings in the historic downtown area, including:

Custom House (1827) During California's Mexican era, the Monterey Custom House presided over Mexico's main port of entry on the Alta California coast. It was built to serve as the primary government building for the collection of customs duties as well as a meeting place for government officials. It was often the site of celebrations known as 'fandangos'. It was here that Commodore John Drake Sloat raised the American flag in July of 1846, claiming over 600,000 square miles of territory for the United States.

Pacific House (1847) This fine two-story adobe houses a museum of California History and the Holman Collection of American Indian artifacts. The self-guided and interactive exhibits present visitors with the flow of California history, from the Native American era through the Spanish, Mexican, and finally, American governance.

Boston Store (Casa Del Oro) (1845) It was built by Thomas O. Larkin, and operated by Joseph Boston and Company during the 1850s. The building was later called the Casa del Oro (House of Gold) because the big safe was used as a depository for the gold brought back from the goldfields. The store still maintains the safe for visitors to see. Today, the Boston Store is again open for business and is operated by the Historic Garden League.

Casa Soberanes (1842) With its thick walls, interconnecting rooms, cantilevered balcony, and lovely garden, Casa Soberanes reminds visitors of the gracious Monterey lifestyle of early California families.

Cooper-Molera Adobe (1827-1900) First occupied by the Cooper family in 1827 and owned by descendants until 1968, the Cooper-Molera Adobe tells the story of Monterey through the life and times of John Rogers Cooper, a New England sea captain, his wife Encarnacion Vallejo de Cooper and their family members through three generations. The large property includes an historic exhibit room, a carriage display, a recreated 'period' garden, a museum, and a gift store which is operated by volunteers of the Monterey State Historic Park Association.

Spear's Warehouse Located at the Cooper-Molera complex, it is currently used as an historic exhibit room. It has pictures and information panels on the history of Monterey, as well as the Cooper family.

Diaz Adobe Originally part of the adobe built by Capt. John Rogers Cooper, it was included in a debt settlement. It was separated by a wall from the original house and eventually leased to the Manuel Diaz family in 1845. Also a part of the Cooper-Molera complex, the Diaz Adobe is adjacent to the Cooper Museum Store, and is open to public viewing from the store.

First Brick House (1847) Inhabited by its builder, Gallant Dickenson, the First Brick House represents the kiln-fired brick construction brought to California by settlers in the early American period. Dickenson occupied the home for a short period, then abandoned his house to go to the goldfields.

<u>First Theater</u> (1844) Jack Swan's saloon and boarding house became the site of Monterey's first paid theatrical performance. The Troupers of the Gold Coast once presented melodramas here. However, the theater is closed until further notice, pending structural renovations.

<u>Larkin House</u> (1834) This two-story adobe built during Monterey's Mexican period by Thomas O. Larkin, American merchant and U.S. Consul to Alta California, has stood witness to intrigues, business deals, and lively social occasions. Today its early 19th century rooms hold antiques from many parts of the world, acquired by the builder's granddaughter, Alice Larkin Toulmin, who lived there from 1922 to 1957. The building is often known as the prototype for the Monterey Colonial architectural style.

<u>Sherman's Quarters</u> This little adobe was built for some unknown initial purpose. U.S. troops stayed there during the occupation of California. William Tecumseh Sherman stayed there in 1847 while supervising the construction of the fort that is now the Presidio Military Reservation. The adobe is located in the gardens of the Larkin House.

<u>Robert Louis Stevenson House</u> (1840-1897) Reading more like a Robert Louis Stevenson tale of travel and romance than real events, the story of Stevenson's courtship of Fanny Osbourne, his future wife, comes alive amid Stevenson family paintings, furniture, and Stevenson memorabilia. Information about the house's beginnings as a Mexican Era home, a late 19th century boarding house (The French Hotel), and early 20th century uses, such as an artists' studio and workshop, are included in the building's foyer.

<u>Casa Gutierrez</u> (1846) This is one of the few remaining adobes built in the simpler Mexican style that once lined the streets of Monterey. Casa Gutierrez has served many uses over the years, including as a Mexican restaurant.

<u>Casa Serrano</u> Construction of Casa Serrano was started by Thomas Larkin in 1845, but was finished by the next owner, Florencio Serrano. Florencio succeeded Walter Colton as the *alcade*, (a position which combines judge, mayor, and sheriff). Casa Serrano served as one of the first schools after the U.S. flag was flown over the Custom House. Casa Serrano is located at 412 Pacific St. and is owned and operated by the Monterey History and Art Association.

<u>Old Whaling Station</u> (1847) Today the Old Whaling Station boasts Monterey's only remaining whalebone sidewalk, a reminder of one of the town's most important industries from 1850-1900. The charming adobe and its gardens are now under the stewardship of the Junior League of Monterey County.

9. Special Exhibits: these vary depending upon the building.

10. Historical era that is featured the best: 1800s.

11. Targeted age groups: all ages.

12. Special activities for children: school tours and special events. Native American and Early California hands-on program for 3rd and 4th grade students in the Monterey area. Los Ninos Summer Camp for students in grades 3 through 6.

13. Guided tours: some of the buildings have park staff or docents that guide you through the building.

14. Hands-on activities: none.

15. The best-kept secrets at the museum: some of the buildings currently are private homes or businesses with limited public access.

16. Hidden treasures at the museum: there are many interesting artifacts from the Mexican and American Pioneers periods. The Customs House is laid out very realistically with trade goods and Native American items.

17. What is unique about the museum that can't be found anywhere else: it is rare to find so many important historical buildings that are in such close proximity to each other. The buildings have been remarkably well preserved.

18. The most important things about local, state, or American history that can be learned at the museum: many important events in California's history happened in this area. Monterey was California's first capitol. Many key Mexican and American settlers had their homes in this district.

19. Annual events held at the site or elsewhere in the community: 4th of July, Living History Day, History Fest, Christmas in the Adobes, and Art in the Adobes (see website for details).

20. Research facilities or archives at the site: at the Pacific House. Contact park staff for information.

21. Type of gift shop and what is for sale: there are gift shops in the Pacific House and Cooper Store. You can purchase books, videos, and many interesting historic toys, crafts, and souvenirs. I am partial to the sarsaparilla!

22. Additional information: once a crown jewel of the state historic parks, Monterey State Historic Park has suffered greatly from state budget cuts. Many buildings that were once open to the public are now closed or only open sporadically. Thanks to the valiant efforts of park staff and community volunteers, the park has been reorganized and efforts are under way to reopen as many buildings as possible. In general, it is better to visit on weekends or with a school group to get into the historic sites. More buildings are open in the summer and during special events. It is best to visit the Monterey State Historic Parks Association website for information before planning a visit.

The following historic sites in Monterey are not part of the State Historic Parks, but are run by the City of Monterey:

Colton Hall U.S. Navy Chaplain Walter Colton was appointed to serve as Monterey's first American *alcade*. He designed and supervised the construction of Colton Hall, the first public building constructed under the American flag. Opened in March 8, 1849, it was built to serve as a school and town meeting hall. California's first constitution was written and signed here. Colton Hall was Monterey's county seat until 1873, when Salinas was chosen. Colton Hall is located at 570 Pacific St., and is owned and operated by the City of Monterey.

See http://www.monterey.org/museums/ for information about hours and location.

Old Monterey Jail Located next to Colton Hall is the old jail, constructed in 1854. It served as a city jail until 1956.

Pacific Biological Laboratories owned and operated by marine biologist and pioneering ecologist Edward Flanders Robb Ricketts (1897-1948), the best friend and collaborator of writer John Steinbeck.

Presidio Museum (see separate listing).

Royal Presidio Chapel Located at 550 Church St. in Monterey, the Royal Presidio Chapel is also known as San Carlos Church and Cathedral of San Carlos Borromeo. It was founded on June 3, 1770, by Father Junipero Serra and Don Gaspar de Portola. The chapel is called "royal" because Alta California's Spanish governor worshipped there in his role as representative of the King of Spain. It is administered by the Diocese of Monterey. See http://www.sancarloscathedral.org/ for visiting hours.

1. **Mothball Fleet-Martinez**

2. Location: passengers meet outside the Harbor Masters building at the Martinez Marina located at 7 North Court Street, Martinez, CA. 94553.

3. Website: http://bayviewcharters.com/us-navy-mothball-fleet/public-tour/

4. Phone number: (707) 747-5443.

5. E-mail: info@bayviewcharters.com

6. Hours of operation: tours usually check in at 10:30 a.m. on Saturdays. See the website for dates.

7. Cost: Tickets are $32 per person and $29 for seniors and children under 5 years of age.

8. Permanent Exhibits: it is a 2-hour tour that includes a light picnic lunch with a beverage. Up-close viewing of the Suisun Navy Reserve Fleet, otherwise known as the Mothball Fleet. You will see the *SS Cape Fear*, the *SS Cape Bover*, the *SS Cape Girardeau*, the *SS Cape Jacob*, the *SS Green Mountain State*, and other ships.

9. Special Exhibits: none.

10. Historical era that is featured the best: WWII.

11. Targeted age groups: all ages.

12. Special activities for children: none.

13. Guided tours: private and group tours narrated by sailors who served on the ships.

14. Hands-on activities: none.

15. The best-kept secrets at the museum: many people driving across the Martinez Bridge have seen the ships, but most people don't know that you can get this close to the venerable ships.

16. Hidden treasures at the museum: the fleet once contained hundreds of ships, but now there are only about a dozen left.

17. What is unique about the museum that can't be found anywhere else: these WWII era ships are some of the last ones still afloat.

18. The most important things about local, state, or American history that can be learned at the museum: these historic vessels took part in four wars: WWII, the Korean War, the Vietnam War, and Desert Storm. They are being removed for salvage, parts, and scrap. It is estimated that by 2017, they will all be gone.

19. Annual events held at the site or elsewhere in the community: Fleet Week (see website for details).

20. Research facilities or archives at the site: none.

21. Type of gift shop and what is for sale: there is a small shop at the dock with souvenirs.

22. Additional information: this is the only way to get close to these famous ships. Passengers may not board the ships, however.

1. **Mount Diablo State Park**

2. Location: Mount Diablo State Park, Walnut Creek, CA. 94598.

3. Websites: http://www.parks.ca.gov/?page_id=517 and http://www.mdia.org/site/park-information/park-info/summit-museum

4. Phone number: (925) 837-2525.

5. E-mail: info@parks.ca.gov

6. Hours of operation: 7 days a week from 10 a.m. – 4 p.m.

7. Cost: $6 per car.

130

8. Permanent Exhibits: the Visitor Center is located in the historic stone building atop Mount Diablo's highest peak. The tower was constructed during the late 1930's of fossiliferous sandstone blocks quarried in the park. The Visitor Center highlights the cultural and natural history of the park. Impressive exhibits chronicle the history of the mountain and capture its majesty. A rock wall with instructional video examines the geological forces that created the mountain. A diorama, complete with sound, offers an overview of the park's ecosystems and its cultural history. A model of the mountain acquaints visitors with important park locations. Splendid artwork and photographs enhance the visitor's experience.

9. Special Exhibits: art shows.

10. Historical era that is featured the best: prehistoric times to the present.

11. Targeted age groups: all ages.

12. Special activities for children: rock-climbing areas such as Rock City are popular with kids. They are like natural playgrounds.

13. Guided tours: ranger-led hikes are occasionally offered. Call for information.

14. Hands-on activities: some of the displays at the visitor center are interactive.

15. The best-kept secrets at the museum: the controversy over the origins of the name, Mt. Diablo is discussed. It is not "Devil's Mountain" as some would say!

16. Hidden treasures at the museum: the displays are a nice combination of natural and human history.

17. What is unique about the museum that can't be found anywhere else: the view from the top of Mt. Diablo is one of the most spectacular in the Bay Area. On a clear day, one can see parts of the San Francisco Bay, the surrounding mountains as far as Mt. Hamilton, and sometimes even the Sierra Nevadas or Mt. Shasta.

18. The most important things about local, state, or American history that can be learned at the museum: the mountain has been very important to the development of the region.

19. Annual events held at the site or elsewhere in the community: contact the park for information.

20. Research facilities or archives at the site: none.

21. Type of gift shop and what is for sale: books, postcards, posters, and state park souvenirs.

22. Additional information: Also visit the Mitchell Canyon Information Center on the north side of the mountain at the south end of Mitchell Canyon Road in Clayton, Ca. The center is currently open on Saturdays and Sundays, and some holidays 8 a.m. to 4 p.m. during spring and summer months and 9 a.m. to 3 p.m. during fall and winter months. The center has displays about various aspects of Mt. Diablo State Park, such as geology, wildlife, trails, and plant life.

1. **Mt. Hamilton-Lick Observatory**

2. Location: Lick Observatory is located on the summit of Mt. Hamilton in the Diablo Range east of San Jose.

3. Website: http://mthamilton.ucolick.org/

4. Phone number: (831) 459-2991.

5. E-mail: ptowle@ucolick.org

6. Hours of operation: Memorial Day - Labor Day: Visitor Center open every day: 12:00 noon - 5:00 p.m., Shane Gallery: 10:00 a.m. - 5:00 pm. The Shane 3-m Telescope Building is open for self-guided viewing of exhibits and the telescope through a window. Labor Day - Memorial Day: Visitor Center open Thurs.-Sun.: 12:00 noon - 5:00 p.m., Shane Gallery every day: 10:00 a.m. - 5:00 p.m.

7. Cost: free.

8. Permanent Exhibits: view exhibits in the Main Observatory building (see details below), built in 1888. Note the original oak and marble interior. Take a short walk to the Shane Dome to view the 120-inch reflector from the Visitors' Gallery. Displays explain the Shane Reflector, one of the major telescopes used to discover extrasolar planets.

9. Special Exhibits: other telescopes may be viewed only during special events.

10. Historical era that is featured the best: 1888-present.

11. Targeted age groups: all ages.

12. Special activities for children: none on site.

13. Guided tours: enjoy a short informal talk about Lick history while taking a look at the Great Lick Refractor in the 36-inch telescope dome (no charge). Talks begin at the gift shop throughout the afternoon, starting at 1:00p.m. on weekdays and 12:30p.m. on weekends, continuing until 4:30p.m.

14. Hands-on activities: some of the displays in the visitors' center are interactive.

15. The best-kept secrets at the museum: some of the newer telescopes are opened to the public during the annual open house.

16. Hidden treasures at the museum: interesting scientific instruments and astronomy pictures.

17. What is unique about the museum that can't be found anywhere else: its location. It is a working scientific research center. The views of the Santa Clara Valley and sometimes the Sierra Nevada Mountains are spectacular.

18. The most important things about local, state, or American history that can be learned at the museum: this is one of the oldest observatories in California with a rich history of important discoveries.

19. Annual events held at the site or elsewhere in the community: the annual open house is in the summer time. Purchase tickets early because they go fast (see website for details).

20. Research facilities or archives at the site: not open to the public.

21. Type of gift shop and what is for sale: Lick Observatory sweatshirts, T-shirts, mugs, wineglasses, astronomical photos, posters, educational toys, and other astronomy-related items.

22. Additional information: the observatory is more than 20 miles from downtown San Jose along Mt. Hamilton Road at an elevation of 4200 feet. The road follows a gradual grade laid out over a century ago for horses and carts. It has many sharp

131

curves and is quite narrow in places. At 4209 feet, weather on Mt. Hamilton may be cool and changeable, so bring a sweater or coat. There is wheelchair access to the main building from the back. There are no gasoline or food services at Mt. Hamilton or anywhere along the road outside of San Jose. During the winter the road may be closed temporarily due to snowfall.

1. **Murrietta's Well-Livermore**
2. Location: Murrietta's Well Winery, 3005 Mines Road, Livermore, CA. 94550.
3. Website: http://www.murrietaswell.com/
4. Phone number: (925) 456-2395.
5. E-mail: none.
6. Hours of operation: May 1 – October 31: daily 11 a.m. to 4:30 p.m.
 November 1 – April 31: Wednesday through Sunday 11 a.m. to 4:30 p.m.
7. Cost: Viewing the well is free, but the entry fee into the wine tasting room is $10.
8. Permanent Exhibits: a recreated artesian well used by Joaquin Murrieta, the Gold Rush Era bandit. A historic winery built on the spot by Louis Mel in 1883.
9. Special Exhibits: none.
10. Historical era that is featured the best: the Gold Rush.
11. Targeted age groups: all ages, except the wine tasting room is only available to adults over the age of 21.
12. Special activities for children: none.
13. Guided tours: none.
14. Hands-on activities: none.
15. The best-kept secrets at the museum: many sites have been attributed to Murrieta in legend, but this one is fairly well documented.
16. Hidden treasures at the museum: just the well.
17. What is unique about the museum that can't be found anywhere else: it is not often that one gets to taste wine and history in the same spot!
18. The most important things about local, state, or American history that can be learned at the museum: Joaquin Murrieta is a controversial figure. He appears in many legends and accounts as a bandito who raided Gold Rush areas from 1850-1853. Many places in California claim to have been his hideout. Some people viewed him as an outlaw and some as a Robin Hood figure. The extent of his crimes and the circumstances of his death and capture are still in dispute.
19. Annual events held at the site or elsewhere in the community: none.
20. Research facilities or archives at the site: none.
21. Type of gift shop and what is for sale: wine.

1. **Musee Mecanique-San Francisco**
2. Location: on Pier 45 at the foot of Taylor Street in San Francisco's Fisherman's Wharf.
3. Website: http://www.museemecaniquesf.com/
4. Phone number: (415) 346-2000.
5. E-mail: use the contact form on the website.
6. Hours of operation: Mon-Fri 10:00 a.m.-7:00 p.m.; Sat., Sun., and holidays 10:00 a.m.-8:00 p.m. Open all year long.

7. Cost: free.

8. Permanent Exhibits: one of the world's largest (over 200) privately owned collection of coin-operated mechanical musical instruments and antique arcade machines in their original working condition.

9. Special Exhibits: none.

10. Historical era that is featured the best: 1800s-1900s.

11. Targeted age groups: all ages.

12. Special activities for children: many of the games are kid-oriented.

13. Guided tours: none, but the museum can be rented for private parties.

14. Hands-on activities: Everything!

15. The best-kept secrets at the museum: there are some very rare and collectible machines in the museum. Many are one-of-a-kind in the world.

16. Hidden treasures at the museum: many treasures have been preserved from the lost San Francisco arcades at Playland at the Beach, Sutro Baths, and the Cliff House.

17. What is unique about the museum that can't be found anywhere else: all of the coin-operated games are available to play. Prices range from 1¢ to $1. Most games cost 25¢ to 50¢.

18. The most important things about local, state, or American history that can be learned at the museum: an important element of American entertainment is chronicled. Arcades are rapidly disappearing in the U.S. This museum preserves this heritage.

19. Annual events held at the site or elsewhere in the community: none.

20. Research facilities or archives at the site: none.

21. Type of gift shop and what is for sale: a video about the collection, CD's of arcade music, and lost and found pictures from the arcade's photo booths over the years!

1. **The Museum of Local History-Fremont**

2. Location: 190 Anza Street, Fremont, CA. 94539.

3. Website: http://www.museumoflocalhistory.org/

4. Phone number: (510) 623-7907.

5. E-mail: info@museumoflocalhistory.org

6. Hours of operation: 10 a.m. to 4 p.m. every Wednesday and Friday and 10 a.m. to 4 p.m. every second weekend in every month.

7. Cost: donations accepted.

134

8. Permanent Exhibits: early elementary schools, the first high school in the Washington Township, Mission Mercantile, Livery Stable, Film-making in Niles, Early Post Offices, the Benbow Family, Ice Age mammal fossils found at the nearby Bell Quarry, horse carriages, farm and ranch equipment, school exhibits, and a well furnished home kitchen exhibit.

9. Special Exhibits: Four Winds Grower, Cloverdale Dairy and Creamery, and IOOF (Independent Order of Odd-fellows).

10. Historical era that is featured the best: 1850 to the present.

11. Targeted age groups: all ages.

12. Special activities for children: 3rd grade tours. A children's program is under development, targeted for completion in 2015.

13. Guided tours: group tours can be arranged. Third grade and Ohlone College student tours. Rancho Higuera Adobe tours by appointment (510) 623-7907.

15. The best-kept secrets at the museum: many unique maps, local aerial photos, and City of Fremont sourced photos and items that cover the area from before incorporation to the present. A display about Teddy Ruxpin, which was made in Fremont.

16. Hidden treasures at the museum: the fossil collection is impressive. The Robert Fisher Collection and the collection of maps from the 1800s to 1970s.

17. What is unique about the museum that can't be found anywhere else: a cross-section of Fremont history is depicted. Lots of information is available about all of the historical sites in Fremont. An extensive photo collection draws from several key local historians and photo-documentarians: Robert B. Fisher, Judge H. Durham, Julie Ann Howe, and Phil Holmes are just a few of the photo collection highlights. Phil Holmes' research files are also kept at the MLH. A broad range of locally - derived items tell the history of many local people, families, and businesses in the area.

18. The most important things about local, state, or American history that can be learned at the museum: Fremont has played many roles over the years, from mission to farming to technology. Many small communities merged to become Fremont. Each of them has its own interesting history. The MLH showcases the early development of Alameda County, and how agriculture, business, and the many townships contributed to the prosperity, growth and development of California.

19. Annual events held at the site or elsewhere in the community: the Washington Township Historical Society holds a bi-monthly speaker series at the MLH.

20. Research facilities or archives at the site: a reference library with several thousand books, magazines, newspapers, ephemera, and various publications. It promotes and offers assistance on many historical research projects.

21. Type of gift shop and what is for sale: books and videos are available about the history of Fremont and surrounding communities. Publications primarily focusing on local history.

22. Additional information: The Museum of Local History is actively involved with many history-focused groups at the state, county, and local community level to promote an interest and lifelong study of history.

1. **Museum of the San Ramon Valley-Danville**
2. Location: at the corner of Railroad and Prospect Avenues in downtown Danville. 205 Railroad Ave. Danville, CA. 94526.
3. Website: http://www.museumsrv.org/
4. Phone number: (925) 837-3750.
5. E-mail: srvmuseum@sbcglobal.net
6. Hours of operation: Tuesday through Friday: 1 - 4pm, Saturday: 10a.m. - 1p.m., Sunday: noon to 3p.m.
7. Cost: Family - $5; adults - $3; children $1 (under 5 are free), students (kindergarten through 12th grade with ID) - $2.
8. Permanent Exhibits: the museum features a permanent exhibit of local valley history. This exhibit begins with the geology of the area in prehistoric times and

135

concludes with contemporary times. An historical narrative frieze near the ceiling traces valley history in drawings. Artifacts, illustrations, photographs, captions, history brochures, and hands-on opportunities enrich the visitor experience.

9. Special Exhibits: six or seven rotating professional exhibits a year with a model train exhibit, an Indian Life exhibit every fall (Bay Miwok and Ohlone Indians, historic baskets, animal mounts, acorn preparation, skins, interpretive signage), and a Christmas Memories exhibit from mid-Nov. to early January (trees, special interactive features, antique toys, life-sized Santa, children's activities). Previous exhibits include: Early Valley Families, Mount Diablo Perspectives, Model Trains, Quilts, Indian Life, and Christmas Memories (see website for details).

10. Historical era that is featured the best: 1800s-1900s.

11. Targeted age groups: all ages.

12. Special activities for children: a passport program that includes Indian life, one room school, local history, treasure hunts, coloring, Q&A doors, and films.

13. Guided tours: available upon request.

14. Hands-on activities: none.

15. The best-kept secrets at the museum: the museum is an old rail depot, so it has many interesting railroad items. It is the only authentically restored Southern Pacific depot along the San Ramon Branch Line.

16. Hidden treasures at the museum: the historical narrative frieze traces the history of the valley.

17. What is unique about the museum that can't be found anywhere else: it is also a visitor's center for local tourist attractions, such as the nearby home of Eugene O'Neill.

18. The most important things about local, state, or American history that can be learned at the museum: the development of local communities from Indian settlements to Spanish ranches to farming villages, and finally, modern cities, is chronicled at the museum.

19. Annual events held at the site or elsewhere in the community: fairs, wind festivals, street art and craft fairs, and oak tree lightings in Alamo, Danville, and San Ramon during the holiday season. A lecture series is provided by the museum and library (see website for details).

20. Research facilities or archives at the site: there is a small library of local history books and papers available to researchers.

21. Type of gift shop and what is for sale: it has an attractive gift shop with many local history books, toys, and souvenirs highlighting Mount Diablo, flora and fauna.

22. Additional information: the museum is run primarily by volunteers and it offers a unique experience to visitors.

1. **Museum of Monterey**
2. Location: 5 Custom House Plaza, Monterey, CA. 93940.
3. Website: http://museumofmonterey.org/
4. Phone number: (831) 372-2608.
5. E-mail: mark.baer@museumofmonterey.org
6. Hours of operation: Winter: 11 a.m.-5 p.m., Wednesday-Saturday noon-5p.m. Summer: 10a.m.-7p.m., Tuesdays-Saturday noon-5 p.m.

136

7. Cost: $8 - General Admission (non-members); $5 - Military, Students, Seniors & Locals; Free - Children 12 and under. 1st Wednesday of every month free 11 a.m. – 5p.m.

8. Permanent Exhibits: In the Footsteps of Legacy: Art History of Monterey, the Maritime Collection, and various art exhibits.

9. Special Exhibits: art shows and historical exhibits (see website for details).

10. Historical era that is featured the best: 1800-1900s.

11. Targeted age groups: all ages.

12. Special activities for children: storytelling, art activities, school tours.

13. Guided tours: available with reservations. Historic walking tours of Monterey.

14. Hands-on activities: none.

15. The best-kept secrets at the museum: there are many fine pieces of art as well as many interesting nautical items.

16. Hidden treasures at the museum: the spectacular original Fresnel first-order lens from the Big Sur lighthouse.

17. What is unique about the museum that can't be found anywhere else: it is located right next to Fisherman's Wharf. The museum building is quite striking.

18. The most important things about local, state, or American history that can be learned at the museum: Monterey has a long tradition of art, the importance of the sea to the community is well documented.

19. Annual events held at the site or elsewhere in the community: the Merienda, Monterey's birthday party, is a colorful fiesta of delicious foods, red wine, gallant dons, lovely senoritas, lively music, and festive dance. Traditionally held in the Memory Garden in the patio of the Old Pacific House, a State Historical Monument, it is the gem of the Monterey History and Art Association's annual celebrations.

20. Research facilities or archives at the site: none.

21. Type of gift shop and what is for sale: art-related items.

22. Additional information: it was formerly known as the Monterey Maritime & History Museum.

1. **Museum of the American Indian-Novato**

2. Location: 2200 Novato Blvd. Novato, CA. 94947.

3. Website: http://museumoftheamericanindian.org/index.html

4. Phone number: (415) 897-4064.

5. E-mail: office@marinindian.com

6. Hours of operation: Tu. - Fr. 12-5p.m., Sat. - Sun. 12-4p.m.

7. Cost: Members: free, Adults: $5, Children/Seniors: $3, Families: $10

8. Permanent Exhibits: Outdoors: Full-scale Kotcha Miwok Indian dwelling, mural, path featuring an actual village site. Indoors: Pottery, basketry, clothing, tools, and many other kinds of artifacts from many different Indian cultures. A permanent display on local Miwok Indians featuring a replica village, interpretative displays, and artifacts.

9. Special Exhibits: rotating special exhibits featuring various Indian themes

10. Historical era that is featured the best: pre-European contact to modern Indian cultures.

11. Targeted age groups: all ages.

137

12. Special activities for children: a hands-on room filled with a rich collection of replica artifacts.

13. Guided tours: available with reservations.

14. Hands-on activities: in the Children's Room.

15. The best-kept secrets at the museum: the large scope of collections for a small museum.

16. Hidden treasures at the museum: local Indian artifacts as well as those from other parts of the country.

17. What is unique about the museum that can't be found anywhere else: the combination of an actual Miwok village site and a museum.

18. The most important things about local, state, or American history that can be learned at the museum: the contributions of Native Americans to our history.

19. Annual events held at the site or elsewhere in the community: the Novato Multi-Cultural Festival and Camp Coyote.

20. Research facilities or archives at the site: a research library is available upon request.

21. Type of gift shop and what is for sale: a wide selection of Indian-related items.

22. Additional information: guest lectures and traveling exhibits are available from the director.

1. **Napa Firefighters Museum**

2. Location: 1201 Main Street, Napa, CA. 94559.

3. Website: www.napafirefightersmuseum.org

4. Phone number: (707) 259-0609.

5. E-mail: info@napafirefightersmuseum.org

138

6. Hours of operation: 11a.m.-4p.m., Wednesday thru Saturday, and occasional Sundays.

7. Cost: free

8. Permanent Exhibits: fire trucks, fire fighting equipment, call boxes, sirens, and firefighter-related toys.

9. Special Exhibits: the museum provides space for a wide variety of rotating displays from other community members, activities, and interests.

10. Historical era that is featured the best: 1800s-the present.

11. Targeted age groups: all ages.

12. Special activities for children: school tours are available.

13. Guided tours: available upon request.

14. Hands-on activities: none.

15. The best-kept secrets at the museum: the toy collection is superb.

16. Hidden treasures at the museum: emergency radio systems and civil defense equipment are featured.

17. What is unique about the museum that can't be found anywhere else: many local items are featured. The museum has a wide variety of objects and vehicles.

18. The most important things about local, state, or American history that can be learned at the museum: it emphasizes the important role that firefighters played in the region and how their equipment changed over time.

19. Annual events held at the site or elsewhere in the community: see website for details.

20. Research facilities or archives at the site: some fire records and photographs and books are available for research.

21. Type of gift shop and what is for sale: some fire-related books and fire department souvenirs are available.

1. **Napa Valley Museum-Yountville**

2. Location: 55 Presidents Circle, PO Box 3567, Yountville, CA. 94599.

3. Website: http://www.napavalleymuseum.org/

4. Phone number: (707) 944-0500.

5. E-mail: info@NapaValleyMuseum.org

6. Hours of operation: Tuesday-Sunday, 10a.m.-4p.m.

7. Cost: free for members, $5 adults, $3.50 seniors, $2.50 youth under 17. Free admission on the second Saturday of every month.

8. Permanent Exhibits: Land and People of Napa Valley is the museum's permanent exhibition about the history and people of Napa Valley. Learn how Napa Valley's unique geology made this valley's agricultural and viticulture industries flourish. Learn about: Geology, Native Americans, Transportation, Early Pioneers, The Rancho Period, The Hot Springs, and Chinese and Jews of Napa Valley

9. Special Exhibits: the Main Gallery has rotating exhibitions of art and history.

10. Historical era that is featured the best: 1800s to the present.

11. Targeted age groups: all ages.

12. Special activities for children: Free Family Fun Days and school outreach programs.

13. Guided tours: tours of the museum's grounds and exhibitions are available the third Saturday of every month at 11 a.m. The tour is included in admission. Special group tours are available upon request.

14. Hands-on activities: none.

15. The best-kept secrets at the museum: displays on Jewish and Chinese settlers in the area.

16. Hidden treasures at the museum: Wappo Indian artifacts.

17. What is unique about the museum that can't be found anywhere else: it has the best comprehensive display of the many farms, resorts, and industries that have shaped the area.

18. The most important things about local, state, or American history that can be learned at the museum: the geology, history, and settlement patterns that made the area into Wine Country.

19. Annual events held at the site or elsewhere in the community: (Prohibition) Repeal Day Party, Oktoberfest & Car Show, Annual Gala and Top Drink: The Art of the Cocktail (see website for details).

20. Research facilities or archives at the site: none. Contact the collection manager for research questions.

21. Type of gift shop and what is for sale: books, CD's, art books and other gift items related to the current exhibit.

1. **NASA Ames Visitor Center-Sunnyvale**
2. Location: NASA Ames Research Center, Moffett Field, CA. 94035.
3. Website: http://www.nasa.gov/centers/ames/home/exploration.html
4. Phone number: (650) 604-6497.
5. E-mail: cara.dodge@nasa.gov
6. Hours of operation: Tuesday - Friday 10 a.m. - 4 p.m. and Saturday-Sunday noon - 4 p.m.
7. Cost: free.
8. Permanent Exhibits: Ames Spacecraft Missions: NASA's Ames Research Center has been involved in pivotal spacecraft missions that have redefined our view of our planetary neighbors and beyond! Models of previous and recent spacecraft missions from NASA Ames.
Mercury Redstone 1A (MR-1A) – This capsule, launched on December 19, 1960, attained an altitude of 130.7 statute miles. MR-1A was the last unmanned test flight before the Mercury 7 astronauts took flight. Five months after MR-1A flew, on May 5, 1961, Alan Shepard became the first American to fly in space aboard Friendship 7, a Mercury capsule nearly identical to MR-1A.
9. Special Exhibits: SOFIA – NASA developed the Stratospheric Observatory for Infrared Astronomy - or SOFIA - as a world-class airborne observatory that will complement the Hubble, Spitzer, Herschel and James Webb space telescopes and major Earth-based telescopes. The original wind-tunnel model of SOFIA is now on display. Kepler – The Kepler Mission is designed to survey our region of the Milky Way Galaxy and has discovered over a thousand potential new planets orbiting nearby stars. Living and Working in Space – Microgravity research has benefited our understanding of the universe. Discovering the Moon – On loan from Marshal Space Flight Center, features NASA mission data. Discovering the Moon covers interesting discoveries about the moon, and what we want to learn next! Science on a Sphere – See our world, and many others, from a new perspective with the Science on a Sphere Visualization System. Originally developed by NOAA, the Science on a Sphere offers visitors a new look at the planets in the universe with a large, spherical projection system. See weather patterns, earthquake data, and much more.
10. Historical era that is featured the best: 20th century-present.
11. Targeted age groups: all ages.
12. Special activities for children: field trips for grades 3-8, educator materials, and some kid-friendly displays.
13. Guided tours: available with reservations.
14. Hands-on activities: a high-resolution Immersive Theater with a 14-foot tall and 36-foot wide screen and a Shuttle Cockpit Simulator. In addition to these, several other exhibits are interactive.
15. The best-kept secrets at the museum: there are many original items used in space, spacesuits, and other interesting displays.
16. Hidden treasures at the museum: a real moon rock, retrieved by the crew of Apollo 15 from the moon's Hadley-Apennine region.
17. What is unique about the museum that can't be found anywhere else: the museum highlights NASA Ames's specific role in the overall space program.

140

18. The most important things about local, state, or American history that can be learned at the museum: this key facility has been very influential in the development of aircraft, spacecraft, and the exploration of our solar system.
19. Annual events held at the site or elsewhere in the community: Day of Remembrance, guest lectures, and other events (see website for details).
20. Research facilities or archives at the site: none.
21. Type of gift shop and what is for sale: space-related toys, gifts, films, books, etc.
22. Additional information: please note that The NASA Ames Research Center is closed to the public.

1. **National Steinbeck Center-Salinas**
2. Location: One Main Street, Salinas, CA. 93901.
3. Website: http://www.steinbeck.org/
4. Phone number: admission: (831) 775-4721.
5. E-mail: Use the contact form on the website.
6. Hours of operation: open seven days a week from 10 a.m. to 5 p.m.

7. Cost: Adults: $14.95; Monterey County residents: $10.95; seniors (over 62), students, teachers, and military with ID: $8.95; youth 13-17: $7.95; children 6-12: $5.95, 5 & under: free.
8. Permanent Exhibits: the John Steinbeck Exhibition Hall, which has displays on each of Steinbeck's books in chronological order. The Rabobank Agricultural Museum is a field-to-fork experience through the Salinas Valley's agricultural industry. With a strong focus on the individuals, immigrant groups, and families who shaped Salinas Valley agriculture, this exhibition features audio clips, photographs, film footage, personal memorabilia, unique tools, and artifacts used throughout the decades.
9. Special Exhibits: rotating exhibits on art, local history, and agriculture.
10. Historical era that is featured the best: the 20th century.
11. Targeted age groups: middle school to adults.
12. Special activities for children: special activities are available for field trips. The Steinbeck Young Authors Program, ACT's Young Conservatory program, and the Grapes of Wrath Journey.
13. Guided tours: available upon request.
14. Hands-on activities: most of the displays are highly interactive with many hands-on features.
15. The best-kept secrets at the museum: personal effects of the author are scattered throughout the museum.
16. Hidden treasures at the museum: Steinbeck's books in foreign languages, mini-theaters with film and stage adaptations of the book. There are also films with interviews with people who knew him.
17. What is unique about the museum that can't be found anywhere else: it is the best comprehensive overview of Steinbeck's life and work available anywhere.
18. The most important things about local, state, or American history that can be learned at the museum: a good deal of Monterey County's history is also contained in the museum.

19. Annual events held at the site or elsewhere in the community: there are many annual events (see website for details).

20. Research facilities or archives at the site: an extensive archive of documents, films, photographs, etc. is available for researchers by appointment.

21. Type of gift shop and what is for sale: all of Steinbeck's books, other memorabilia and gifts.

1. **New Almaden Quicksilver Mining Museum-San Jose**

2. Location: Almaden Quicksilver County Park, 21350 Almaden Road, San Jose, CA. 95120.

3. Website: http://www.sccgov.org/sites/parks/parkfinder/Pages/Almaden-Quicksilver-Mining-Museum.aspx

4. Phone number: (408) 323-1107.

5. E-mail: tamara.clark@prk.sccgov.org

6. Hours of operation: Mondays, Tuesdays, Fridays: 12p.m. - 4p.m. Saturdays and Sundays: 10a.m. - 4p.m.

7. Cost: free.

8. Permanent Exhibits: use of cinnabar by the Ohlone people, Mexican mining, mining equipment, ore samples, various items that use mercury, life in the camps, historic photographs, and the mine superintendant's office.

9. Special Exhibits: nature trails run through the park. There are also remnants of mining structures throughout the park. All mines have been sealed, but the San Cristobal Mine may be viewed from behind a locked gate.

10. Historical era that is featured the best: 1800s.

11. Targeted age groups: all ages.

12. Special activities for children: school tours and educational materials for teachers. A Junior Ranger program.

13. Guided tours: ranger-guided nature and history walks are available upon request. Call (408) 268-3883 for more information.

14. Hands-on activities: some of the displays may be touched.

15. The best-kept secrets at the museum: most people don't know that the Ohlone Indians used the crushed ore for pigmentation.

16. Hidden treasures at the museum: many interesting pieces of mining equipment and mercury related items may be viewed.

17. What is unique about the museum that can't be found anywhere else: it is the only mining museum in Santa Clara County. Most people assume that only gold was mined in California. The hills of the park contain the only ghost towns in the Bay Area as well.

18. The most important things about local, state, or American history that can be learned at the museum: simply put, the Gold Rush, as we know it, could not have taken place without New Almaden. Gold cannot be extracted from hard rock ores such as quartz without mercury. Flasks of mercury from this mine can be seen in almost every mining museum throughout the Gold Country and into Nevada. The mines drew miners from around the world. This mine was a huge part of the local economy. Many mine structure ruins and miners' houses remain in the park. A century later, it is still not safe to eat fish caught in some of the creeks of the Santa

Clara Valley and the San Francisco Bay because of the mercury poisoning from this mine.

19. Annual events held at the site or elsewhere in the community: see the County of Santa Clara Parks and Recreation website for details.

20. Research facilities or archives at the site: none.

21. Type of gift shop and what is for sale: many interesting books, gift items, and souvenirs related to the Ohlone Indians, history, mining, and the nature of the area can be purchased.

1. **The Niles Depot Model Railroads and Museum-Fremont**

143

2. Location: 37592 Niles Boulevard, Fremont, CA. 94536.

3. Website: www.nilesdepot.org

4. Phone number: (510) 797-4449.

5. E-mail: museum@nilesdepot.org

6. Hours of operation: 10 a.m. to 4 p.m. Sundays.

7. Cost: Suggested donation of $2 adults, $1 children & seniors.

8. Permanent Exhibits: equipment & photographs from Niles Tower, operating railroad signals, passenger train uniforms and artifacts, railroad lanterns, historic track tools, telegraph & railroad communications equipment, artifacts and photos of Niles and other local areas, history and photographs of other local area depots, WP467, and a Western Pacific Railroad caboose.

9. Special Exhibits: model railroad displays.

10. Historical era that is featured the best: 1860s to 1940s.

11. Targeted age groups: all ages.

12. Special activities for children: none.

13. Guided tours: not available, but docents are often available to guide and answer questions.

14. Hands-on activities: operating telegraph equipment.

15. The best-kept secrets at the museum: this was part of the Transcontinental Railroad.

16. Hidden treasures at the museum: local maps and railroad items.

17. What is unique about the museum that can't be found anywhere else: the museum is housed in the twice-moved 1901 railroad depot. It was moved about a half-mile away in 1981, and then returned to its original location in 2008.

18. The most important things about local, state, or American history that can be learned at the museum: the importance of railroads in the development of the area.

19. Annual events held at the site or elsewhere in the community: Niles Antique Fair, Niles Tree Lighting Ceremony.

20. Research facilities or archives at the site: the Jim Sullivan Memorial Library contains thousands of railroad-related items, including books, films, videos, DVDs, photographs, local track plans, area maps, technical plans, and timetables.

21. Type of gift shop and what is for sale: a few souvenirs and railroad-related items are available.

22. Additional information: there are occasional train rides through the Niles Canyon Railway, which is not affiliated with the Niles Depot but is located nearby. See the website: http://www.ncry.org/.

1. **Niles Essanay Silent Film Museum & Edison Theater-Fremont**
2. Location: 37417 Niles Boulevard, Fremont, CA. 94536.
3. Website: www.nilesfilmmuseum.org
4. Phone number: (510) 494-1411.
5. E-mail: info@nilesfilmmuseum.org
6. Hours of operation for docent-led tours: Saturday and Sunday 12-4.
7. Cost: free; donations appreciated and are tax-deductible.
8. Permanent Exhibits: cameras and other film equipment, original movie one-sheet posters, props, costumes, and historical photos.
9. Special Exhibits: silent movies are shown regularly in the historic theater.
10. Historical era that is featured the best: Early 20th century.
11. Targeted age groups: all ages
12. Special activities for children: tours for school groups include activities. There are occasional film screenings specifically for children.
13. Guided tours: available during regular hours or for groups with reservations.
14. Hands-on activities: simple costumes for photo opportunities; cameras & projectors to hand-crank.
15. The best-kept secrets at the museum: Charlie Chaplin photos, props, etc.
16. Hidden treasures at the museum: many original films are stored in the museum vaults.
17. What is unique about the museum that can't be found anywhere else: the complete history of the Western branch of the Chicago-based Essanay studios, the home of Broncho Billy, the first Western movie star.
18. The most important things about local, state, or American history that can be learned at the museum: Niles was chosen as a filming location due to its optimal weather and proximity to the picturesque canyon, railroad, and small town atmosphere that had an Old West feel to them. Chaplin's breakthrough movie, "The Tramp" was filmed nearby.
19. Annual events held at the site or elsewhere in the community: film festivals.
20. Research facilities or archives at the site: available upon request.
21. Type of gift shop and what is for sale: a well-stocked gift store with silent film and movie related items.

1. **Novato History Museum**
2. Location: 815 DeLong Avenue, Novato, CA. 94945.
3. Website: http://www.cityofnovato.org/Index.aspx?page=387
4. Phone number: (415) 897-4320.
5. E-mail: none.
6. Hours of operation: Wednesday, Thursday, and Saturday 12 p.m.-4 p.m., or by appointment.
7. Cost: free.

8. Permanent Exhibits: Miwok Indians, Spanish and Mexican settlements, American pioneers, Victorian household items, and farms and ranches.

9. Special Exhibits: none.

10. Historical era that is featured the best: 1800s-1900s.

11. Targeted age groups: all ages.

12. Special activities for children: school tours for 3rd graders, March-June.

13. Guided tours: docents are available during visiting hours.

14. Hands-on activities: some of the farming items are labeled, "please touch".

15. The best-kept secrets at the museum: historic maps and photos.

16. Hidden treasures at the museum: there is a very fine dollhouse and an historic saddle.

17. What is unique about the museum that can't be found anywhere else: it is set in a historic post office.

18. The most important things about local, state, or American history that can be learned at the museum: Novato's growth from a sleepy farming community to a modern city is well documented.

19. Annual events held at the site or elsewhere in the community: see website for details.

20. Research facilities or archives at the site: the entire upstairs is dedicated to historical maps, documents, and records.

21. Type of gift shop and what is for sale: local history books and videos, note cards, T-shirts, and sweatshirts are available at the museum.

1. **Oakland Aviation Museum**

2. Location: 8252 Earhart Road, Oakland, CA. 94621.

3. Website: http://www.oaklandaviationmuseum.org/

4. Phone number: (510) 638-7100.

5. E-mail: oamdirector@oaklandaviationmuseum.org

6. Hours of operation: 10a.m. - 4p.m. Wednesday - Sunday

7. Cost: Adults - $10, seniors (55+) - $9, military/teens - $7, children (6-12) - $5, under 6 free.

8. Permanent Exhibits: 8th Air Force, Aircraft Engines, Amelia Earhart, The American Legion - WWI & WWII, The 356 Aero Service Squadron, Oakland International Airport Aviation Hall of Fame, Aviation History Room, The Evolution of Black Americans in Aviation and Space, F-14 Pinball Machine, General James "Jimmy" Doolittle, McDonnel Douglas Commercial Aviation, Norden Bombsight, The Theatre Room, Transocean Air Lines, Women in Aviation, and World Airways.

9. Special Exhibits: none.

10. Historical era that is featured the best: WWI to the Cold War.

11. Targeted age groups: all ages.

12. Special activities for children: Kids and Airplanes play area.

13. Guided tours: tour groups must consist of 12 people or more.

14. Hands-on activities: flight simulators.

15. The best-kept secrets at the museum: the flying boat used by Indiana Jones in Raiders of the Lost Ark & several of Amelia Earheart's personal items.

16. Hidden treasures at the museum: women aviators, The Tuskegee Airmen, a Soviet MiG, and the Doolittle room.

17. What is unique about the museum that can't be found anywhere else: the flying boat.

18. The most important things about local, state, or American history that can be learned at the museum: the historical significance of the Oakland airport and the Boeing School of Aeronautics.

19. Annual events held at the site or elsewhere in the community: Open Cockpit Days, dinner aboard the flying boat, and guest speakers.

20. Research facilities or archives at the site: the aviation library is available with reservations.

21. Type of gift shop and what is for sale: aviation items, model planes, apparel, and Indiana Jones hats!

22. Additional information: space is available for events.

1. **The Oakland Museum of California**

2. Location: 1000 Oak Street, Oakland, CA. 94607.

3. Website: http://www.museumca.org/

4. Phone number: (510) 318-8400.

5. E-mail: info@museumca.org

147

6. Hours of operation: Wednesday–Thursday 11 a.m.–5 p.m., Friday 11 a.m.–9 p.m., Saturday–Sunday 10 a.m.–6 p.m.

7. Cost: General Admission: $15, seniors (ages 65+) and students (with current ID): $10, Youth ages 9–17: $6, OMCA members and children 8 and under: free.

8. Permanent Exhibits: Gallery of California History. The strength of the collections is in photography; California native baskets and other material; California Gold Rush era artifacts; and material that relates to California technology, agriculture, business and labor, domestic life, and significant events such as World War II. Recent acquisitions tell the stories of many ethnic and cultural groups, recent immigrants, and the counterculture. There is also the Gallery of California Art and the Gallery of California Natural Sciences.

9. Special Exhibits: available on a rotating basis (see website for details).

10. Historical era that is featured the best: all eras.

11. Targeted age groups: all ages.

12. Special activities for children: school groups tours and programs designed for specific grade levels (see website for details).

13. Guided tours: available upon request (see website for details).

14. Hands-on activities: many of the displays are interactive and very interesting. There are also weekly public programs and events that relate to the galleries (see website for details).

15. The best-kept secrets at the museum: there are many priceless artifacts.

16. Hidden treasures at the museum: the giant interactive historical map is always a favorite with kids and adults. You can look at many layers of maps of a community over time.

17. What is unique about the museum that can't be found anywhere else: this is by far the largest and finest comprehensive historical museum in the state. It has a

long-standing reputation as a leader in the field. The quality of the displays and the number of artifacts are not surpassed by any other West Coast institution.

18. The most important things about local, state, or American history that can be learned at the museum: this is the best comprehensive museum of California history anywhere.

19. Annual events held at the site or elsewhere in the community: field trips, guest speakers, workshops, and many other events (see website for details).

20. Research facilities or archives at the site: contact the museum for information.

21. Type of gift shop and what is for sale: there is a fine gift shop, which has items reflecting all of the galleries and special exhibits. There is a wide variety of art, books, and gift items available.

1. **Olompali State Historic Park**

2. Location: The park is located three miles north of Novato on U.S. 101. The entrance is accessible only to southbound traffic from Highway 101.

3. Website: http://www.parks.ca.gov/?page_id=465 and http://www.olompali.org/index.html

4. Phone number: (415) 898-4362.

5. E-mail: Jill.Miller2@parks.ca.gov

6. Hours of operation: Wednesdays - Sundays 9:00 a.m. - 5:00 p.m.

7. Cost: A $5 day use fee.

8. Permanent Exhibits: the visitors' center outlines the site's history under many owners and uses.

9. Special Exhibits: none.

10. Historical era that is featured the best: pre-history to 1990s.

11. Targeted age groups: all ages.

12. Special activities for children: school tours available.

13. Guided tours: available during special events or by request. See the websites for details.

14. Hands-on activities: none.

15. The best-kept secrets at the museum: an historic garden, rock fountain, and the ruins of the original adobe.

16. Hidden treasures at the museum: the Miwok village and native plant garden.

17. What is unique about the museum that can't be found anywhere else: the site has had many uses over the years and it is well preserved.

18. The most important things about local, state, or American history that can be learned at the museum: the site has been a Miwok village, Spanish rancho, a productive ranch for the Burdell family, and in the early 1900s became an exclusive estate with construction of a mansion around the original Burdell wood frame house and adobe. Through subsequent ownerships, Olompali was used as a Jesuit retreat, a dairy ranch, and a private swim club. In the late 1960s, the site was home to a hippie commune until fire severely damaged the Burdell mansion in 1969.

19. Annual events held at the site or elsewhere in the community: Native American events, historic tours nature walks, and other events (see website for details).

20. Research facilities or archives at the site: none.

21. Type of gift shop and what is for sale: t-shirts and other souvenirs are available at the visitors' center.

1. **Octagon House-San Francisco**
2. Location: 2645 Gough Street (at Union Street) San Francisco, CA. 94123.
3. Website: http://www.nscda.org/museums2/ca-octagonhouse.html
4. Phone number: (415) 441-7512.
5. E-mail: none.
6. Hours of operation: the second Sunday, second and fourth Thursdays: noon to 3:00 p.m.
7. Cost: Suggested donation: $4.
8. Permanent Exhibits: Colonial furniture and artwork, original house furnishings, and dinnerware.
9. Special Exhibits: a beautiful garden is next to the house.
10. Historical era that is featured the best: 1700s-1920s.
11. Targeted age groups: all ages.
12. Special activities for children: none.
13. Guided tours: docents provide tours during visiting hours. Group tours are by arrangement only.
14. Hands-on activities: none.
15. The best-kept secrets at the museum: the collection of American furnishings includes a Baltimore sideboard and a Salem secretary-desk, both dating from the Federal Period, portraits, samplers, silver, pewter, and ceramics.
16. Hidden treasures at the museum: a remarkable collection of documents bearing signatures of 54 of the 56 signers of the Declaration of Independence that is of great interest.
17. What is unique about the museum that can't be found anywhere else: it is one of two surviving octagon-shaped houses in San Francisco and the only one that is open to the public.
18. The most important things about local, state, or American history that can be learned at the museum: the house itself was built in 1861 in a style that was once popular nationwide. The exterior remains essentially in its original condition, while the interior has been extensively modified for use as California Society headquarters and a hospitable setting for social occasions.
19. Annual events held at the site or elsewhere in the community: call for details.
20. Research facilities or archives at the site: the library emphasizes colonial history, genealogy and the decorative arts.
21. Type of gift shop and what is for sale: books on the history of octagon houses and the McElroy family.
22. Additional information: no photography is allowed inside the home.

1. **Orinda Historical Society**
2. Location: on the ground floor of the Orinda Library, Room 106, 24 Orinda Way in Orinda, CA. 94563.
3. Website: http://www.orindahistory.org/
4. Phone number: (925) 254-1353.

5. E-mail: none.

6. Hours of operation: Monday, Wednesday, and Friday: 3 p.m. to 5 p.m. Also open by appointment. It's best to call ahead if planning a visit. The museum is staffed by volunteers, and thus, museum hours may vary.

7. Cost: free.

8. Permanent Exhibits: historical artifacts, documents and images related to the Orinda area.

9. Special Exhibits: none.

10. Historical era that is featured the best: 1800s-1900s.

11. Targeted age groups: all ages.

12. Special activities for children: none.

13. Guided tours: call for information.

14. Hands-on activities: none.

15. The best-kept secrets at the museum: WWII era civil defense items.

16. Hidden treasures at the museum: historic photos.

17. What is unique about the museum that can't be found anywhere else: it is part of a library.

18. The most important things about local, state, or American history that can be learned at the museum: Orinda's growth and role as a crossroads between the Diablo Valley and the East Bay.

19. Annual events held at the site or elsewhere in the community: the Holiday Dinner.

20. Research facilities or archives at the site: items are available for researchers. Call for details.

21. Type of gift shop and what is for sale: historic photos, Afghan blankets, tote bags, coasters, note cards and books.

1. **Pacific Heritage Museum-San Francisco**

2. Location: 608 Commercial St., San Francisco, CA. 94111.

3. Website: none.

4. Phone number: (415) 399-1124.

5. E-mail: none.

6. Hours of operation: Tue-Sat 10 a.m. - 4 p.m.

7. Cost: free

151

8. Permanent Exhibits: a reconstructed cut-away display in the historic US Subtreasury Building depicts the building's origins as a currency depository for the US Mint. Strong walls reinforced by steel allowed it to survive the 1906 earthquake when all the others around it collapsed. A display of moneybags, the guards' walkway, and some rare silver dollars.

9. Special Exhibits: despite its far-reaching name, the rotating exhibits are related to mostly just East Asian artwork, culture, etc.

10. Historical era that is featured the best: San Francisco in the 1870's and historic and contemporary Asia.

11. Targeted age groups: all ages.

12. Special activities for children: none.

13. Guided tours: none, although the docents are eager to show you around.

14. Hands-on activities: none.

15. The best-kept secrets at the museum: the vaults. This was the site of the first US Mint in San Francisco.

16. Hidden treasures at the museum: the silver dollar collection.

17. What is unique about the museum that can't be found anywhere else: the age and architecture of the building.

18. The most important things about local, state, or American history that can be learned at the museum: the reason why most brick buildings in San Francisco did not survive the earthquake.

19. Annual events held at the site or elsewhere in the community: none.

20. Research facilities or archives at the site: none.

21. Type of gift shop: none.

22. Additional information: this museum definitely had a glorious past with important visiting exhibits of Chinese and other East Asian art, but is mostly just a photo gallery now.

1. **Pajaro Valley Historical Association-Watsonville**

2. Location: 332 East Beach St. Watsonville, CA. 95077.

3. Website: http://www.pajarovalleyhistory.org/

4. Phone number: (831) 722-0305.

5. E-mail: info@pajarovalleyhistory.org

6. Hours of operation: Tue, Wed, and Thurs.: 11a.m. to 3p.m.

7. Cost: free.

8. Permanent Exhibits: the Bockius-Orr House built in 1870, The Tank House, The Synder Archive, and the Volck Museum.

9. Special Exhibits: rotating exhibits (see website for details).

10. Historical era that is featured the best: 1800s.

11. Targeted age groups: all ages.

12. Special activities for children: the Volck Museum has interactive school programs.

13. Guided tours: there is a virtual tour on the website. School tours are available upon request.

14. Hands-on activities: farm chores and household equipment from the Victorian era are done by school children at the Volck Museum.

15. The best-kept secrets at the museum: the rare square grand piano.

16. Hidden treasures at the museum: many interesting historic household items are on display.

17. What is unique about the museum that can't be found anywhere else: it is one of the best preserved Victorian homes in the area.

18. The most important things about local, state, or American history that can be learned at the museum: the importance of the farming community to the area's development.

19. Annual events held at the site or elsewhere in the community: see the online calendar for details.

20. Research facilities or archives at the site: the Borina Archive & Alzora Synder and Jane Borg Research Center are top-notch historical research facilities. They

have very well organized collections of documents, books, photos, objects, and clothing.

21. Type of gift shop and what is for sale: historical books of local interest, tapestries and posters are for sale.

1. **Palace of the Legion of Honor-San Francisco**
2. Location: 100 34th Avenue, San Francisco, CA. 94121.
3. Website: http://legionofhonor.famsf.org/
4. Phone number: (415) 750-3600.
5. E-mail: contact@famsf.org
6. Hours of operation: Tuesdays through Sundays: 9:30 a.m. to 5:15 p.m.
7. Cost: Adults: $10, Seniors 65+:$7, Youths 13–17 and College Students with valid ID: $6, Children 12 and under: Free. Free on the first Tuesday of the month.
8. Permanent Exhibits: ancient art, European painting, ceramic, photography, decorative and graphic art.
9. Special Exhibits: rotating exhibits, including major visiting exhibitions.
10. Historical era that is featured the best: ancient times-20th century.
11. Targeted age groups: all ages.
12. Special activities for children: school tours, art classes, summer art camp, guest speakers, and curriculum supported visits. Contact schooltours@famsf.org or call (415) 750-7696.
13. Guided tours: audio, docent-led, and private docent-led tours are available.
14. Hands-on activities: art and poetry classes feature hands-on creative activities. Some exhibits feature interactive elements.
15. The best-kept secrets at the museum: there are thousands of priceless treasures at the museum.
16. Hidden treasures at the museum: the museum is often the location of world-class visiting exhibitions. Treasures from around the world are often on loan there.
17. What is unique about the museum that can't be found anywhere else: this is the finest Western art collection in the state of California.
18. The most important things about local, state, or American history that can be learned at the museum: a very good overview of the history of Western art can be gained from the museum. Specific works can be studied in more detail. The docent-led tours are very informative about this.
19. Annual events held at the site or elsewhere in the community: see website for details.
20. Research facilities or archives at the site: there is an art preservation facility built into the museum.
21. Type of gift shop and what is for sale: a state of the art gift shop contains many interesting items at every price level from common souvenirs to fine art.

1. **Pardee Home Museum-Oakland**
2. Location: 672 Eleventh Street, Oakland, CA. 94607.
3. Website: http://www.pardeehome.org/
4. Phone number: (510) 444-2187.
5. E-mail: office@pardeehome.org

6. Hours of operation: regular tours are given every Wednesday and the second Saturday of each month at 10:30 a.m. and on the second Sunday of each month at 2:00 p.m.

7. Cost: $10.

8. Permanent Exhibits: the house was built in 1868-69 by Enoch Pardee, a Gold Rush immigrant to California from the Midwest, who became an eye doctor in San Francisco after mining gold. He also pursued a vigorous public career in the East Bay during the 1870s and 1880s, including mayor of Oakland, state assemblyman, and state senator. Enoch's only child by his first wife Mary, George C. Pardee, followed ever so closely in his father's footsteps, also becoming an eye doctor in San Francisco and mayor of Oakland. Unlike his father, George did not serve in the state legislature in Sacramento. However, he was elected governor of California in 1902.

9. Special Exhibits: none.

10. Historical era that is featured the best: 1860s-early 1900s.

11. Targeted age groups: all ages.

12. Special activities for children: school tours available for grades 3-6. Call for a reservation.

13. Guided tours: all regular admission tours are guided. Group tours may be arranged on any day anytime between 9:00 a.m. and 4:00 p.m. Tours are approximately one hour. If possible, make reservations for group tours at least a week in advance.

14. Hands-on activities: none.

15. The best-kept secrets at the museum: original furnishings from the late 1800's including the Pardee women's dresses and hats. Mrs. Helen Pardee's priceless and fascinating artifacts from around the world.

16. Hidden treasures at the museum: every drawer and closet is jammed with items that belonged to the family. Ask your tour guide for permission to see them.

17. What is unique about the museum that can't be found anywhere else: it is one of the largest and best-preserved Italianate Victorian mansions in the state, dating to the late 1800's. It has 22 rooms and all of the furnishings and objects in it actually belonged to the Pardee family.

18. The most important things about local, state, or American history that can be learned at the museum: the Pardee family was very wealthy and influential. They produced prominent doctors, legislators, and a governor of California.

19. Annual events held at the site: light and high tea fundraisers, ghost investigation, Vintage Porcelain Show, and the annual 4th of July celebration with live ragtime music, food, games, and vintage costumes. Reservations can be made for high teas or dessert teas in the dining room (4 to 12 people) and in the garden in the summer months for groups from 15 to 40 (see website for details).

20. Research facilities or archives at the site: there are some documents and artifacts that are available to researchers upon request.

21. Type of gift shop and what is for sale: a variety of goods that reflects the beauty of the home and the history of Oakland including postcards and books.

22. Additional information: the Preservation Park of Oakland is right across the street. Visitors may take a nice stroll and see many fine historical homes. They are

businesses and not museums, but the public may view the exteriors of the homes free of charge.

1. **The Peña Adobe -Vacaville**

2. Location: Pena Adobe Rd. Vacaville, CA. 95687.
3. Website: http://www.penaadobe.org/.
4. Phone number: (707) 447-0518.
5. E-mail: penaadobe@gmail.com.
6. Hours of operation: the first Saturday of each month, 11:00 a.m. to 2:00 p.m.
7. Cost: free.
8. Permanent Exhibits: the Peña Adobe. The Goheen-Mowers Museum next door holds historic artifacts dating back to the early settlers and Native Americans of the region.
9. Special Exhibits: artwork from the famed sculptor Gordon Huff.
10. Historical era that is featured the best: 1800s.
11. Targeted age groups: all ages.
12. Special activities for children: school tours.
13. Guided tours: available with reservations. Some guided walks are available on open house days.
14. Hands-on activities: rubber stamps that replicate the brands used by the ranch.
15. The best-kept secrets at the museum: The Native American bedrock mortar that the children call "smiley face" because it resembles a human face.
16. Hidden treasures at the museum: a wooly mammoth bone and other fossils.
17. What is unique about the museum that can't be found anywhere else: the Peña Adobe is one of the few pre-Gold Rush era structures remaining in the county.
18. The most important things about local, state, or American history that can be learned at the museum: Peña Adobe is the oldest building in Solano County. The original adobe was built on this property in 1842-1843.
19. Annual events held at the site or elsewhere in the community: monthly Open House.
20. Research facilities or archives at the site: none.
21. Type of gift shop: none.

1. **The Peralta House Museum of History-Oakland**

2. Location: 2465 34th Avenue (at the corner of Coolidge Ave and Hyde St) Oakland, CA. 94601.
3. Website: http://www.peraltahacienda.org/pages/main.php?pageid=1&pagecategory=1
4. Phone number: (510) 532-9142.
5. E-mail: info@peraltahacienda.org
6. Hours of operation: Wednesday through Saturday, 2:30-5:30 p.m.
7. Cost: Admission is $5. Free for Fruitvale community members, museum members, and children 10 and under.
8. Permanent Exhibits: the kitchen, Native American Land Loss, Peralta Land Loss, Your Story, Native Plants Garden, and outdoor displays.

155

156

9. Special Exhibits: rotating exhibits on local history and the many cultures that have settled in the area.

10. Historical era that is featured the best: 1800s.

11. Targeted age groups: all ages.

12. Special activities for children: children's storybooks, school tours including Peralta Rancho Life (4th grade), Ohlone Daily Life (3rd grade).

13. Guided tours: 45-minute guided tours at 2:30 and 4:00p.m.

14. Hands-on activities: special events have hands-on activities. One exhibit encourages visitors to share their story of immigration.

15. The best-kept secrets at the museum: an historic saddle and sword.

16. Hidden treasures at the museum: historic photos, home furnishings, and items excavated from the site.

17. What is unique about the museum that can't be found anywhere else: It is one of the few surviving adobe houses in Oakland. The museum staff lets you don a poncho and Mexican hat while touring the house!

18. The most important things about local, state, or American history that can be learned at the museum: Peralta Hacienda Historical Park is on the Juan Bautista de Anza National Historic Trail. The Peralta family has many descendants in the Bay Area and in other parts of the world (including Che Guevara). This house is one of the oldest in Oakland.

19. Annual events held at the site or elsewhere in the community: there are many (see website for details).

20. Research facilities or archives at the site: contact the staff for further information.

21. Type of gift shop and what is for sale: t-shirts, mugs, and books about the Peralta family are available through the website.

1. The Peralta Adobe - Fallon House Historic Site-San José

2. Location: 175 West Saint John Street, San José, CA. 95110.

3. Website: http://historysanjose.org/wp/plan-your-visit/

4. Phone number: (408) 287-2290.

5. E-mail: education@historysanjose.org

6. Hours of operation: currently only open for special events and reserved tours.

7. Cost: varies by event or tour reservation.

157

8. Permanent Exhibits: built in 1797, the Peralta Adobe is the last remaining structure from El Pueblo de San José de Guadalupe. See the Adobe's horno, an outside working oven, or venture inside the home and see two rooms furnished as they might have been when they were occupied by the Gonzales and Peralta families. The exquisite Fallon House was built in 1855 by one of San José's earliest mayors. The Victorian mansion showcases 15 fully furnished rooms typical of the Victorian period. Learn about Thomas Fallon, a frontiersman in the John C. Fremont expedition, and Carmel Fallon, the daughter of one of the most prominent Mexican landowners in California.

9. Special Exhibits: rotating exhibits are in the basement of the Fallon House.

10. Historical era that is featured the best: 1700s-1800s.

11. Targeted age groups: all ages.

12. Special activities for children: school tours available with reservations.

13. Guided tours: available with reservations.

14. Hands-on activities: during special events participants can grind corn, make dolls, or form adobe bricks.

15. The best-kept secrets at the museum: the basement of the Fallon House was once a bar!

16. Hidden treasures at the museum: both houses are filled with period furnishings and historical exhibits.

17. What is unique about the museum that can't be found anywhere else: the Peralta Adobe is the best-preserved building from the Mexican period in San Jose. The Fallon House is one of the finest Victorian mansions in the area.

18. The most important things about local, state, or American history that can be learned at the museum: these two families were important pioneers in San Jose and the two buildings together provide an interesting contrast to two different eras of development.

19. Annual events held at the site or elsewhere in the community: there are many interesting events hosted by History San Jose. Many of these feature this site (see website for details).

20. Research facilities or archives at the site: none.

21. Type of gift shop and what is for sale: at present, gifts are only available through the website.

1. **Petaluma Adobe State Historic Park**

2. Location: Petaluma Adobe State Historic Park, 3325 Adobe Road, Petaluma, CA. 94954.

3. Website: http://www.petalumaadobe.com/index.html.

4. Phone number: (707) 762-4871.

5. E-mail: petadobe@parks.ca.gov

6. Hours of operation: Tuesday through Sunday from 10 a.m. to 5 p.m.

7. Cost: $3.00 for adults, $2.00 for children between 6 and 16, children under 5 free. The paid admission is also good, on the same day, at Sonoma State Historic Park.

8. Permanent Exhibits: the large two-story ranch house contains a loom and weaving room, bread ovens, leather processing and storage areas, a gristmill, dining room, parlor, and living quarters where fandangos were held.

9. Special Exhibits: a visitors' center that has displays on the Miwok Indians, Mexican Land Grants, The Hide and Tallow Trade, and Cattle, Sheep, and Cowboys. It has portraits of the Vallejo family and many ranch artifacts.

10. Historical era that is featured the best: early 1800s.

11. Targeted age groups: all ages.

12. Special activities for children: school tours and special activities include re-enacting mission life and environmental living programs.

13. Guided tours: docent-led tours are available most Saturdays and Sundays between 1 p.m. and 3 p.m.

14. Hands-on activities: school children are allowed to card and comb wool and do other ranch activities on visits.

15. The best-kept secrets at the museum: the amount of hides stored in the place is huge!

16. Hidden treasures at the museum: many original tools and furnishings of the ranch. They are realistically staged in such a way as to make a visitor feel as if the inhabitants just left.

17. What is unique about the museum that can't be found anywhere else: it was the largest privately owned adobe building in Northern California in the 1830-40's. It dwarfs most other Bay Area adobes in size.

18. The most important things about local, state, or American history that can be learned at the museum: the building served as the headquarters for General Vallejo's vast cattle rancho. It was about 66,000 acres (100 square miles) with 600-2,000 workers, 25,000 head of cattle, 3,000 sheep, and many crops. Vallejo was a key character in the history of the region. He played an important role in the era in which the area changed from Mexican to American rule. The ranch played an important role in the local and international trade of the region.

19. Annual events held at the site or elsewhere in the community: Sheep Shearing Day, Living History Day, All Nations Big Time, and the Fandango.

20. Research facilities or archives at the site: none.

21. Type of gift shop and what is for sale: local history books, state park items, historical toys, and other gift items.

1. **Petaluma Historical Library and Museum**

2. Location: 20 Fourth Street (Corner of 4th and B Street) in downtown Petaluma, CA. 94952.

159

3. Website: http://www.petalumamuseum.com

4. Phone number: (707) 778-4398.

5. E-mail: use the contact form on the website.

6. Hours of operation: Thursdays through Saturdays: 10 a.m. to 4 p.m., Sundays 12:00 to 3:00, and by appointment.

7. Cost: free.

8. Permanent Exhibits: Miwok Indians, shipping and industry, Vallejo and other pioneer families, schoolroom, kitchen, carriage and firearms, and poultry farms

9. Special Exhibits: there are rotating special exhibits on the main floor (see website for details).

10. Historical era that is featured the best: 1800s-present.

11. Targeted age groups: all ages.

12. Special activities for children: school tours are offered to all third grade classes as part of the Social Studies curriculum. These include a visit to the museum and a short walk around Historic Downtown Petaluma.

13. Guided tours: Historic Downtown Walking Tours. Free walking tours of historic Petaluma led by costumed docents. You will hear the history of Petaluma from the mouths of early settlers. Held on most Saturdays, May through October. Meet on the steps of the museum at 10:30 a.m. to begin. Bus and travel group tours are also offered. Contact bmarshwest@aol.com

14. Hands-on activities: none.

15. The best-kept secrets at the museum: the museum itself is a well-preserved Carnegie Library. The colorful stained-glass dome is the largest in California.
16. Hidden treasures at the museum: the collection of Miwok artifacts is quite extensive.
17. What is unique about the museum that can't be found anywhere else: the poultry exhibit displays the agricultural heritage of the region very well.
18. The most important things about local, state, or American history that can be learned at the museum: the role of Petaluma as a farming and transportation region that supported the growth of San Francisco.
19. Annual events held at the site or elsewhere in the community: there are several (see website for details).
20. Research facilities or archives at the site: books and files that assist in history, genealogy, and architectural research of Petaluma and close environs. They include such treasures as: early maps; the Vallejo land grant; books relating to topics as the Miwok Indians, poultry and dairy industries; histories of surrounding communities.
21. Type of gift shop and what is for sale: books about local history and other gift items.

1. **The Phoebe A. Hearst Museum of Anthropology -Berkeley**
2. Location: UC Berkeley, 103 Kroeber Hall, Berkeley, CA. 94720.
3. Website: http://hearstmuseum.berkeley.edu/
4. Phone number: (510) 642-3682.
5. E-mail: use the contact form on the webpage.
6. Hours of operation: currently closed for remodeling. The projected reopening will be in the fall of 2015.
7. Cost: free.
8. Permanent Exhibits: cultural and historical objects from around the globe.
9. Special Exhibits: rotating special exhibits will be available.
10. Historical era that is featured the best: all eras.
11. Targeted age groups: adults, although tours will be available for school children.
12. Special activities for children: none.
13. Guided tours: not currently available.
14. Hands-on activities: none

160

15. The best-kept secrets at the museum: The collection of Ishi's weapons and implements and other Indian items is superb.
16. Hidden treasures at the museum: mummies and many other interesting artifacts.
17. What is unique about the museum that can't be found anywhere else: it is one of the few museums dedicated exclusively to anthropology in the area.
18. The most important things about local, state, or American history that can be learned at the museum: a wide range of historical and contemporary cultures are on display from around the world.
19. Annual events held at the site or elsewhere in the community: none currently.
20. Research facilities or archives at the site: the museum encourages research on its collections by members of the university community and of researchers from anthropology and related disciplines from outside the university. The research

facilities are closed during renovation. Only online resources are currently available.

21. Type of gift shop and what is for sale: gift items related to art, cultures, and archaeology.

22. Additional information: closed for renovation. Will reopen in the fall of 2015.

1. **Pine Ridge Museum-Henry Coe State Park**

2. Location: The main entrance into Henry W. Coe State Park 13-miles east of Morgan Hill on East Dunne Avenue. From Highway 101 in Morgan Hill (1/2 hour south of San Jose), take the East Dunne Avenue exit and go east past Anderson Lake to the end of the county road to the park headquarters. The road to the park beyond Anderson Lake is 10 miles of narrow winding road. The trip will take about 30 minutes.

3. Websites: http://www.parks.ca.gov/?page_id=25818 and http://www.coestatepark.com/recreation_at_henry_w__coe_state_park.htm#history _study and http://coepark.net/pineridgeassociation/about-coe-park/history

4. Phone number: (408) 779-2728.

5. E-mail: use the online contact form.

6. Hours of operation: the Visitor Center is open on weekends from at least 8:00a.m. to 4:00p.m. In the spring and summer months, hours are 8:00a.m. to 8:00p.m. on Friday and 8:00a.m. to 6:00p.m. Saturday and Sunday. Please note that times may change without notice.

7. Cost: $8 per vehicle. Additional camping fees if so desired.

8. Permanent Exhibits: park headquarters for Henry W. Coe State Park is located on Pine Ridge, site of a working cattle ranch from the late 1800s until the early 1950s.

9. Special Exhibits: various exhibits about the nature and history of the park.

10. Historical era that is featured the best: late 1800s until the early 1950s.

11. Targeted age groups: all ages.

12. Special activities for children: Coe Connections is an all-year program that provides public school students quality environmental education. Classroom visits are also available.

13. Guided tours: ranger-led activities, interpretive programs. See the calendars on the websites for details.

14. Hands-on activities: there are some items in the visitors' center that can be touched.

15. The best-kept secrets at the museum: its location. It is quite remote and very beautiful.

16. Hidden treasures at the museum: ranching items, historic farm equipment.

17. What is unique about the museum that can't be found anywhere else: this was a working ranch until the 1950's. It is very well preserved.

18. The most important things about local, state, or American history that can be learned at the museum: the area was home to the Ohlone Indians and then various ranchers. The area has remained undeveloped since becoming a state park. It is the largest park in Northern California and has vast wilderness areas. If you really want to get away from it all, this is the place.

161

19. Annual events held at the site or elsewhere in the community: Fall Tarantula Fest, Ranch Day, nature hikes, foot races, and other events. See the online calendars for details.

20. Research facilities or archives at the site: none.

21. Type of gift shop and what is for sale: there are books about the park and other gifts available at the visitors' center.

22. Additional information: Ranch Day is probably the best time to visit to appreciate the history of the park. It is usually held in May at the peak of the wildflower season. There are many demonstrations and hands-on activities for children.

1. **Pittsburg Historical Society**

2. Location: 515 Railroad Ave. Pittsburg, CA. 94565.

3. Website: http://www.pittsburghistoricalsociety.com/

4. Phone number: (925) 439-7501.

5. E-mail: pittsburgcamuseum@att.net

6. Hours of operation: Wednesday 1 - 4 p.m., Saturday 11 - 3 p.m. Winter Hours Saturday 10 a.m.-2 p.m. Nov.-May.

7. Cost: free.

8. Permanent Exhibits: the museum hosts a collection of artifacts, historical photos, a well-organized library of papers, maps and reference books. Of special interest to visitors are the Sports Hall of Fame Room, Family Room, Military Room, Bridal Room, and Theater Room.

9. Special Exhibits: occasional special exhibits.

10. Historical era that is featured the best: 1800s-1900s.

11. Targeted age groups: all ages.

12. Special activities for children: school tours for students and a 3rd grade passport program.

13. Guided tours: available upon request.

14. Hands-on activities: none.

15. The best-kept secrets at the museum: the old fire truck and the saloon exhibit are nice.

16. Hidden treasures at the museum: the local sports hall of fame is exceptional.

17. What is unique about the museum that can't be found anywhere else: it has a fine collection of local history items.

18. The most important things about local, state, or American history that can be learned at the museum: this is a place to learn about Pittsburg's people and their changing lives through ranching, mining, fishing, canning, military base, and large industries which came here for its location on the river. It is a crossroads of rail and water transportation. Settlers here were people from many backgrounds and ethnicities who were willing to work together to build the community.

19. Annual events held at the site or elsewhere in the community: Thursday Night Car Shows, pasta dinners, Bunco games, concerts, etc. (see website for details).

20. Research facilities or archives at the site: the museum hosts a large collection of artifacts, historical photos, a well-organized library of papers, maps and reference books.

21. Type of gift shop and what is for sale: afghans, mugs, books, t-shirts, jackets, and sweatshirts.

1. Pleasanton's Museum on Main
2. Location: 603 Main Street, Pleasanton, CA. 94566.
3. Website: www.museumonmain.org
4. Phone number: (925) 462-2766.
5. E-mail: info@museumonmain.org
6. Hours of operation: Tues. – Sat. 10:00 a.m. – 4:00 p.m.; Sun. 1:00 – 4:00 p.m.
7. Cost: free.
8. Permanent Exhibits: the permanent exhibit tells the story of the Tri Valley area, including the City of Pleasanton from prehistoric to the present.
9. Special Exhibits: the museum hosts temporary exhibits throughout the year.
10. Historical era that is featured the best: Early Californio and American settlers.
11. Targeted age groups: all ages.
12. Special activities for children: a children's corner with activities that often build on the temporary exhibit; a downtown walking backpack activity that is intergenerational for families; a pre-school reading and activity time on the 2nd Wednesday of each month at 10:00 a.m.; educational programs for school groups and scouts.
13. Guided tours: walking tours of the historic downtown as well as a "Guide by Cell" phone tour that highlights historic buildings along Main Street.
14. Hands-on activities: the Children's Corner has low-tech, hands-on activities. There are also "Try It" stations in the permanent gallery space.
15. The best-kept secrets at the museum: the building was originally the town hall and police station.
16. Hidden treasures at the museum: the entire historic downtown in Pleasanton is a hidden treasure that few people realize. It is one of the few Bay Area communities that have a historic downtown that adds charm and character to the community.
17. What is unique about the museum that can't be found anywhere else: they conduct an annual Ghost Walk as a fun way to teach local history while telling the tales of "ghosts" who inhabit some of the historic buildings.
18. The most important things about local, state, or American history that can be learned at the museum: everyone has a story of their journey to get to their community - from the Native Americans thousands of years ago to the new immigrants from Asia and Central America – and each one of those journeys is as important as the other.
19. Annual events held at the site or elsewhere in the community: Wines and Valentines, Dance of the Decades, Brothels, and Bar Rooms and Bandits.
20. Research facilities or archives at the site: there is an archive that contains over 6,000 photos, newspapers, books, manuscripts, and other ephemera that is available for on-site research. It is best to make an appointment.
21. Type of gift shop and what is for sale: a small gift shop that sells books, postcards, copies of historic photos, and mission related items.

1. **Point Bonita Light House**
2. Location: Marin Headlands. On Bunker Road, pass through one-way Baker-Barry Tunnel. Follow Bunker Road 3-miles; turn left on Field Road. Follow Field Road 0.8-miles to the Point Bonita parking lot and trailhead. Walk the 0.5-mile trail to the lighthouse.
3. Website: http://www.nps.gov/goga/pobo.htm
4. Phone number: (415) 331-1540.
5. E-mail: use contact form on the website.
6. Hours of operation: Saturdays, Sundays, and Mondays from 12:30 p.m. to 3:30 p.m.
7. Cost: free.
8. Permanent Exhibits: the lighthouse and the ruins of an historic Coast Guard rescue station.
9. Special Exhibits: none.
10. Historical era that is featured the best: 1870s-1900s.
11. Targeted age groups: all ages.
12. Special activities for children: none.
13. Guided tours: Point Bonita's wild landscape, geology, and fascinating history can be seen with a guided tour. Visit www.parksconservancy.org/calendar for details.
14. Hands-on activities: none.
15. The best-kept secrets at the museum: the second order Fresnel lens (developed by French physicist, Augustin Fresnel in 1822) sends out its powerful beam 18 miles across the water.
16. Hidden treasures at the museum: the views from the point are stupendous.
17. What is unique about the museum that can't be found anywhere else: unlike other historic lighthouses, this one, the third lighthouse on the West Coast, is still in use. The lighthouse was built in 1855 and moved to the current location in 1877.
18. The most important things about local, state, or American history that can be learned at the museum: the importance of lighthouses to coastal trade and travel.
19. Annual events held at the site or elsewhere in the community: see website for details.
20. Research facilities or archives at the site: none.
21. Type of gift shop and what is for sale: see the Marin Headlands Visitor Center, just one mile away.

1. **Point Lobos Whaling Station**
2. Location: inside of Point Lobos State Natural Reserve, on the central coast of California in Monterey County. The entrance is three miles south of Carmel on Highway 1.
3. Website: http://www.pointlobos.org/general-info/trail-maps/whalers-cabin
4. Phone number: (831) 624-4909.
5. E-mail: pointlobos@parks.ca.gov
6. Hours of operation: Summer Hours: Open at 8 a.m., no entry after 7:00 pm. Winter Hours: Open at 8 a.m., no entry after sunset. All visitors must exit the reserve ½ hour after sunset (when sunset is 7:00 pm and earlier).
7. Cost: included in the cost of park admission: $10.

8. Permanent Exhibits: this continuously busy area was the site of a whaling station from 1862 to 1879. Where visitors now park, an abalone cannery once operated. Traces remain of a granite quarry, said to have supplied the stone for the San Francisco Mint.

9. Special Exhibits: none.

10. Historical era that is featured the best: 1850s-1900.

11. Targeted age groups: all ages.

12. Special activities for children: none.

13. Guided tours: docents are sometimes available to answer questions.

14. Hands-on activities: some of the whale bones and baleen may be touched.

15. The best-kept secrets at the museum: displays of collected artifacts show different sizes of harpoons and whaling tools, whale-oil barrels, a model of a shore whaling boat, diagrams of whale-oil processing, and photographs of the old Monterey Peninsula whalers. Outside the Whaling Station you can see a variety of whale bones, a magnificent specimen of humpback whale baleen, and the "try pots" that were used at Point Lobo to render the oil from the whale blubber.

16. Hidden treasures at the museum: among the diverse collection of artifacts you can see Native American jewelry and grinding mortars, Chinese fishing equipment, a display recalling the Portuguese dairies, Japanese "hard hat" diving equipment, photographs, models, and numerous other items.

17. What is unique about the museum that can't be found anywhere else: this is one of the few spots in California that documents whaling activities at the site. This was an important early industry in California.

18. The most important things about local, state, or American history that can be learned at the museum: the Carmel Bay Whaling Company was operated in Point Lobos by a group of Portuguese seamen from 1862 until 1879. Whaling was one of the first activities that drew Americans to the Monterey area. Whaling provided ties to New England and the Hawaiian Islands and attracted settlers to California.

19. Annual events held at the site or elsewhere in the community: see the park website for details.

20. Research facilities or archives at the site: none.

21. Type of gift shop: none.

1. **Point Pinos Lighthouse-Pacific Grove**

2. Location: 90 Asilomar Avenue, Pacific Grove, CA. 93950.

3. Website: http://www.pointpinoslighthouse.org/

4. Phone number: (831) 648-3176.

5. E-mail: info@pointpinoslighthouse.org

6. Hours of operation: Thursday-Sunday 1:00 p.m. – 4:00 p.m.

7. Cost: Suggested donation is $2 for adults, $1 for children (6-17), and free for children under 6.

8. Permanent Exhibits: at the lighthouse keeper's living quarters, admire the well-appointed Victorian parlor, the original Fresnel lens from the grounds, and displays on how lighthouses work and the location of other lighthouses.

9. Special Exhibits: coastal patrols during WWII.

10. Historical era that is featured the best: 1800s-present.

166

11. Targeted age groups: all ages.

12. Special activities for children: school tours.

13. Guided tours: docents are placed in various rooms to explain the features of the lighthouse and answer questions.

14. Hands-on activities: many of the displays downstairs are interactive.

15. The best-kept secrets at the museum: there were two female lighthouse keepers, Emily Fish and Charlotte Layton. Mrs. Layton got the job when her husband Charles died. She later remarried and her new husband, George Harris, became the new lighthouse keeper.

16. Hidden treasures at the museum: foghorns, lenses, buoys, and other lighthouse equipment.

17. What is unique about the museum that can't be found anywhere else: Point Pinos is the oldest lighthouse in continuous operation on the West Coast. It's not the oldest lighthouse ever built, but it is the oldest one that has never been torn down or decommissioned. In fact, it's rarely even been turned off. It has operated virtually non-stop since it was first lit in 1855 — a span of over 150 years!

18. The most important things about local, state, or American history that can be learned at the museum: the protection of maritime traffic has been essential to commerce and travel along the California coast.

19. Annual events held at the site or elsewhere in the community: see website for details.

20. Research facilities or archives at the site: none.

21. Type of gift shop and what is for sale: there are t-shirts, souvenirs, books and other lighthouse related gifts for sale.

1. **Point Reyes Light Station District**

2. Location: The Point Reyes Lighthouse is located on the western-most point of the Point Reyes Headlands at 27999 Sir Francis Drake Blvd. Inverness, CA. 94937.

3. Website: http://www.nps.gov/pore/historyculture/people_maritime_lighthouse.htm

4. Phone number: (415) 669-1534.

5. E-mail: none.

6. Hours of operation: the Lighthouse Visitor Center is open from 10 a.m. to 4:30 p.m., Thursday through Monday.

7. Cost: free.

8. Permanent Exhibits: the Point Reyes Lighthouse, built in 1870. In the Lighthouse Visitor Center, you can see historic photographs of shipwrecks and lighthouse keepers. A display of local birds will introduce you to the birds you might see just off the cliffs.

9. Special Exhibits: none.

10. Historical era that is featured the best: 1800s-1900s.

11. Targeted age groups: all ages.

12. Special activities for children: none

13. Guided tours: occasional ranger talks (see website for details).

14. Hands-on activities: you can handle items on the touch table, including whale baleen.

15. The best-kept secrets at the museum: the lighthouse keeper's life is well documented. The views of the ocean are spectacular.

16. Hidden treasures at the museum: the lenses of the lighthouse are a very beautiful site to behold.

17. What is unique about the museum that can't be found anywhere else: this is one of the most remote lighthouse locations on the coast.

18. The most important things about local, state, or American history that can be learned at the museum: the historic Point Reyes Lighthouse served mariners for 105 years before it was replaced. It endured many hardships, including the April 18, 1906 earthquake, during which the Point Reyes Peninsula and the lighthouse moved north 18 feet in less than one minute!

19. Annual events held at the site or elsewhere in the community: seasonally, there are "tours" of the lantern room and evening lighting programs (see website for details).

20. Research facilities or archives at the site: none.

21. Type of gift shop and what is for sale: a small bookstore offers books, maps and other educational products.

22. Additional information: on weekends and holidays during whale-watching season, the road to the lighthouse is closed to private vehicles. Visitors must ride a shuttle bus. Please call the Lighthouse Visitor Center for details at (415) 669-1534. Climbing the 300 stairs can be quite strenuous and high winds sometimes cause the trail to be closed. Dress in warm clothes.

1. **Presidio Museum of Monterey**

2. Location: Presidio of Monterey Museum, Corporal Ewing Road, Bldg. 113, Monterey, CA. 93944 (Pacific Street to Artillery, follow the signs).

3. Website: http://www.monterey.org/museums/CityMuseums/PresidioofMontereyMuseum.aspx

4. Phone number: (831) 646-3456.

5. E-mail: copeland@monterey.org

6. Hours of operation: Monday 10 a.m. to 1 p.m., Thursday - Saturday 10 a.m. - 4 p.m., Sunday 1 - 4 p.m. Closed Thanksgiving, Christmas, and New Years Day.

7. Cost: free.

8. Permanent Exhibits: museum exhibits lead visitors through Monterey's various stages of military development, from the indigenous period, which highlights the area's native populations; through the Spanish and Mexican periods; and up to present day. Because of the important role of the military in Monterey between 1902 and today, the majority of the museum is dedicated to the development of the Presidio as a training base.

9. Special Exhibits: none.

10. Historical era that is featured the best: 1770s-present.

11. Targeted age groups: all ages.

12. Special activities for children: none.

13. Guided tours: contact the Presidio Museum or the City of Monterey Museums office (831-646-5648) for details.

14. Hands-on activities: none.

15. The best-kept secrets at the museum: it is located on a U.S. Army base, yet open to the public on the Lower Presidio Historic Park, managed by the city of Monterey in a unique agreement with the U.S. Army known as the "Monterey Model".

16. Hidden treasures at the museum: a life-size horse and lieutenant depicts the Presidio. All the tack and the officer's uniform are original for the period between World War I and WWII. The saddle is a 1928 McClellan. There are also historic cannons out front and at Fort Mervine on the hill above.

17. What is unique about the museum that can't be found anywhere else: the museum is a former armory which was sheathed in metal.

18. The most important things about local, state, or American history that can be learned at the museum: the presidios of Monterey have been in continuous use since the days of Spanish California to the present American Presidio, home of the Defense Language Institute. It has had many different names and uses.

19. Annual events held at the site or elsewhere in the community: Civil War Encampments with musket, cannon, and cavalry demonstrations during Monterey's History Fest in October.

20. Research facilities or archives at the site: none.

21. Type of gift shop and what is for sale: a small gift area with books and cards.

1. **Presidio Visitor's Center and The Officers' Club-San Francisco**
2. Location: Headquarters at the Presidio Visitor Center, 105 Montgomery Street, (Main Post) San Francisco.
3. Website: http://www.presidio.gov/Pages/default.aspx
4. Phone number: (415) 561-4323.
5. E-mail: presidio@presidiotrust.gov
6. Hours of operation: Visitor's Center-Thursdays to Sundays, 10 a.m. to 4 p.m. Officers' Club- Tuesday-Sunday 10 a.m.- 6 p.m.
7. Cost: free.
8. Permanent Exhibits: a few displays at the Visitor's Center. A recent addition to the park is the newly re-opened Officer's Club at 50 Morage Avenue. It features The Presidio Heritage Gallery, which contains films, images, and artifacts that tell the story of the last 10,000 years at the site. Rotating seasonal exhibits are also housed at the gallery. Other sites are in the planning stages and will be open soon.
9. Special Exhibits: A room that shows the different layers of construction of the Officers' Club over the years.
10. Historical era that is featured the best: all periods are represented.
11. Targeted age groups: all ages
12. Special activities for children: Archaeology Education Programs, Camping at the Presidio, Environmental Service Learning, Kids and Family, nature walks and tours on National Trails Day.
13. Guided tours: some are available during special events (see website for details). There is an audio walking tour available.

169

14. Hands-on activities: Archaeology Education Programs and nature activities. There are also multi-media displays and "please touch" items at the Officer's Club.

15. The best-kept secrets at the museum: there are many works in progress. New exhibits and refurbished buildings are opening all the time.

16. Hidden treasures at the museum: there are many historic gun batteries and cannons scattered throughout the Presidio. The Heritage Gallery has a historic cannon, military uniforms, artifacts from archeological digs, and a video clip of a visit from Teddy Roosevelt. There are also beautiful nature trails on the grounds.

17. What is unique about the museum that can't be found anywhere else: it is the oldest continuously occupied military base in the U.S. It was active from 1776-1989.

18. The most important things about local, state, or American history that can be learned at the museum: it covers the Indian settlements, and the Spanish, Mexican, and American periods. Many historic expeditions were associated with the base. The De Anza Expedition, Mexican American War, Buffalo Soldiers who patrolled national parks, Modoc Indian Wars, major staging ground for WWII, a center for WWII Japanese translators, a hospital used for returning Vietnam vets, etc.

19. Annual events held at the site or elsewhere in the community: numerous public events are hosted by the Park Service and other public agencies (see website for details).

20. Research facilities or archives at the site: The Presidio Trust Library houses two primary collections. The general collection contains public documents created by the Presidio Trust and its contractors, as well as books, videos, and documents on the Presidio's rich history, its buildings, and environmental resources. A second collection contains environmental cleanup program materials, including the Base Realignment and Closure (BRAC) documents transferred by the U.S. Army to the Presidio Trust in August 1999, as well as reports created since that time. The Golden Gate National Recreation Area Archive and Record Center houses the archival collections of the Golden Gate National Recreation Area.

21. Type of gift shop and what is for sale: some books are available at the Visitor's Center.

22. Additional information: many organizations have buildings on the site that are not directly involved with the history of the site. Call ahead before visiting them. Improvements in food services and lodgings in the area are forthcoming. The Walt Disney Family Museum is right next-door to the Visitor's Center. It tells the story of Disney's life and accomplishments. It has many interesting items, original artwork and videos about Disney's projects. The highlight is a huge model of Disneyland. See http://www.waltdisney.org/ for information.

1. **Prusch Farm-San Jose**
2. Location: 647 S. King Road, San Jose, CA. 95116.
3. Website: http://www.pruschfarmpark.org/ and http://www.sanjoseca.gov/Facilities/Facility/Details/Emma-Prusch-Farm-Regional-Park-131
4. Phone number: (408) 794-6262.
5. E-mail: use the online contact form for the city of San Jose.
6. Hours of operation: Tuesday - Sunday: 8 a.m. – sunset.

170

7. Cost: free.

8. Permanent Exhibits: the park is home to San José's largest barn, where 4H livestock projects are housed; animals vary throughout the year, so keep going back to see what is around. The park also features robust community gardens, a rare fruit orchard, and acres of open grass perfect for picnicking, kite flying, games, and relaxing.

9. Special Exhibits: the farmhouse has some of the Prusch family's items. It was built in the mid 1880s and has ten rooms. It has a lovely garden. The community center and grounds have historical farming equipment on display.

10. Historical era that is featured the best: 1800s-1900s.

11. Targeted age groups: all ages.

12. Special activities for children: the park offers a variety of educational programs for school children and other groups, and hosts a Summer Camp during the months of May to August. Summer Camp kids get to spend each day caring for the farm animals and growing vegetables in their own garden. The "Hatchery" is a class for pre-school aged children where they learn motor skills and how to socialize in a farm environment. Saturday classes introduce children to cooking, gardening, animal care, and other fun activities. School groups up to the third grade can schedule time with a docent to see the animals up close and learn about the rich history of the Valley of Heart's Delight.

13. Guided tours: available upon request.

14. Hands-on activities: some of the animals can be fed or petted, community gardens.

15. The best-kept secrets at the museum: the museum grows its own food. It is also the composting center for the city's recycling program.

16. Hidden treasures at the museum: the historic farm equipment.

17. What is unique about the museum that can't be found anywhere else: it is a large working farm in the midst of a large urban area near a major freeway intersection. Most city kids never get a chance to get this close to farm animals and find them quite entertaining.

18. The most important things about local, state, or American history that can be learned at the museum: Santa Clara Valley's agricultural heritage is preserved here. It is the largest museum of its type in the county.

19. Annual events held at the site or elsewhere in the community: educational programs, farming and gardening classes.

20. Research facilities or archives at the site: none.

21. Type of gift shop and what is for sale: some produce is sold at special events.

1. **Quail Hollow Ranch County Park-Felton**

2. Location: 800 Quail Hollow Road, Felton, CA. 95062.

3. Website: http://www.scparks.com/quail_hollow.html

4. Phone number: (831) 335-9348.

5. E-mail: prc120@scparks.com

6. Hours of operation: open daily from dawn to dusk. The visitor center is open Saturday and Sunday from 8:30 a.m. to 5:00 p.m.

7. Cost: free (special events cost extra).

171

8. Permanent Exhibits: nestled deep in the Santa Cruz Mountains, this 300-acre historic horse ranch and nature preserve is home to 15 habitats and 4.5 miles of hiking and equestrian trails. In the center of this tear-drop shaped valley, one will find the ranch complex consisting of the visitor center housed in a historic ranch house, picnic areas, horse barns and turnouts, lawn area, and orchard.

9. Special Exhibits: local wildlife, The Lane Family and Sunset Magazine, and Life in the 1950s.

10. Historical era that is featured the best: 1900s.

11. Targeted age groups: all ages.

12. Special activities for children: field trips, classes, and camps (see website for details).

13. Guided tours: free walks, classes, and workshops about the natural and cultural history of the park are offered on Sundays and occasionally on Friday evenings.

14. Hands-on activities: depends upon the special class or activity.

15. The best-kept secrets at the museum: the August 1948 issue of Sunset magazine featured the barns at the ranch.

16. Hidden treasures at the museum: historic photos of the house and other buildings.

17. What is unique about the museum that can't be found anywhere else: the variety of activities held there.

18. The most important things about local, state, or American history that can be learned at the museum: Joseph and America Kenville homesteaded 44 acres in 1866, along with their 9 children, and began a 70-year farming tradition of growing everything from apples to melons. The site is best known, however, as the home of Sunset magazine owners Larry and Ruth Lane. The ranch also served the magazine by becoming the site of test gardens and a test kitchen.

19. Annual events held at the site or elsewhere in the community: educational birthday parties, science enrichment programs, field trips, and a summer day camp are offered for a fee.

20. Research facilities or archives at the site: a collection of old Sunset magazines is available to visitors.

21. Type of gift shop: none.

1. **Ravenswood Historical Site-Livermore**

2. Location: 2647 Arroyo Road, Livermore, CA. 94550.

3. Website: http://www.larpd.org/programs/ravenswood.html

4. Phone number: (925) 443-0238.

5. E-mail: use the online contact form.

6. Hours of operation: Noon - 4:00 p.m. the second and fourth Sundays of each month (except December).

7. Cost: free.

8. Permanent Exhibits: the 1885 Buckley Cottage, 1891 main house, and farm buildings.

9. Special Exhibits: The Carriage Barn.

10. Historical era that is featured the best: 1880s-1920s.

11. Targeted age groups: all ages.

12. Special activities for children: during the Old-Fashioned Ice Cream Social there are pony rides, a petting zoo, a live orchestra, and other musical groups.

13. Guided tours: available during visiting hours.

14. Hands-on activities: see above.

15. The best-kept secrets at the museum: the cottage is actually nicer than the big house where the servants lived.

16. Hidden treasures at the museum: a built-in communication pipe that allowed the Buckleys to talk to the servants next door.

17. What is unique about the museum that can't be found anywhere else: it is one of the finest historical buildings in Livermore. It has been very well restored.

18. The most important things about local, state, or American history that can be learned at the museum: the importance of the estate to the development of the local wine industry. Also, Christopher Buckley was a famous San Francisco politician known as "The Blind Boss".

19. Annual events held at the site or elsewhere in the community: The Old-Fashioned Ice Cream Social and the Victorian Yuletide.

20. Research facilities or archives at the site: none.

21. Type of gift shop: none.

1. **Red Oak Victory Ship-Richmond**
2. Location: 1337 Canal Blvd., Berth 6A, Richmond, CA. 94804.
3. Website: www.ssredoakvictory.com/index.htm
4. Phone number: 510-237-2933.
5. E-mail: ROV235@SBCGlobal.Net

173

6. Hours of operation: 10:00a.m. to 3:00p.m. on Tuesdays, Thursdays, Saturdays, and Sundays.

7. Cost: $5.

8. Permanent Exhibits: the whole ship!

9. Special Exhibits: there is a small museum about the ship near the gift shop.

10. Historical era that is featured the best: WWII.

11. Targeted age groups: all ages.

12. Special activities for children: school tours are available.

13. Guided tours: the only entrance to the ship is through guided tours.

14. Hands-on activities: you will travel throughout the ship on your tour. Some areas are permissible to touch.

15. The best-kept secrets at the museum: the docents are mostly WWII veterans themselves, who tell some fascinating tales of their experiences. They donate many hours to restore the ship. It will soon sail again!

16. Hidden treasures at the museum: a display near the gift shop with items from the Kaiser Shipyards explaining the origins and construction of the ship, its christening, and the voyages it made.

17. What is unique about the museum that can't be found anywhere else: this is an actual ship from WWII, one of the few remaining afloat in the US.

18. The most important things about local, state, or American history that can be learned at the museum: Richmond's importance to the war effort and home front.

19. Annual events held at the site or elsewhere in the community: "What's in a Name", The Battle of Kasserine Pass, the Memorial Day Event, ROV Film Series, Pancake Breakfasts, dances, and The Home Front Festival.

20. Research facilities or archives at the site: a small research library is available upon request. Many books from the era are also placed throughout the ship.

21. Type of gift shop and what is for sale: a wide selection of WWII and nautical items are for sale.

1. **The Rengstorff House- Mountain View**

2. Location: 3070 N. Shoreline Blvd., Mountain View, CA. 94043.

3. Website: http://www.r-house.org/

4. Phone number: (650) 903-6392.

5. E-mail: rengstorff.events@gmail.com

6. Hours of operation: Tuesdays and Wednesdays from 11 a.m. to 5 p.m., and Sundays from 1 p.m. to 4 p.m.

7. Cost: free.

8. Permanent Exhibits: kitchen, dining room, 2 parlors, music room, office, water tower, and windmill.

9. Special Exhibits: none.

10. Historical era that is featured the best: 1860s-1890s.

11. Targeted age groups: all ages.

12. Special activities for children: school tours are available. Pictures with Father Christmas.

13. Guided tours: docent-led tours are available during regular hours.

14. Hands-on activities: none.

15. The best-kept secrets at the museum: taxidermy of local animals.

16. Hidden treasures at the museum: paintings by family members, clothing, furnishings, documents, and memorabilia of family members.

17. What is unique about the museum that can't be found anywhere else: the location in Shoreline Park is quite scenic.

18. The most important things about local, state, or American history that can be learned at the museum: the house is one of the best examples of Italianate Victorian architecture in the West.

19. Annual events held at the site or elsewhere in the community: Haunted Mansion Halloween, Holiday Open House, Arts Festival (see website for details).

20. Research facilities or archives at the site: none.

21. Type of gift shop and what is for sale: books and gift items pertaining to the house and Mountain View.

1. **Richmond Museum of History**

2. Location: 400 Nevin Avenue, Richmond, CA. 94801.

3. Website: http://www.richmondmuseumofhistory.org/

4. Phone number: (510) 235-7387.

5. E-mail: Use the online contact form.

6. Hours of operation: Wednesday through Sunday, 1 p.m. to 4 p.m.

7. Cost: free

8. Permanent Exhibits: a large collection of items from Indians to modern times. Ohlone arrowheads, bowls, basketry, replica tule boat, pioneer wagon, tools, furniture, clothing, 19th century store, kitchen, a model A Ford, fire equipment, and toys. Exhibits featuring local oil industry, ferries, bridges, and the Kaiser Shipyards of WWII. The history of Richmond including Native American/Archaeology exhibit, Mexican Period, Early American Period, World War II Home Front Experience, Post-War Richmond, and some of exhibits on contemporary Richmond.

9. Special Exhibits: rotating exhibits such as: Semi-pro Baseball in Richmond. Temporary exhibits in the Seaver Gallery change twice annually.

10. Historical era that is featured the best: 19th-20th centuries.

11. Targeted age groups: all ages.

12. Special activities for children: none.

13. Guided tours: Call for tour information, docent-led tours are available.

14. Hands-on activities: none.

15. The best-kept secrets at the museum: the museum also operates the Red Oak Victory ship in a nearby harbor. This is a fully refurbished transport from the Mothball Fleet that will soon be able to sail again!

16. Hidden treasures at the museum: the exhibits on the Kaiser shipyards and WWII homefront are exceptional. They are even better than the ones at the nearby Rosie the Riveter museum. The museum has a large collection of artifacts from the prehistoric shellmounds in Richmond.

17. What is unique about the museum that can't be found anywhere else: a large collection of well-maintained items crammed in a two-story building. The 1931 Ford that was first car to roll off the line at the Ford Richmond Assembly Plant.

18. The most important things about local, state, or American history that can be learned at the museum: Richmond's unique role as the crossroads of the Bay Area. Its importance in WWII is especially emphasized.

19. Annual events held at the site or elsewhere in the community: Richmond Tales Literary Festival and the Home Front Festival.

20. Research facilities or archives at the site: it has the largest local research library in the area and a huge photograph archive. The library is available by appointment only Wednesday through Sunday between 1 p.m. to 4 p.m.

21. Type of gift shop and what is for sale: a small bookstore near the entrance features local history books, gifts, and a quilt depicting Richmond's heritage.

1. **Rio Vista Museum**

2. Location: 16 N. Front Street, Rio Vista, CA. 94571.

3. Website: http://www.riovistamuseum.com/

4. Phone number: (707) 374-5169.

5. E-mail: riovistamuseum@yahoo.com

6. Hours of operation: Saturday and Sunday, 1:30 to 4:30 p.m.

7. Cost: free.

8. Permanent Exhibits: parlor, pioneer items, dairy farming, kitchen, sports teams,

9. Special Exhibits: none.

10. Historical era that is featured the best: 1800s-1900s.

176

11. Targeted age groups: all ages.

12. Special activities for children: none.

13. Guided tours: call the museum for information.

14. Hands-on activities: none.

15. The best-kept secrets at the museum: the city has had to rebuild itself due to floods. These efforts are well documented at the museum.

16. Hidden treasures at the museum: an antique buggy and mail carriage, and an organ.

17. What is unique about the museum that can't be found anywhere else: it is in the first of many small historic towns along the Sacramento River. The history of the city is intimately tied in to the fortunes of the river. There are many charming buildings in these small towns.

18. The most important things about local, state, or American history that can be learned at the museum: Rio Vista has a history going back to Spanish land grants. It is considered the easternmost city in the Bay Area and is a gateway to the Delta and Sacramento River areas. This means that it is an important transportation hub for the state.

19. Annual events held at the site or elsewhere in the community: Olde Time Christmas Faire (see website for details).

20. Research facilities or archives at the site: none.

21. Type of gift shop and what is for sale: books about Rio Vista, blanket throws, postcards with photos from Rio Vista's past, t-Shirts, coffee mugs, and assorted movies filmed locally.

22. Additional Information: If you would like to "dig up" more local history visit The Dutra Museum of Dredging. See http://www.dutragroup.com/museum.html for further information.

1. **The Robert Louis Stevenson Museum-St. Helena**

2. Location: 1490 Library Lane in St. Helena, CA. 94574.

3. Website: http://www.StevensonMuseum.org

4. Phone number: (707) 963-3757.

5. E-mail: director@stevensonmuseum.org

6. Hours of operation: Tues. through Sat. - noon to 4 p.m.

7. Cost: free.

177

8. Permanent Exhibits: visitors can follow the life of Robert Louis Stevenson chronologically through the exhibit and experience firsthand the personal possessions of RLS and his family. Contextualizing Stevenson's works during his life, the exhibit particularly highlights the time he spent in Napa Valley in 1880, just before writing the classic, *Treasure Island*. With over 11,000 objects in its collection, many acquired directly from heirs and friends of the Stevenson family, visitors can expect to see: original letters; manuscripts; a library full of first and rare editions; paintings and drawings; sculptures; photographs; and the personal possessions of RLS and his family, such as childhood toys, family scrapbooks, Stevenson's wedding ring, and the furniture and decorative items the Stevensons used to decorated their home.

9. Special Exhibits: they are changed every six months, a small rotating exhibit highlights special topics related to Robert Louis Stevenson.

10. Historical era that is featured the best: 1850s to 1890s.

11. Targeted age groups: all ages.

12. Special activities for children: a hands-on worksheet related to the temporary exhibits is available for children, and range from drawing activities to puzzles and games. Also, every July, the museum hosts a free family treasure hunt around the town of St. Helena.

13. Guided tours: appointments must be made in advance by contacting museum staff. Tours are generally held during normal operating hours, but can be scheduled for any time that staff may be available. There is a recommended donation of $25 for guided tours.

14. Hands-on activities: none.

15. The best-kept secrets at the museum: Stevenson's manuscripts, first editions, and other personal items.

16. Hidden treasures at the museum: Stevenson's toy soldiers he played with as a boy, which inspired his poem "The Land of Counterpane".

17. What is unique about the museum that can't be found anywhere else: this is the largest collection devoted to Robert Louis Stevenson on public display anywhere in the world. There are more items and information here than in his homeland of Scotland.

18. The most important things about local, state, or American history that can be learned at the museum: how the region inspired his literature. Stevenson's enduring influence on literature and culture. What life and travel were like at the end of the 19th century.

19. Annual events held at the site or elsewhere in the community: International Talk Like a Pirate Day every September 19th, a Free Family Treasure Hunt every July, and other events. Call for information.

20. Research facilities or archives at the site: scholars and researchers of Robert Louis Stevenson's life and works are encouraged and welcomed to spend time at the museum while pursuing their academic interests. Research fees are $15/hour. Scheduled appointments are required in advance by calling (707) 963-3757.

21. Type of gift shop and what is for sale: Stevenson's books and other gift items.

22. Additional information: a trail marker in nearby Robert Louis Stevenson State Park is the place where the famous author spent his honeymoon in 1880. Although nothing remains of Stevenson's cabin, the site is identified on the trail to the summit.

1. **Rosie the Riveter WWII Home Front Museum-Richmond**

2. Location: 1414 Harbour Way South, Suite 3000. Richmond, CA. 94804.

3. Website: http://www.nps.gov/rori/index.htm

4. Phone number: (510) 232-3108.

5. E-mail: use the online contact form.

6. Hours of operation: every day from 10:00 a.m. to 5:00 p.m. Cost: free.

178

7. Permanent Exhibits: the Rosie the Riveter Memorial. None of the exhibits at the visitor's center are permanent yet. The museum is new and the collections will soon be greatly expanded.

8. Special Exhibits: temporary displays on Kaiser shipyards, Liberty and Victory ships, propaganda posters, victory gardens, Japanese Relocations, Hispanics, women, civil defense, rationing, scrap drives, housing shortages, etc.

9. Historical era that is featured the best: WWII.

10. Targeted age groups: all ages.

11. Special activities for children: Junior Ranger program. Civil Rights trading cards.

12. Guided tours: free ranger tours of the park. The rangers provide both scheduled bus and Visitor Education Center tours. You may also tour the Visitor Education Center on your own, or enjoy the free Auto Tour brochure, which will guide you around the park sites.

13. The best-kept secrets at the museum: a movie theater has great films with interviews of shipyard workers and others active on the home front of WWII.

14. Hidden treasures at the museum: the oral history collection.

15. What is unique about the museum that can't be found anywhere else: it shows the unique perspectives of those who worked so hard to contribute to the war effort at home.

16. The most important things about local, state, or American history that can be learned at the museum: there was a lot more to WWII than just the battles that were fought. People at home made great sacrifices to advance the cause of the war. The war had a permanent impact on minorities, women, and the poor as they got jobs in the war industries for the first time. These led to the Civil Rights movement after the war.

17. Annual events held at the site or elsewhere in the community: none yet.

18. Research facilities or archives at the site: not available yet.

19. Type of gift shop and what is for sale: Rosie the Riveter memorabilia, books, WWII, and Park Service souvenirs.

1. **Salinas Valley Memorial Hospital Museum of Medical History**

2. Location: Located in the Downing Resource Center, 450 E Romie Ln., Salinas, CA. 93901.

3. Website: http://www.svmh.com/community/medicalhistorymuseum.aspx

4. Phone number: (831) 755-0772.

5. E-mail: webmaster@svmh.com

6. Hours of operation: self-guided tours available 9:00 a.m. to 4:00 p.m. Monday through Friday.

7. Cost: free.

8. Permanent Exhibits: a Civil War surgical kit, a doctor's office circa 1920 featuring furniture and instruments used to perform a tonsillectomy, and a surgery case complete with an operating table owned by Dr. Henry Murphy, John Steinbeck's family doctor (other larger diagnostic machines are also included). Two cases of medical items dating from the 1700s to World War I (1918), including many instruments used during the Civil War. A display of memorabilia spanning the 50-

179

year history of the Salinas Valley Memorial Hospital Service League and the nursing profession.

9. Special Exhibits: exhibits include nurses and candy stripers, a library of historic medical books, and murals depicting Native American and Spanish colonial medical practices in the area.

10. Historical era that is featured the best: 1700s-present.

11. Targeted age groups: all ages.

12. Special activities for children: school tours.

13. Guided tours: tours for adults and community groups and the interactive program for second and third grade students are available by appointment.

14. Hands-on activities: some displays have interactive audio components. Many more activities are available during school tours.

15. The best-kept secrets at the museum: operating table and other equipment used by John Steinbeck's doctor.

16. Hidden treasures at the museum: Civil War era medical instruments, a skeleton in the closet, and the lancet used by Benjamin Rush to bleed George Washington!

17. What is unique about the museum that can't be found anywhere else: most of this type of equipment was discarded long ago. This is one of the few museums of its kind in California.

18. The most important things about local, state, or American history that can be learned at the museum: it strives to provide an interesting and educational window to our scientific past so that we can more easily understand and contribute to the continued progress of healthcare. The museum offers a rare and interesting look at the evolution of medicine and medical equipment over the past three centuries

19. Annual events held at the site or elsewhere in the community: see the hospital website for details.

20. Research facilities or archives at the site: none.

21. Type of gift shop: none.

1. **San Anselmo Historical Museum**

180

2. Location: 110 Tunstead Ave., San Anselmo, CA. 94960.

3. Website: http://www.sananselmohistory.org

4. Phone number: (415) 258-4659.

5. E-mail: info@sananselmohistory.org

6. Hours of operation: Tuesdays from 10:00 a.m. to noon, Saturdays from 10:00 a.m. to 4:00 p.m.

7. Cost: free.

8. Permanent Exhibits: the museum offers historical records of the town's notable people, neighborhoods, businesses, celebrations, and events, including its occasional floods.

9. Special Exhibits: special displays of local historical interest are on view on a rotating basis.

10. Historical era that is featured the best: 1800s-1900s.

11. Targeted age groups: all ages.

12. Special activities for children: the museum offers a Children's Corner with crayons and San Anselmo-themed coloring books.

13. Guided tours: none.

14. Hands-on activities: none.

15. The best-kept secrets at the museum: a delightful student-made film points out many interesting trivia facts about the locations in town that George Lucas used in his movies.

16. Hidden treasures at the museum: an historic timeline from Miwok times to the present. A diorama of the historic downtown.

17. What is unique about the museum that can't be found anywhere else: it is located in the town library. It has many historic photographs and oral histories.

18. The most important things about local, state, or American history that can be learned at the museum: the town has been an important agricultural center, home of the San Francisco Theological Seminary, and a railroad junction.

19. Annual events held at the site or elsewhere in the community: walking tour of historic buildings.

20. Research facilities or archives at the site: a small research library is available.

21. Type of gift shop and what is for sale: historic photos and books.

22. Additional information: Imagination Park next to the museum has statues of Yoda and Indiana Jones that are popular tourist attractions.

1. **San Jose Fire Museum**

2. Location: 1661 Senter Road, #D1, San Jose, CA. 95112.

3. Website: http://www.sjfiremuseum.org/

181

4. Phone number: (408) 793-4321.

5. E-mail: use the online contact form.

6. Hours of operation: Tue. and Thurs. except holidays, 9:00 a.m. to 1:00 p.m.

7. Cost: free.

8. Permanent Exhibits: there are over 30 apparatus, including hose carts, hand pumpers, hook & ladders, fire engine pumpers & steamers, chemical hose wagons, fire chief's cars, and aerial ladder trucks. Also, there are historic written documents, including journals, constitutions and documented Common Council Minutes for the city of San Jose. There are badges, ground ladders, helmets, fire fighting tools, and equipment. Most of these items are specific to the City of San Jose Fire Department and its great history.

9. Special Exhibits: none.

10. Historical era that is featured the best: 1810-present.

11. Targeted age groups: all ages

12. Special activities for children: none.

13. Guided tours: available upon request.

14. Hands-on activities: none.

15. The best-kept secrets at the museum: photographs of historical fires.

16. Hidden treasures at the museum: civil defense and fire fighting equipment from San Jose.

17. What is unique about the museum that can't be found anywhere else: most of the equipment is from San Jose. Many other fire museums have out-of-town equipment.

18. The most important things about local, state, or American history that can be learned at the museum: how fire-fighting technology has changed over the years, how the department expanded to meet the growing city's needs.

19. Annual events held at the site or elsewhere in the community: the vehicles are taken out for display at the auto show at History San Jose, parades, and other events.

20. Research facilities or archives at the site: some fire records and related documents are available.

21. Type of gift shop and what is for sale: t-shirts, belt buckles and other Fire Department-related gift items.

22. Additional information: The museum will soon move to Firestation #1 in downtown San Jose.

1. **Sanchez Adobe-Pacifica**

2. Location: 1000 Linda Mar Boulevard, Pacifica, CA. 94044.

3. Website: www.historysmc.org

4. Phone number: (650) 299-0104.

5. E-mail: sanchezadobe@historysmc.org

6. Hours of operation: Tuesday-Thursday from 10 a.m. – 4 p.m., Saturday-Sunday from 1 – 5 p.m.

7. Cost: free.

8. Permanent Exhibits: the adobe built by Francisco Sanchez between 1842-1846 and the surrounding grounds.

9. Special Exhibits: there are numerous historical items from the Ohlone, Spanish and Mexican eras on display inside the adobe.

10. Historical era that is featured the best: 1800s.

11. Targeted age groups: all ages.

12. Special activities for children: school program features hands-on activities such as roping cattle, grinding corn, and making adobe bricks.

13. Guided tours: available upon request.

14. Hands-on activities: see the children's activities above.

15. The best-kept secrets at the museum: it is one of the best-preserved Mexican adobes in California.

16. Hidden treasures at the museum: there some fine Ohlone artifacts and original furnishings from the Mexican and American eras.

17. What is unique about the museum that can't be found anywhere else: Archaeological discoveries from the Ohlone village of Pruristac, once located on the site, are on display.

18. The most important things about local, state, or American history that can be learned at the museum: the site has been a Native American settlement, support farm for Mission Dolores in San Francisco, a Mexican ranch, and an American hotel. Each phase of its occupation is well documented.

19. Annual events held at the site or elsewhere in the community: Rancho Day Fiesta (see website for details).

20. Research facilities or archives at the site: none.

21. Type of gift shop and what is for sale: there are some interesting history books, videos, and other gift items for sale.

1. **San Leandro History Museum & Art Gallery**
2. Location: 320 West Estudillo Avenue, San Leandro, CA. 94577.
3. Website: https://www.sanleandro.org/depts/library/about_us/history/
history_museum.asp
4. Phone number: (510) 577-3990.
5. E-mail: asilveira@sanleandro.org
6. Hours of operation: first Saturday of each month, 11:00 a.m. - 3:00 p.m.
7. Cost: free.
8. Permanent Exhibits: a timeline of San Leandro begins with the first people, the Ohlone/Costanoan Indians, and follows the changes through Spanish/Mexican California, the Gold Rush, the beginnings of a new American town, and the developments of the 20th Century through World War II. Concept exhibits include People from Many Lands, Oysters and the Bayshore, and Agriculture and Industry.
9. Special Exhibits: Rotating exhibits.
10. Historical era that is featured the best: 1800s-1900s.
11. Targeted age groups: all ages.
12. Special activities for children: 3rd and 4th grade school tours.
13. Guided tours: call for reservations. Walking tours of the historic downtown.
14. Hands-on activities: a wall that says, "Add Your Story".
15. The best-kept secrets at the museum: the 1909 Cherry Festival Exhibit.
16. Hidden treasures at the museum: an antique school desk in the children's area.
17. What is unique about the museum that can't be found anywhere else: it is an art gallery and a history museum.
18. The most important things about local, state, or American history that can be learned at the museum: the development of the community over time. Its settlers came from many lands.
19. Annual events held at the site or elsewhere in the community: the Cherry Festival. See the city website for information.
20. Research facilities or archives at the site: available through the city library.
21. Type of gift shop and what is for sale: postcards with historic photos, local history books, and DVDs.

1. **The San Lorenzo Valley Museum-Boulder Creek**
2. Location: 12547 Highway 9, Boulder Creek, CA. 95006.
3. Website: http://www.slvmuseum.com/index.html
4. Phone number: (831) 338-8382.
5. E-mail: slvmuseum@sbcglobal.net
6. Hours of operation: Wednesday -Sunday: 12:00 p.m. - 4:00 p.m.
7. Cost: free, donations are welcomed.
8. Permanent Exhibits: school items, kitchen and household tools, redwood trees and logging, historic photos, Native Americans.
9. Special Exhibits: rotating exhibits (see website for details).
10. Historical era that is featured the best: 1800s-1900s.
11. Targeted age groups: all ages.
12. Special activities for children: school outreach programs, Children's Christmas Tree Trimming, and special family events.

13. Guided tours: available upon request.

14. Hands-on activities: none.

15. The best-kept secrets at the museum: Turn-of-the-century schoolroom, interesting logging photos, and antique kitchen tools.

16. Hidden treasures at the museum: the logging equipment display is exceptional. Antique hand-carved redwood furniture, oxen yokes, and extra large blacksmith bellows.

17. What is unique about the museum that can't be found anywhere else: it is housed in an historic church.

18. The most important things about local, state, or American history that can be learned at the museum: the important role that the valley played in supplying several types of lumber and limestone throughout America.

19. Annual events held at the site or elsewhere in the community: SLV Museum sponsors The Veterans Day Dinner, Children's Christmas Tree Trimming, Spirit of '45, Models & Miniatures Exhibition, and National Museum Day. It also participates in Felton Remembers Parade on Memorial Day, Boulder Creek July 4th Parade, curates an art exhibition on The Community Wall, The Pop-Up Museum, Historic Talk Series, and Evening Lectures with guest speakers (see website for details).

20. Research facilities or archives at the site: a small research library is available inside the museum with an oral history program. A researcher is available for assistance by appointment.

21. Type of gift shop and what is for sale: an extensive book selection on local history, railroad history, local nature, local Ohlone culture, and biking / hiking trails.

1. **San Mateo County History Museum-Redwood City**

2. Location: 2200 Broadway, Redwood City, CA. 94063.

3. Website: www.historysmc.org

4. Phone number: (650) 299-0104.

5. E-mail: info@historysmc.org

6. Hours of operation: Tuesday – Sunday, 10 a.m. - 4 p.m.

7. Cost: $6 adults, $4 seniors & students, kids under 5 free. Free on the Free First Fridays of the month.

8. Permanent Exhibits: Nature's Bounty, Journey to Work, Living the California Dream, Land of Opportunity, San Mateo County History Makers, Charles Parsons' Ships of the World, Courtroom A, and The Mavericks surfing exhibit.

9. Special Exhibits: rotating exhibits.

10. Historical era that is featured the best: prehistoric times-present.

11. Targeted age groups: all ages.

12. Special activities for children: school tours, school outreach programs, and child-oriented special events such as Family Past Times.

13. Guided tours: Victorian Days Walking Tours.

14. Hands-on activities: there are many fascinating, state-of-the-art interactive displays at the museum.

15. The best-kept secrets at the museum: the Mavericks surfing simulation lets you try your hand on a surfboard riding the giant waves of local fame.

185

16. Hidden treasures at the museum: there are many fascinating items, such as Ohlone artifacts, Mexican ranch items, model ships, and immigrants' possessions.

17. What is unique about the museum that can't be found anywhere else: the exhibits on Bay Area industries and the postwar housing boom are some of the best in the state. The displays are well designed, colorful, and interactive. They even contain lighting and sound elements that help immerse you in the experience.

18. The most important things about local, state, or American history that can be learned at the museum: this is one of the best comprehensive history museums in the state. It does an especially good job of explaining the growth of the Bay Area and the development of its resources.

19. Annual events held at the site or elsewhere in the community: Victorian Days, holiday and other events (see website for details).

20. Research facilities or archives at the site: there is a full-sized research library with extensive records available.

21. Type of gift shop and what is for sale: the gift shop has many interesting books, videos, toys, souvenirs, and other gift items. The items in the store are exceptionally well coordinated with the themes of the museum. It is one of the nicest museum gift shops around.

1. Santa Cruz Beach Boardwalk Historium-Santa Cruz

2. Location: The Santa Cruz Beach Boardwalk, 400 Beach Street, Santa Cruz, CA. 95060. On the second Floor of Neptune's Kingdom.

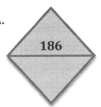

3. Website: http://news.beachboardwalk.com/press-kit/boardwalk-arcade#.UzCbqV6uF7k

4. Phone number: (831) 423-5590.

5. E-mail: publicity@scseaside.com

6. Hours of operation: Mon-Thu: 11a.m.-10p.m., Fri: 11a.m.-11p.m., Sat: 10a.m.-11p.m., Sun: 10a.m.-10p.m. Call to confirm the hours.

7. Cost: admission to the Historium is free (see website for details regarding admission to the park).

8. Permanent Exhibits: images and photographs of the first 100 years of the Santa Cruz Boardwalk.

9. Special Exhibits: none.

10. Historical era that is featured the best: the 20th Century.

11. Targeted age groups: all ages.

12. Special activities for children: none.

13. Guided tours: a self-guided history tour of the Santa Cruz Boardwalk. The brochure includes points of interest and fun facts about the historic Boardwalk and Cocoanut Grove. The brochure map includes the locations of 18 interpretive signs posted throughout the park. The Historic Walking Tour brochure is available at the Miniature Golf station inside Neptune's Kingdom for $2.00, or you can download a free printable PDF version from the website.

14. Hands-on activities: none.

15. The best-kept secrets at the museum: rare historic photographs of the beach and boardwalk.

16. Hidden treasures at the museum: there are many famous former attractions that are long gone, such as an immense indoor swimming pool and classic roller coasters. The Cocoanut Grove Ballroom, a big band ballroom that drew some of the biggest names of the swing era, still exists and looks much the same – see www.cocoanutgrovesantacruz.com. The most famous attraction, the Giant Dipper rollercoaster (1924) is still running. The oldest ride in the park is the Looff Carousel (1911). There are two important antique band organs on display in the carousel building. "Laffing Sal" came from Playland at the Beach (a defunct amusement park in San Francisco).

17. What is unique about the museum that can't be found anywhere else: it is the only museum that records the past of this famous tourist attraction.

18. The most important things about local, state, or American history that can be learned at the museum: Santa Cruz is the largest seaside resort in California and it has a storied past that includes famous swimmers, surfing, beauty pageants, WWII, and concerts.

19. Annual events held at the site or elsewhere in the community: there are many concerts and special events through out the year (see website for details).

20. Research facilities or archives at the site: private archives.

21. Type of gift shop and what is for sale: there are many souvenir shops in the park. A book entitled *The Santa Cruz Beach Boardwalk: A Century by the Sea* and a DVD entitled *100 Years, Millions of Memories* are for sale.

22. Additional information: guided, behind-the-scenes tours are offered through Santa Cruz Parks & Recreation Department.

1. **Santa Cruz Natural History Museum**
2. Location: 1305 East Cliff Drive, Santa Cruz, CA. 95062.
3. Website: http://santacruzmuseum.org/explore-the-museum/permanent-exhibits/
4. Phone number: (831) 420-6115.
5. E-mail: staff@santacruzmuseums.org
6. Hours of operation: Tuesday – Saturday 10:00 am - 5:00 pm.
7. Cost: $4 Adults, $2 seniors (over 60), $2 students, free for youth (under 18). Admission is free for individuals and families on the first Friday of every month.
8. Permanent Exhibits: while this is primarily a nature museum, they have a good display on the Ohlone Indians.
9. Special Exhibits: rotating exhibits on various nature themes.
10. Historical era that is featured the best: prehistory-1800s.
11. Targeted age groups: all ages.
12. Special activities for children: school tours.
13. Guided tours: available with reservations for a fee of $15.
14. Hands-on activities: real mortar and pestles are available for young and old to try their hand at grinding acorns. Acorns were an important food source for the Ohlone people prior to the Mission Period.
15. The best-kept secrets at the museum: an enormous mural depicting every-day life in an Ohlone village.

16. Hidden treasures at the museum: artifacts, baskets and images bring to life the cultural traditions of local native people, both past and present. Examples of native basketry, beadwork, and stone implements can be found throughout the exhibit.

17. What is unique about the museum that can't be found anywhere else: It has a giant whale sculpture on the front lawn!

18. The most important things about local, state, or American history that can be learned at the museum: the ways in which the Ohlone Indians interacted with the environment.

19. Annual events held at the site or elsewhere in the community: field trips, art shows, camps, classes and more (see website for details).

20. Research facilities or archives at the site: none of a historical nature.

21. Type of gift shop and what is for sale: there are many interesting nature-related books, films, and toys. There are a few books on the Ohlone Indians for sale.

1. **Santa Cruz Surfing Museum**

2. Location: In the Mark Abbott Memorial Lighthouse at Lighthouse Point on West Cliff Drive, Santa Cruz, CA. 95060.

3. Website: http://www.santacruzsurfingmuseum.org/

4. Phone number: (831) 420-6115.

5. E-mail: none.

6. Hours of operation: July 4-Sept.1: Wednesday-Monday, 10-5. The rest of the year: Thursday-Monday, 10-4.

7. Cost: free.

8. Permanent Exhibits: rare and historic surfboards. There are interesting photos and objects chronicling the history of surfing in Santa Cruz.

9. Special Exhibits: exhibit at the Museum of Art and History in Santa Cruz on the making of historic surfboards.

10. Historical era that is featured the best: 20th century-present.

11. Targeted age groups: all ages.

12. Special activities for children: none.

13. Guided tours: none.

14. Hands-on activities: none.

15. The best-kept secrets at the museum: it was the first surfing museum in the world.

16. Hidden treasures at the museum: historic surfboards and photos.

17. What is unique about the museum that can't be found anywhere else: you can watch the surfers in action just outside of the museum's doors!

18. The most important things about local, state, or American history that can be learned at the museum: surfing has had a tremendous impact on our popular culture. Many pioneers of the sport were active in Santa Cruz's waters. Santa Cruz has been commemorated in film and song. It is one of the most popular surfing sites in the world.

19. Annual events held at the site or elsewhere in the community: see website for details.

20. Research facilities or archives at the site: none.

21. Type of gift shop: none.

1. **Saratoga Historical Park & Museum**

2. Location: 20450 Saratoga-Los Gatos Road, Saratoga, CA. 95070-5935.

3. Website: http://www.saratogahistory.com

4. Phone number: (408) 867-4311.

5. E-mail: info@saratogahistory.com

6. Hours of operation: Friday, Saturday, and Sunday 1-4.

7. Cost: free.

8. Permanent Exhibits: Ohlone Indians, Spanish and Mexican settlement, Saratoga orchards and vineyards, schools and business, local notables, Saratoga Springs, Paul Masson, farm equipment and vehicles, etc.

9. Special Exhibits: McWilliams house, a fully furnished 1850s historic home and a one room schoolhouse, also furnished. Quarterly rotating special exhibits.

10. Historical era that is featured the best: 1800-1900s.

11. Targeted age groups: all ages.

12. Special activities for children: school tours, classroom trunks. Pioneer living classes for schools, scout groups, adults.

13. Guided tours: available upon request. Walking tours of the historic homes of the city, historic bicycle tour, and museum garden tour.

14. Hands-on activities: every special exhibit has interactive activities.

15. The best-kept secrets at the museum: local settlers had connections to John Brown, the Donner party, Theodore Wores, and other famous people.

16. Hidden treasures at the museum: the items from the Paul Masson Winery are some of the best preserved from this former local landmark.

17. What is unique about the museum that can't be found anywhere else: it has information about the once-famous Saratoga Pacific Congress Springs resort.

18. The most important things about local, state, or American history that can be learned at the museum: Saratoga has been an important crossroads between the valley orchard and mountain redwoods communities. It has a rich agricultural and cultural heritage.

19. Annual events held at the site or elsewhere in the community: Blossom Festival, guest speakers and other activities (see website for details).

20. Research facilities or archives at the site: a small research library is available upon request.

21. Type of gift shop and what is for sale: history books, postcards, and small gift items.

1. **San Francisco Maritime National Historical Park**

2. Location: The Visitor Center address is: 499 Jefferson Street, San Francisco, CA 94109. The Maritime Museum address is: 900 Beach Street, San Francisco, CA 94109. The park's historic ships are located at Hyde Street Pier at the foot of Hyde Street, across from the Visitor Center.

3. Website: http://www.nps.gov/safr/index.htm

4. Phone number: (415) 447-5000.

5. E-mail: use the online contact form.

6. Hours of operation: Visitor's Center and Hyde Street pier: 9:30 a.m.-5:00 p.m. (last entry onto the pier is 4:30 p.m.). Maritime Museum: 10:00 a.m. -4:00 p.m.

7. Cost: $5 (This may increase to $10 in the near future)

8. Permanent Exhibits: the award-winning Waterfront Exhibit in the Visitor Center and the award-winning Cargo is King exhibit on the historic sailing ship *Balclutha*.

9. Special Exhibits: the Maritime Museum hosts rotating exhibits.

10. Historical era that is featured the best: Gold Rush to 1930s.

11. Targeted age groups: all ages.

12. Special activities for children: all-ages, ranger-led sails on the historic scow schooner *Alma*; overnight stay on *Balclutha* for students as part of the San Francisco Maritime National Park Association's Age of Sail program.

13. Guided tours: ranger-led tours include the "Historic Waterfront Walking Tour," "Rangers in the Rig," "Adventures at Sea: Life Aboard a 19th Century Sailing Ship," and special programs that vary by month. An audio tour is also available.

14. Hands-on activities: rangers present and interpret a wide variety of maritime artifacts and skills, including rope making, fancywork, compass navigation, caulking, and capstan and pump demonstrations aboard *Balclutha*. A chantey sing-along takes place aboard the historic ferryboat *Eureka* monthly.

15. The best-kept secrets at the museum: a unique opportunity to sail on the National Historic Landmark ship *Alma* from the 1800s. Visitors can help raise the sails.

16. Hidden treasures at the museum: the Maritime Museum hosts changing exhibits that provide new learning opportunities. The museum's deck offers a beautiful view of the San Francisco Bay and the park's historic ships.

17. What is unique about the museum that can't be found anywhere else: visitors have a chance to board a variety of historic ships and sail on the 1891 scow schooner *Alma*.

18. The most important things about local, state, or American history that can be learned at the museum: how maritime culture shaped San Francisco and the Pacific Coast, as well as maritime connections visitors can make to their own lives.

19. Annual events held at the site or elsewhere in the community: Sea Music Festival, Sea Music Concert Series, lectures in the park's Maritime Research Center, and Fleet Week.

20. Research facilities or archives at the site: The Maritime Research Center (Building E, Third Floor, Lower Fort Mason) is open by appointment only. Please call (415) 561-7030 to schedule an appointment.

21. Type of gift shop and what is for sale: the nonprofit park partner, Western National Parks Association, has a store featuring maritime items and books on Hyde Street Pier. The Friends of the San Francisco Maritime Museum Library sells used and duplicate books on site (Building E, Third Floor, Lower Fort Mason) as well as online at www.maritimelibraryfriends.org. Please call (415) 561-7040 for hours of operation.

1. **San Francisco Fire Department Fire Museum**
2. Location: 655 Presidio Avenue, San Francisco, CA. 94115-2424.
3. Website: http://guardiansofthecity.org/sffd/

4. Phone number: (415) 563-4630.

5. E-mail: use the online contact form.

6. Hours of operation: Thursday through Sunday 1:00 p.m. to 4:00 p.m. as staffing permits.

7. Cost: free.

8. Permanent Exhibits: fire equipment and vehicles, historic photos, and records.

9. Special Exhibits: the 1906 Earthquake and Fire.

10. Historical era that is featured the best: 1800s-1900s.

11. Targeted age groups: all ages.

12. Special activities for children: some displays are child-friendly.

13. Guided tours: call for information.

14. Hands-on activities: none.

15. The best-kept secrets at the museum: there are many historic vehicles and objects crammed into this small building.

16. Hidden treasures at the museum: items from the 1906 earthquake.

17. What is unique about the museum that can't be found anywhere else: it is the only one of its kind in San Francisco County.

18. The most important things about local, state, or American history that can be learned at the museum: San Francisco has had a long history of volunteer and paid fire departments. The crucial role the department has served in the city is highlighted.

19. Annual events held at the site or elsewhere in the community: car shows, remembrances of the 1906 earthquake, and other events (see website for details).

20. Research facilities or archives at the site: submit a request using the online form.

21. Type of gift shop and what is for sale: the gift shop features various books and small souvenirs, including fire badge pins.

22. Additional information: the museum is sometimes not open during published hours. Make sure you call ahead before visiting.

1. **The San Francisco History Museum**

2. Location: 449 Powell Street, San Francisco, CA. 94108.

3. Website: none.

4. Phone number: (415) 981-1955.

5. E-mail: francisco@lorisdiner.com

6. Hours of operation: Mon–Sun: 9:00a.m–5:00 p.m.

7. Cost: $5.

8. Permanent Exhibits: California Indians, Spanish and Mexican periods, Gold Rush, Pan-American Exhibit, Sutro Baths, The Cliff House, The Golden Gate Bridge, Alcatraz, WWII, radios, local celebrities, Hippies and the 60's, and the Gay Rights Movement.

9. Special Exhibits: rotating exhibits.

10. Historical era that is featured the best: all eras.

11. Targeted age groups: all ages.

12. Special activities for children: none.

13. Guided tours: none.

14. Hands-on activities: none.

192

15. The best-kept secrets at the museum: it's location! It is upstairs on the fourth floor of a building on Powell Street, above Lori's Diner.

16. Hidden treasures at the museum: model of the Cliff House, several famous celebrity items of clothing, tools used to build the Golden Gate Bridge, and many other interesting items.

17. What is unique about the museum that can't be found anywhere else: it is the only comprehensive museum of San Francisco's history that is currently open.

18. The most important things about local, state, or American history that can be learned at the museum: San Francisco's emerging status as a world-class city. How it has grown and developed over time.

19. Annual events held at the site or elsewhere in the community: none.

20. Research facilities or archives at the site: none.

21. Type of gift shop and what is for sale: a small gift shop near the entrance has San Francisco souvenirs.

1. **Shadelands Ranch Historical Museum-Walnut Creek**

2. Location: 2660 Ygnacio Valley Road, Walnut Creek, CA. 94598-3445

3. Website: http://walnutcreekhistory.info/visit.php

4. Phone number: (925) 935-7871.

5. E-mail: wcshadelands@sbcglobal.net

6. Hours of operation: Wednesday and Sunday between 1 p.m. and 4 p.m.

7. Cost: $3.

8. Permanent Exhibits: built by Walnut Creek pioneer Hiram Penniman (1824-1907), the main house on the Shadelands Ranch grounds is a 1903 redwood-framed Colonial Revival structure that now showcases numerous historical artifacts, many of which belonged to the Pennimans. It also houses a rich archive of Contra Costa and Walnut Creek history in its collections of old newspapers, photographs, and government records.

9. Special Exhibits: none.

10. Historical era that is featured the best: early 1900s.

11. Targeted age groups: all ages.

12. Special activities for children: local history programs for area third-graders.

13. Guided tours: available during visiting hours.

14. Hands-on activities: none.

15. The best-kept secrets at the museum: pictures of the Pennimans at their second home at Scotty's Castle in Death Valley.

16. Hidden treasures at the museum: local history photographs, maps, and turn-of-the-century furniture and clothing.

17. What is unique about the museum that can't be found anywhere else: the architecture of the house is exceptional. The rooms are replete with period furnishings.

18. The most important things about local, state, or American history that can be learned at the museum: the role the Pennimans played as pioneers in the area.

19. Annual events held at the site or elsewhere in the community: a rotating exhibit at the downtown Walnut Creek Library.

20. Research facilities or archives at the site: the Sherwood Burgess Room is open Wednesdays from 1 p.m. to 4 p.m. for individuals who wish to do research on local history.

21. Type of gift shop and what is for sale: postcards of the house.

1. **The Sharpsteen Museum of Calistoga History**

2. Location: 1311 Washington St., Calistoga, CA. 94515.

3. Website: http://www.sharpsteenmuseum.org/

4. Phone number: (707) 942-5911.

5. E-mail: sharpsteenmuseum@att.net

6. Hours of operation: daily from 11 a.m. to 4 p.m., closed for Thanksgiving & Christmas.

7. Cost: free, suggested donation of $3.

8. Permanent Exhibits: Ben Sharpsteen's art and career, a geothermal exhibit, collection of cultural artifacts from the Wappo, the area's original inhabitants. Large and impressive dioramas depict Sam Brannon's resort and the town in its heyday. There are also exhibits on stagecoaches, resorts, farms, and blacksmith shops, Robert Louis Stevenson, Sam Brannan's cottage, and other items of local interest.

9. Special Exhibits: rotating exhibits twice a year.

10. Historical era that is featured the best: 1800s to the present.

11. Targeted age groups: all ages

12. Special activities for children: summer programs for children.

13. Guided tours: special tours for groups, schools, and associations can be arranged in advance by calling (707) 942-5911.

14. Hands-on activities: the train exhibit has a model train that rolls through an elaborate course, if quarters are fed into the machine.

15. The best-kept secrets at the museum: part of the museum is made up of one of the original cabins from the Hot Springs Resort.

16. Hidden treasures at the museum: original Disney drawings that Ben Sharpsteen drew and one of his Oscar trophies. A kettle that traveled with the Graves family, members of the Donner-Reed Party.

17. What is unique about the museum that can't be found anywhere else: it is the largest and most elaborate historical museum in Napa Valley. The large dioramas are very intricate and detailed.

18. The most important things about local, state, or American history that can be learned at the museum: the complete history of the region from prehistoric times to the present is covered in detail. It has a large collection of artifacts that are well displayed.

19. Annual events held at the site or elsewhere in the community: Through Doors and Gates tour of historical homes and the annual Instant Wine Cellar in August.

20. Research facilities or archives at the site: many photos and books are available to researchers. An appointment must be made in advance by calling the museum.

21. Type of gift shop and what is for sale: local history books are published by the museum and only available there. Other books are specific to the history of Calistoga, the Napa Valley, Sam Brannan, the Gold Rush, California history, the Wappo and other Native American tribes from this area, and the history of our

country beginning with the great migration of 1846. There is also a wide variety of gift items.

22. Additional information: after Ben Sharpsteen completed the building of the museum, opened in Sept. of 1978, he gifted it to the city of Calistoga.

1. **Shinn Historic Park and Arboretum-Fremont**

2. Location: 1251 Peralta Blvd. Fremont, CA. 94539.
3. Website: https://www.fremont.gov/index.aspx?nid=325
4. Phone number: (510) 795-0891.
5. E-mail: none.
6. Hours of operation: every day 8:00 a.m. - 30 minutes before dusk.
7. Cost: free.
8. Permanent Exhibits: the gardens and exterior of the house are available for viewing any day. The interior is only available on special events.
9. Special Exhibits: none.
10. Historical era that is featured the best: the late 1800s.
11. Targeted age groups: all ages.
12. Special activities for children: none.
13. Guided tours: some are available during events. See the website.
14. Hands-on activities: none.
15. The best-kept secrets at the museum: the historic gardens.
16. Hidden treasures at the museum: the antique furnishings of the house.
17. What is unique about the museum that can't be found anywhere else: it is an historic house in its original setting.
18. The most important things about local, state, or American history that can be learned at the museum: the Shinn family was important in the nursery business in the area.
19. Annual events held at the site or elsewhere in the community: Ice Cream Social
20. Research facilities or archives at the site: none.
21. Type of gift shop: none.

1. **S.S. Jeremiah O'Brien-San Francisco**

2. Location: Pier 45, Fisherman's Wharf, San Francisco, CA. 94133.
3. Website: http://www.ssjeremiahobrien.org/
4. Phone number: (415) 544-0100.
5. E-mail: liberty@ssjeremiahobrien.org
6. Hours of operation: daily 9 a.m. to 4 p.m. Closed Christmas and New Year's Day
7. Cost: Adults: $12, Seniors 62+: $8, Children 6-12: $6, Children under 5: free with adult supervision, Family (2 adults, 2 children): $25, US Student (with ID): $8, and US Active Military (with ID): Free.
8. Permanent Exhibits: most of the ship is open to visitors.
9. Special Exhibits: there is an onboard museum that tells the history of the ship.
10. Historical era that is featured the best: WWII.
11. Targeted age groups: all ages.

12. Special activities for children: overnight programs are available for youth groups. Young people learn how the ship was involved in WWII and stay on board overnight.

13. Guided tours: guided tours are available for groups of 10 or more with advance notice. Call (415) 544-0100 for reservations. Self-guided tours are available daily for less than ten people.

14. Hands-on activities: none.

15. The best-kept secrets at the museum: the vessel is constantly maintained by hundreds of volunteers.

16. Hidden treasures at the museum: most of the furnishings and equipment are original to WWII ships.

17. What is unique about the museum that can't be found anywhere else: this is one of the few WWII ships that still sails; it is the only ship from the D-Day Invasion that still sails.

18. The most important things about local, state, or American history that can be learned at the museum: this ship participated in the Normandy invasions. It is one of two functional Liberty ships remaining from the 2,710 that were built for the war effort. She is named after the first maritime Revolutionary War hero.

19. Annual events held at the site or elsewhere in the community: several San Francisco Bay cruises are scheduled each year (see website for details).

20. Research facilities or archives at the site: none.

21. Type of gift shop and what is for sale: clothing, books, videos, and souvenirs related to the ship and WWII.

1. **Sonoma State Historic Park**

197

2. Location: six midtown locations near Sonoma's Plaza.

3. Website: http://www.parks.ca.gov/?page_id=479

4. Phone number: (707) 938-9560.

5. E-mail: info@parks.ca.gov

6. Hours of operation: Open 7 days a week, 10 a.m. – 5 p.m.

7. Cost: a single fee of $3 gets you into all of the historic buildings.

8. Permanent Exhibits: Mission San Francisco Solano, the Blue Wing Inn, Sonoma Barracks, the Toscano Hotel, the Servants Quarters (the remains of La Casa Grande), and Vallejo's Home.

9. Special Exhibits: periodic displays at the mission are available.

10. Historical era that is featured the best: the 1800s.

11. Targeted age groups: all ages

12. Special activities for children: school group tours. Note: book far in advance.

13. Guided tours: Mission Tours: Friday, Saturday, and Sunday: 11 a.m., 12 p.m., 1p.m., and 2 p.m. Vallejo Home Tours: Saturday and Sunday: 1 p.m., 2 p.m., and 3 p.m. Toscano Hotel and Kitchen Tours: Saturday, Sunday, and Monday: 1 p.m. to 4p.m.

14. Hands-on activities: none.

15. The best-kept secrets at the museum: great Mission Era relics.

16. Hidden treasures at the museum: many interesting items from early Sonoma.

256

17. What is unique about the museum that can't be found anywhere else: It is one of the best-preserved historical plazas in California. It has many interesting sites and most are within walking distance of each other.
18. The most important things about local, state, or American history that can be learned at the museum: many key events in California history took place here, such as the northernmost mission and the Bear Flag Revolt.
19. Annual events held at the site or elsewhere in the community: see website for details.
20. Research facilities or archives at the site: none.
21. Type of gift shop and what is for sale: there are some gift and state park items for sale at the mission.

1. **Porter Library/Soquel Pioneer and Historical Association Museum**
2. Location: 3050 Porter St., Soquel, CA. 95073.
3. Website: http://www.soquelpioneers.com/
4. Phone number: Judy Parsons, President, (831) 476-1871 or Lynda Lewit, Secretary, (831) 818-1809.
5. E-mail: juudy@aol.com
6. Hours of operation: Library hours are 12-4 p.m. Monday through Friday and 10:00 a.m. to 2:00 p.m. Saturday.
7. Cost: free.
8. Permanent Exhibits: the building was built in 1913. It contains artifacts, books, and pictures related to the history of Soquel.
9. Special Exhibits: none.
10. Historical era that is featured the best: 1700s-present.
11. Targeted age groups: all ages.
12. Special activities for children: none.
13. Guided tours: none.
14. Hands-on activities: none.
15. The best-kept secrets at the museum: historical photos and maps of the area.
16. Hidden treasures at the museum: Ohlone Indian artifacts, farming and logging tools.
17. What is unique about the museum that can't be found anywhere else: it is a library and a museum.
18. The most important things about local, state, or American history that can be learned at the museum: the area has gone through many transitions, from Spanish land grants to timber camp, to beach resort and redwood parks.
19. Annual events held at the site or elsewhere in the community: Annual Pioneer Picnic at Pringle Grove and history talks at the library.
20. Research facilities or archives at the site: none.
21. Type of gift shop and what is for sale: the Arcadia book, *Soquel*, is sold at the museum and through the Arcadia Publishing website.

1. **The South Bay Historical Railroad Society-Santa Clara**
2. Location: 1005 Railroad Avenue, Santa Clara, CA. 95050.
3. Website: http://www.sbhrs.org/

4. Phone number: (408) 243-3969.

5. E-mail: use the contact form on the website.

6. Hours of operation: Tuesday evenings from 6:00 p.m. to 9:00 p.m. and on Saturdays from 10:00 a.m. to 3:00 p.m.

7. Cost: free.

8. Permanent Exhibits: the museum is set in the historic Santa Clara Depot; its various structural parts were built between 1863 and 1877. The museum also includes the former Southern Pacific Santa Clara Tower (built in 1926), along with the Maintenance-of-Way Speeder Shed (built in 1926), and Section Tool House (built in 1894). The museum houses a collection of railroad artifacts, some of which date back to the 1870s and earlier. The museum concentrates on Western railroads, but does have a reasonable collection of Midwest and Eastern railroad hand lanterns and switch lamps. Outside, there is a historic rail car from the Oregon & Washington Navigation RR.

9. Special Exhibits: a large room full of model train displays. Numerous trains run through varied and detailed terrain, including bridges, tunnels, towns, mountains, logging camps, etc. Friendly club members will tell you how the train layout is built and operated.

10. Historical era that is featured the best: 1863-present.

11. Targeted age groups: all ages

12. Special activities for children: birthday parties and school age tours.

13. Guided tours: available during hours that the museum is not open to the public. Call for reservations.

14. Hands-on activities: none.

15. The best-kept secrets at the museum: the collection of historic rail maps, schedules, photos, and other documents from the area.

16. Hidden treasures at the museum: electro-mechanical signaling devices, lanterns, and other historic rail equipment.

17. What is unique about the museum that can't be found anywhere else: there are many rail museums, but this is the only one that focuses on Santa Clara Valley and its railways exclusively.

18. The most important things about local, state, or American history that can be learned at the museum: the importance of railways to the development of the area. The location of historic railways in the area is explained and how they shaped the subsequent landscape, road layout, etc. The passenger rail depot is the oldest west of the Mississippi River.

19. Annual events held at the site or elsewhere in the community: train shows in April and November.

20. Research facilities or archives at the site: there is a rail library for members. The SBHRS has a fairly extensive library of railroad related materials. The collection currently holds over 3500 books and over 500 videos. Although many of the books concentrate on the Northern California area, the library covers non-California railroads also. There are books and videos covering the many how-to facets of model railroading. The collection of videos spans most of the Great Model Railroad series and most of the western first class roads. Library materials are indexed in a database to make research easy. Membership in the SBHRS allows you to check out

most of the books and videotapes. Non-members may view the materials with reservations, but may not check out items.

21. Type of gift shop: none.

22. Additional information: the museum is located right across the tracks from the modern Caltrain line, so it makes a fun trip to ride the train to the museum.

1. **South San Francisco Historical Museum**

2. Location: 80 Chestnut Avenue, South San Francisco, CA. 94080.

3. Website: http://www.ssf.net/index.aspx?NID=1295

4. Phone number: (650) 829-3825.

5. E-mail: ssfpladm@plsinfo.org

6. Hours of operation: Tuesdays and Thursdays, 2 p.m. - 4 p.m. Every second & fourth Saturday, 1 p.m. - 3 p.m.

7. Cost: free.

8. Permanent Exhibits: vintage wedding gowns and other clothing that belonged to early families in the community. A beautiful teacup collection donated by local residents. Photos and artifacts dating from the 1850's to the present, tracing the history of the "Industrial City", an historic kitchen, local industries and businesses.

9. Special Exhibits: rotating Special Exhibit Room with displays such as the history of women in the community and other themes.

10. Historical era that is featured the best: 1900s.

11. Targeted age groups: all ages.

12. Special activities for children: school age tours.

13. Guided tours: tours are available by appointment.

14. Hands-on activities: none.

15. The best-kept secrets at the museum: a fine collection of personal household objects from the early 1900s and historical photos of shipbuilding in WWII.

16. Hidden treasures at the museum: a large Victorian dollhouse that is very detailed. There is a large amount of information about founding families of the city.

17. What is unique about the museum that can't be found anywhere else: the museum provides a good contrast to development patterns of the more famous city to the north. It shows how much the area changed in the 20th century.

18. The most important things about local, state, or American history that can be learned at the museum: the city was formed after refugees fled the San Francisco Earthquake of 1906. It has been the home of many important industries.

19. Annual events held at the site or elsewhere in the community: see the city website for details.

20. Research facilities or archives at the site: oral history tapes, The Audio/Visual Room with historic school yearbooks, relevant newspaper articles, maps, Bay Area historical reference materials, and paintings from local artists. A public database is available for researching historical photographs.

21. Type of gift shop and what is for sale: the museum store includes the videos/DVDs "Sign of the Times" (1987), a documentary of the history of Sign Hill; "Baden to Biotech" (2008), a documentary of the history of South San Francisco; and "The 2008 Centennial Celebration" (2009), a short video highlighting the festivities that occurred during the centennial year. Numerous books on the history of South

San Francisco are available, including souvenir pins, coffee mugs, t-shirts, postcards, and the 2008 Centennial postage stamp.

22. Additional Information: The Historical Society also operates the The Plymire-Schwarz Center, a 1905 colonial revival style house. It is located at 519 Grand Avenue, Ph: (650) 879-6988. Admission is free. Open Wednesdays 2 - 4 p.m. (or by appointment).

1. **Spanishtown Jail-Half Moon Bay**
2. Location: 505 Johnston St., Half Moon Bay, CA. 94019.
3. Website: http://www.visithalfmoonbay.org/half-moon-bay-california-history-culture
4. Phone number: (650) 726-7084.
5. E-mail: use the online contact form.
6. Hours of operation: open for special events such as the Art & Pumpkin Festival.
7. Cost: free.
8. Permanent Exhibits: two jail cells from 1911. There are also posters about the history of the area, historic clothing, and farm implements.
9. Special Exhibits: none.
10. Historical era that is featured the best: 1911.
11. Targeted age groups: all ages.
12. Special activities for children: none.
13. Guided tours: none.
14. Hands-on activities: none.
15. The best-kept secrets at the museum: it is the home of the Spanishtown Historical Society.
16. Hidden treasures at the museum: there are two dummies dressed up as prisoners in the cells.
17. What is unique about the museum that can't be found anywhere else: it was the first jail in the area. It was only used for a few years.
18. The most important things about local, state, or American history that can be learned at the museum: it is one of the oldest surviving buildings in the area. The development of the town and its surroundings is described.
19. Annual events held at the site or elsewhere in the community: The Half Moon Bay Art & Pumpkin Festival.
20. Research facilities or archives at the site: none.
21. Type of gift shop: none.

1. **Sunnyvale Heritage Park Museum**
2. Location: 570 East Remington Drive, Sunnyvale, CA. 94087.
3. Website: http://heritageparkmuseum.org/
4. Phone number: (408) 749-0220.
5. E-mail: info@heritageparkmuseum.org
6. Hours of operation: 12-4 p.m., Tuesday/Thursday/Sunday.
7. Cost: free.

8. Permanent Exhibits: the reconstructed Martin Murphy home has many different displays ranging from the Ohlone Indians to the postwar era, with extensive displays of Sunnyvale's orchard heritage.

9. Special Exhibits: regularly rotating exhibits on local history, such as churches, local businesses, the Great Depression, Low Tech to High Tech, Holiday Memorabilia, historic wedding dresses, and much more (see website for details).

10. Historical era that is featured the best: 1800s-1900s.

11. Targeted age groups: all ages.

12. Special activities for children: there is a special school program for third graders. There are also school outreach programs and kid-friendly special events.

13. Guided tours: Available daily.

14. Hands-on activities: some of the displays are interactive.

15. The best-kept secrets at the museum: there is a huge, colorful display upstairs on the history of Silicon Valley innovations. There are also some interesting Ohlone items, including some fascinating death masks. There is a panoramic floor-to-ceiling mural room depicting Santa Clara Valley history.

16. Hidden treasures at the museum: the Martin Murphy party crossed the plains in 1844 to California. They were the first party to cross the Sierras in a covered wagon, the first to bring oxen across the plains, and the first to use the route now used by Union and Pacific Railroads. The Donner party used the route two years later and Martin Murphy, Jr. was a member of the party who rescued them. Many items related to Murphy and other Sunnyvale pioneers.

17. What is unique about the museum that can't be found anywhere else: it is surrounded by a heritage apricot orchard and community center. If you visit in the summer months, you can even purchase farm-fresh produce!

18. The most important things about local, state, or American history that can be learned at the museum: Sunnyvale's important role in first the orchard and farming industries, followed by science and computer technology is very well documented. The museum highlights the crucial role played by the Murphy family in opening the West and their early educational, business, and political contributions to both state and local history. There is also a fine display on Lockheed and Moffett Field.

19. Annual events held at the site or elsewhere in the community: guest speakers, author's day, display receptions, Antique Appraisal Faire, and other special events of community interest (see website for details).

20. Research facilities or archives at the site: contact the museum staff for access to their archives.

21. Type of gift shop and what is for sale: books, crafts, history books, vintage linens, antiques, a spectacular assortment of both vintage and new jewelry, unique gift ideas, films, and many beautiful gift items are for sale.

1. **The Santa Cruz Museum of Art & History at the McPherson Center**
2. Location: 705 Front Street, Santa Cruz, CA. 95060.
3. Website: http://www.santacruzmah.org/
4. Phone number: (831) 429-1964.
5. E-mail: info@santacruzmah.org
6. Hours of operation: Tuesday – Sunday: 11a.m. – 5p.m. Open late until 9p.m. every

Friday.

7. Cost: $5 adults, $3 students and seniors. Free on the first Friday of the month.

8. Permanent Exhibits: Where the Redwoods Meet the Sea: A History of Santa Cruz County and its People. The museum's installation is devoted to a thematic and topical interpretation of county history, from its earliest days to its more recent past. Dedicated to the uniqueness and diversity of Santa Cruz County and its residents, the exhibit describes native peoples, the Mission period, early immigrants, early industries, and more.

9. Special Exhibits: there are many interesting special exhibits throughout the year (see website for details).

10. Historical era that is featured the best: 1700s-present.

11. Targeted age groups: all ages.

12. Special activities for children: many displays are kid-friendly. School tours and educator materials are also available.

13. Guided tours: self-guided tour of the Evergreen Historical Cemetery. Tours of the museum are available with reservations.

14. Hands-on activities: the museum has several modern, interactive exhibits.

15. The best-kept secrets at the museum: the Ohlone display is one of the best around.

16. Hidden treasures at the museum: there are many interesting artifacts related to logging, WWII, beach and pop culture.

17. What is unique about the museum that can't be found anywhere else: it is an art museum and a history museum. This means that many of the displays also have a pleasant artistic flair to them.

18. The most important things about local, state, or American history that can be learned at the museum: the museum emphasizes the many cultures that call Santa Cruz their home.

19. Annual events held at the site or elsewhere in the community: Guest lectures, art shows, Teen Nite – I.D.E.A. Fest, Pop-Up Museum, cultural festivals, etc. (see website for details).

20. Research facilities or archives at the site: the archive is open by appointment and offers research material pertaining to all aspects of Santa Cruz County history.

21. Type of gift shop and what is for sale: there are many interesting and creative art items as well as some historical books and photos available for sale.

1. **The Museum of San Carlos History**

2. Location: 533 Laurel Street, San Carlos, CA (between San Carlos Ave and Holly).

3. Website: www.sancarloshistorymuseum.org

4. Phone number:(650) 802-4354.

5. E-mail: sancarloshistorymuseum.org

6. Hours of operation: Open every Sat. (except Dec) 1-4 p.m.

7. Cost: free.

8. Permanent Exhibits: Native Americans, Spanish land grant era, the expansion of the railroads, the building boom following WWII, fire and police departments, San Carlos schools, and the Chickens' Ball event.

9. Special Exhibits: a 1927 restored Seagrave fire truck, Sorcha Boru ceramics, Circle Star Theatre, and the early electronic companies.

10. Historical era that is featured the best: 1800s-1900s.

11. Targeted age groups: all ages.

12. Special activities for children: the September Ice Cream Social and photo contest for students.

13. Guided tours: public tours by appointment.

14. Hands-on activities: none.

15. The best-kept secrets at the museum: a native American grinding bowl and the city flag taken aboard the Atlantis II flight by SC High School graduate Rex Walheim.

16. Hidden treasures at the museum: The San Carlos Depot, the WWII dog training site in SC, the electronic companies begun in San Carlos.

17. What is unique about the museum that can't be found anywhere else: a restored 1927 Seagrave fire engine.

18. The most important things about local, state, or American history that can be learned at the museum: the growth of San Carlos through its school building, town clubs, home building, and downtown expansion.

19. Annual events held at the site or elsewhere in the community: the Villager's September Ice Cream Social and other events noted on the web site. Also open during town events, such as May Hometown Days and October Art& Wine Faire.

20. Research facilities or archives at the site: The museum and its archives have been entered into the computer for easy access. The museum has many photographs and artifacts on display to tell the San Carlos Story

21. Type of gift shop and what is for sale: the DVD "The Town of Good Living", the books: *San Carlos Stories* and *Through the Years in San Carlos*, *A Walking Tour of San Carlos*, postcards and posters of the SC Depot, and the game SANCARLOSOPOLY.

1. The Tech Museum of Innovation-San Jose

2. Location: 201 South Market Street, San Jose, CA. 95113.

3. Website: http://www.thetech.org/

4. Phone number: (408) 294-8324.

205

5. E-mail: info@thetech.org

6. Hours of operation: Open Daily: 10:00 a.m. - 5:00 p.m. Closed Thanksgiving, Christmas, and the Tuesday through Friday after Labor Day.

7. Cost: $20 for adults, $15 for students/seniors, kids. Additional costs for Imax Theater or special exhibits.

8. Permanent Exhibits: there are many different galleries covering many different areas of science. While this is primarily a science museum, there are often displays on the history of the technology.

9. Special Exhibits: some of the best visiting expositions in the Bay Area are held in the large special exhibits area of the Tech Museum. These often feature historical themes. Some of the past exhibits have included Leonardo da Vinci, The Mongols, Star Trek and Star Wars. See the website for current exhibits.

10. Historical era that is featured the best: the post-war technology boom.

11. Targeted age groups: all ages.

12. Special activities for children: the museum is very kid-friendly. It is a frequent destination for school field trips. There are many school outreach and educator program (see website for details).

13. Guided tours: available upon request.

14. Hands-on activities: the entire museum is designed to be highly interactive.

15. The best-kept secrets at the museum: some of the workshops given by the museum are taught by Silicon Valley innovators. They may not be famous, but they have nonetheless invented some pretty important things. They can share some interesting insights into the history of technology in the area.

16. Hidden treasures at the museum: there are some nice examples of early Silicon Valley technology on display, but displays change frequently and you may have to hunt for them.

17. What is unique about the museum that can't be found anywhere else: this is the best showcase in the Bay Area for the many kinds of technology that originated in the Silicon Valley.

18. The most important things about local, state, or American history that can be learned at the museum: the museum demonstrates how this technology has changed, and continues to change the world.

19. Annual events held at the site or elsewhere in the community: after-school labs, The Tech Awards, The Tech Challenge, summer camps, weekend Maker-style workshops and many other activities (see website for details).

20. Research facilities or archives at the site: science lab and classrooms. There is no historical archive on site.

21. Type of gift shop and what is for sale: there is a large gift shop with all kinds of scientific gadgets, toys, books, films, etc. If there is a visiting exhibition, there are usually items for sale in the special exhibit hall.

22. Additional information: the Imax theater occasionally offers films with historical content as well. In the past it has shown films about the exploration of the Grand Canyon and the space program, for example.

1. **Tomales Regional History Center**

2. Location: 26701 Highway One, Tomales, CA. 94971.

3. Website: http://www.tomaleshistory.com/

4. Phone number: (707) 878.9443.

5. E-mail: info@tomaleshistory.com

6. Hours of operation: Saturday and Sunday 1-4.

7. Cost: free.

8. Permanent Exhibits: Before the Pioneers: the Coast Miwoks, The Pioneers, The Story of Tomales, Agriculture, the Narrow Gauge Railroad, and Tomales High School History.

9. Special Exhibits: Tomales Neighbors and other rotating exhibits.

10. Historical era that is featured the best: 1800-1900s.

11. Targeted age groups: all ages.

12. Special activities for children: school tours. A special display on the schools of the area.

13. Guided tours: available upon request.

206

14. Hands-on activities: none.

15. The best-kept secrets at the museum: Miwok Indian artifacts, narrow gauge railroad items, and extensive school records.

16. Hidden treasures at the museum: rare trade beads thought to have been given to the Miwok Indians by Russian traders.

17. What is unique about the museum that can't be found anywhere else: it is located in the former Tomales High School Auditorium. This is the only building remaining from the high school.

18. The most important things about local, state, or American history that can be learned at the museum: the museum is the largest and most comprehensive in the region. It provides a good overview of the history of the region, local landmarks and industries.

19. Annual events held at the site or elsewhere in the community: TRHC's annual Tea and Fashion Show and other events. Contact the museum for details.

20. Research facilities or archives at the site: there is a small archive and a research library available upon request.

21. Type of gift shop and what is for sale: regional history books.

1. **Tor House-Carmel**

2. Location: 26304 Ocean View Ave., Carmel, CA. 93923.

3. Website: http://www.torhouse.org/index.htm

4. Phone number: (831) 624-1813.

5. E-mail: thf@torhouse.org

207

6. Hours of operation: Friday and Saturday. The first tour begins at 10 a.m. and the final tour at 3 p.m.

7. Cost: $10 adults, $5 full-time students 12 and older.

8. Permanent Exhibits: the Tor House, gardens, and Hawk Tower.

9. Special Exhibits: none.

10. Historical era that is featured the best: early 20th Century.

11. Targeted age groups: ages 12 and up.

12. Special activities for children: none.

13. Guided tours: docent-led tours of Tor House, Hawk Tower, and the old-world gardens are conducted hourly every Friday and Saturday. Tour reservations should be made in advance via email at thf@torhouse.org.

14. Hands-on activities: none.

15. The best-kept secrets at the museum: many influential literary and cultural celebrities were guests of the Jeffers family. Among them were Sinclair Lewis, Edna St. Vincent Millay, Langston Hughes, Charles Lindbergh, George Gershwin, and Charlie Chaplin. Later visitors have included William Everson, Robert Bly, Czeslow Milosz, and Edward Abbey.

16. Hidden treasures at the museum: original family furnishings and possessions.

17. What is unique about the museum that can't be found anywhere else: In 1914, when they first saw the unspoiled beauty of the Carmel-Big Sur coast south of California's Monterey Peninsula, Robinson Jeffers (1887-1962) and his wife, Una (1884-1950), knew they had found their "inevitable place." Over the next decade, on a windswept, barren promontory, using granite boulders gathered from the

rocky shore of Carmel Bay, Jeffers built Tor House and Hawk Tower as a home and refuge for himself and his family.

18. The most important things about local, state, or American history that can be learned at the museum: it was in Tor House that Jeffers wrote all of his major poetical works: the long narratives of "this coast crying out for tragedy", as well as the shorter meditative lyrics and dramas on classical themes, culminating in 1947 with the critically acclaimed adaptation of "Medea" for the Broadway stage, with Dame Judith Anderson in the title role.

19. Annual events held at the site or elsewhere in the community: poetry readings and other events (see website for details).

20. Research facilities or archives at the site: none.

21. Type of gift shop and what is for sale: the works of Jeffers are for sale.

1. **Travis Air Force Base Heritage Center**

2. Location: Building 80, 461 Burgan Blvd., Travis AFB, CA. 94535.

3. Website: travisheritagecenter.org

4. Phone number: (707) 424-5883.

5. E-mail: heritagecenter1214@live.com

6. Hours of operation: Tuesday-Saturday 10 a.m. to 5 p.m., Sundays 12 p.m. to 5 p.m. For non-Department of Defense cardholders, an escort is required. Please stop at the visitor's center and let them know that you would like to visit the Heritage Center. A shuttle van will transport you from the Visitor Center to the Heritage Center and return you to the Visitor Center. The last pick-up at the Visitor Center is 4 p.m. The Static Displays outside are open to those with base access during all daylight hours.

7. Cost: free (The Heritage Center is an all-volunteer staff, with support from the Active Duty staff. The Heritage Center runs on donations to the Jimmy Doolittle Air and Space Museum Foundation).

8. Permanent Exhibits: the history of flight from WWI to the present, with a special emphasis on missions flown by planes from the base. Dozens of aircraft both large and small are featured from WWII to the present.

9. Special Exhibits: anniversaries of the Berlin Airlift and the Korean War, General Doolittle, and The Tuskegee Airmen exhibits.

10. Historical era that is featured the best: 20th century.

11. Targeted age groups: all ages.

12. Special activities for children: trainer planes and space capsule that you can climb into, both for children and adults who are kids at heart. Scavenger Hunts for all ages, including picture hunts and history hunts. Static Displays outside are accessible to be touched and crawled under.

13. Guided tours: special arrangements must be made in advance for groups of 10+ (see website for details).

14. Hands-on activities: some of the displays have QR codes for additional information on smart devices. Trainer plane and a space capsule that you can climb into.

15. The best-kept secrets at the museum: rare WWII currency, WWI aircraft machine guns, items from the Berlin airlift, and much, much more.

16. Hidden treasures at the museum: a replica of an atom bomb, space capsules, aircraft engines, one of the largest displays of restored aircraft in Northern California, etc.

17. What is unique about the museum that can't be found anywhere else: flights from this air base have flown all over the world. Some of the famous missions include WWII and Korean War bombing and transport runs, Vietnam POW and refugee evacuations, humanitarian missions, and the space program.

18. The most important things about local, state, or American history that can be learned at the museum: flights from the base were involved with every major conflict in the 20th century.

19. Annual events held at the site or elsewhere in the community: Mustangs and More is a big fundraiser at the Nut Tree airport (P-51 Mustang to the Ford Mustang, along with other WWII fighters). Air shows, special exhibits, auctions, shows, and many other events. There are also a few displays at the Nut Tree shopping mall (see website for details). Special events can also be held at the Heritage Center by contacting the office and making arrangements for guests and scheduling. Donations are highly encouraged for events.

20. Research facilities or archives at the site: there is a research library in the museum, open Tuesday and Thursday, but can be opened with prior arrangements on any day.

21. Type of gift shop and what is for sale: patches, model airplanes, clothing, coins, and aviation artwork. The gift shop features a model of a B-52 signed by Doolittle Raider, Lt. Col. Richard Cole. It is open from 10 a.m.-4 p.m. Tues-Friday, and some weekends.

22. Additional information: all non-Department of Defense ID card holders visiting the Heritage Center age 18 and over are required to present a photo ID and submit to a criminal background check at the Visitor Center. On occasion, this process can take up to 45 minutes. Once this process is completed, an escort will be requested from the Heritage Center to meet the visitors at the Visitor Center. Visitors will only be escorted directly to the Heritage Center and back to the Visitor Center. No deviations from this route are authorized. Please contact the Heritage Center for groups of 10 or more 2 weeks prior to your visit to set up a pre-screening and avoid the Visitor Center wait time. Groups of 9 or smaller must go to the visitor center and complete the process the day of your visit.

1. **Ulistac Natural Area-Santa Clara**
2. Location: 4901 Lick Mill Boulevard, Santa Clara, CA. 95050.
3. Website: http://santaclaraca.gov/index.aspx?page=1455#ulistac
4. Phone number: (408) 615-2260.
5. E-mail: ParksandRecreation@santaclara.gov
6. Hours of operation: every day from sunrise to one-half hour after sunset.
7. Cost: free.
8. Permanent Exhibits: Ulistac Natural Area, 40 acres of open space that showcases seven distinctive natural habitats, opened in Santa Clara in 2001 after months of

volunteer efforts to restore California native vegetation and preserve wildlife habitat. This land was originally used as a seasonal encampment for the Ohlone Indians (Ulistac was the name of an Ohlone chief). The trails have interpretive panels to provide additional information on the natural history of the area.

9. Special Exhibits: none.

10. Historical era that is featured the best: pre-history-1800s.

11. Targeted age groups: all ages.

12. Special activities for children: none.

13. Guided tours: none.

14. Hands-on activities: none.

15. The best-kept secrets at the museum: the signs in the park help identify the plants and how the Ohlone Indians and other settlers used them.

16. Hidden treasures at the museum: wildlife abounds in the park.

17. What is unique about the museum that can't be found anywhere else: an open space in an urban area that preserves historic native plants from the area.

18. The most important things about local, state, or American history that can be learned at the museum: the site was an Ohlone seasonal encampment, a Spanish Rancho, American farm, and then golf course before becoming a nature preserve.

19. Annual events held at the site or elsewhere in the community: volunteer opportunities for plant restoration and trail building. There are occasional civic events (see website for details).

20. Research facilities or archives at the site: none.

21. Type of gift shop: none.

1. **Union City Historical Museum**

2. Location: 3841 Smith St. Union City, CA. 94587.

3. Website: http://unioncityhistoricalmuseum.org/

4. Phone number: (510) 378-6376.

5. E-mail: none.

6. Hours of operation: Thursdays to Saturdays, 10 a.m. to 4 p.m.

7. Cost: free (donations accepted).

8. Permanent Exhibits: small displays on everything from local Native Americans to businesses, schools, industries, and former local buildings. There are tons of artifacts crammed in a small place.

9. Special Exhibits: none.

10. Historical era that is featured the best: 20th Century

11. Targeted age groups: all ages.

12. Special activities for children: none.

13. Guided tours: none.

14. Hands-on activities: none.

15. The best-kept secrets at the museum: drive-in movie relics and other unusual antiques that are not always seen in museums. It is easy to miss some things because there are so many of them.

16. Hidden treasures at the museum: a strange mixture of historic and ordinary objects.

17. What is unique about the museum that can't be found anywhere else: the odd mix of objects loosely mixed in a small area. The museum has some recent historical items that other museums often overlook.

18. The most important things about local, state, or American history that can be learned at the museum: the history of the city as a cultural crossroads.

19. Annual events held at the site or elsewhere in the community: none.

20. Research facilities or archives at the site: the general collection contains books, videos, and documents on the city's history.

21. Type of gift shop and what is for sale: there are some used books available for sale.

1. **U.S.S. Hornet-Alameda**

2. Location: 707 W Hornet Ave, Alameda, CA. 94501.

3. Website: http://www.uss-hornet.org/

4. Phone number: (510) 521-8448.

5. E-mail: Info@uss-hornet.org

6. Hours of operation: daily, 10:00a.m. – 5:00p.m.

7. Cost: Adults: $16.00; Seniors (65+) military w/ I.D., students w/ I.D $13:00; youth (5-17) $7.00; children (4 & under) free with paying adult.

8. Permanent Exhibits: the aircraft carrier, historic aircraft, and Apollo mission display.

9. Special Exhibits: Hornets Before Wings (Officers' Wardroom Lounge) traces the legacy of the ships named *Hornet* since the Revolutionary War.

Black Aces Ready Room (Ready Room 2) is a close approximation of the VFA-41 Ready Room in use onboard *USS Nimitz*; used only for Merit Badge Classes.

Hornet in the Pacific, WWII (Ready Room 3) Opening soon, this exhibit chronicles the *Hornet*'s role in the Pacific during WW II. By the end of the war, *Hornet* had destroyed 1,410 enemy aircraft and earned a Presidential Unit Citation, becoming one of the most decorated ships in naval history.

Fighter and Attack Aircraft (Ready Room 4) displays ready room photos from WWII to present.

Raymond J. Vyeda Memorial Room (Officer's Stateroom, Second Deck) has memorabilia of a CVA-12 crewmember and his shipmates.

Apollo Splashdown (Jet Engine Repair Shop, Hangar Deck) features memorabilia and photos from the *Apollo 11* and *Apollo 12* recoveries.

442 Regimental Combat Team (Gallery Deck, Hangar Bay 3) honors the contributions made by Nisei soldiers during WWII. The main focus is on the 20,000-plus American men of Japanese ancestry who served in the 442 Regimental Combat Team in Europe and the 6,000 men who served in the Military Intelligence Service in the Pacific.

WAVES & Women in the Sea Service (Second Deck, Portside).

10. Historical era that is featured the best: WWII-The Cold War.

11. Targeted age groups: all ages.

12. Special activities for children: guided tours and overnight camps.

13. Guided tours: available upon request.

14. Hands-on activities: some items on board can be manipulated.

15. The best-kept secrets at the museum: this is the site of the *Apollo 11* return to earth. The carrier also took part in many WWII campaigns in the Pacific.

16. Hidden treasures at the museum: many interesting aircraft, uniforms, weapons, etc. are on board.

17. What is unique about the museum that can't be found anywhere else: it is one of the few remaining WWII vessels still afloat.

18. The most important things about local, state, or American history that can be learned at the museum: it provides a unique perspective on WWII and the Cold War. It has been lovingly restored by veterans. Listening to their stories is worth the price of admission alone.

19. Annual events held at the site or elsewhere in the community: Flashlight Tours, Living Ship Days, Big Band dances, Monster Bash, and New Year's Eve parties (see website for details).

20. Research facilities or archives at the site: none.

21. Type of gift shop and what is for sale: books, films, and souvenirs related to the Navy, WWII, the space program, aircraft, etc.

1. **USS Pampanito - San Francisco Maritime National Park**

2. Location: Pier 45, Fisherman's Wharf, San Francisco, CA. 94133.

3. Website: http://www.maritime.org/pamphome.htm

4. Phone number: (415) 775-1943.

5. E-mail: use the online contact form.

6. Hours of operation: daily at 9:00 a.m. Closing times vary. Call ahead.

7. Cost: Adults $12.00; Children ages 6-12 $6.00; Children under 6 free with an adult, Students, $8.00, Senior Citizens (over 62) $8.00, Active Duty Military with current ID $6.00; HNSA and Ca.m.M members are free. A self-guided audio tour can be rented for an additional $3.00

8. Permanent Exhibits: *USS Pampanito* (SS-383) is a World War II Balao class Fleet submarine museum and memorial.

9. Special Exhibits: none.

10. Historical era that is featured the best: WWII.

11. Targeted age groups: all ages.

12. Special activities for children: the educational programs include daytime and environmental living programs at the Hyde Street Pier and daytime and overnight programs aboard *USS Pampanito*. An onboard Science Program for grades 6 - 8 that follows CA state curriculum allows kids to participate in hands-on activities dealing with buoyancy, navigation, SONAR, periscopes, and batteries.

13. Guided tours: self-guided. A virtual tour is also available online.

14. Hands-on activities: see the educational programs above.

15. The best-kept secrets at the museum: most of the furnishings and equipment on board are from the time period.

16. Hidden treasures at the museum: many interesting artifacts from WWII are on board.

17. What is unique about the museum that can't be found anywhere else: it is a floating museum that needs to go into dry dock for repairs periodically.

18. The most important things about local, state, or American history that can be learned at the museum: the *Pampanito* made six patrols in the Pacific during World War II during which she sank six Imperial Japanese ships and damaged four others.
19. Annual events held at the site or elsewhere in the community: Fleet Week and the annual Lost Boat and Memorial Day ceremony (see website for details).
20. Research facilities or archives at the site: research and archive facilities are available to be viewed by appointment only. Appointments can be made by calling (415) 775-1943.
21. Type of gift shop: none.
22. Additional information: a dockside museum is being planned for additional display space and educational purposes.

1. **U.S.S. Potomac-Oakland**

2. Location: 540 Water Street, Oakland, CA. 94607.
3. Website: http://www.usspotomac.org/
4. Phone number: (510) 627-1215.
5. E-mail: usspotomacnews@gmail.com
6. Hours of operation: dockside tours: Wednesday, Friday, and Sunday 11:00 a.m. to 3:00 p.m.
7. Cost: $10.
8. Permanent Exhibits: the "Floating White House" was originally commissioned the USCG Cutter *Electra* in 1934. In 1936, it was renamed the *USS Potomac* and served as Franklin Delano Roosevelt's Presidential Yacht until his death in 1945. The boat features several items from Roosevelt's life and career, as well as WWII era furnishings.
9. Special Exhibits: a special exhibit of an original battle plan off the deck of the D-Day command ship *USS Augusta*.
10. Historical era that is featured the best: 1930-1940s.
11. Targeted age groups: all ages.
12. Special activities for children: school tours and excursions. Teacher's guides are available.
13. Guided tours: docent-led tours on dockside days and on special cruises.
14. Hands-on activities: some of the ship's equipment may be handled by visitors.
15. The best-kept secrets at the museum: Roosevelt's dog is featured on the ship as well.
16. Hidden treasures at the museum: some of the original equipment that was aboard the *Potomac* when Roosevelt used the ship and a display of Roosevelt's personal fishing gear.
17. What is unique about the museum that can't be found anywhere else: this is one of the few surviving presidential yachts that is open to the public.
18. The most important things about local, state, or American history that can be learned at the museum: Roosevelt's life and career are well documented by the visitor's center and docents. Connections to local history are also made on the tours.
19. Annual events held at the site or elsewhere in the community: there are many special events and cruises available for additional fare (see website for details).

20. Research facilities or archives at the site: there are some documents available at the visitor's center.

21. Type of gift shop and what is for sale: souvenirs, gift items with the Potomac logo, and other items related to the ship are available.

1. **Vacaville Museum**

2. Location: 213 Buck Ave. Vacaville, CA. 95688.

3. Website: http://www.vacavillemuseum.org/current

4. Phone number: (707) 447-4513.

5. E-mail: vminfo@vacavilemuseum.org

6. Hours of operation: Wednesday - Sunday from 1:00 to 4:30.

7. Cost: Adults: $3.00, Students and Seniors: $2.00, School tours: $1 per student.

8. Permanent Exhibits: none.

9. Special Exhibits: the museum offers a series of rotating exhibits from its collections. A recent exhibit was "In Her Shoes, Women Who Walked West 1841-1865".

10. Historical era that is featured the best: 1800s-1900s.

11. Targeted age groups: all ages.

12. Special activities for children: school tours. Some interactive displays are suitable for children to use.

13. Guided tours: available with advance reservations. Historic home tours of Vacaville are also held occasionally. Contact the museum for details.

14. Hands-on activities: there are usually some interactive displays, depending upon the current exhibit.

15. The best-kept secrets at the museum: the dress of pioneer Sallie Fox, who brought the original walnut to Vacaville that became the famous "nut tree" for which the restaurant and shopping mall are named.

16. Hidden treasures at the museum: pioneer artifacts and clothing.

17. What is unique about the museum that can't be found anywhere else: the Vacaville Museum, a center for Solano County history, is the only institution whose mission includes cultural and historical preservation for all of Solano County. Through exhibits, publications, and educational programs, the museum continuously promotes the value of community heritage. Since 1984, Vacaville Museum has produced 40 exhibits, as well as numerous publications important to the history and sense of place of Solano County.

18. The most important things about local, state, or American history that can be learned at the museum: settlers from the Oregon and Santa Fe Trails came to the area. There was also an early Spanish home nearby called the Pena Adobe.

19. Annual events held at the site or elsewhere in the community: Sallie Fox Day, Dinner at the Dump Fundraiser, Celebrate Solano! art exhibit and fundraiser, and the Annual Children's Party.

20. Research facilities or archives at the site: there is a small research library upstairs. Contact research@vacavilemuseum.org for information.

21. Type of gift shop and what is for sale: a fine selection of gift items, including books, art, crafts, and many other beautiful items.

1. **The Vallejo Adobe-Fremont**
2. Location: 36500 Niles Blvd., Fremont, CA. 94536.
3. Website: https://www.fremont.gov/325/Historic-Parks-Facilities
4. Phone number: (510) 494-4300.
5. E-mail: RegeRec@fremont.gov
6. Hours of operation: every day from 7:00 a.m. - 30 minutes before dusk, but the adobe is not open to the public. It is surrounded by a chain-link fence.
7. Cost: free.
8. Permanent Exhibits: the Vallejo Adobe was built in 1842 and it is located in the heart of the California Nursery Historical Park in Niles.
9. Special Exhibits: none.
10. Historical era that is featured the best: 1840s.
11. Targeted age groups: all ages.
12. Special activities for children: none.
13. Guided tours: none.
14. Hands-on activities: none.
15. The best-kept secrets at the museum: none.
16. Hidden treasures at the museum: none.
17. What is unique about the museum that can't be found anywhere else: it is one of the few original structures left from the Mexican Era in the Bay Area.
18. The most important things about local, state, or American history that can be learned at the museum: the Rancho Era was an important step in the development of the area. A few large land grants were given to a select few. These later fell into dispute as American settlers challenged their claims.
19. Annual events held at the site or elsewhere in the community: the adobe is not available for rent until after a Park Master Plan is complete. The opening is tentatively projected for January 2016. This plan will include a much larger historical park incorporating the historic nursery.
20. Research facilities or archives at the site: none.
21. Type of gift shop: none.

1. **Vallejo Naval and Historical Museum**
2. Location: 734 Marin Street, Vallejo, CA. 94590.
3. Website: http://www.vallejomuseum.org/
4. Phone number: (707) 643-0077.
5. E-mail: valmuse@pacbell.net
6. Hours of operation: Tuesday-Saturday, 12- 4 p.m.
7. Cost: $5 adults; $3 seniors & students; children under 12 free.
8. Permanent Exhibits: the museum occupies over 25,000 square feet and has exhibits that are maintained in five galleries. Highlights include Native American artifacts, California artwork, folk art, textiles, household furnishings, and a huge collection of fascinating items related to naval history and sailors.
9. Special Exhibits: local private collections, traveling exhibitions, and borrowed artifacts from the extensive collection at Mare Island.
10. Historical era that is featured the best: 1800s-1900s.
11. Targeted age groups: all ages.

12. Special activities for children: field trips for school children.

13. Guided tours: available upon request.

14. Hands-on activities: some of the items, such as the periscope, may be manipulated.

15. The best-kept secrets at the museum: "miniaturized" Styrofoam cups crushed by tremendous ocean pressure during record-breaking deep submersible dives in the Pacific Ocean.

16. Hidden treasures at the museum: a Russian cannon brought to Mare Island from Sitka, Alaska.

17. What is unique about the museum that can't be found anywhere else: a working submarine periscope is installed in the building. It passes though the roof and gives an excellent view of the city and Mare Island.

18. The most important things about local, state, or American history that can be learned at the museum: the region's importance in naval history is very well documented. The importance of Mare Island in WWII in particular is highlighted.

19. Annual events held at the site or elsewhere in the community: the Antiques & Collectibles Evaluation Day, The annual Vallejo Garden Tour, concerts and recitals in the Heritage Chamber, lectures, audio-visual presentations, and other special events for the benefit of the community.

20. Research facilities or archives at the site: the Research Library is open every Tuesday from noon to 4:00 and other days by appointment.

21. Type of gift shop and what is for sale: books about Vallejo, naval history and other gift items.

1. **Montalvo Arts Center (formerly Villa Montalvo)-Saratoga**

2. Location: 15400 Montalvo Road, Saratoga, CA. 95070.

3. Website: http://montalvoarts.org/

4. Phone number: (408) 961-5800.

5. E-mail: use the online contact form.

6. Hours of operation: April 1 - September 30: Monday - Thursday 8 a.m. – 7 p.m., Friday - Sunday and holidays 9 a.m. – 5 p.m.; October 1 - March 31: Monday - Thursday 8 a.m. – 5 p.m., Friday - Sunday and holidays 9 a.m. – 5 p.m.

NOTE: The park may close on certain holidays and up to 2 hours early for concerts and evening events.

Gallery Hours: Thursday - Sunday, 11a.m.-3p.m.

7. Cost: the park is free. Parking is sometimes charged. Ticketed events are on sale at the box office.

8. Permanent Exhibits: the villa, the gardens, and various concert and stage venues.

9. Special Exhibits: there are many different shows featuring art, theater, poetry, music, etc., year round (see website for details).

10. Historical era that is featured the best: early 1900s.

11. Targeted age groups: all ages.

12. Special activities for children: field trips, classes, camps, etc.

13. Guided tours: walking tours are led by volunteer docents and occur most Sundays and Tuesdays at 10a.m. Cost $10. Self-guided tours are free.

14. Hands-on activities: varies by exhibit.

217

15. The best-kept secrets at the museum: the sculptures in the gardens are often neo-classical; others are created by contemporary artists.

16. Hidden treasures at the museum: Villa Montalvo was named for the popular 16th-century Spanish writer Garci Ordóñez de Montalvo, who coined the name "California". In one of his fables, he described an island rich with gold and jewels, peopled by Amazons whose queen was Califia. On this storybook island of California, Montalvo's Amazons rode griffins, the mythical winged guardians of precious treasure. Griffins can still be found throughout the Montalvo grounds, standing guard over one of California's true precious treasures.

17. What is unique about the museum that can't be found anywhere else: it is one of the few Italian style villas in the Bay Area. The facility has many different cultural uses. The interior of the villa is only open for special events.

18. The most important things about local, state, or American history that can be learned at the museum: Montalvo Arts Center was previously known as Villa Montalvo, a historic landmark built in 1912 by James Duval Phelan (1861-1930). Phelan, a passionate Californian who had been a three-term progressive mayor of San Francisco, went on to become California's first popularly-elected U.S. Senator. Villa Montalvo was Senator Phelan's favorite home and a center of artistic, political and social life in Northern California. Phelan invited leading writers and artists to Villa Montalvo to work on individual artistic projects in an environment rich in dialogue and fellowship. Jack London, Ethel Barrymore, Mary Pickford, Douglass Fairbanks, and Edwin Markham were among Phelan's many guests.

19. Annual events held at the site or elsewhere in the community: the Food & Wine Classic is every year in early June, and ArtSplash occurs annually in April (see website for details).

20. Research facilities or archives at the site: none.

21. Type of gift shop and what is for sale: there are art and gift items for sale at the villa.

1. **Watsonville Fire Department Chief Gene Friend Museum**
2. Location: 105 Second Street, Watsonville, CA. 95076.
3. Website: http://www.santacruzcountymuseums.org/History-Museums.htm
4. Phone number: (831) 768-3202.
5. E-mail: none.
6. Hours of operation: Thurs – Sat, 10:00 a.m. – 12:00 p.m. Visits are available by appointment.
7. Cost: free.
8. Permanent Exhibits: historic fire trucks and a wide variety of fire fighting equipment.
9. Special Exhibits: the original firemen's bunkhouse.
10. Historical era that is featured the best: 1800s-present.
11. Targeted age groups: all ages.
12. Special activities for children: school tours are popular.
13. Guided tours: a firefighter will give you a tour of the facility if time permits.
14. Hands-on activities: none.

218

15. The best-kept secrets at the museum: they still have the original fire pole used by the station, but alas, guests are not allowed to use it!

16. Hidden treasures at the museum: the historic control room, antique fireman hats, ladders, fire extinguishers, and uniforms. The1915 Seagrave Engine was the first mechanized firefighting equipment purchased by the City of Watsonville in 1914.

17. What is unique about the museum that can't be found anywhere else: the museum offers an up close and personal view of the apparatus and equipment used during the history of the Watsonville Fire Department. The building was in use by the fire department from 1924 until 1982, when the new building adjacent to the museum was opened.

18. The most important things about local, state, or American history that can be learned at the museum: the ever-changing technology that is used to fight fires is demonstrated.

19. Annual events held at the site or elsewhere in the community: the fire trucks are sometimes featured in local parades.

20. Research facilities or archives at the site: none, but there are some records of historic fires.

21. Type of gift shop: none.

1. **Wells Fargo History Museum- San Francisco**

2. Location: 420 Montgomery Street [A0101-106] San Francisco, CA 94163.

3. Website: http://www.wellsfargohistory.com/museums/san-francisco/

4. Phone number: (415) 396-2619.

5. E-mail: none.

6. Hours of operation: Monday – Friday, 9:00 a.m. – 5:00 p.m.

7. Cost: free.

8. Permanent Exhibits: a Wells Fargo stagecoach that carried passengers and gold across the western plains, an impressive display of gold dust and ore from California's Gold Country, and works of art by noted Western artists.

9. Special Exhibits: a special collection of Gold Rush letters carried by hundreds of express companies.

10. Historical era that is featured the best: 1800s.

11. Targeted age groups: all ages.

12. Special activities for children: a "please touch" box for children.

13. Guided tours: by appointment.

14. Hands-on activities: a working telegraph machine that allows you to send a message to another Wells Fargo museum.

15. The best kept secrets at the museum: it is located in Wells Fargo's world headquarters, in the heart of San Francisco's financial district.

16. Hidden treasures at the museum: real gold from California gold country regions.

17. What is unique about the museum that can't be found anywhere else: this is the site where Wells Fargo first opened for business in 1852.

18. The most important things about local, state, or American history that can be learned at the museum: Wells Fargo played a critical role in the Gold Rush and subsequent growth of the banking industry in California. It is still active today.

19. Annual events held at the site or elsewhere in the community: concerts and educational event (see the website for details).
20. Research facilities or archives at the site: The Wells Fargo Corporate Archives keeps artifacts and records that bring Wells Fargo history to life.
21. Type of gift shop: none.

1. **Western Railway Museum-Suisun City**

2. Location: Western Railway Museum, 5848 State Highway 12, Suisun, CA. 94585.
3. Website: http://www.wrm.org/
4. Phone number: (707) 374-2978.
5. E-mail: use the contact form on the website.
6. Hours of operation: Saturday and Sunday from 10:30 a.m. to 5 p.m. From Memorial Day through Labor Day, the museum expands its hours for the summer, and is open Wednesdays through Sundays from 10:30 a.m. to 5 p.m.
7. Cost: Adults: $10; seniors over 65: $9; children (2-14): $7.
8. Permanent Exhibits: the opportunity to ride historic streetcars and interurban electric trains from all over California and other western states. Streetcars loop the shaded picnic grounds. Interurban cars run over the restored main line of the old Sacramento Northern Railway. There are over 50 historic cars on display, railway exhibits, and picnic grounds.
9. Special Exhibits: there are rotating exhibits in the visitor's center, including how electric trains work, energy usage, and other exhibits.
10. Historical era that is featured the best: the late 1800s to early 1900s.
11. Targeted age groups: all ages.
12. Special activities for children: the train rides are a must for children. Friendly old conductors let you ring the trolley bell and climb aboard historic trains. This is a favorite destination for school tours, birthday parties, and family outings.
13. Guided tours: offered several times a day. Check the website for the exact times.
14. Hands-on activities: there are several interesting interactive displays in the visitor's center.
15. The best-kept secrets at the museum: you can ride the exhibits!
16. Hidden treasures at the museum: there are many familiar trains from around the Bay Area and Sacramento Area. Older folks will remember when some of these were still in operation and younger visitors will be intrigued by an unfamiliar technology.
17. What is unique about the museum that can't be found anywhere else: there are miles of track around the museum where the trains run. Some of them are historic lines.
18. The most important things about local, state, or American history that can be learned at the museum: there are several rail museums in California, but this is the only one dedicated exclusively to electric trains, interurban railroads, and trolleys. These were an important form of transportation in many Bay Area communities and were only replaced when buses and cars became commonplace after WWII.

19. Annual events held at the site or elsewhere in the community: there are many special events year around, featuring scenic tours and vintage trains (see website for details).

20. Research facilities or archives at the site: The F. M. Smith Memorial Library is open to the public on the 2nd and 4th Saturday of each month, from 11a.m. - 4p.m. A circulating collection of books is available to members when the library is open, and they often present programs and films on railroad history.

21. Type of gift shop and what is for sale: there is a large gift shop with a wide variety of train-related books, films, and gifts.

1. **Western Sonoma County Historical Society West County Museum**

2. Location: 261 South Main St. Sebastopol, CA. 95472.
3. Website: http://www.wschsgrf.org/west-county-museum or http://www.sebastopol-farm-museum.org
4. Phone number: (707) 829-6711.
5. E-mail: use the online contact form.
6. Hours of operation: Thursday – Sunday: 1 to 4 p.m.
7. Cost: free.
8. Permanent Exhibits: the museum curates two exhibits per year with a focus on West Sonoma County history. There are two permanent mini exhibits: "Sebastopol's Story" and "The Petaluma and Santa Rosa Railroad History".
9. Special Exhibits: past exhibits have explored movies filmed in Sonoma County, historical toys, eclectic collections from the community, the World War II experience on the home front, the apple industry and apple festivals and fairs, early lighting devices, etc.
10. Historical era that is featured the best: 1900s.
11. Targeted age groups: all ages.
12. Special activities for children: school tours.
13. Guided tours: docent-led tours are available by appointment.
14. Hands-on activities: none.
15. The best-kept secrets at the museum: a Southern Pacific refrigerator boxcar that stands behind the museum houses the archive collections.
16. Hidden treasures at the museum: historic photographs, Pomo and Miwok Indian artifacts, and pioneer and railroad items.
17. What is unique about the museum that can't be found anywhere else: it is located in the 1917 former Petaluma & Santa Rosa Railroad Depot that was placed on the National Register of Historical Places in 1996.
18. The most important things about local, state, or American history that can be learned at the museum: Willard Libby, the inventor of radio carbon dating, and Luther Burbank, the botanist and horticulturalist were from this city. It was an important rail hub for the surrounding farm communities and helped make the Gravenstein apple known worldwide.
19. Annual events held at the site or elsewhere in the community: Annual Cemetery Walk and Apple Blossom Parade (see website for details).

20. Research facilities or archives at the site: the Triggs Reference Room contains historical reference books, pioneer and local family histories, and newspaper clipping files, along with oral histories of local people.

21. Type of gift shop and what is for sale: the museum's gift shop has interesting reproductions of jewelry, greeting cards made by local artists, many unique books and pamphlets, some by local historians. Other souvenirs include railroad caps, T-shirts, and jam from Burbank's farm.

1. **Wilder Ranch State Park**

2. Location: the park is north of Santa Cruz, immediately west of Highway One, approximately 1.8 miles past the Western Drive stoplight.

3. Website: http://www.parks.ca.gov/?page_id=549

4. Phone number: (831) 423-9703.

5. E-mail: use the online contact form.

6. Hours of operation: 8 a.m. – sunset.

7. Cost: $10 per car.

8. Permanent Exhibits: several restored buildings once belonging to the Wilder family are preserved. The park has tours and living history demonstrations to help visitors explore the history of early ranchers and farmers along the Central Coast. The surrounding grounds include Victorian homes, gardens, and an historic adobe.

9. Special Exhibits: none.

10. Historical era that is featured the best: 1800s.

11. Targeted age groups: all ages.

12. Special activities for children: the living history days have many fun, hands-on activities for children.

13. Guided tours: Wilder Ranch Living History Demonstrations and Ranch Tours: Weekends from 11 a.m. to 3 p.m. Tours of the ranch houses are at 1 p.m.

14. Hands-on activities: During living history days, there are Victorian games, farm animals, hand quilting, blacksmithing, or wood stove baking techniques, depending upon the event.

15. The best-kept secrets at the museum: antique buggies, wagons, and automobiles in the cow barn and garage

16. Hidden treasures at the museum: Victorian-era furnishings and historic dairy equipment.

17. What is unique about the museum that can't be found anywhere else: the natural setting is quite beautiful. There are many fine nature trails in the park.

18. The most important things about local, state, or American history that can be learned at the museum: the site was originally the main rancho supplying Santa Cruz Mission. It later became a successful and innovative dairy ranch.

19. Annual events held at the site or elsewhere in the community: Garden Planting and Wool Day, Spring Garden Planting Day and Sheep Sheering, Old-fashioned Independence Day, Heritage Harvest Festival, Holidays on the Ranch, and various nature and historic walks.

20. Research facilities or archives at the site: none.

21. Type of gift shop: none.

1. **Winchester Mystery House-San Jose**

2. Location: 525 S Winchester Blvd. San Jose, CA. 95128.

3. Website: http://winchestermysteryhouse.com/index.cfm

4. Phone number: (408) 247-2000.

5. E-mail: info@winchestermysteryhouse.com

6. Hours of operation: January 1-May 23: 9-5. May 24-September 1: 9-7. September 2-December 31: 9-5.

7. Cost: $25 - $40, depending on which tour is taken.

8. Permanent Exhibits: a 160-room mansion built by Sarah Winchester, the heiress of the Winchester Rifle Company. Sarah's obsession with non-stop building has led to many different theories about the mansion. Some are supernatural and some practical. The mystery continues. Tours are also available of the gardens, basement and firearms museum.

9. Special Exhibits: none.

10. Historical era that is featured the best: 1800s-early 1900s.

11. Targeted age groups: all ages.

12. Special activities for children: none.

13. Guided tours: all tours are guided. Book in advance during the busy summer season or at Halloween time.

14. Hands-on activities: none.

15. The best-kept secrets at the museum: hidden passages, stairs that go nowhere and many strange building elements that are amazing to behold.

16. Hidden treasures at the museum: the gun collection is one of the best in California.

17. What is unique about the museum that can't be found anywhere else: it is one of the largest Victorian mansions in the Bay Area. It has many unique architectural features and a fascinating back-story.

18. The most important things about local, state, or American history that can be learned at the museum: Sarah was a very wealthy and influential person. She even had Teddy Roosevelt visit her house, but she did not come out to greet him!

19. Annual events held at the site or elsewhere in the community: special events are held related to Christmas, Halloween, and catering to the haunted house crowd (see website for details). Book early because these events often sell out.

20. Research facilities or archives at the site: none.

21. Type of gift shop and what is for sale: There is a large gift shop and snack bar with many interesting books, films, and gift items related to the mansion and the Winchester family.

1. **Wings of History-San Martin**

2. Location: 12777 Murphy Avenue, San Martin, CA. 95046.

3. Website: http://www.wingsofhistory.org/

4. Phone number: (408) 683-2290.

5. E-mail: inquiry@wingsofhistory.org

6. Hours of operation: Saturday, Sunday 11 a.m. to 4 p.m.; Tuesday, Thursday: 10 a.m. to 3 p.m.

7. Cost: Adults: $ 5.00, Children (6-12): $ 3.00, Children (under 6) and Military (in service) are free.

8. Permanent Exhibits: The Early Days of Flight, WWI-WII, real and model aircraft, engines, flight equipment, county airports, small planes, and commercial aviation.

9. Special Exhibits: the Prop Shop and restoration workshop.

10. Historical era that is featured the best: WWI– WWII.

11. Targeted age groups: all ages.

12. Special activities for children: school tours. Some of the model aircraft are available for children to play in.

13. Guided tours: call for reservations.

14. Hands-on activities: Climb into the cockpit of a B-25!

15. The best-kept secrets at the museum: The WWI items are some of the best available in the Bay Area.

16. Hidden treasures at the museum: an exact replica of the Wright Brothers airplane and models from the former Flying Lady restaurant.

17. What is unique about the museum that can't be found anywhere else: it documents the locations of past airports that are no longer in service. It has historical photos of local airports.

18. The most important things about local, state, or American history that can be learned at the museum: the importance of aviation to the area.

19. Annual events held at the site or elsewhere in the community: Annual Open House.

20. Research facilities or archives at the site: The Aviation Library.

21. Type of gift shop and what is for sale: aviation-related items, souvenirs, and gifts.

22. Additional information: the clubhouse is available for events.

1. **The Woodside Store**

2. Location: 3300 Tripp Road, Woodside, CA. 94062.

3. Website: www.historysmc.org

4. Phone number: (650) 851.7615.

5. E-mail: woodsidestore@historysmc.

6. Hours of operation: Tuesday & Thursday 10 a.m. - 4 p.m., Saturday - Sunday 12 - 4 p.m.

7. Cost: free

8. Permanent Exhibits: the general store, dentist office, hardware shed, and blacksmith shop.

9. Special Exhibits: none.

10. Historical era that is featured the best: 1854-1909.

11. Targeted age groups: all ages

12. Special activities for children: school tours are available with reservations.

13. Guided tours: during hours of operation

14. Hands-on activities: sawing logs, making shingles, washing clothes the old-fashioned way, and operating a store.

15. The best-kept secrets at the museum: historic maps and photos, antique penny banks, coffee grinder etc.

225

16. Hidden treasures at the museum: lots of interesting antiques including animal pelts and logging equipment.

17. What is unique about the museum that can't be found anywhere else: it is the original store in the original location.

18. The most important things about local, state, or American history that can be learned at the museum: how a general store operated in the 1800's and the importance of logging in the area. This was an important early center of activity for the area. The store served many useful purposes.

19. Annual events held at the site or elsewhere in the community: Old Woodside Store Day the first Sunday in May.

20. Research facilities or archives at the site: none

21. Type of gift shop and what is for sale: old-fashioned candy and toys.

1. **The Woodside Community Museum**

2. Location: 2961 Woodside Road, Woodside, CA. 94062.

3. Website: http://www.woodsidetown.org/community/woodside-community-museum

4. Phone number: (650) 851-1294.

5. E-mail: woodsidehistory@woodsidetown.org

6. Hours of operation: April – October 1st & 3rd Saturday (1:00-4:00); November – March 1st Saturday (1:00-4:00).

7. Cost: free.

8. Permanent Exhibits: none.

9. Special Exhibits: the current exhibit is entitled: "Days of Grandeur", which features artifacts from the historic Jackling House. Rotating exhibits are changed every 2-3 years.

10. Historical era that is featured the best: 1850s-1950s.

11. Targeted age groups: all ages.

12. Special activities for children: none.

i13. Guided tours: docent-led tours during visiting hours.

14. Hands-on activities: none.

15. The best-kept secrets at the museum: the museum building is a restored farmhouse, built by a Woodside pioneer who owned the local hotel.

16. Hidden treasures at the museum: a local history collection containing photographs, maps, clippings, books, and primary- source documents.

17. What is unique about the museum that can't be found anywhere else: it has a unique collection of items of local interest.

18. The most important things about local, state, or American history that can be learned at the museum: Woodside was the center of Peninsula lumbering activity in the 19th century.

19. Annual events held at the site or elsewhere in the community: May Day Parade (1st Saturday in May) and Day of the Horse (1st Saturday in October).

20. Research facilities or archives at the site: a small research library is available with reservations.

21. Type of gift shop: none.

1. **Villa Mira Monte** (the **Morgan Hill Historical Society**)
2. Location: 17860 Monterey Street, Morgan Hill, CA 95037. Mailing address: Mail: P.O. Box 1258, Morgan Hill, CA 95038- 1258.
3. Website: www.morganhillhistoricalsociety.org
4. Phone number: (408) 779-5755.
5. E-mail: See the contacts on the website.
6. Hours of operation: Fridays: 12:00 – 3:00 p.m. and Saturdays: 10:00 – 1:00 p.m.
7. Cost: free.
8. Permanent Exhibits: none. The Centennial History Trail, Museum and Historic Home of Hiram Morgan Hill and Diana Murphy Hill. Artifacts, maps, photos, manuscripts, clippings and memorabilia.
9. Special Exhibits: the current exhibit is entitled: Amah Mutsun Exhibit: features the local Native American tribe, the Ohlone.
10. Historical era that is featured the best: late 1800s to the mid 1900s.
11. Targeted age groups: all ages.
12. Special activities for children: Living History Field Trips for grades 3-5.
13. Guided tours: call the museum for information.
14. Hands-on activities: none.
15. The best-kept secrets at the museum: The town is named for the builder and owner of Villa Mira Monte, Hiram <u>Morgan Hill</u> - not a geographic landmark. The town acquired its name because train conductors would call out, "Morgan Hill's" when making special stops for the Hill's guests to disembark.
16. Hidden treasures at the museum: A landscape water color painting by Mary Robinson Blair – resident of Morgan Hill during her high school years in the 1920s. She was known as an illustrator, colorist, and artist working for Disney on such projects as: The Three Caballeros, Cinderella and Dumbo. She is best known for her unique color styling and design.
17. What is unique about the museum that can't be found anywhere else: Poppy Jasper – a semi-precious stone found only in Morgan Hill.
18. The most important things about local, state, or American history that can be learned at the museum: Facts about the early inhabitants, the Amah Mutsuns. The site's connection to the famous Townsend, Stephens, Murphy Party – the first wagon train to successfully cross the Rockies. (Diana Murphy Hill was the granddaughter of Martin Murphy Sr.) The cultivation of orchards and vineyards in the early 1900s.
19. Annual events held at the site or elsewhere in the community: Founder's Dinner, Spring and Winter Holiday Craft Boutiques, Teas, and Wine Tastings.
20. Research facilities or archives at the site: archival materials are available for research by appointment only; please call to make reservations.
21. Type of gift shop: children's coloring books and flashcards for learning the Amah Mutsun language, history books, oral history videos, prints of historic photos, and quilts.

227

Conclusion

This book would not be complete without some suggestions for enhancing the experience of visitors to Bay Area museums and historical sites. I would like to offer some recommendations for both local residents and museum owners regarding ways in which they might help to improve the experience at their local site.

What can I do to help my local museum or historical site?

1. Donate time: Many museums are looking for volunteers. You do not have to be a professional historian, curator, or archivist to help. You merely need to have a love for local history and a desire to serve the community. Most have docent-training programs of some kind that will get you up to speed on the most important facts about the site and how best to present them to the public. Retired teachers and actors are particularly valued in this role. If you are not comfortable with public speaking, there are many more ways you can help besides being a docent. Many museums need people to do handy work, such as gardening, repair, and restoration of the buildings and artifacts. Chances are, there is already an overworked specialist in this area working at the historical site who would be eager to train some helpers. Other volunteers can help with setting up and cleaning up for public events held at the site. Others can help with office work, publicity, and fundraising. No matter what your skill set is, if you contact your local historical site, they will put you to work. Finally, most historical site volunteers tend to be elderly or retired folks. This is good because they often have lived in the community for many years and have valuable oral history to share. They are passionate about their community's history, but they have their physical limitations. Many of them could also use the aid of some strong young people or career-age folks to help out.

2. Donate money or gifts: Most sites have some kind of community group that supports them. You can do as I have done, and take out a membership in this group. Since many sites do not charge an admission fee, this is the main source of their income. Many businesses or corporations also make donations to local historical museums and sites. Check with your employer, there may also be a matching gift program that allows you double your donation amount! You may also be able to donate goods and services to a museum, such as office equipment, furniture, painting, landscaping, etc. You may even be able to donate an antique or historical document. Many museums have plenty of older historical items, but are lacking items from recent history. They may be looking to fill a particular gap in their collection. Don't feel that an item has to be a valuable antique to be of interest to the museum. I once donated an early calculator from the 1970's and the museum was thrilled to have it! One particular category of item that museums are always looking for is called ephemera. These are ordinary items that usually get thrown away, such as tickets, programs, brochures, yearbooks, postcards, etc., that reflect a particular time or event in local history. These are particularly valued if the facility is no

longer in operation. Examples include items from Santa's Village, Frontier Village, Neptune Island, or closed businesses, schools, or hospitals, just to name a few. All of these types of gifts listed above are tax deductible as well. Check with your local museum or historic site for details.

3. Tell your friends to visit the sites: Most of these sites are starving for publicity, but can't afford to advertise or publicize. Invite your friends and neighbors to visit them. If you are a local, make it a point to take out-of-town guests to see a site that would interest them. Mention these sites as potential outings to travel agents, journalists, church groups, or club members. Contact your children's teacher about going there for a field trip. Better yet, volunteer to be a chaperone or driver on the field trip! Even if you cannot fit a field trip into your school calendar, many museums have traveling historical trunks that teachers can check out when they are doing a certain historical unit in their classrooms. These are usually giant chests filled with historical replicas from a certain time period. They give kids a chance to try on costumes, handle artifacts, and read documents that they usually wouldn't be able to touch. They are similar to a large play set with curriculum guides and activities for the teacher.

4. Attend the special events offered by the museum or historical site: Most sites have an interesting variety of community events throughout the year. These are important fundraisers for the site, as well as often being fun family-oriented activities.

5. Patronize the gift shop: Many sites also depend heavily on their gift shops as a source of income. These shops often contain interesting gift items that can be found nowhere else. Don't just think of them as a place for books for the history buff. They also have many interesting antiques, souvenirs, clothing, toys, or food items. Purchase a holiday or birthday item there that will be unique, unlike anything you will find in a department store.

6. Rent the facility: Many sites have rooms or gardens that can be rented for public events. This can provide an attractive alternative site for a meeting, party, or wedding. The rental fees will also help support the museum.

My advice to museum owners:

People often ask me what I have learned from visiting all of these museums. I have gained a unique perspective on how the communities of the Bay Area are all tied together. Starting with the Gold Rush, many communities sprung up around the Bay Area to provide materials and services to San Francisco and other cities that were staging areas for the gold fields. Later, these areas took on a life of their own as new waves of settlers decided to stay in the area and add their unique talents to its growth. Finally, during World Wars I and II, technological innovations and international migrations drew many new settlers to the area, most of whom reinvented themselves during a period of unprecedented postwar growth. This has led to a host of museums, great and small, which attempt to capture the area's history and interpret it for visitors before it is lost.

While all of the sites are passionate about what they do, some naturally do a better job of it than others. While I make no claims to be a museum professional, I can't help but offer some suggestions on how to better run a local museum, based on years of museum visits while researching this book. I understand that there are limitations to funding, staff availability, and display space. However, whenever possible, I think that implementing the following policies will help create a more enjoyable experience for your visitors and would increase patronage as well.

Therefore, I humbly offer the following suggestions, based upon my many visits to local museums:

1. Expand your visiting hours: I know that many sites are dependent upon volunteers to keep the doors open and that the museum can only be open when the volunteers are available, but having hours of operation that are too restrictive only hurts your attendance in the long run. If you are only open on a weekday in the afternoon, for example, most working people will never make it to your museum. If you must pick a single day to be open, at least make it on a weekend, when more people are available.

Also, please try to keep consistency in your opening hours. If you have some kind of unusual schedule, like only being open the third Tuesday of the month, very few people are going to remember that and get the day right.

Finally, if your sign and/or your website say you are going to be open at a certain time, you really should honor that. I understand that volunteers don't all always show up when they are supposed to, but there is nothing more frustrating to a visitor than driving for hours to get to a place that is supposed to be open, only to find that it is closed and that he or she has wasted a trip. That visitor is very unlikely to return.

2. Charge something for admission: Many places are so good-hearted in their dedication to local history that they don't want to turn anyone away. Consequently, they don't charge admission or only accept donations. The problem with this concept is what marketers call perceived value. If a person pays nothing for admission, then they think that the museum must not be very good. If, on the other hand, you charge an admission fee, even if it is a small one, he or she thinks they are getting something of value. All of the museums or sites have something worth seeing, so it's okay to make people pay a little to see it. This is also a good source of income for the museum. If you really want to keep your site open to everyone, offer discounted rates for children and seniors or have an advertised free day once a month. If you do prefer to have a donation box, it should be placed prominently near the entrance. Mark it with a notation such as, "Suggested donation: $5". That way, if people are needy, they won't feel badly about putting in a little less, and if they are generous, they will often put in a lot more.

3. Invest in a good gift shop: Be creative in what you offer for sale. T-shirts, historical books, and other items with a local tie-in are good, but if you sell unique items that can't be found anywhere else, this will really help sales. One of the better examples I have seen is the Niles Essanay Film Museum. They have a wide selection of film-related items, with a special emphasis on Charlie Chaplin. You can get books about movies, silent movies, a life-sized cut out of Chaplin, even a reel from an old projector! Other places with good tie-ins to a notable person are the Jack London State Historic Park, The National Steinbeck Center, and John Muir National Historic Site.

Another brilliant idea is to take advantage of the fact that your visitors are viewing antiques or art, vintage toys, etc. and offer these items for sale at your gift shop. This is done very effectively at the Alameda Museum. Patrons donate antiques and collectibles and the museum sells them. They can't buy the items on display in the museum, of course, but this allows them feel like they are taking a little piece of it home with them. This is the museum's best source of income.

Other museums have also done a good job of selling replicas of nostalgic books and films, toys, food items, and house wares. The gift shop near the San Francisco Maritime National Historical Park has hundreds of nautical items for sale, ranging from typical San Francisco souvenirs to ships in a bottle. The better your gift shop ties in with the theme of your museum, the more fun it will be to shop there. A good example of this is the Oakland Air Museum. They have a plane used by Indiana Jones in his first movie, so they sell hats like the one Harrison Ford wore in the movies. What a fun way for a visitor to take home a memento of their visit!

4. Improve your publicity: If you don't have one already, you really need to get a website. Make sure your website is up to date and visitors can quickly find important information such as visiting hours, fees, and directions. If you can, load up the website with photos of your displays, or even better, a virtual museum tour. Include archival sources for online visitors and educational resources for parents and teachers. Make sure that your fliers, website and signage all have the same updated information to avoid confusion for visitors. Talk to travel agents and make sure that they know about what your museum has to offer. That way they will be more likely to recommend it to visitors.

Also, please keep the lines of communication open with your visitors. If they call or send an e-mail, get them the information they need promptly, so that they will visit right away before they lose interest. You should also try to stage interesting events throughout the year at the museum for all ages. Scholarly talks and seminars are fine for adults, but you need to also have family-oriented events where people feel comfortable bringing their children. I have seen museums do a wide variety of fun activities to draw crowds like staging a haunted Halloween house, historical characters speaking out at cemeteries, putting out Christmas decorations, Native American day, pioneer living history day, gold panning, and many other great events. Issue press releases whenever you have a new exhibit or social event for the community to get people to attend. If you are fortunate enough to have regular school group visits, have a tie-in that gets the adults to bring the whole family back at a later time.

5. Upgrade your displays: Make them well labeled, easy to read, and, preferably, hands-on or kid-friendly. There is nothing more frustrating for visitors than to try to make out faded labels in tiny print behind old glass display cases that have been collecting dust for years. Most will give up and pass over these items, even if they are important. You really need to get the items out where they are well lit, clearly labeled, and accessible to the public. This is especially important to visitors with disabilities. Local oral history recordings, music, lighting and sound that change as a narrator speaks, touch screens, dress up and "please touch me" items for children are all great ideas that add excitement to your exhibits. Visit museums such as The Oakland Museum of California or the National Steinbeck Center to see good examples of how this is done. Join a professional association of museums and attend their conference to see what other institutions are doing.

6. Get some good historical interpreters or "re-enactors": This really makes the experience come alive for visitors. Tourists consistently rank these as their most memorable experiences at a historical site. If you cannot afford to hire some, enlist the help of local actors or drama students to help portray historical characters that were important to your site. There are societies for historical re-enactors online or you can solicit help from leaders in the field, such as renaissance fairs, the National Park Service, or the Colonial Williamsburg Foundation.

7. Organize your collection into clearly themed displays: Many small museums mean well when they try to cram as many items as possible into their display space, but a cluttered collection only confuses people. If one historical era overlaps into another, or if people do not understand what they are looking at, then the display has lost its educational value. It is better to have a few well-identified items than an overstuffed collection where important items get overlooked.

8. Provide the historical context of the museum: Explain to visitors how this site fits into the historical era that you feature most prominently. Sometimes displays are so idiosyncratic to a certain place, individual, or family, that it is difficult for visitors to see how the site fits into the big picture of the historical era portrayed by the museum.

9. Rotate your collection: Tired displays don't keep people coming back. You should make sure that there is always something new for them to see each time they visit. An excellent example of the effective use of rotating displays is the Museum of Modern History in Palo Alto.

10. Tie in with other regional sites and attractions: Explain to visitors how your site fits into the overall history of the region, of California, and of the nation and the world. Arrange your visiting hours so that you are open on the same days as other historical sites in your area so that visitors can easily see multiple sites on the same day. This is especially important if you want to attract people who have to drive a long way to get to your site.

Feedback Form

If you have any suggestions for places we might have missed, updates, corrections, or other suggestions for this book, please feel free to contact Magnifico Publications at 2486 Aram Ave. San Jose, Ca. 95128. You may also e-mail krinibar@aol.com

Name of the museum or historical site: _____
_____

Listing update or correction: _____
_____
_____
_____
_____
_____
_____
_____
_____
_____

Suggestions: _____
_____
_____
_____
_____
_____
_____
_____
_____
_____
_____
_____
_____
_____
_____

Your name and contact information: _____
_____
_____
_____
_____
_____

Bibliography

Geologic prehistory:
1. http://pubs.usgs.gov/bul/b2188/b2188ch4.pdf.
2. http://geomaps.wr.usgs.gov/sfgeo/geologic/stories/dinosaur_fossils.html.
3. Alt, David D., and Donald William Hyndman. *Roadside Geology of Northern California*. 17th Printing. ed. Missoula, Mont: Mountain, 1994.

Native Americans:
1. Di Giacomo, Richard. *Ohlone Teacher's Resource*. 2nd ed. San Jose, CA: Magnifico Publications, 2010. ISBN 09706237-6-3.
2. Margolin, Malcolm. *The Ohlone Way: Indian Life in the San Francisco-Monterey Bay Area*. Berkeley: Heyday Books, 2002.
ISBN: 0-930588-01-0.
3. Milliken, Randall. *A Time of Little Choice-The Disintegration of Tribal Culture in the San Francisco Bay Area 1769-1810*. Menlo Park, CA.: Ballena Press, 1995.
ISBN-10: 0879191325.
4. Yamane, Linda, ed. *A Gathering of Voices: The Native Peoples of the Central California Coast*. Santa Cruz County History Journal, Issue Number 5. Santa Cruz, California: The Museum of Art & History, 2002. ISBN 0-949283-11-5.

California History:
1. *California Historical Landmarks*. [11th ed. Sacramento: Office of Historic Preservation, Dept. of Parks and Recreation, 1990.
2. Hoover, Mildred Brooke. *Historic Spots in California*. 5th ed. Stanford, Calif.: Stanford UP, 2002. ISBN 0804744831.
3. Pittman, Ruth. *Roadside History of California*. Missoula, MT: Mountain Pub., 1995. ISBN 0878423184.
4. Rawls, James and Bean, Walton. California: An Interpretive History 10th ed., California: McGraw-Hill, 2011. ISBN-13: 9780073406961.
5. "Saving the Bay" television documentary, PBS, 2011.
6. "Becoming California" television documentary, PBS, 2014.

Museum guides:
Akers, Charlene, and Jobyna Akers Dellar. *Open to the Public: A Guide to the Museums of Northern California*. Berkeley, Calif.: Heyday: 1994. ISBN 093058872X.

California State Parks:
Ostertag, Rhonda, and George Ostertag. *California State Parks: A Complete Recreation Guide*. 2nd ed. Seattle, WA: Mountaineers, 2001. ISBN9780898867626.

Military History:
1. http://www.history.navy.mil/faqs/faq80-1.htm.
2. http://www.nps.gov/poch/faqs.htm.
3. http://www.militarymuseum.org/HistoryWWII.html.

4. Distasi, Lawrence, ed. *Una Storia Segreta : The Secret History of Italian American Evacuation and Internment During World War II*, Heyday Books; First edition. June 1, 2001.

The Golden Gate Bridge-San Francisco

Other titles available from Magnifico Publications:

1. *The New Man and the New World: The Influence of Renaissance Humanism on the Explorers of the Italian Era of Discovery* ISBN 978-0-9706237-2-0.
2. *The History Teacher's Joke Book* ISBN 978-0-9706237-3-7.
3. *The History Teacher's Movie Guide* ISBN 978-0-9706237-7-5.
4. *Ohlone Teacher's Resource* ISBN 978-0-9706237-6-8.
5. *When Am I Ever Going to Use This Stuff? How Social Studies Skills are Used in Everyday Jobs* ISBN 978-0-9706237-8-2.
6. *Tales of Time* ISBN 978-0-9834267-1-4.

See www.magnificopublications.com for further information.

Additional titles by Richard Di Giacomo are now available from Interact. These include role-playing simulations for United States and World History, creative geography activities, and history and grammar activities for English language learners. For ordering information see www.socialstudies.com.

Meet the Author

Richard Di Giacomo graduated from San José State University with a BA in Ancient and Medieval history, a BA in Social Science and an MA in American History. He has been a teacher for over 25 years and has taught in a variety of schools from private and continuation schools to public high schools. He has taught everything from at risk and limited English students to honors and college preparatory classes. The subjects he has taught include US and World History, Government, Economics, Bible and Ethics, History of the Cold War, and Contemporary World History. He has been a reviewer and contributor to textbooks, and a frequent presenter at social studies conferences on the use of simulations, videos, and computers in education. Rich's love for California history and museums led to the creation of this book.

Folger Estate Stable Carriage Room Museum- Woodside